T0144136

Implementing Digital Forensic Readiness

Implementing Digital Forensic Readiness

From Reactive to Proactive Process

Second Edition

Jason Sachowski

CRC Press
Taylor & Francis Group
Boca Raton London New York

CRC Press is an imprint of the
Taylor & Francis Group, an **informa** business

CRC Press
Taylor & Francis Group
6000 Broken Sound Parkway NW, Suite 300
Boca Raton, FL 33487-2742

Printed on acid-free paper

International Standard Book Number-13: 978-1-1383-3895-1 (Hardback)

Visit the Taylor & Francis Web site at
http://www.taylorandfrancis.com

and the CRC Press Web site at
http://www.crcpress.com

Contents

12   Enabling Targeted Monitoring   141

13   Mapping Investigative Workflows   157

Section III
INTEGRATING DIGITAL FORENSICS

19   Forensics Readiness with Mobile Devices   243

20   Forensics Readiness and the Internet of Things   268

Section IV
ADDENDUMS

Section V
APPENDIXES

Section VI
TEMPLATES

Preface

The art of war teaches us to rely not on the likelihood of the enemy's not coming, but on our own readiness to receive him; not on the chance of his not attacking, but rather on the fact that we have made our position unassailable.

—Sun Tzu
The Art of War

Acknowledgments

I would like to most of all thank my wife and my children for showing me that no matter what I do in my lifetime, they will always be my greatest success.

Thank you to my parents for providing me with countless opportunities to become who I am today and for encouraging me to keep pushing my boundaries.

Thank you to my colleagues for allowing me the honor of working with you and for the infinite wisdom and knowledge you have given me.

Lastly, thank you to Blair for opening doors.

Introduction

Digital forensics has been a discipline of information security for decades. Since the digital forensics profession was formalized as a scientific discipline, the principles, methodologies, and techniques have remained consistent despite the evolution of technology and can ultimately be applied to any form of digital data. Within a corporate environment, digital forensics practitioners are often relied upon to maintain the legal admissibility and forensic viability of digital evidence in support of a broad range of different business functions.

Why This Book

Regardless of how strong an organization's defenses are, there will come a time when the weakest link is exposed, leading to some type of incident or event. When that time comes, organizations turn to the highly specialized skills of digital forensics practitioners to parse through and extract evidence from the complex volumes of data.

Unfortunately, there are times when an incident or event occurs and organizations are unable to support the digital investigation process with the electronic data needed to conduct analysis and arrive at conclusions. Not only does this slow down the digital investigation process, it also places additional overhead on people and systems to reactively identify where relevant electronic data is and work to have it properly collected and preserved to support the investigation. In comparison, the ability to collect and preserve electronic data before something happens enhances the digital investigation process by streamlining activities, reducing overhead, and enabling a proactive approach to incidents or events.

Who Will Benefit from This Book

This book was written from a non-technical business perspective to provide readers with realistic methodologies and strategies related to how the people, process, and technology aspects of digital forensics are integrated throughout an enterprise to support different business operations.

While this book does cover the fundamental principles, methodologies, and techniques of digital forensics, it largely focuses on outlining how the people, process, and technology areas are used to defend the enterprise through integrating digital forensics capabilities with key business functions.

The information contained in this book has been written to benefit people who:

- Are employed, both directly or indirectly, in the digital forensics profession and are working to implement digital forensics readiness capabilities within their organization
- Are employed in the information security profession and are interested in implementing security controls that enable proactive digital forensics capabilities
- Are academic scholars pursuing non-technical business knowledge about requirements for enabling proactive digital forensics capabilities throughout an enterprise environment

Who Will NOT Benefit from This Book

This book is not designed to provide readers with technical knowledge about digital forensics, including the "hands-on" and "how-to" aspects of the discipline; such as how to forensically acquire a hard drive.

How This Book Is Organized

This book is organized into six thematic sections:

Section 1: Enabling Digital Forensics outlines the fundamental principles, methodologies, and techniques applied unanimously throughout the digital forensic discipline.

Section 2: Enhancing Digital Forensics analyses additional considerations for enabling and enhancing digital forensic capabilities throughout an enterprise environment.

Section 3: Integrating Digital Forensics addresses best practices for integrating the people, process and technologies components of digital forensics across an enterprise environment.

Section 4: Addendums provides complimentary content that discusses topics and subject areas not directly related to Digital Forensics.

Section 5: Appendixes provides supplementary content that expand topics and subject areas discussed in throughout other sections of this book.

Section 6: Templates supply structured templates and forms used in support of the digital forensic and business functions/processes covered throughout.

Author

Jason Sachowski is a seasoned professional in the fields of information security and digital forensics. He has an extensive history of working in a fast-paced corporate environment where he has led digital forensics investigations, directed incident response activities, developed and maintained processes and procedures, managed large information security budgets, and governed the negotiation of third-party contracts.

In addition to his professional career, Jason is the author of the books *Implementing Digital Forensic Readiness: From Reactive to Proactive Process* and *Digital Forensics and Investigations: People, Process, and Technologies to Defend the Enterprise*. He has also served as a contributing author and content moderator for DarkReading, a subject matter expert for information security and digital forensic professional exam development, and volunteering as an advocate for cyberbullying prevention and cybersecurity awareness.

Jason holds several information security and digital forensics certifications, including Certified Information Systems Security Professional—Information Systems Security Architecture Professional (CISSP-ISSAP), Certified Secure Software Lifecycle Professional (CSSLP), Systems Security Certified Practitioner (SSCP), and EnCase Certified Examiner (EnCE).

Enabling Digital Forensics

I

Understanding Digital Forensics

1

Introduction

What is now commonly referred to as *digital forensics* is a profession that was once made up of unstructured processes, custom home-grown toolsets, and knowledge based on the collective work of hobbyists. Over the past 50 years, the profession of digital forensics has evolved significantly alongside technological advancements to become a mature discipline where a common body of knowledge (CBK)—made up of proven scientific principles, methodologies, and techniques—has brought about a globally adopted level of standardization and formal structure.

While it is relatively well known that there are legal aspects involved with digital forensics, most people are surprised to learn that the profession involves a great deal of scientific principles, methodologies, and techniques. Not only does digital forensics require a significant amount of specialized training and skills to properly apply these scientific fundamentals, digital forensics is also somewhat of an art form where analytical experience comes into play.

The Role of Technology in Crime

In relation to crime, technology can play multiple roles that in turn produce many types of digital artifacts that can be used as digital evidence. Depending on how much digital evidence is contained within any given piece of technology, it may or may not be authorized for seizure and subsequent collection of evidence as part of an investigation. In any case, when technology plays a role in criminal activity, it is much easier to justify its seizure so evidence can be processed.

Through the years, several authors have tried to develop a standard classification scheme for the distinct roles technology can play in crime. In the 1970s, Donn Parker was one of the first individuals to recognize the potential seriousness of technology-relates crimes which led him to create the following four categories which remain relevant today:

1. *Object of Crime* applies when technology is affected by the crime (e.g., when a device is stolen or damaged).
2. *Subject of Crime* applies when technology is in the environment in which the crime was committed (e.g., system infected by malware).

3. *Tool of Crime* applies when technology is used to conduct or plan crime (e.g., illegally forged documents).
4. *Symbol of Crime* applies when technology is used to deceive or intimidate (e.g., falsified investment profits).

Distinguishing when technology plays one role or another is important on many levels. For example, knowing when technology is an object or subject is important because, from the perspective of the practitioner, this demonstrates intent of the perpetrator. Also, when technology is a tool, like a gun or other weapon, this could lead to additional charges or increased punishment. However, although technology as a symbol may seem irrelevant because no actual system is involved in the crime, when categorized under this role technology is represented as an idea, belief, or any entity that can be useful in understanding motivations for committing the crime. As an example, CEOs are a symbol of their organization and as such can become either the victim or target of crime because of what they symbolize.

In 1994, the U.S. Department of Justice (USDOJ) developed their own categorization scheme that made a clear distinction between hardware, being physical components, and information, being data and programs that are stored or transmitted. It is important to note that with a single crime there is the potential to fall into one or more of these categories; for example, when a system is used as the instrument of crime, it may also contain information as evidence. The categories proposed by the USDOJ include:

- *Hardware as Contraband or Fruits of Crime* (i.e., any item that is illegal to be possessed or was obtained illegally)
- *Hardware as an Instrumentality* (i.e., when technology played a role in committing the crime; such as a gun or weapon)
- *Hardware as Evidence* (i.e., scanners with unique characteristics that can be used and linked to the creation of digitized content)
- *Information as Contraband or Fruits of Crime* (i.e., computer programs that can encrypt content to conceal evidence)
- *Information as an Instrumentality* (i.e., programs used to break into other systems)
- *Information as Evidence* (i.e., digital artifacts revealing a user's activities on a system)

In 2002, the USDOJ updated their categorization scheme as part of their publication titled *Searching and Seizing Computers and Obtaining Electronic Evidence in Criminal Investigations*. The most notable difference in the updated categorization was the realization that data and program content, not the hardware, are usually the target of the crime; but even when information is the target it may be necessary to collect the hardware.

History of Digital Crime and Forensics

Information technology has been involved in criminal activities for more than half of a century. Dating as far back as the 1960s, computer crimes were first committed as either physical damage or as sabotage to computer systems. But when technology first arrived, most people did not think that it would one day become such an integral part of our everyday lives. If history has taught us anything, it's that as information technology advances there will always be new and evolved digital crimes.

With the growing commercialization of technology and the expansion of the Internet, computer crimes continue to take the next step in an ever-evolving threat landscape. Moving forward from the 1970s and into the new millennium, computer crimes expanded from just damage and sabotage to digital crimes such as fraud, denial of service (DoS), SPAM, advanced persistent threats (APT), and extortion.

Prologue (1960s–1980s)

From the 1960s to 1980s, computers were owned and operated by corporations, universities, research centers, and government agencies. Computers were used primarily as industrial systems largely supporting data processing functions and were, for the most part, not connected to the outside world. Responsibility for securing these computer systems was left to administrators who would perform routine audits to ensure the efficiency and accuracy of the data processing functions. These activities were essentially the first systematic approach to a computer security discipline.

It was during this time that the computer first became a point of interest to the information security, legal, and law enforcement communities. Several government agencies started creating small ad hoc groups of individuals who were then provided with basic training on computer systems. These "investigators" would work with administrators to gather information from the computer systems to be used as evidence in criminal matters.

In 1968, in Olympia, Washington, an IBM 1401 Data Processing System was shot twice by a pistol-toting intruder.

Following closely behind in February 1969, the largest student riot in Canada ignited when police were called in to stop a student occupation of several floors of the Hall Building at Concordia University. When the police arrived to control the protest, a fire broke out, resulting in computer data and university property being destroyed. The damages totaled $2 million, and 97 people were arrested.

Prior to the 1980s, computer crimes were largely dealt with under existing laws. However, in response to an increasing number of computer crimes, law enforcement agencies began establishing new laws to address computer crimes. The first computer crime law, the *Florida Computer Crimes Act*, was created in 1978 to address fraud, intrusion, and all unauthorized access to computer systems. The evolution of crime into computer systems during this time led to new terms such as *computer forensics, forensics computer analysis,* and *forensics computing.*

Infancy (1980–1995)

With the arrival of the IBM personal computer (PC), there was a sudden explosion of computer hobbyists around the world. These PCs had very few applications and were not user friendly, which enticed hobbyists to write program code and access the internals of both the hardware and operating system (OS) to better understand how they worked. Amongst the hobbyists were individuals from law enforcement, government agencies, and other organizations who collectively shared their understanding of computer systems and how technology could play a larger role as a source of evidence. Much of the time and money spent by these individuals to learn about these modern technologies was done of their own accord because their respective agencies did not necessarily support their efforts.

Investigations performed by these pioneers were rudimentary from today's perspective. The Internet was not yet widely available for consumer use, which limited the scope of most investigations to data recovery on standalone computer systems. Cyber criminals mostly consisted of a mix of traditional criminals who used technology to support their activities (e.g., phreaking) and people who used their technical skills to illegally access other computers.

During this time, there were very few tools available, which left investigators to either build their own or use available data protection and recovery applications to perform analysis. Additionally, the only means of preserving evidence was taking logical backups of data onto magnetic tape, hoping that the original attributes were preserved, and restoring the data to another disk, where analysis was performed using command-line utilities.

Throughout the 1990s, forensics tools began to emerge from both the hobbyists (e.g., Dan J. Mare's Maresware, Gord Hama's RCMP Utilities) and larger software vendors (e.g., Norton's Utilities, Mace Utilities). These applications and software suites were developed to solve specific forensics activities (e.g., imaging, file recovery) and proved to be powerful tools for the computer forensics practice.

As technology became more widely available and reports of different types of computer crimes were becoming more widely known, law enforcement agencies around the world started responding by enacting laws similar to that passed by Florida. In 1983, Canada was the first to respond by amending their criminal code to address computer crimes. Following their lead, several other nations began implementing legislation in response to computer crimes, including the *1984 U.S. Federal Computer Fraud and Abuse Act*, the 1989 amendment of the *Australian Crimes Act* to include *Offenses Relating to Computers*, and the *1990 British Computer Abuse Act*.

Parallel to the establishment of computer laws, interest in the forensics community was growing, as was its popularity. Agencies recognized that many forensics investigations were performed by individuals who had minimal training, operated on their own terms, used their own equipment, and did not follow any formal quality control. From this, efforts began to create a CBK of principles, methodologies, and techniques that could be applied to standardize and bring formal structure to computer forensics.

Childhood (1995–2005)

The next decade proved to be a major step forward in the maturity of digital forensics. Technology quickly became pervasive amongst consumers, where it was embedded in many facets of our daily lives, which drove significant technology innovation (e.g., mobile devices). Plus, the Internet had gained enough momentum for it to become more readily available for use in homes and businesses, introducing personal accessibility to email and web browsing.

Accompanied by these advances in technology was the opportunity for criminals to commit new cybercrimes. An example of this opportunity being made available through technology occurred following the events on September 11, 2001, when investigators realized that digital evidence of the attack was recoverable on computers located across the world. This revelation reinforced the fact that criminals were using technology in the same ubiquitous ways as the everyday consumer.

From the technology-sponsored growth of digital crime, the term *computer forensics* became increasing challenging to use because both crimes and evidence could now be found throughout networks, printers, and other devices. In 2001, the first annual Digital Forensics Research Workshop (DFRWS) recognized that computer forensics was considered a specialization and proposed the use of the term *digital forensics* to describe the discipline as a whole.

Expansion of the field into the all-encompassing *digital forensics* resulted in the creation of specializations for investigating different technologies. In addition to the traditional computer forensics becoming a concentration, there was the introduction of *network forensics* and *mobile forensics*. However, with the formation of these specializations came increased technical sophistication and legal scrutiny over requirements to follow standardized principles, methodologies, and techniques.

The formalization of digital forensics led to the first publication of standardized principles being issued between 1999 and 2000 from the combined work of the International Organization on Computer Evidence (IOCE), the G-8 High Tech Crime Subcommittee, and the Scientific Working Group on Digital Evidence (SWGDE). Likewise, forensics tools evolved from simple home-grown applications used by hobbyists into sophisticated commercial suites of tools. At the same time, the digital forensics community continued to mature, with professional certification programs being created not only to recognize individuals with the appropriate knowledge and experience but also to acknowledge laboratory environments that met the requirements of forensic science principles, methodologies, and techniques.

Adolescence (2005–2015)

Due to the academic preparation required and formal training requirements, the maturity of digital forensics has grown exponentially to a point where it is now recognized by the information security profession as a core skill area. Colleges and universities have recognized the popularity and appeal of digital forensics, which has led to the creation of numerous academic and professional education programs around the world. Furthermore, the number of international conferences dedicated to the field of digital forensics continues to increase as the integration of digital forensics with other professions evolves.

During this time, the American Academy of Forensic Sciences (AAFS), one of the most widely recognized professional organizations for establishing the forensics disciplines, created a new section specific to digital and multimedia sciences (DMS). This development led to a major advancement in recognizing digital forensics as a scientific discipline by providing a common foundation for specialized groups of people who can share knowledge and address current forensics challenges.

Technology has now reached a point in its evolution where almost every device has some type of storage medium and can, in some fashion, be connected to the Internet. Naturally this has driven the development of systems and applications that are increasingly adaptive and accessible from virtually anywhere and, if not secured properly, by anyone. Capitalizing on technology's modern pervasiveness, cybercriminals once again have expanded their portfolio to incorporate new and sophisticated attacks such as varying levels of phishing campaigns (e.g., spear, whaling, cloning), advanced persistent threats (APT), and even cyber espionage.

With the change in cyberattacks comes new ways that digital evidence is created, gathered, and processed. Adapting to the new wave of digital evidence sources, commercial software suites began to transform from offering functionality specific to digital forensics and now benefit other professions where digital forensics is used. Including professions like cybersecurity, electronic discovery (e-discovery), and incident response, digital forensics has become an underlying foundation driving several information security disciplines.

The Future (2015 and Beyond)

The digital forensics discipline has come a long way in the past 50 years. What started out as a hobby made up mostly of home-grown tools and quite often insufficient processes has arrived at a convergence of various law enforcement organizations and intelligence agencies in which everybody is following the same consistent principles, methodologies, and techniques.

Predicting what the future holds for digital forensics is not overly challenging. Rather, if history has taught us anything about how the past has shaped what digital forensics is today, the most realistic and accurate prediction that can be made is this: every person and group involved with digital forensics today will have some type of influence on what the future brings.

For the most part, digital forensics has become what it is today because of the tactical influences that have consistently driven its development and maturity, such as technology advancements, creation of commercial tools, and integration with other professions. On the other hand, while the list of strategic influences might be somewhat smaller, the alignment to forensic science and subsequent creation of principles, methodologies, and techniques to abide by brought about a standardization and formality to the structure of digital forensics. There are also influences that exist in both tactical and strategic realms that should be considered for the future of digital forensics, for example:

- The continued development of the CBK based on research, knowledge, and experiences of the digital forensics community. At the end of the day, the digital forensics investigators of the future will be better trained and educated because the CBK that was established before them will be extensive and readily available. Organizations will need to ensure that they employ digital forensics professionals who not only are accredited to conduct digital forensics investigations, but also have strong business and technical qualities.
- Historically, advancements introduced innovative ways for technology to be used as either the fruit, tool, or instrument of crime, resulting in an evolution in how digital forensics has been used to investigate these crimes. Until recently, cybercrime was traditionally committed with a focus primarily on content (e.g., data exfiltration) and done so with little context (e.g., where attacks are being perpetrated). Naturally, cybercriminals of the future will be better trained, funded, and organized to the point that the value of their collective efforts will be realized, resulting in heightened situational awareness involving their attacks.
- To counter the evolving threat landscape, commercial digital forensics tools will need to evolve to be able to:

- Easily adapt with the ever-growing volumes of data that need to be analyzed
- Further automate known, verified, and validated analytic functions to alleviate manual processing time and reduce error probability
- Understand and interpret both the content and context of human language and communications for better analytical results
- Given the fact that some investigations encompass an international scope, such as data residing under multiple jurisdictions, laws and regulations must evolve to enable a global standard for digital forensics.

Evolutionary Cycle of Digital Forensics

Digital forensics has become the scientific discipline it is today because of the work done by all those involved since its inception back in the 1970s. Driving structure and maturity in the discipline and community is the product of influences both tactical, such as technology advancements, and strategic, such as the creation of global working groups dedicated to digital forensics.

If we've learned anything about how the past activities have shaped digital forensics into what it is today, the best and most educated prediction is that history will repeat itself. This doesn't mean that the digital forensics profession will revert to the way it was in the 1970s; rather the maturity of the discipline will be subject to continuous improvement transformations that follow a cyclical methodology like the one illustrated in Figure 1.1.

"Ad Hoc" Phase

The *ad hoc* phase is the starting point in the continuous transformation of the digital forensics discipline. Also referred to as *pre-forensics* or

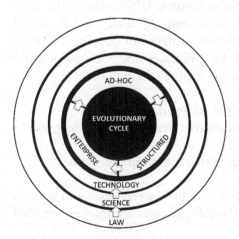

Figure 1.1 Digital forensics evolutionary cycle.

proto-forensics, this phase is characterized by the absence of structure, ambiguous goals, and an overall lack of tools, processes, and training. This phase can be related to the time from the 1970s and into the mid-1980s.

Looking back at the history of digital forensics and crime, it is evident that both technology advancements and legal precedence are the major contributors to any type of evolution relating to the digital forensics discipline. Generally, the term *ad hoc* refers to the methodology via which something new has been created (e.g., law) and because of this the approach is disorganized or not theory driven. This is not to say that we ignore everything that came previously and start anew, but that with new developments in technology there is a need to circle back to ensure structure is provided in terms of digital forensics capabilities.

"Structured" Phase

The *structured* phase is the next step in the continuous transformation of digital forensics, as seen from the mid-1980s into the 1990s. This phase is characterized by the development of complex solutions that bring harmony and structure to processes and tools that were identified as challenges faced during the ad hoc phase. Elements specifically addressed during this phase include:

- Establishment of policy-based programs (i.e., laws, regulations);
- Definition and coordination of processes that align with established policies; and
- Requirements for forensically sound tools.

First, for investigative processes to be clearly defined and documented there need to be policies in place, such as laws and regulations, to establish a foundation from which to work. In turn, these policies drive the need to legitimize processes and tools to ensure they are consistently applied to warrant repeatable and reproducible outcomes. Ultimately, if the tools used cannot consistently reproduce results, their legitimacy can be called into question and the viability of evidence gathered or processed cannot be guaranteed. All things considered, for processes and tools to produce credible evidence that is forensically sound requires them to be:

- Verifiable as authentic to the original source data;
- Collected and preserved in a manner that preserves their integrity; and
- Analyzed using tools and techniques that maintain their integrity.

At the end of this phase, the formal structure brings processes and tools in line with the scientific principles, methodologies, and techniques required for achieving a state of maturity.

"Enterprise" Phase

The *enterprise* phase is the last step in the maturity of a digital forensics; like the progress made at the start of the new millennium (2000s) and beyond. This phase is characterized by the recognition of processes and tools being an actual science that involves the real-time collection of evidence, the general acceptance of the development of effective tools and processes, and the application of formally structured principles, methodologies, and techniques.

Ultimately, this phase of the digital forensics evolution came about from the need to automate digital forensics processes. Not only does this automation support the ability to perform proactive evidence collection, but it also allows for methodologies and techniques to be consistently applied to maintain standards set out by the legal system to ensure the legal admissibility of evidence.

The evolution of digital forensics is cyclical when it comes to maturing existing scientific principles, methodologies, and techniques to adapt with modern technologies or standards (i.e., laws and regulations). However, at the same time the evolution of digital forensics is linear in the sense that the as scientific principles, methodologies, and techniques are being matured, the continued development and contribution to the digital forensics CBK persists.

Principles of Digital Forensics

Digital forensics is the application of science to law and subsequently must follow the scientific principles, methodologies, and techniques required for admissibility in a court of law. Even if legal prosecution is not the end goal of an investigation (e.g., corporate policy violations), there may be a requirement for legal action at some point. Therefore, it is important to handle all potential digital evidence in a manner that guarantees it will remain legally admissible.

Evidence Exchange

One of the main goals when conducting a forensics investigation is to establish factual conclusions that are based on credible evidence. According to *Locard's exchange principle*, illustrated in Figure 1.2, anyone or anything entering a crime scene takes something with them and leaves something behind when they leave. In general, Locard's exchange principle states that with contact between entities, there will be an exchange.

In the physical world, an example of this exchange can occur when a perpetrator inadvertently leaves fingerprints or traces of blood at the crime scene. Or a perpetrator might take a crucial piece of evidence away from the crime scene, such as a knife, to make the job of identifying evidence more challenging.

Figure 1.2 Locard's exchange principle triad.

In both examples, these exchanges produce tangible forms of evidence that demonstrate both class and individual characteristics. Evidence that possesses class characteristics, otherwise referred to as class evidence, has features that group items by type, such hair color. On its own, this type of evidence does not provide conclusive identification of a perpetrator and individualizing characteristics. What individualizes evidence, such as hair color, are those characteristics with unique qualities that differentiate one from another and help to narrow the group to a single item. Using the analogy of hair color, examples of individual characteristics include length, style (e.g. straight, wavy), and highlights.

In the digital world, evidence exists in a logical state that is much more intangible than physical evidence is. However, exchanges like those in the physical world can persist and are equally as relevant in the digital world. Email communication and web browsing are clear examples of how these exchanges occur within the digital world. If a threatening email message is sent, the individuals computer will contain artifacts of this, as will the email servers used to transmit the message. Practitioners can identify and gather a copious amount of evidence relating to this threatening email in the form of access logs, email logs, and other artifacts within computer systems.

Forensics Soundness

Evidence can make or break an investigation. Equally important in both the physical and digital worlds, it is critical that evidence is handled in a way that will not raise questions when being presented in a court of law.

Forensically sound is a term used to qualify and, in some cases, justify the use of a technology or methodology. Likewise, *forensic soundness* occurs when electronically stored information (ESI), as digital evidence, remains complete and materially unaltered as result of using a technology or methodology. This means that during every digital investigation, proper techniques must be used, following consistent methodologies that are based on established scientific principles, to achieve forensic soundness specific to digital evidence:

- *Minimally handle the original.* Digital forensics processes should be minimally applied to original data sources. To achieve this, forensics images of ESI should be taken and used to perform investigative procooooc and techniques.
- *Account for any ohango.* In some instances, digital evidence can change from its original state. When change occurs, it should be documented to note the nature, extent, and reason for the change.
- *Comply with the rules of evidence.* Throughout an investigation, applicable rules of evidence (e.g., laws and regulations) should be considered. Refer to Chapter 16, "Ensuring Legal Review," for additional information.
- *Avoid exceeding one's knowledge.* Do not undertake any activity or task that is beyond your current level of knowledge and skill.

Perhaps one of the biggest reasons digital evidence does not maintain *forensic soundness* is human error. To guarantee digital evidence remains *forensically sound*, ESI must be gathered, processed, and maintained following principles, methodologies, and techniques that do not alter its state at any time, thus demonstrating that it is authentic and has integrity.

Authenticity and Integrity
The authenticity of digital evidence is maintained to demonstrate it is the same data that was originally seized. From a technical perspective, there are times digital evidence cannot be compared to its original state, such as with random access memory (RAM) that is constantly in a state of change. For these occurrences, point in time snapshots are taken that demonstrate the state of the technology at that moment. From a legal perspective, authentication means satisfying the legal systems that the:

- Content of the record has remained unchanged;
- Information in the record does in fact originate from its original source; and
- Extraneous information about the record is accurate (e.g., time stamp).

Supporting the need to establish authenticity, the goal of maintaining the integrity of digital evidence is to demonstrate that it has not been changed since the time it was first gathered. In digital forensics, verifying integrity generally involves comparing the digital fingerprint of digital evidence when it is first gathered and subsequently throughout its entire lifecycle. Currently, the most common means of generating a digital fingerprint in digital forensics is to use a one-way cryptographic hash algorithm such as the Message Digest Algorithm family (i.e., MD5, MD6) or the Secure Hashing Algorithm family (i.e., SHA-1, SHA-2, SHA-3).

In 2004–2005, experts identified that the MD5 and SHA-1 algorithms contained flaws where two unique inputs, having distinctively different properties and characteristics, would result in the same computational hash value being outputted.

Dubbed a "hash collision," this meant that the same computational hash value could be engineered in such a way that multiple pieces of digital evidence could return the same hash value. Naturally, this raised concerns in the digital forensics community about the potential impact on the legal admissibility of digital evidence.

In 2009, during the matter of *United States v. Joseph Schmidt III*, the court ruled that the chance of a hash collision is not significant and is not an issue. Specifically, a digital fingerprint of a file still produces a unique digital algorithm that uniquely identifies that file.

This ruling allows the integrity of digital evidence that was done using either the MD5 or SHA1 algorithms to be relied upon as legally admissible.

The near uniqueness of these cryptographic algorithms makes them an important technique for documenting the integrity of digital evidence. While the potential for hash collisions exists, use of the Message Digest Algorithm family or Secure Hashing Algorithm family remains an acceptable way of demonstrating the authenticity and integrity of digital evidence.

Chain of Custody

Perhaps the most important aspect of maintaining authenticity and integrity is documenting the continuity of possession for digital evidence. This chain of custody is used to demonstrate the transfer of ownership over digital evidence between entities and can be used to validate the integrity of evidence being presented in court. Without a chain of custody in place, arguments can be made that evidence has been tampered with, altered, or improperly handled, which can lead to potential evidence contamination with other consequences. It is best to keep the number of custody transfers to a minimum, as these individuals can be called upon to provide testimony on the handling of evidence during the time they controlled it.

A sample template that can be used as a chain of custody form has been provided in the *Templates* section of this book.

As the digital forensics discipline continues to evolve along with technology advancements, one of the most challenging activities is to ensure that the fundamental principles, methodologies, and techniques are updated. There is a constant struggle to maintain a balance between collecting digital evidence as efficiently as possible without modifying the integrity of the data in the process. Fortunately, the principles and methodologies of forensic science have been clearly defined and well established over several decades, allowing them to be applied relatively seamlessly to any form of digital evidence.

Types of Forensics Investigations

Traditionally, digital forensics is performed in response to an event and focuses on determining the root cause of the event. The purpose of performing a digital forensics investigation is to establish factual conclusions from digital evidence existing on any number of different technologies (e.g., game consoles, mobile devices, computer systems), across dissimilar network architectures (e.g., private, public, cloud), or in varying states (e.g., volatile, static).

Since the beginning of computer forensics in the 1980s, the application of forensic science has become an underlying foundation that has seen an integration of consistent principles that support repeatable methodologies and techniques within several other information security disciplines. The application of digital forensic science in other disciplines provides organizations with an acceptable level of assurance that validated and verified processes are being followed to gather, process, and safeguard digital evidence. Examples of disciplines where digital forensic science is used include:

- *Computer forensics,* which relates to the gathering and analysis of digital information as digital evidence on computer systems and electronic storage media
- *Network forensics,* which relates to the monitoring and analysis of network traffic for the purposes of information gathering, gathering of digital evidence, or intrusion detection
- *Incident response,* which relates to reducing business impact by managing the occurrence of computer security events
- *Memory forensics,* which relates to the gathering and analysis of digital information as digital evidence contained within a system's RAM
- *Electronic discovery (e-discovery),* which relates to the discovery, preservation, processing, and production of electronically stored information (ESI) in support of government or litigation matters
- *Cloud forensics,* which relates to the gathering and analysis of digital information as digital evidence from cloud computing systems

Legal Aspects

Even if legal prosecution is not the end goal of the investigation, such as with a corporate policy violation, there may be some form of legal action, such as employee termination. It is important that principles, methodologies, and techniques of forensic science are consistently followed because the investigation may wind up in a court of law at some point. Regardless of criminal proceedings, every digital forensics investigation must ensure that:

- An exact copy of digital data is created to ensure no information is lost or overlooked;
- The authenticity of digital data is preserved using cryptographic algorithms;
- A chain of custody is established to maintain integrity through the evidence's life cycle; and
- Actions taken by people through the different investigative phases are recorded.

The legal aspects of technology crimes have many overlapping areas of laws and regulations. While there are commonalities amongst them, the number of international laws and regulations enacted do vary when it comes to their respective statutes, standards, and precedence. Generally, these laws and regulations were created with the intention of bridging the gap between risk (i.e., criminal activity) and technology (i.e., fruit or tool). The laws and regulations were also designed to anticipate the potential for dispute and reduce the likelihood of such dispute.

Jurisdiction

Jurisdiction is the power, or right, of a legal system (i.e., court, law enforcement) to exercise its authority in deciding over a (1) person, relating to the authority for trying individuals as a defendant; (2) subject matter, relating to authority originating from the country's laws and regulations; or (3) territory, relating to the geographic area where a court has authority to decide. In some cases, depending on the crime committed, concurrent jurisdiction can exist where two different legal systems have simultaneous authority over the same case.

In the simplest of scenarios, a legal matter can be tried in the location (i.e., country) where the crime took place. However, with the ways in which technology, such as the Internet, has an extensive global reach and crimes are committed using this delivery channel spanning several countries, it has become somewhat challenging to determine where to prosecute. In cases when there is contention over where a case should be tried, the jurisdiction of the court needs to be assessed and alternatives considered.

Although modern technology adds an additional layer of complexity to jurisdiction issues, international courts are becoming more familiar with laws and regulations relating to technology and are making more informed decisions about which legal system has jurisdiction.

Digital Forensics Resources

This book is written from a non-technical, business perspective and is intended for use as an implementation guide to prepare any organization to enhance its digital forensics readiness by moving away from reacting to incidents/events and becoming proactive with investigations.

While the basic principles, methodologies, and techniques of digital forensics are covered, this book focuses on outlining—in detail—how an organization can enhance its knowledge, processes, and technologies to implement effective and proactive digital forensics readiness.

There are countless resources available that are designed specifically to teach different the basics or specifics contained within the digital forensics discipline. The volume of reference material on digital forensics topics is beyond the scope of this text, which intends to identify and include them as a reference in this book. Contained within the bibliography of this book are numerous publications on the topic of digital forensics that can be consulted for more information.

Summary

The rise and continued evolution of cybercrime has made a significant contribution to the formation of what digital forensic science is today. Growing from the pastime of hobbyists, the establishment of forensically sound principles, methodologies, and techniques has turned it into a respected and authoritative discipline.

Investigative Process Methodology

2

Introduction

From what was covered in Chapter 1, "Understanding Digital Forensics," the digital forensics disciple is built on an extensive common body of knowledge (CBK) of well-established and proven scientific principles, methodologies, and techniques. With the evolution of digital forensics throughout the years, consistent advancements have been made in areas such as education, technologies, and processes, all of which painted a picture that bypassing, switching, or not following proper processes could result in missed, incomplete, or inadmissible evidence.

As early as 1984, law enforcement agencies began developing processes and procedures to use as part of their computer forensics investigations. This eventually led to the realization that, from bypassing, switching, or not following correct processes, digital investigations can result in missed, incomplete, or inadmissible evidence. Since then, several authors have attempted to develop and propose digital forensics process models to address a specific need, such as law enforcement, or with a generalized scope with the intention that it could be adopted internationally.

Existing Process Models

When technology was first used as part of criminal activities, practitioners did not follow any standardized principles, methodologies, or techniques when it came to collecting and processing digital evidence. It was only in the 1980s that law enforcement agencies realized there was a need to have an established set of processes that could be consistently followed to support of their forensics investigations and guarantee the legal admissibility of digital evidence.

Since then, there have been several authors who have taken on the task of developing and proposing a process model by which digital forensics practitioners can follow as assurance that digital evidence remains authentic, maintains integrity, and is legally admissible by following repeatable methodologies and techniques. Over the years, several different process models were proposed to formalize the digital forensics discipline and transform "ad hoc" tasks and activities into tested and scientifically proven methodologies.

Displayed in Table 2.1 is a list of process methodologies that have been developed and proposed for digital forensics investigations. It is important to note that while this list may not be complete, the inclusion of a process methodology does not suggest it is better or recommended over other methodologies that were not included in the table.

Every digital forensics process model noted in Table 2.1 was developed with distinct characteristics and with the purpose of addressing a specific need of the digital forensics investigative workflow. There are, however, no criteria for stipulating which of these process models is the one and only right way for conducting a digital forensics investigation.

Depending on why the process model was developed, such as law enforcement, there are advantages and disadvantages depending on the investigative scenario, for example, being too rigid, linear, or generalized. In Appendix A, "Investigative Process Models," further dissect the digital forensics process models identified Table 2.1 to understand the tasks performed in phases and better understand the uniqueness and commonalities with investigative workflow phases. Despite the differences noted amongst the process models, there are still significant commonalities in how some phases are used across multiple process models. These similarities confirm that while the process models address different investigative requirements, the underlying forensic science principles, methodologies, and techniques are applied consistently throughout.

As illustrated in Figure 2.1, we can get a better sense for how some phases are frequently used across multiple digital forensics process models. Without getting caught up in the subtle differences in naming conventions, it is quite apparent that there is an opportunity to consolidate all phases identified throughout each process model into these common phases. Of special note, highlighted in the graphic below are seven phases that have the highest frequency of re-occurrence:

- *Preparation* includes activities to ensure equipment and personnel are prepared.
- *Identification* involves detection of an incident or event.
- *Collection* of relevant data is done using approved techniques.
- *Preservation* establishes proper evidence gathering and chain of custody.
- *Examination* evaluates digital evidence to reveal data and reduce volume.
- *Analysis* examines the context and content of digital evidence to determine relevancy.
- *Presentation* includes preparing reporting documentation.

Process models developed to support the digital forensics investigative workflow focus on establishing the activities and tasks performed throughout to ensure that processes are not bypassed, switched, or disregarded.

Table 2.1   Digital Forensics Process Models

ID	Name	Author(s)	Year	Phases
M01	Computer Forensics Investigative Process	M. Pollitt	1995	4
M02	Computer Forensics Process Model	U.S. Department of Justice	2001	4
M03	Digital Forensics Research Workshop Investigative Model (Generic Investigation Process)	Palmer	2001	6
M04	Scientific Crime Scene Investigation Model	Lee et al.	2001	4
M05	Abstract Model of the Digital Forensics Procedures	Reith et al.	2002	9
M06	Integrated Digital Investigation Process	Carrier and Spafford	2003	5
M07	End to End Digital Investigation	Stephenson	2003	9
M08	Enhanced Integrated Digital Investigation Process	Baryamureeba and Tushabe	2004	5
M09	Extended Model of Cyber Crime Investigation	Ciardhuain	2004	13
M10	A Hierarchical, Objective Based Framework for the Digital Investigations Process	Beebe and Clark	2004	6
M11	Event Based Digital Forensics Investigation Framework	Carrier and Spafford	2004	5
M12	Four Step Forensics Process	Kent et al.	2006	4
M13	Framework for a Digital Forensics Investigation	Kohn et al.	2006	3
M14	Computer Forensics Field Triage Process Model	Roger et al.	2006	12
M15	FORZA—Digital Forensics Investigation Framework	Ieong	2006	6
M16	Common Process Model for Incident and Computer Forensics	Freiling and Schwittay	2007	3
M17	Dual Data Analysis Process	Bem and Huebner	2007	4
M18	Digital Forensics Model Based on Malaysian Investigation Process	Perumal	2009	7
M19	Generic Framework for Network Forensics	Pilli et al.	2010	9
M20	Generic Computer Forensics Investigation Model	Yusoff	2011	5
M21	Systematic Digital Forensics Investigation Model	Agarwal et al.	2011	11

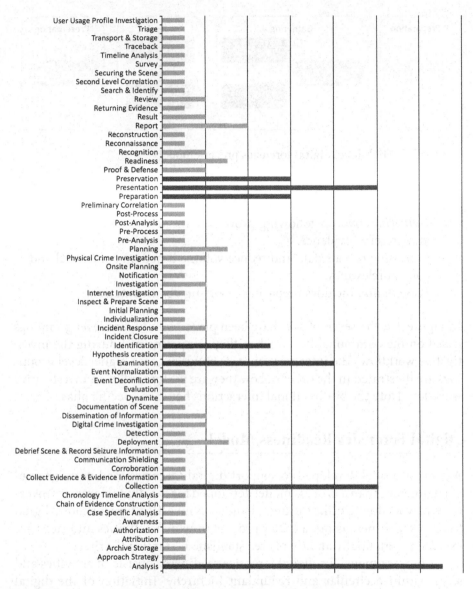

Figure 2.1 Phases as used across digital forensics process models.

As outlined in the previous section, there are seven common phases of a digital forensics investigation workflow: *preparation, identification, collection, preservation, examination, analysis,* and *presentation.* From the descriptions of each of these phases, we see that there are further commonalities between them that allow for further consolidation of these phases into a higher-level grouping of workflow categories:

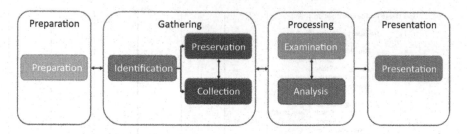

Figure 2.2 High-level digital forensics process model.

- *Preparation* includes activities to ensure administrative, technical, and physical provisions are in place.
- *Gathering* involves following proven techniques to identify, collect, and preserve evidence.
- *Processing* reveals data and reduce volume based on contextual and content relevancy.
- *Presentation* includes preparing reporting documentation.

In Figure 2.2, the seven phases have been placed into higher-level groupings based on the commonalities of when they are performed during the investigative workflow. The inter-relationships between these higher-level groupings are illustrated in the order of how they are performed in an investigative workflow. Note the bi-directional interactions between specific phases.

Digital Forensics Readiness Model

A process model developed to support digital forensics readiness is somewhat different than a process model developed for the digital forensics investigative workflow. Unlike the digital forensics investigative workflow, digital forensics readiness is not a linear process in which activities and steps are executed sequentially and there are established "start/end" criteria.

A process model for digital forensics readiness consists of activities and steps within a circular and redundant hierarchy. Initiation of the digital forensics readiness process model can originate from any activity or step and can subsequently lead to any other phase. The digital forensics readiness process model must establish administrative, technical, and physical foundations to effectively support the activities and tasks performed in all phases of the digital forensics process model by:

- Maximizing the potential use of digital evidence
- Minimizing the cost(s) of digital forensics investigations
- Minimizing the interference disruption of business processes
- Preserving and improving the information security posture

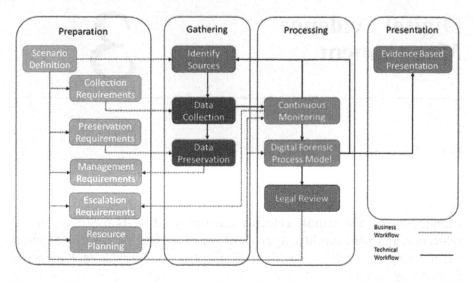

Figure 2.3 Digital forensics readiness process model.

High-level groupings of a digital forensics readiness process model follow the same naming convention as in the digital forensics process model. Figure 2.3 illustrates the activities and steps that make up the digital forensics readiness process model. Within this process model, there is a combination of sequential steps within each phase as well as redundant workflows that are dependent on the nature of the investigation at hand. This digital forensics process model serves as the basis for the detailed topics addressed in *Section B* of this book.

Summary

Digital forensic science has long established itself as a discipline that adheres to consistent, repeatable, and defensible processes. Although there have been several models developed to meet the unique needs of how digital forensics is practiced, they are all homogenous in the design methodology. Following a process methodology that is ambiguous to the context of its implementation, the digital forensics community adopts a common model as the basis for conducting consistent, repeatable, and defensible processes.

Digital Evidence Management 3

Introduction

Evidence is a critical component of every digital forensics investigation. Whether it is physical or digital, the methodologies and techniques used to gather, process, and handle evidence ultimately affect its meaningfulness, relevancy, and admissibility. Appropriate safeguards must exist throughout the investigative work to provide assurance that the lifecycle of evidence is forensically sound.

Following the High-Level Digital Forensics Process Model outlined in Chapter 2, "Investigative Process Methodology," each phase of the investigative workflow will be examined to determine the requirements for managing evidence through its lifetime.

Like how the Confidentiality, Integrity, and Availability (CIA) Triad outlines the most critical components for implementing an information security program; the Administrative, Physical, and Technical (APT) Triad describes the most critical components for implementing information security controls in support of digital forensics investigations.

Types of Digital Evidence

Historically, the legal system has viewed digital evidence as hearsay evidence because for the longest time there were no scientific techniques to ascertain that the data were factual. This meant that digital evidence being presented before the courts would commonly be dismissed because its authenticity and integrity could not be determined beyond a reasonable doubt. However, as digital evidence became more prevalent with the global adoption of technology, and its use in criminal activities, exceptions to admissibility began to arise. For example, under the *Federal Rules of Evidence 803(6)*, an exception to viewing digital evidence as hearsay evidence exists whereby digital evidence is admissible if it demonstrates "records of regularly conducted activity" as a business record, such as an act, event, condition, opinion, or diagnosis.

However, to qualify digital evidence as a business record within this exception requires digital evidence to be demonstrated as authentic, reliable, and trustworthy. Criteria for what type of data constitutes an admissible business record falls within the following categories:

- *Technology-generated data*, or background evidence, is any electronically stored information (ESI) that has been created and is being maintained because of programmatic processes or algorithms (i.e., log files). These records fall within the rules of hearsay exception on the basis that the data are proven to be authentic because of properly functioning programmatic processes or algorithms.
- *Technology-stored data* is any ESI that has been created and is being maintained because of user input and interactions (e.g., word productivity document). These records fall within the rules of hearsay exception on the basis that the individual creating the data is reliable, is trustworthy, and has not altered the data when it any way.

Building off these evidence categories, the following groupings can also be applied to provide another perspective on types of evidence:

- *Background evidence* is any ESI that has been created as part of normal business operations that are used to establish facts and conclusions during an investigation. Examples of this type of evidence include:
  - Network devices such as routers, switches, or firewalls;
  - Authentication records such as directory services or physical access systems;
  - Data management solutions such as backups, archives, or classification engines; and
  - Audit information such as system, application, or security logs.
- *Foreground evidence* is any ESI that has been created as a result of an object's—whether human, application, or system—interactions or activities that directly support an investigation or identify perpetrators. Examples of this type of evidence include:
  - Real-time monitoring systems such as intrusion prevention systems (IPS), packet sniffers, or anti-malware technologies;
  - Application software such as file integrity monitoring (FIM) and data loss prevention (DLP);
  - Business process systems such as fraud monitoring;

- Address books, calendar entries, to-do lists, memos; and
- Electronic communication channels such as email, text, chat, instant messaging, or web browsing history.

With both technology-generated and technology-stored data, it is important to keep in mind that historically the legal system viewed all digital artifacts as hearsay evidence and would not admit them as evidence. However, given how technology evolved to become so pervasive, the courts amended their rulings as to where exceptions can be made, given the authenticity and trustworthiness of the digital evidence being presented. Further discussion on legal and regulatory precedence relating to digital evidence can be found in Chapter 16, "Ensuring Legal Review."

Common Sources of Digital Evidence

Traditionally, digital evidence was primarily gathered from computer systems such as desktops, laptops, and servers. However, the reality now is that digital evidence exists in the form of structured and unstructured ESI across many different technologies that are inclusive to traditional computer systems, such as networks, removable devices (e.g., universal serial bus [USB]), mobile devices, and cloud computing environments.

   With the widespread use of technology in business operations, every organization will have ESI that is considered potential digital evidence generated across various sources. Because of this, careful consideration needs to be given when identifying data sources of potential digital evidence. While the examples below are by no means exhaustive or a complete representation of where digital evidence can be identified, the following data sources should be included as sources of relevant and meaningful ESI to be used as digital evidence.

> **Note:** While this book does cover the fundamental principles, methodologies, and techniques of digital forensics, it largely focuses on outlining how the people, process, and technology areas are used to defend the enterprise through integrating digital forensics capabilities with key business functions. This book is not designed to provide readers with technical knowledge about digital forensics, that is, including the "hands-on" and "how to" aspects of the discipline such as how to forensically acquire technology devices.

Log Files

As a form of background evidence, log files are typically generated from the operation of many different systems and applications. When used as evidence, these logs can be a valuable source of information for correlating and reconstructing events to determine what occurred (and in what order). For example, different technology-generated logs that can exist within an enterprise environment include the following:

- *Access* logs contain records of authentication, authorization, and admittance by systems and users into systems and information assets.
- *Audit* logs contain records of specific operations, procedures, or activities associated with interactions and communications between systems and users.
- *Error* logs contain records of faults, unexpected events, or abnormal behaviors that occur during normal system operations.
- *External* logs contain records of interactions and communications between an entity and external systems or users.
- *Infrastructure* logs contain records of specific operations, procedures, or activities associated with operational systems and services.
- *Transactional* logs contain records associated with the interaction with and transmission of information assets between systems and users.
- *Security* logs contain records of events associated with continuous security monitoring of systems and users.

Depending on the type of log file, there will be different data attributes available that can be logged as part of a single event record. However, across all log types there are common data attributes that should be recorded including the following:

- *Unique identifier* is a distinctive value representing a single event record (e.g., A1728C27F0)
- *Log timestamp* is the full date and time the event was recorded in the log file, and it includes relevant time-zone information if not in Coordinated Universal Time (UTC).
- *Event timestamp* is the full date and time the event occurred, and it includes relevant time-zone information if not in Coordinated Universal Time (UTC).
- *Event type* ranks the event specific to the type of record entry created.
- *Event priority* ranks the event specific to its potential impact.

- *Event category* ranks the event specific to the type of interaction and communication occurring between systems and users.
- *Event message* provides additional detailed information about the event not contained within any other attribute field of the event record.
- *Account name* is the full name of the account associated with the event.
- *Source IP address* is the IP address from which the event originated.

Computer Systems

Perhaps the oldest technology where digital evidence existed includes traditional computing systems such as servers, workstations, and laptops. For decades, these form factors were predominantly used to support both personal and business users where many formats of digital evidence can exist in some variation, including both technology-generated (background) and technology-stored (foreground) ESI.

Within computer systems, there are many different digital artifacts created, some of which are unbeknown to users, that can be used as digital evidence. For example, the following are digital artifacts that can be gathered from computer systems as background evidence:

- Random access memory (RAM) containing information such as username and passwords, running processes, and network connections
- Event log files maintaining records of security, system, or access events
- Temporary files such as caches (i.e., browsing history), dump files, or paging/swap files
- Registry hives and keys containing artifacts associated with applications and the host operating system (OS)

In addition to the background evidence artifacts, computer systems have also incorporated and support a wide variety of third-party software applications that allow users to create, interact with, and store many types of ESI. For example, the following are digital artifacts that can be gathered from computer systems as foreground evidence:

- Configuration and application-specific files (i.e., data outputs, runtime instructions)
- Malicious code or applications (i.e., root kits, backdoors)
- Unstructured documents (i.e., word processing)

With all digital evidence on computer systems, it is important to consider the order of volatility when deciding which digital evidence needs to be gathered, as is discussed in Chapter 2, "Investigative Process Methodology." Understanding that there are several different OS used with traditional computer systems, the types of digital artifacts that can exist will be inherent to each and may not be present in all instances.

Infrastructure Devices

From the time network communications were introduced, the potential sources of digital evidence have expanded beyond stand-alone computer systems. In today's technological world, most notably within an enterprise environment, infrastructure devices (i.e., routers, firewalls, proxies, etc.) are actively monitoring and capturing all communications and actions passing through their backplane. The events captured and recorded by these technologies, as technology-generated data, are an excellent source of background evidence that can be used to correlate and corroborate the movement of an attack through the organization.

In line with the statements made in the previous section, it is important to remember that legal admissibility of technology-generated data requires that the authenticity and trustworthiness of the digital evidence is demonstrable. Further discussion on legal and regulatory precedence relating to digital evidence can be found in Chapter 16, "Ensuring Legal Review."

Virtual Systems

Virtualization has become an extremely attractive option to operate both computer systems and infrastructure devices because they are a cost-effective means of quickly provisioning technology resources. For the most part, the systems hosted in these virtual environments will produce similar digital artifacts as found in traditional computer systems with physical hardware. However, within these rapidly elastic virtual environments exists a networking backplane of system communications that do travel beyond the physical host system where virtualization is being run.

Because of how this internal backplane operates, all indicators that an attack is moving between virtualized systems is not going to be available—in typical technology-generated log files—because of the way in which virtualization works. Where this type of internal communication exists, digital forensics practitioners need to remember that the network communications between virtualized systems can only be observed using network forensics tools and techniques directly on the physical host system.

As illustrated in Figure 3.1, virtualized systems have an underlying host environment (hardware and software) where digital evidence can be generated and collected. When a virtual system is involved in an incident, or discovered during an investigation, it is important that all data objects associated with the virtual systems are gathered from both host and guest systems, for example:

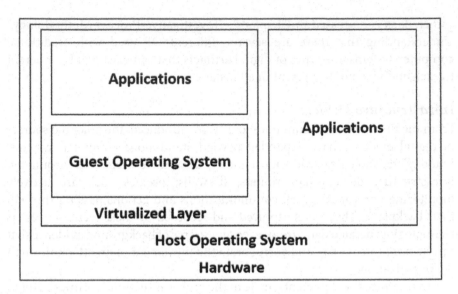

Figure 3.1 Virtualization architecture.

- Virtual machine images (files that contain a guest operating system, file system, and data objects);
- Log files containing information such as virtual disk partitioning, virtual networking settings, or state configurations; or
- Dump files from random access memory (RAM) or paging files.

Cloud Computing

Through the combination of several major technology concepts, cloud computing has evolved over several decades to become the next stage in computing models. As cloud computing continues to mature, providing organizations with an inexpensive means of deploying computing resources, it is driving a fundamental change in the ways technology is becoming a common layer of service-oriented architectures. Cloud computing presents a unique challenge because of the dynamic nature in which information exists; and it has motivated a shift to where organizations have less control over physical infrastructure assets. This leads to the inherent challenge of maintaining best practices for cloud computing while continuing to enable digital forensics capabilities.

Cloud computing has revolutionized the ways ESI is stored, processed, and transmitted. There are numerous challenges facing the digital forensics community when it comes to gathering and processing digital evidence in cloud computing environments. These challenges—broadly categorized as technical, legal, or organizational—can impede or ultimately prevent the ability to conduct digital forensics. While cloud computing possesses similarities to its predecessor technologies, the introduction of this operating model presents challenges to digital forensics.

With cloud-based systems managed by cloud service providers (CSP), organizations may not have direct access to the hardware to gather and process evidence following traditional methodologies and techniques. As result, collection and preservation of cloud-based evidence that is relevant to a specific organization's investigation can be challenging where factors such as multi-tenancy, distributed resourcing (cross-borders), or volatile data are persistent.

Mobile Devices

From significant technology advancements made over the last decade, business has evolved into a much more dynamic and mobile workforce. Since its inception, the world of mobile technologies has evolved quickly to the point that new devices, operating systems, and threats are emerging every day. Mobile devices present a unique challenge because of how quickly these technologies are changing and the shifting of traditional concepts, such as establishing a perimeter around systems and data. This leads to the inherent challenge of maintaining best practices for mobile device usage while continuing to enable digital forensics capabilities.

In today's world of technology, mobile devices (including smartphones and tablets) have allowed business to transform into a much more mobile and dynamic workplace where employees can work anywhere at any time. However, with a mobile workforce it is quite common that mobile devices, both personally and corporate owned, have been used to access business information that may need to be gathered and processed during an investigation.

Since mobile devices have become commonplace since the late 1990s, the digital forensics community has seen an increasing demand to gather and process digital evidence from these devices, which has presented numerous challenges. With the proliferation of mobile devices as technologies designed for consumers and businesses alike, they increasingly contain much more potential for digital evidence that needs to be gathered and collected during an investigation.

External Sources

Aside from cloud computing environments, there will cases where digital evidence exists beyond the boundaries of the organization's control that is both relevant and meaningful to an investigation. Understanding the scope of what could constitute an external source, examples of where digital evidence can be found include collaboration and communication platforms such as web-based email or social media platforms, or managed service providers (MSP), who provide defined sets of services to clients.

Within these external sources, much like the other sources of evidence, much of the same type of background and foreground digital evidence can exist, and it differs vis a vis what ESI the systems or application within these sources create. Where digital evidence has been identified to exist in an external source, like cloud environment, it is not as easily or readily available for organizations. In most cases, it is necessary to involve law enforcement agencies to facilitate gathering digital evidence from external sources, which can prove to be a troublesome and challenging task. Alternatively, formalized legal contracts can be drafted as a mechanism for guaranteeing that third parties will cooperate in gathering digital evidence when required by the organization.

The above examples are by no means a definitive representation of every location where potential digital evidence can exist because every organization is unique and will need to determine the relevance and usefulness of each data source as it is identified. Additional information about different legal and regulatory governance around the proof of fact, as relates to evidence, can be found in Chapter 16, "Ensuring Legal Review."

Federal Rules of Evidence

Laws of evidence govern the proof of facts, and the conclusions drawn from these facts, during legal proceedings. Up until the twentieth century, evidence presented during trial was largely the result of laws derived from case law, or decisional law. During the twentieth century, work began to arrange these common laws into formal evidence rules. Enacted in 1975, and last amended in 2015, the United States (U.S.) *Federal Rules of Evidence (FRE)* applies to legal proceedings by regulating when, how, and for what purpose evidence can be placed before a trier of fact for consideration.

Issues of relevance and authenticity are commonly put into question about whether, when validated as part of a general acceptance testing program, evidence is justifiable to be presented before a court of law. Within this context, relevancy is not inherently a characteristic of a specific piece of evidence, but instead exists within its relationship with other pieces of evidence that demonstrate proof of fact. For example, *FRE 401* states that evidence is deemed relevant if it has *any tendency to make a fact more or less probable than it would be without the evidence* and that *the fact is of consequence in determining the action.* Reinforcing this, *FRE 901* states that in order *to satisfy the requirement of authenticating or identifying an item of evidence, the proponent must produce evidence sufficient to support a finding that the item is what the proponent claims it is.*

Traditionally, legal systems—such as those of the United States—have viewed digital evidence, otherwise referred to as ESI, as being hearsay evidence because there was no scientific technique to demonstrate that the data are indeed factual. This meant that digital evidence being presented before the courts would commonly be dismissed because its authenticity could not be determined beyond a reasonable doubt. However, as digital evidence became more prevalent with the global adoption of technology and its use in criminal activities, exceptions to admissibility begun to arise. Under *FRE 803(6)*, an exception to viewing ESI as hearsay evidence exists whereby digital evidence is admissible if it demonstrates *records of regularly conducted activity* as a business record, such as an act, event, condition, opinion, or diagnosis.

Qualifying business records under this exception require that the digital data be demonstrated as authentic, reliable, and trustworthy. As described in U.S. *Federal Rules of Evidence 803(6)*, the requirements for qualifying business record are achieved by proving:

1. The record was made at or near the time by—or information was transmitted by—someone with knowledge;
2. The record was kept in the course of a regularly conducted activity of a business, organization, occupation, or calling, whether or not for profit;
3. Making the record was a regular practice of that activity;
4. All these conditions are shown by the testimony of the custodian or another qualified witness, or by a certification that complies with Rule 902(11) or (12) or with a statute permitting certification; and
5. Neither the source of information nor the method or circumstances of preparation indicate a lack of trustworthiness.

Supporting the requirements of *FRE 803(6)* for testimony of the custodian or another qualified witness, *FRE 902(11) and 902(12)* describes the requirements for certifying domestic records of regularly conducted activity as follows:

- *Rule 902(11)*: The original or a copy of a domestic record that meets the requirements of Rule 803(6)(A)–(C), as shown by a certification of the custodian or another qualified person that must be signed in a manner that, if falsely made, would subject the signer to criminal penalty under the laws where the certification was signed. Before the trial or hearing, the proponent must give an adverse party reasonable written notice of the intent to offer the record—and must make the record and certification available for inspection—so that the party has a fair opportunity to challenge them.

- *Rule 902(12)*: The original or a copy of a foreign record that meets the requirements of Rule 803(6)(A)–(C), as shown by a certification of the custodian or another qualified person that must be signed in a manner that, if falsely made, would subject the signer to criminal penalty under the laws where the certification was signed. Before the trial or hearing, the proponent must give an adverse party reasonable written notice of the intent to offer the record—and must make the record and certification available for inspection—so that the party has a fair opportunity to challenge them.

Business records are commonly challenged on issues of whether the data were altered or damaged after creation (integrity) and validation/verification of the programmatic processes used (authenticity). As a means of lessening these challenges, *Federal Rules of Evidence 1002* describes the need for proving the trustworthiness of digital evidence through the production of the original document. To meet this requirement, organizations must implement a series of safeguards, precautions, and controls to ensure that when digital evidence is admitted into a court of law it can be demonstrably proven as authentic against its original source.

Investigative Process Methodology

As illustrated previously in Figure 2.3 and as discussed further in Chapter 2, "Investigative Process Methodology," the high-level digital forensics process model consists of the following phases:

- *Preparation* includes activities to ensure administrative, technical, and physical provisions are in place
- *Gathering* involves following proven techniques to identify, collect, and preserve evidence
- *Processing* reveals data and reduces volume based on the contextual and content relevancy
- *Presentation* includes preparing reporting documentation

This process model supports the investigative workflow by establishing the sequence and relationship between phases to ensure that activities and tasks that must be completed are not bypassed, switched, or disregarded. By not consistently following an investigative methodology, there is potential for dire consequences with respect to the authenticity, integrity, and legal admissibility of digital evidence. Throughout the sections to follow, each phase of the high-level digital forensics process model has been expanded to explore requirements for digital evidence management.

Preparation

As the first phase of the investigative workflow, preparation is essential for the activities and steps performed in all other phases of the workflow. Ultimately, if the preparation activities and steps are deficient in any way, whether they are not comprehensive enough or not reviewed regularly for accuracy, there is a greater risk that evidence may be interfered with, altered in some form, or even unavailable when needed.

Information Security Management

The establishment of information security management is a must so that the organization has defined its overall goals. Management, with involvement from key stakeholders such as legal, privacy, security, and human resources, works to define a series of documents that describe exactly how the organization will go about achieving these goals. Figure 3.2 illustrates the hierarchy of the information security governance framework and the relationship between these documents in terms of which have direct influence and precedence over others.

In the context of digital forensics, the implementation of these documents serves as the administrative groundwork for indirectly supporting the subsequent phases where digital evidence is involved. The sections to follow explore these documents individually and provide specifics on the types that contribute to digital forensics readiness.

Policies At the highest level of documentation policies are built as formalized blueprints used to describe the organization's goals affecting evidence. These documents address general terms and are not intended to contain the level of detail found in standards, guidelines, procedures, or processes.

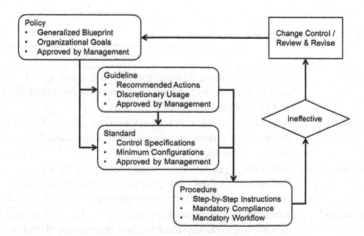

Figure 3.2 Information security governance framework.

Before writing a policy the first step is to define the scope and purpose (why the document is required), what technical and physical evidence is included, and why it is being included. This allows the organization to consider all possibilities and determine what types of policies must be written and how many policies are required.

A common mistake organizations face is writing a single policy document that encompasses a broad scope which is not easily understood and is difficult to distribute. Instead of having one large document to support all digital forensics requirements, multiple policies should be written to focus on specific evidence sources.

The type of policies to be written is subjective to the organization and its requirements for gathering and maintaining evidence. While there might be a specific type of policy document absent from Table 3.1, it does contain a list of common policies your organization must have in place to support digital forensics.

Guidelines   Following the implementation of a policy, guidelines provide recommendations for how the generalized blueprints can be implemented. In certain cases, security cannot be described through the implementation of specific controls, minimum configuration requirements, or other mechanisms. Unlike standards, these documents are created to contain guidelines for end users to use as a reference to follow proper security.

Consider a policy that requires a risk assessment to be routinely completed against a specific system. Instead of developing standards or procedures to perform this task, a guideline document is used to determine the methodologies that must be followed, thus allowing the teams to fill in the details as needed.

Table 3.1   Common Policies

Policy	Scope
Acceptable use	Defines acceptable use of equipment and computing services and the appropriate end-user controls to protect the organization's resources and proprietary information
Business conduct	Defines the guidelines and expectations of individuals within the organization to demonstrate fair business practices and encourage a culture of openness and trust
Information security	Defines the organization's commitment to globally manage information security risks effectively and efficiently, and in compliance with applicable regulations wherever it conducts business
Internet and email	Defines the requirements for proper use of the organization's Internet and electronic mail systems to make users aware of what is considered acceptable and unacceptable use

Table 3.2   Common Guidelines

Guideline	Scope
Data loss prevention	Awareness of end users on how to safeguard organizational data from unintentional or accidental loss or theft
Mobile/portable devices	Recommendations for end users to protect the organization's data stored on mobile and/or portable devices
Passcode selection	Considerations for end users to select strong passcodes for access into organizational systems
Risk assessments	Direction for assessors to use documented methodologies and proven techniques for assessing organizational systems

The type of guidelines to be written is subjective to the organization and its requirements for gathering and maintaining evidence. While there might be a specific type of guideline document absent from Table 3.2, it does contain a list of common guidelines your organization must have in place to support digital forensics.

Standards   After policies are in places, or because of a guideline, a series of standards can be developed to define more specific rules used to support the implemented policies. Standards are used as the drivers for policies; and by setting standards, policies that are difficult to implement—or that encompass the entire organization—are guaranteed to work in all environments. For example, if the information security policy requires all users to be authenticated to the organization, the standard for using a solution is established here.

Standards can be used to create a minimum level of security necessary to meet the predetermined policy requirements. Standard documents can contain configurations, architectures, or design specifications that are specific to the systems or solutions they directly represent, such as firewalls or logical access. While standards might or might not reflect existing business processes, they represent a minimum requirement that must be able to change to meet evolving business requirements.

The type of standard to be written is subjective to the organization and its requirements for gathering and maintaining evidence. While there might be a specific type of standard document absent from Table 3.3, it does contain a list of common standards your organization must have in place to support digital forensics.

Procedures   From the guidelines and standards that have been implemented, the last documents to be created are the procedures used by administrators, operations personnel, analysts, etc. to follow as they perform their job functions.

Policies, standards, and guidance documents all have a relationship with digital evidence whereby they do not have direct interactions with the

Table 3.3 Common Standards

Standard	Scope
Backup, retention, and recovery	Defines the means and materials required to recover from an undesirable event, in a timely and reliable manner, that causes systems and/or data to become unavailable
Email systems	Define the configurations necessary to minimize business risk and maximize use of email content because of the available and continuous nature of the supporting infrastructure
Firewall management	Defines the configurations necessary to ensure the integrity and confidentiality of the organization's systems and/or data is protected as a result of the available and continuous nature of the supporting infrastructure
Logical access	Defines the requirements for authenticating and authorizing users' access to mitigate exposure of the organization's systems and/or data
Malware detection	Defines the configurations necessary to ensure the attack surface of vulnerable systems is mitigated against known malicious software
Network security	Defines the requirements for controlling external, remote, and/or internal access to the organization's systems and/or data
Platform configurations	Defines the minimum-security configurations necessary to ensure the organization's systems mitigate unauthorized access or unintended exposure of data
Physical access	Defines the methods used to ensure adequate controls exist to mitigate unauthorized access to the organization's premises

systems and/or data. On the other hand, procedures are documents whereby interactions with digital evidence are directly associated through clearly defined activities and steps.

To better understand the different procedures involved with digital evidence management, each procedure will be explored throughout the remainder of this chapter as they apply to the different phases within the high-level digital forensics process model.

Essentially, the culture and structure of each organization influences how these governance documents are created. Regardless of where (internationally) business is conducted or the size of the organization, there are five simple principles that should be followed as generic guidance for achieving a successful governance framework:

- *Keep it simple.* All documentation should be as clear and concise as possible. The information contained within each document should be stated as briefly as possible without omitting any critical pieces of information. Documentation that is drawn out and wordy is typically more difficult to understand, less likely to be read, and harder to interpret and implement.

- *Keep it understandable.* Documentation should be developed in a language that is commonly known throughout the organization. By leveraging a taxonomy, as discussed in Addendum D, "Building a Taxonomy," organizations can avoid the complication of using unrecognized terms and jargon.
- *Keep it practicable.* Regardless of how precise and clear the documentation might be, if it cannot be practiced then it is useless. An example of unrealistic documentation would be a statement indicating that incident response personnel are to be available 24 hours a day, even though there is no adequate means of contacting them when they are not in the office. For this reason, documentation that is not practicable is not effective and will be quickly ignored.
- *Keep it cooperative.* Good governance documentation is developed through the collaborative effort of all relevant stakeholders, such as legal, privacy, security, and human resources. If a key stakeholder has not been involved in the development of these documents, it is more likely that problems will arise during implementation.
- *Keep it dynamic.* Useful governance documents should be, by design, flexible enough to adapt with organizational changes and growth. It would be impractical to develop documentation that is focused on serving the current needs and desires of the organization without considering what could come in the future.

Lab Environment

Generally, a forensics lab environment is a secured facility used to process and, depending on the organization, store evidence gathered from a crime scene, security event, or incident. Foundationally, these facilities are built following a methodology similar to that applied when building a data center where strict security measures are implemented to guarantee contents are protected from unauthorized access and external contamination.

Planning   The foremost concern, as with any new project, is proper planning of the lab environment so that, as the project progresses, issues arising later can be reduced and the project will result in successful completion. This means taking necessary actions to carefully and deliberately set out the scope, schedule, and cost for the forensics lab environment before any work begins on construction.

Within the planning activities, it is important to follow a systematic approach when performing the following sequence of activities:

- Identify and analyze the organization's needs for building a forensics lab environment. Having previously understood the business risk scenarios for having digital forensics capabilities, along with establishing a governance framework, the work done at this stage should be not be exhaustive.
- Assemble a team of individuals who will provide knowledge and support (e.g., management funding approval) in the subsequent activities and tasks. Having previously identified key stakeholders, as discussed in Chapter 14, "Establish Continuing Education," identifying the project team should not be exhaustive.
- Define the strategy, structure, and schedule by which the remaining activities and tasks will follow. For example, a register of all activities should be developed to include a complete list of tasks that need to be completed, and this should be accompanied by the individual (or team) who is responsible for completing each task, the allotted timeline for completing the task, and any dependencies that exist between individual tasks so that critical paths to success can be identified.

Designing Next comes the task of designing the structure and layout of the forensics lab environment. Unfortunately, there is no "cookie cutter" approach that can be universally applied when designing a forensics lab because each environment is subjective as to the types of evidence, governance framework, and needs of the organization. Considering the functional requirements of the forensics lab, such as equipment and workspace, organizations should design their lab environment to be flexible enough so that it supports evolving business needs and continued growth in digital forensics capabilities.

As a foundational principle, the forensics lab environment must be both physically and logically secured from the organization's general network and office space so that the work being done with digital evidence does not result in contamination, lost material, or unauthorized disclosure. Working from the principles and concepts of data centers, the following design elements must be incorporated to guarantee the integrity, authenticity, and admissibility of evidence:

- Construction in a fully enclosed room located in the interior of a building with true floor to ceiling walls and no windows
- Access doors with internally facing hinges and fire safety windows reinforced with wire mesh material
- Walls constructed with permanent materials (i.e., concrete)
- Raised flooring with a fire suppression system

Building off the above physical design considerations, the following are logical design elements that need to be considered when designing a lab environment:

- Principles of least-privilege access are applied so that only authorized individuals are permitted unattended access.
- Unattended physical access is granted using multi-factor authentication mechanisms, including something you know (e.g., passcode), something you have (e.g., smartcard), and something you are (e.g., manager).
- Visitor access must be logged, and visitors must always be escorted.
- Evidence lockers and safes must always remain locked.
- Chain of custody logs for tracking evidence ownership must always be tracked.
- Inventory control mechanisms must be implemented to track and maintain complete, accurate, and up-to-date records of all lab equipment (i.e., software, forensics workstations, servers, etc.).
- Governance documents, such as standard operating procedures (SOP) and runbooks, must be readily available to lab personnel (i.e., software currency, evidence management).
- A lab manager who is responsible for the ongoing maintenance and safeguarding of the lab and its contents (i.e., digital evidence) must be assigned.

In addition to the physical and logical design elements required to secure the lab environment, this is where the identification and placement of hardware and software comes into play. When determining what equipment is needed as part of the forensics toolkit, it is important to refer to the work completed when documenting the business risk scenarios as the basis for acquiring forensics equipment. Also, it is important to keep in mind that each investigation is unique and, as noted previously, might require specific activities to be conduct either in the field or within the lab environment. Therefore, a variety of different tools and equipment may be required to fulfill a broad scope of potential investigative circumstances.

Selecting the right tools and equipment to properly support digital forensics capabilities requires having a good understanding of the organization's business risk scenarios and the technologies used to support their respective business functions. As part of the selection process, it is important that tools and equipment not be blindly purchased without first validating and verifying that they provide the functionality required to gather or process evidence existing throughout the organization.

Digital forensics practitioners must go through proper evaluation and assessment of tools and equipment before purchasing to demonstrate that these technologies will generate repeatable and reproducible results when following their governance documentation to gather or process their respective digital evidence. By completing a proof of concept (POC), the organization will have a level of assurance that the tools and equipment being used to support their digital forensics capabilities are forensically sound and will not introduce doubt into the evidence's integrity.

Whether selecting open-source or commercial-off-the-shelf (COTS) technologies for the forensics toolkit, there are many different solutions that can fit within the requirements of the organization's needs. As outlined in the introduction to this book, the focus of topics discussed throughout is not on getting into detailed technical execution discussions about how to perform digital forensics. In keeping with this scope, references have been made available in the *Resources* chapter at the end of this book, where lists of forensics tools and equipment can be found. It is important to note that, given how technology is a constantly evolving landscape, the inclusion of one specific forensics tool or piece of equipment over another does not suggest that any one item is better than or recommended over others that were not included.

Piecing all physical and logical components together, the team must thoroughly document their design plan so they have a complete view of the final lab environment design. With this plan in place, the team should review what has been identified for inclusion in the lab facility to ensure that what has been included meets the original requirements defined by the organization. If there are missing components identified, it is important for the team to take time to sort out the design before proceeding to the next step so that issues arising during construction will be reduced and the project will result in a successful completion.

Construction   Transforming the plan and design into a physical lab environment is where organizations will invest most of their resources (i.e., time, effort, cost). However, before any construction work can begin, the team needs to secure management approval and the funding necessary to build the facility. This is done by creating a business case that illustrates the costs and benefits so that stakeholders have enough details to support their decision making on whether the organization should proceed with implementing the final recommendation. A business case template has been provided in the *Templates* section of this book.

With the business case approved and funding available, construction of the lab environment can begin. It is important for the construction work to stay within the expected scope, schedule, and cost as outlined in the business case because any additional funding needed due to delays or other issues will require the team to go back to management for an explanation of the unaccounted overage(s) and approval of new requests. Keeping to the expected scope, schedule, and cost requires having a dedicated individual, such as a project control officer (PCO), to oversee all work being done on the lab. Ultimately, the PCO will be responsible for managing all project resources (e.g., people, funding) to ensure that agreed-upon deliverables meet the requirements within defined timelines and budget. As a strategy, keeping to the project plan might require multiple streams of work to be done in parallel by different members of the project team to procure and build:

- The physical lab environment, such as walls, floors, and access points (doors)
- Internal workspace equipment, such as desks, evidence lockers, and server racks
- Forensics hardware and software, such as workstations, write-blockers, and storage units

As work is being completed and project milestones are met, it is important to remember that there can be dependencies for how each stream of work can come together for a final deliverable. For example, the physical lab environment must be finished before any equipment or tools can be set up in the facility's workspace; and in some cases, obtaining workspace equipment needs to come before setting up the forensics hardware and software. However, when configuration and setup activities are required before hardware and software can be set up, use of a staging area can help to do this while waiting for equipment to be finalized.

Throughout the construction work, communication is essential to achieving a successful project completion. It is important that the PCO track and maintain an up-to-date record of the work being done/completed by scheduling periodic spot-checks at critical milestones during the construction.

Hardware and Software

With the digital forensics lab built, the team should begin to acquire a series of hardware equipment and software tools that will be needed to conduct investigations in a forensically sound manner. It is important that the digital forensics team keep in mind that each investigation is unique and may require a variety of different tools and equipment to maintain evidence integrity.

To identify and select the proper tools and equipment to perform their investigative activities and steps, the digital forensics team must have a good understanding of how different business environments function with respect to the hardware and operating system(s) they use. This assessment will determine what tools and equipment are required to gather and process evidence from the organization's data sources. While there might be some tools or equipment absent due to new ones being constantly developed, the

Resources section at the end of this book includes websites for some companies that have commercial offerings for digital forensics tools and equipment.

All digital forensics tools and equipment work differently, and behave differently, when used on different evidence sources. Before using any tools or equipment to gather or process evidence, investigators must be familiar with how to operate these technologies by practicing on a variety of evidence sources. This testing must demonstrate that the tools and equipment used generate repeatable and reproducible results. This process of testing introduces a level of assurance that the tools and equipment being used by investigators are forensically sound and will not introduce doubt into the evidence's integrity.

Refer to Addendum A, "Tool and Equipment Validation Program," for guidance on how digital forensics practitioners can test their forensics tools and equipment.

Forensics Workstations   Forensics workstations are a combination of specialized hardware and software technologies that, together, allow for digital evidence to be gathered and processed in a forensically sound manner. In the marketplace, there are several COTS manufacturers of forensics workstations that come pre-built with the hardware and software required to gather and process digital evidence. References have been made available in the *Resources* chapter at the end of this book, where lists of forensics tools and equipment can be found. It is important to note that, given how technology is a constantly evolving and changing landscape, the inclusion of one particular forensics tool or piece of equipment over another does not suggest that these are better or recommended over others that were not included.

If a decision is made to build a custom forensics workstation internally, it is important to note that this has some obvious advantages—and disadvantages—when compared to COTS hardware. On one hand, when building a forensics workstation, the forensics team can ensure that they have all the right hardware and software required to support their needs. However, pre-built systems come with a level of assurance that all components have been configured and integrated correctly to ensure the integrity, authenticity, and legal admissibility of digital evidence is maintained when being used. Whether a COTS system or one that is custom built, a forensics workstation should include the following components to provide the required digital forensics capabilities:

- Standard operating hardware such as a central processing unit (CPU), random access memory (RAM), and primary hard drive. The performance and capacity required of these components is dependent on the forensics team's requirements to support the needs of their organization.
- Add-on hardware components considered optional, subjective to the forensics team's needs, such as:

- Optical disc bays to read a variety of compact discs (CD) formats, digital video discs (DVDs), and Blu-Rays
- Network adaptors to interface with evidence storage networks (refer to the section below in this chapter for discussion of evidence storage networks)
- Connectors to access a variety of removable devices (i.e., universal serial bus [USB] drives, FireWire)
- Additional internal or external hard drive bays, verified as write-block enabled, to access a variety of hard drive formats (i.e., integrated drive electronics [IDE], serial advanced technology attachment [SATA], small computer system interface [SCSI], solid state drive [SSD])
- A primary operating system (OS) that supports the execution of required forensics software. Where needed, additional OS versions can be run using virtual machine (VM) or emulation software applications from the primary OS.

Before putting the forensics workstation into use, it is important that the forensics team complete thorough testing to verify and validate that the hardware and software components are working as expected and that they do not result in the forensics viability of digital evidence being lost.

Gathering

As the second phase of the investigative workflow, gathering is made up of the activities and steps performed to identify, collect, and preserve evidence. These activities and steps are critical in maintaining the meaningfulness, relevancy, and admissibility of evidence for the remainder of its lifecycle.

Operating Procedures

Prior to gathering evidence, there must be a series of written and approved operating procedures to assist the forensics team when performing evidence gathering activities and steps. The combination of governance that was developed through the information security management program, along with the validation and verification results from tool and equipment testing; these operating procedures are the backbone for investigators to follow as they work through the investigation.

Identification   Identification of evidence involves a series of activities and steps that must be performed in sequence. It is important to know what data sources, such as systems, peripherals, removable media, etc. are associated with or have an impacting role on the investigation.

When a data source has been identified, proper evidence handling must always be followed. If the evidence is handled incorrectly, there is a high probability that the evidence will no longer be meaningful, relevant, or admissible.

Operating procedures are required to support the investigative workflow and provide investigators with direction on how to execute their tasks in a repeatable and reproducible way.

Securing the Scene   Although one of the main focuses of digital forensics is digital evidence, it is critical that digital forensics practitioners consider both electronic and physical evidence within the scope of every investigation they conduct. Like how the first step law enforcement takes is to establish a perimeter around a crime scene to secure evidence, the same first step must be done during a digital forensics investigation. Whoever is responsible for securing the scene must be trained in and knowledgeable of the accepted activities, steps, and procedures to be followed.

By securing the physical environment, the current state of evidence can be documented and a level of assurance is established that evidence will be protected against tampering or corruption. While the activities, steps, and procedures used will vary and are subjective depending on the environment, it is critical that they are followed to minimize the potential for errors, oversights, or injuries.

An important rule to remember with all crime scenes is that everyone who enters or leaves a crime scene will either deposit something or take something with them. It is crucial that no unauthorized individuals be within a reasonable distance of the secured environment, as these persons can interfere with evidence and potentially disrupt the investigation.

At this phase, information and details are collected about the state of the scene at the highest level. Proper planning must take place to develop and implement operating procedures that address the different scenarios for how to physically and logically secure crime scenes.

Documenting the Scene   Having secured the physical environment, the next step is to document the scene and answer questions about what is present, where it is located, and how it is connected.

The most effective way to answer these questions is by videotaping, photographing, or sketching the secured environment before any evidence is handled. When capturing images of the physical environment, the following aspects of the scene must be documented:

- A complete view of the physical environment (e.g., floor location, department, workspace)
- Individual views of specific work areas as needed (e.g., bookshelves, systems, open cabinets, garbage cans)

- Hardwire connections to systems and where they lead (e.g., USB drives, printers, cameras)
- Empty slots or connectors not in use in the system as evidence that no connection existed
- Without pressing mouse or keypad buttons, what is visible on the monitor (e.g., running processes, open files, wallpaper)

Just like police officers record events in their notebooks, forensics investigators must maintain documentation for every interaction on the presumption that the investigation could end up in a court of law. The investigator's notes must include (at a minimum) date, time, investigator's full name, and all interactions. The notes should also have page or sequence numbers and have no whitespace present—fill that space with a solid line to prevent supplementary comments from being inserted. A logbook template has been provided as a reference in the *Templates* section of this book.

Search and Seizure   Once the scene is secured and thoroughly documented, investigators work on seizing evidence. But the goal of seizing evidence is not to seize everything at the scene. Through the knowledge and experience of trained investigators, educated decisions can be made about what forms of evidence need to be seized and then the justifications for doing so can be documented.

Digital evidence comes in many forms, such as application logs, network device configurations, badge reader logs, and audit trails. Given that these are only examples and depending on the scope of the investigation, there are potentially significantly more relevant evidence forms. Identifying and seizing all evidence can prove to be a challenging task for which technical operating procedures will provide guidance and support. However, from time to time investigators might encounter situations in which these technical operating procedures do not address collecting a specific evidence source. In these situations, having trained digital forensics professionals is essential in providing the knowledge and skills necessary to apply the fundamental principles, methodologies, and techniques of forensic science to seizing the evidence.

Documentation is at the center of the investigative workflow and is equally important when it comes to seizing evidence. When a physical (e.g., computer) or a logical (e.g., text file) artifact has been identified as relevant to an investigation, the act of seizing it as evidence initiates the chain of custody to establish authenticity by tracking where it came from, where it went after it was seized, and who handled it for what purpose. Custody tracking must accompany the evidence and be maintained throughout the lifetime of the evidence. A chain of custody template has been provided as a reference in the *Templates* section of this book.

All digital evidence is subject to the same rules and laws that apply to physical evidence in that prosecutors must demonstrate, without a doubt, that evidence is in the exact unchanged state it was in when the investigator seized it. The *Good Practices Guide for Computer Based Electronic Evidence* was developed by the Association of Chief of Police Officers (ACPO) in the United Kingdom to address evidence handling steps for the types of technologies commonly seized during an investigation. Within this document, there are four overarching principles that investigators must follow when handling evidence to maintain evidence authenticity:

- *Principle #1*: No action taken by law enforcement agencies or their agents should change data held on a computer or storage media which may subsequently be relied upon in court.
- *Principle #2*: In circumstances where a person finds it necessary to access original data held on a computer or on storage media, that person must be competent to do so and be able to give evidence explaining the relevance and the implications of their actions.
- *Principle #3*: An audit trail or other record of all processes applied to computer-based electronic evidence should be created and preserved. An independent third party should be able to examine those processes and achieve the same result.
- *Principle #4*: The person in charge of the investigation (the case officer) has overall responsibility for ensuring that the law and these principles are adhered to.

Collection and Preservation   The transition between a physical investigation and digital forensics activities starts with the collection of digital evidence. Digital evidence is volatile by nature and investigators are responsible for ensuring that the original state of seized evidence is preserved because of any tool or equipment used to collect it. Working in a controlled lab environment, investigators must create an exact, bit-level duplicate of original evidence using digital forensics tools and equipment that have been subject to validation and verification testing programs.

FRE Rule 1001 explains that a duplicate of digital evidence is admissible in court instead of the original when it is "the product of a method which insures accuracy and genuineness." To guarantee that the bit-level copy is an accurate and genuine duplicate of the original evidence source, one-way cryptographic algorithms such as the Message Digest Algorithm family (i.e., MD5, MD6) or the Secure Hashing Algorithm family (i.e., SHA-1, SHA-2, SHA-3) are used to generate hash values of both the original and the duplicate. Not only does the use of one-way cryptographic hash algorithms provide investigators with assurance that the bit-level copy is an exact duplicate of the original, they provide investigators with the means of verifying the integrity of the bit-level duplicate throughout the subsequent activities and task of the investigative workflow.

Having generated an exact bit-level duplicate to use during the processing phase to follow, the original evidence must be placed back into secure lockup with an update to the chain of custody reflecting the investigators' interactions with the original evidence sources. In addition, a new chain of custody for the bit-level duplicate must be created and maintained throughout the remainder of the evidence's lifetime.

In 2004–2005, it was discovered that both MD5 and SHA-1 algorithms contain flaws whereby two different data files or data sets have cryptographic hash values that are identical even though there are distinctly different properties and characteristics in the data themselves.

Otherwise known as "hash collisions," these flaws created concerns amongst the forensics community about the potential impact on the admissibility of digital evidence in a court of law. From a digital forensics perspective, this meant that a hash collision could be engineered so that separate pieces of digital evidence return the same hash value.

However, during a forensics investigation both the MD5 and SHA-1 algorithms are used as a way of demonstrating to the courts that the digital evidence being presented is in the same state as it was when it was obtained and that it has not been altered in any way, thus demonstrating the authenticity and integrity of the digital evidence.

In the 2009 trial of *United States v. Joseph Schmidt III*, findings of facts and conclusions of law determined that the SHA-1 digital fingerprint for a file produces a unique digital algorithm that specifically identifies the file. Further, it was ruled that the chances of a hash collision are not mathematically significant and this is not at issue.

Legally, this means that if digital evidence was cryptographically hashed using either MD5 or SHA-1 when it was obtained, and then validated later using the same cryptographic algorithm, then the authenticity and integrity of the digital evidence can be relied upon in a court of law.

Processing

As the third phase of the investigative workflow, processing involves the activities and steps performed by the investigator to examine and analyze digital evidence. These activities and steps are used by investigators to examine duplicated evidence in a forensically sound manner to identify meaningful data and subsequently reduce volume based on contextual and content relevance.

All activities and steps performed during the processing phase should occur inside a secure lab environment where digital evidence can be properly controlled and is not susceptible to access by unauthorized personnel or exposure to contamination. Before performing any examination or analysis of digital evidence, investigators must complete due diligence by proving the integrity of the forensics workstations that will be used, including inspecting for malicious software, verifying wiped media, and certifying the host operating system (e.g., time synchronization, secure boot).

Maintaining the integrity of digital evidence during examination and analysis is essential for investigators. By using the one-way cryptographic hash algorithm calculated during the gathering phase, investigators can prove that their interactions do not impact the integrity and authenticity of the evidence. Digital forensics tools and equipment provide investigators with automated capabilities, based on previous professional knowledge and criteria, which can be used to verify and validate the state of evidence.

On occasion, the programmatic processes or algorithms provided through tools and equipment require extended and potentially unattended use of digital evidence. During this time, the investigator remains the active custodian of all digital evidence in use and is responsible for maintaining its authenticity, reliability, and trustworthiness while unattended. Within the controlled lab environment, access to evidence can be restricted from unauthorized access using physical controls, such as individual work areas under lock/key entry, or logical controls, such as individual credentials for accessing tool and equipment.

Presentation

As the fourth and last phase of the investigative workflow, presentation involves the activities and steps performed to produce evidence-based reports of the investigation. These activities and steps provide investigators with a channel of demonstrating that processes, techniques, tools, equipment, and interactions maintained the authenticity, reliability, and trustworthiness of digital evidence throughout the investigative workflow.

Having completed the examination and analysis, all generated case files and evidence must be checked into secure lockers and the chain of custody updated. Unless otherwise instructed by legal authorities, the criteria for retaining digital evidence must comply with, and not exceed, the timelines established through policies, standards, and procedures. Proper disposal of digital evidence must be done using the existing chain of custody form.

Documentation is a critical element of an investigation. In alignment with established operating procedures, each phase of the investigative workflow requires several types of documentation to be maintained that are as complete, accurate, and comprehensive as possible. From the details captured in these documents investigators can demonstrate for all digital evidence the continuity in custody, and interactions with authorized personnel.

The layout and illustration of the final report must clearly articulate to the audience a chronology of events specific to evidence interactions. This chronology should be structured in sequence to the phases of the investigative workflow and accurately communicate through defined section heading the activities and steps performed. A final report template has been provided as a reference in the *Templates* section of this book.

Evidence Storage Networks

With technology being so pervasive across both our personal and business lives, and the rate at which ESI proliferates across different technologies, it is reasonably safe to say that gone are the days when the scope of a digital forensics investigation was limited to a single computer system. The reality is, management of complex investigations where digital evidence is being extracted from multiple sources—such as traditional computer systems, networks, mobile devices, and cloud computing environments—has become a major challenge. In some cases, evidence only needs to be held for the duration of the investigation (or trial). However, in other cases evidence needs to be held beyond the duration of the investigation (or trial). Where this is the case, the result is that organizations need to preserve and store massive amounts of digital evidence for extended periods.

Traditionally, organizations have leveraged digital backup solutions, such as tapes or external hard drives, to preserve digital evidence for the long term. However, digital media technology is constantly changing and what data available now may not be accessible years from now. Also, digital media degrades over time and few, if any, can guarantee the integrity of the evidence stored there beyond a given period. Furthermore, in multi-national enterprise environments, where digital forensics practitioners are in different geographic locations, digital evidence needs to be accessible to all those involved in the investigation to allow for collaboration. Continued storage of digital evidence in isolated or offline environments is introducing challenges given the massive amounts of evidence being gathered today. Ideally, what is needed is an efficient way for storing, preserving, and accessing the growing volumes of digital evidence from any location throughout the enterprise.

Evidence storage networks are centralized repositories where digital evidence can be stored, preserved, and accessed over extended periods. They are designed to support secure access to digital evidence from throughout the enterprise, eliminating the need to maintain digital evidence backup systems. Generally, the primary technologies available today to implement network-based storage solutions include the following:

- *Network area storage (NAS)*: a scalable technology attached to a network and accessible via standard network protocols (i.e., transmission control protocol/internet protocol [TCP/IP]). It comes embedded with an operating system (OS) and, in some cases, comes pre-built in appliances for increased ease of use.
- *Storage area networks (SAN)*: a segmented area of the organization's network that is used to handle and store ESI. SAN removes the need for creating and maintaining any storage devices because it is essentially a part of the enterprise network environment, just one that is dedicated to storage-heavy traffic.

Any combination of NAS and SAN can be used to achieve an evidence storage network for long-term storage of digital evidence. The decision to use any of these technologies for extended preservation of digital evidence goes back to the business need for implementing it as well as the costs and benefits of selecting one over another.

A common solution for supporting an evidence storage network is to build an enterprise data warehouse (EDW) designed specifically for maintaining the authenticity and integrity of digital evidence and, at no time introducing the risk of spoilage that renders evidence legally inadmissible. Refer to Addendum G, "Data Warehousing Introduction," for further discussions on the unique designs, capabilities, and purposes of these ecosystems.

Summary

Evidence is the cornerstone from which fact-based conclusions are established. Guaranteeing that evidence remains legally admissible and forensically viable requires following consistent and repeatable methodologies and techniques throughout the entire lifecycle of evidence. Organizations must employ a complementary series of administrative, physical, and technical controls to effectively maintain the authenticity and integrity of business records that could be used as potential digital evidence.

Ethics and Conduct

4

Introduction

At some point during a forensics investigation, digital forensics practitioners may encounter evidence or information that puts them in a difficult position, challenging their ethics and professional conduct. For the most part, these dilemmas can be resolved by following an approach where they recognize, classify, and manage these issues while respecting the boundaries and obligations they have as a professional.

However, differences amongst individuals, cultures, social classes, and organizations create challenges in establishing what is ethical and what is not. Abiding by a set of consistent professional ethics and code of conduct relating to digital forensics helps to define the moral principles that provide guidance to avoid potential misconduct.

Importance of Ethics

Whatever the cause of illegal, immoral, or unethical behavior, it's the responsibility of every digital forensics practitioner to do everything in their power to be objective, honest, truthful, and demonstrate due diligence during an investigation. That said, perhaps the best way to illustrate the importance of ethics is to explain what it is not. First and foremost, ethics should not be regarded as aspirational, meaning that it should be something applied consistently and not intermittently. Ethics establish a minimum standard of acceptable conduct for all activities performed by all digital forensics practitioners.

Ethics are concerned with the norms of conduct and follows the same rigors of logical reasoning as those of the scientific digital forensics discipline. While some might view ethics as being prescriptive and prohibitive, they provide reasonable guidance for acting in good faith. Although ethics are not law, conduct outside of these guidelines can lead to harm, liabilities, damages, or other consequences.

Principles of Ethics

Digital forensics practitioners possess specialized and unique knowledge which, if not governed or used appropriately, has the potential for misuse and abuse. When practitioners fail to uphold a minimum level of standards, the resulting impact can lead to digital evidence being overlooked, disregarded, spoiled, or disclosed.

Principles of ethical reasoning provide an appropriate means of sorting out the good from the bad. Typically, ethical guidelines are created to be broad and vague and don't outline every prohibited act to prescribe what proper behavior is.

Personal Ethics

Personal ethics are those values that individuals, or groups of people, regard as desirable and commonly apply to their behaviors. These principles reflect general expectations without having to formally articulate them and include:

1. Concern and respect for the well-being of others
2. Honesty and the willingness to comply with the law
3. Fairness and the ability not to take undue advantage of others
4. Goodwill and preventing harm to any creature

Largely, people are motivated to abide by these principles because:

- They want to have a clear conscience and desire to act ethically under normal circumstances;
- It is their nature to ensure their actions and behaviors do not cause injury or harm to others;
- They are obligated to follow laws and regulations of countries and regions; or
- Social and material well-being depends on how one behaves in society.

Professional Ethics

A professional is any individual who performs a specific activity, such as a digital forensics practitioner, within the context of a business environment. Examples of basic ethics principles people are expected to follow in their professional career include:

- Impartiality and objectivity;
- Openness and disclosure;
- Confidentiality and trust;
- Due diligence and duty of care;
- Loyalty to professional responsibilities; and
- Avoidance of potential or apparent conflicts.

Computer Ethics

Published in 1992 by the Computer Ethics Institute (CEI), the *Ten Commandments of Computer Ethics* was developed as a standard set of principles to guide and instruct people on the ethical use of a computer system. These command-ments have been widely quoted and referenced since the original publication as the minimum standards for human conduct when using computer systems.

Ten Commandments of Computer Ethics:

1. Thou shalt not use a computer to harm other people.
2. Thou shalt not interfere with other people's computer work.
3. Thou shalt not snoop around in other people's computer files.
4. Thou shalt not use a computer to steal.
5. Thou shalt not use a computer to bear false witness.
6. Thou shalt not copy or use proprietary software for which you have not paid.
7. Thou shalt not use other people's computer resources without autho-rization or proper compensation.
8. Thou shalt not appropriate other people's intellectual output.
9. Thou shalt think about the social consequences of the program you are writing or the system you are designing.
10. Thou shalt always use a computer in ways that ensure consideration and respect for your fellow humans.

Business Ethics

Business ethics is the application of the general principles discussed above to the behavior portrayed within a business environment. Following a mini-mum standard of ethical business behavior is expected, both by the organi-zation and by the public, to facilitate aspects of business, including improved profitability, nurturing of business relationships, improved employee pro-ductivity, and reduction of risk (i.e., strategic, financial, operational, legal, and other).

Organizations must conduct themselves ethically because they need to exist in a competitive global landscape and demonstrating these values brings about credibility. Generally, organizations should act ethically to:

- Protect the interests of themselves, the business community at large, and public interest;
- Meet the expectations of and build trust with stakeholders, share-holders, and investors; and
- Create an environment whereby employees can act consistently with the organization's values and principles.

A *business code of conduct policy* is a management tool for setting out an organization's values, responsibilities, and ethical obligations. This gov-ernance document provides the organization with guidance for handling difficult ethical situation relating to business conduct. To be truly effective, the business code of conduct needs to be embedded throughout the organization so that employees know exactly how it applies to them.

Like how organizations have a mission statement, sometimes referred to as a vision statement, aligned to their business goals, they should also develop such statements to promote an ethical culture.

Ethics in Digital Forensics

Most education and training available today is focused on the technical aspects of the digital forensics discipline, such as how to examine a hard drive or conduct network traffic analysis. Within the academic curriculum, there is little time spent on the business side of digital forensics which includes teaching ethics and conduct.

Perhaps the reason there is this notable absence in academic curriculum is because the code of ethics that exists does not encompass the digital forensics community as a whole. While there are professional organizations that have established their own codes of ethics, as discussed in the section below, these values and principles are specific to a single entity and are not universally translated to demonstrate the level of competency expected of a digital forensics practitioner internationally.

Above we discussed personal, professional, computer, and business ethics that can be used to establish a set ethics that can be used in the digital forensics profession. While the following are not structured in the manner of a code of ethics, these values and principles should be consistently applied by digital forensics to demonstrate how practitioners can conduct themselves in an ethical manner.

Certifications and Professional Organizations

Internationally, there are several professional organizations that have established ethics, or codes of conduct, which certified digital forensics practitioners are expected to adhere by. Even though these ethics put forward by these professional organizations can have a positive effect on the behavior, actions, and judgment of individuals, many organizations do not mandate that their employees become certified. Holding a professional digital forensics certification can be viewed as a deterrence to professional misconduct at the risk of losing the accreditation due to a violation of the code of ethics defined by the certifying body.

Ultimately, digital forensics practitioners are held accountable for acting ethically and according to their organization's policies (e.g., business code of conduct), their associated professional organizations, and applicable laws where they live and conduct business. While there are professional organizations in addition to those specified below, the following are examples of certifying bodies and their respective codes of ethics to which accredited individuals must adhere.

Digital Forensics Certification Board (DFCB)

The Digital Forensics Certification Board (DFCB) exists to promote public trust and confidence in the digital forensics profession. Specifically, the Digital Forensics Certified Practitioner (DFCP) designation offered by DFCB is a professional certification to enhance professionalism and distinguish individuals who have a broad comprehension of the common body of knowledge (CBK) within the digital forensics industry.

Within the DFCB Code of Ethics, it is stated that a certificant shall:

1. Not engage in, or pressure others to engage in, any conduct that is harmful to the profession of digital forensics including, but not limited to, any illegal or unethical activity, any technical misrepresentation or distortion, any scholarly falsification or any material misrepresentation of education, training, credentials, experience, or area of expertise;
2. Demonstrate, at all times, commitment, integrity, and professional diligence;
3. Avoid any action that could appear to be a conflict of interest;
4. Comply with all lawful orders of courts of competent jurisdiction;
5. Show no bias with respect to findings or opinions;
6. Express no opinion with respect to the guilt or innocence of any party;
7. Not disclose or reveal any confidential or privileged information obtained during an engagement without proper authorization or otherwise ordered by a court of competent jurisdiction;
8. Examine and consider thoroughly all information (unless specifically limited in scope by court order or other authority) and render opinions and conclusions strictly in accordance with the results and findings obtained using validated and appropriate procedures;
9. Report or testify truthfully in all matters and not knowingly make any material misrepresentation of information or otherwise withhold any information that, in so doing, might tend to distort the truth;
10. Accept only engagements for which there is a reasonable expectation of completion with professional competence.

International Association of Computer Investigative Specialists (IACIS)

The International Association of Computer Investigative Specialists (IACIS) is a global non-profit organization that promotes educational excellence in the digital forensics profession. Specifically, both the Certified Forensics Computer Examiner (CFCE) and Certified Advanced Windows Forensics Examiner (CAWFE) designations offered by IACIS are professional certifications for individuals to demonstrate their knowledge of core competencies and practical skills in the field of digital forensics.

The IACIS Code of Ethics states that "members must demonstrate and maintain the highest standards of ethical conduct" by doing the following:

- Maintaining the highest level of objectivity in all forensics examinations and accurately presenting the facts involved.
- Thoroughly examining and analyzing the evidence in a case.
- Conducting examinations based upon established, validated principles.
- Rendering opinions having a basis that is demonstratively reasonable.
- Not withholding any findings, whether inculpatory or exculpatory, that would cause the facts of a case to be misrepresented or distorted.
- Never misrepresenting credentials, education, training, and experience or membership status.

International Society of Forensics Computer Examiners (ISFCE)

The International Society of Forensics Computer Examiners (ISFCE) is a non-profit organization that promotes a community of competent digital forensics practitioners. Specifically, the Certified Computer Examiner (CCE) designation offered by ISFCE is a professional certification that sets a high ethical standard based on the recipient's knowledge and practical experience within the digital forensics discipline.

Within the ISFCE Code of Ethics, a Certified Computer Examiner (CCE) will at all times:

- Demonstrate commitment and diligence in performance of assigned duties
- Demonstrate integrity in completing professional assignments
- Maintain the utmost objectivity in all forensics examinations and accurately present findings
- Conduct examinations based on established, validated procedures
- Abide by the highest moral and ethical standards and abide by the Code of the ISFCE

- Testify truthfully in all matters before any board, court or proceeding
- Avoid any action that would knowingly present a conflict of interest
- Comply with all legal orders of the courts
- Thoroughly examine all evidence within the scope of the engagement

Within the ISFCE Code of Ethics, a Certified Computer Examiner (CCE) will never:

- Withhold any relevant evidence
- Reveal any confidential matters or knowledge learned in an examination without an order from a court of competent jurisdiction or with the express permission of the client
- Express an opinion on the guilt or innocence of any party
- Engage in any unethical or illegal conduct
- Knowingly undertake an assignment beyond his or her ability
- Misrepresent education, training or credentials
- Show bias or prejudice in findings or examinations
- Exceed authorization in conducting examinations

Principles for Digital Forensics

Currently, there is no universally adopted code of ethics that governs the ethical behavior and conduct of digital forensics as a single community; and just because there isn't one today doesn't mean that creating one is a simple task. Perhaps the biggest reason no such code of ethics exists for the entire digital forensics community can be attributed to the challenges that would be faced in establishing one at an international level. Some obstacles that could be faced during this process include:

- What behavior and conduct would the code of ethics cover?
- What values and principles would the code of ethics address?
- What agency or organization would govern and enforce the code of ethics?
- To whom would the code of ethics apply (e.g., just digital forensics practitioners or all individuals involved with digital evidence)?

Despite these questions, it might be fair to say that, from the code of ethics illustrated in the section above, there are key values and principles to which digital forensics practitioners must ensure their behavior and conduct adheres. That said, digital forensics is a profession and as such should follow a similar minimum level of values and principles as required for professional ethics, which is discussed in the section above.

On this basis, the subject matters to follow should be consistently applied, at all times, by digital forensics practitioners as fundamental values and principles of ethical behavior and conduct.

Impartiality and Objectivity

One of the main goals when performing an investigation is to establish factual conclusions based on credible evidence. As part of an investigation, there could arise times when the subject is known to or familiar with the practitioner. It is the responsibility of the practitioner to maintain the utmost fairness during an investigation to draw conclusions based on factual and credible evidence. This means that practitioners should avoid any action that would appear to be a conflict of interest and otherwise create potential bias in establishing their evidentiary conclusions.

Openness and Disclosure

Investigations are not "witch hunts" and should be conducted using the utmost fairness and obligation to report factual conclusions based on credible evidence. While analyzing evidence, practitioners may encounter specific findings that need to be assessed further before factual conclusions can be drawn, such as paying special attention to inculpatory (indication of guilt) or exculpatory (indication of innocence) evidence. It is crucial that practitioners take into consideration the totality of all evidence gathered during an investigation before arriving at factual conclusions.

Confidentiality and Trust

The work of a digital forensics practitioner comes with a high level of trust. From time to time, they can come across extremely sensitive and confidential information that needs to be kept confidential and communicated on a need to know basis. When these types of information are discovered, human nature tends to kick in and the desire to disclose details of these occurrences comes about. As a digital forensics practitioner, it is required that evidence not be disclosed or revealed without proper authorization (e.g., court order).

Due Diligence and Duty of Care

Legal admissibility of evidence requires practitioners to follow a consistent investigative process model that respects the digital forensics best practices of well-established principles, methodologies, and techniques. Informed decision making during an investigation must be carried out in accordance with applicable laws, standards, and regulations to avoid potential negative consequences. With this in mind, digital forensics professionals must consistently demonstrate their behavior and conduct is honest, prudent, and in compliance with laws and professional norms.

Certifications and Accreditations

Internationally, there are many professional organizations that have established certifications and accreditations specific to the digital forensics profession. Predominantly, these certifications are provided by professional organizations with an industry-wide perspective on the digital forensics profession; however, there are a small number of certifications provided by merchants who sell digital forensics products and services.

It is important to keep in mind that while professional certification provides the assurance that an individual meets the required level of knowledge in digital forensics, these accreditations do not provide the in-depth level of education that formal academic programs teach. Refer to Appendix B, "Education and Professional Certifications," for a list of digital forensics certifications.

Summary

Ethical values and principles are a useful way for sorting out what is considered good and bad behavior or conduct. While there is no code of ethics that universally applies to the digital forensics profession, the morals originating from the combination of personal, professional, computer, and business values and principles can be leveraged to establish a code of ethics to adhere by.

Digital Forensics as a Business

5

Introduction

Organizations exist in many different contexts (i.e., size, geography, industry) and within each there are different and unique requirements when it comes to digital forensics capabilities. There are some organizations that, given their operating model and corporate profile, leverage external managed services to supply a digital forensics team when required. The remaining organizations, have decided that having a digital forensics team in-house is the best strategy for given their operating model and corporate profile. After making this decision, the organization needs to kick-start their long-term digital forensics program by implementing a series of administrative, technical, and physical strategies.

The Role of Digital Forensics in an Enterprise

From previous chapters covered in this section of this book, we know that digital forensics is the application of science to law and consists of scientifically proven principles, methodologies, and techniques. While the technical execution of digital forensics within an enterprise environment resembles that seen in other organizations, the purpose and roles it serves can be somewhat different. Consider that, for the most part, when law enforcement agencies are performing digital forensics they are doing so in response to criminal activity. True, enterprises also use digital forensics as a reactionary process, but there are many more opportunities to extend the use and application of digital forensics proactively.

With the opportunity to have both proactive and reactive digital forensics capabilities, first and foremost it is important that organizations follow a systematic approach so that their digital forensics capabilities are properly aligned to business and organizational needs. Throughout this chapter are methodologies organizations can use when exploring in-house digital forensics capabilities.

Starting a Digital Forensics Program

What drives an organization to decide it needs in-house digital forensics capabilities? Largely, this need is determined by both internal and external factors that can include the following:

- Countries or regions that have specific laws and regulations that require a process for dealing with incidents leveraging forensics analysis or investigation; for example, the Sarbanes–Oxley Act (SOX) in the United States
- Regulated industries (e.g., financial, healthcare, insurance) that have specific requirements governing the use, transmission, or storage of information; for example, Payment Card Industry Data Security Standards (PCI DSS)
- Assisting legal and compliance teams with the discovery of electronically stored information (ESI) for production as evidence
- Facilitating human resources (HR) or employee relations (ER) with evidence supporting employee misconduct or other disciplinary actions (e.g., termination)
- Analyzing and correlating ESI to determine root cause or potential of data breaches

In any case, establishing in-house digital forensics capabilities requires following a systematic approach by which implementation is aligned to the organization's needs, with the technical execution aspects following afterward. Below are the steps organizations should follow to answer "who, where, what, when, why, and how" in-house digital forensics capabilities will be implemented.

Step #1: Understand Business Risks

Before implementing digital forensics in an enterprise environment, it is important to take a step back and understand the need for investing time, money, and resources. Doing so requires that organizations clearly understand what their business is (i.e., financial, health, etc.) and the risks that can (in)directly result in any form of business impact.

The type of risks that can potentially impact an organization depends on each organization (e.g., size, geography, industry) and should not be seen as universally equivalent. Generally, risks can be described as any threat event, whether internal (can be controlled within the boundaries of the organization) or external (can occur outside the organization and cannot be controlled), that occurs in one of five major groupings:

- *Strategic risk* is associated with business functions and commonly occurs because of:
  - Business interactions where goods and services are purchased and sold, varying supply and demand, adjustments to competitive structures, and the emergence of new or innovative technologies
  - Transactions resulting in asset relocation from mergers and acquisitions, spin-offs, alliances, or joint ventures
  - Strategies for investment relations management and communicating with stakeholders who have invested in the organization
- *Financial risk* is associated with the financial structure, stability, and transactions of the organization.
- *Operational risk* is associated with the organization's business, operational, and administrative procedures.
- *Legal* risk is associated with the need to comply with the rules and regulations of the relevant governing bodies.
- *Other risks* are associated with indirect, non-business factors such as natural disasters and others as identified based on the relevant circumstances of the organization.

The approach for how to determine business risk is done by completing a risk assessment as an output of the organization's overall risk management program. Determining the need for investing time, money, and resources in digital forensics capabilities comes from completing both qualitative and quantitative risk assessments to ensure that a thorough understanding of the potential risks is achieved. Following these assessments, a complete picture of all potential risk can be used to perform a cost-benefit analysis that will ultimately determine whether it is feasible to implement in-house digital forensics capabilities.

At the end of this step, organizations will have answered the question of "why" they need in-house digital forensics capabilities.

Step #2: Outline Business Scenarios

Generally, if a business risk exists and there is a positive return on investment (ROI) then implementing appropriate digital forensics capabilities is beneficial. As stated previously, every organization is unique and has a different business profile that presents different requirements for in-house digital forensics capabilities. Enhancing digital forensics capabilities within an enterprise must also take into consideration the (in)direct influences of business operations so that strategies can be developed to adequately manage risk.

Outlined below are multiple business scenarios where digital forensics can be applied to manage business risk. While the applicability of all scenarios outlined below might not fit the profile of every organization, it is important that each is illustrated and understood so that they can be considered for relevancy.

Reducing the impact of cybercrime: With information technology (IT) playing an integral part of practically every business operation, the evolving threat landscape continues to increase risks associated with organizational assets. Using a threat modeling methodology, organizations can create a structured representation of the different ways a threat actor can go about executing attacks and how these tactics, techniques, and procedures can be used to create an impact. The output of this exercise can be put to practical use by implementing appropriate countermeasures that create potential digital evidence.

Validating the impact of cybercrime or disputes: When a security incident occurs, organizations must be prepared to quantify impact. To obtain a complete and accurate view of the entire cost of an incident, both direct and indirect contributors must be included in the impact assessment. This means incorporating logs generated from different type of controls (e.g., preventive, detective, corrective) or the overhead cost of managing the incident (e.g., people and technology expenses).

Producing evidence to support organizational disciplinary issues: A business code of conduct document promotes a positive work environment that, when signed, strengthens the confidence of employees and stakeholders by establishing an accepted level of professional and ethical workplace behavior. When the guidelines set out in this document have been violated, employees can be subject to disciplinary actions. Where disciplinary actions escalate into legal problems, organizations must approach the situation fairly and reasonably by gathering and processing credible digital evidence.

Demonstrating compliance with regulatory or legal requirements: Compliance is not a one-size-fits-all process. It is driven by factors such as an organization's industry (e.g., financial services) or the countries where business is conducted (e.g., Canada). Evidence documenting that compliance standards are met must be specific to the requirements of both the regulation or law, and the jurisdiction.

Effectively managing the release of court ordered data: Regardless of how diligent an organization is, there will always be times when disputes end up before a court of law. With adequate preparation, routine follow-ups, and a thorough understanding of what is considered reasonable in a court of law, organizations can effectively manage this risk by maintaining the admissibility of ESI, such as the requirements described within the *U.S. Federal Rules of Evidence*. Ensuring compliance with these requirements demands that organizations implement safeguards, precautions, and controls to ensure their ESI is admissible in court and that it is authenticated to its original source.

Supporting contractual and commercial agreements: From time to time, organizations are faced with disagreements that extend beyond disputes that involve employees. With most of today's business interactions conducted electronically, organizations must ensure they capture and electronically preserve critical metadata about their third-party agreements. This would include details about the terms and conditions or the date the agreement was co-signed. Contract management system can be used to standardize and preserve metadata needed to provide sufficient grounds for supporting a dispute.

In addition to the above scenarios, there are "non-forensics" scenarios where digital forensics techniques and skills can be used to support other business operations and functions, such as recovering data from old or failed media (e.g., hard drives, floppy disks). Even though these "non-forensics" scenarios do not have the same requirements for maintaining legal admissibility, they can present business risks if there is no other means of performing these functions within the organization.

At the end of this step, organizations will have answered the questions of "where and what" in-house digital forensics capabilities are needed, which is further discussed in Chapter 7, "Defining Business Risk Scenarios."

Step #3: Establish Governance Framework

Generally, an enterprise governance framework involves the administration, management, enforcement, and control of policies, standards, and procedures specific to the discipline. It is designed to provide strategic direction by ensuring the successful completion of organizational goals and objectives from a top-down approach. The concept of a governance framework includes several layers of governance sub-disciplines, all of which have relationships with digital forensics.

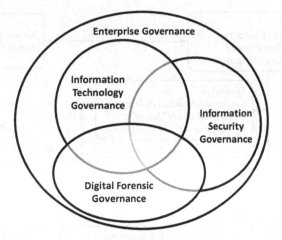

Figure 5.1 Enterprise governance framework.

Illustrated in Figure 5.1 are the relationships between the different governance disciplines implemented throughout the organization, including the following:

- *Enterprise governance*, as the top-level governance discipline, is very broad and is an all-inclusive mechanism to ensure the well-being of the entire organization. It is designed to establish relationships between the organization and its shareholders by defining the strategic direction, objectives, and goals.
- *Information technology (IT) governance* focuses on the use of IT throughout the enterprise to support business operations and functions. It contains a series of documents that are designed to establish how the organization will direct, manage, and control the use of IT resources to support the strategic direction, objectives, and goals.
- *Information security (IS) governance* manages risks relating to information assets that have been entrusted to the organization. It establishes and maintains control of the environments by which information assets are used, transmitted, and stored.

Given the business risks faced by organizations, it is necessary for all stakeholders throughout the organization to understand the importance of digital forensics and the requirements for utilizing key resources to support its integrated business capabilities. Executive management, with involvement from key stakeholders such as legal, privacy, security, and human resources, work to define a series of documents that describe exactly how the organization will go about aligning digital forensics capabilities to address the pre-defined business risk scenarios.

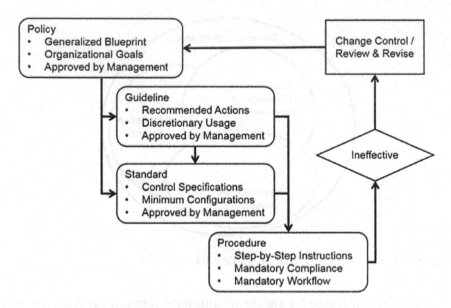

Figure 5.2 Governance documentation hierarchy.

Governance over digital forensics capabilities is essential within corporate environments looking to enable in-house capabilities. Figure 5.2 illustrates the hierarchy of governance documentation and the relationships shared between those specific to direct influence and those that take precedence over others. The implementation of these documents serves as the administrative groundwork for indirectly supporting the subsequent phases where digital evidence is involved. The sections to follow explore these documents individually and provide specifics on the types that contribute to digital forensics.

Enforcing governance over in-house digital forensics capabilities is crucial, considering the legal and regulatory implications involved. Not only will having a governance framework instill trust in the organization's digital forensics capabilities, it will also help to:

- Clearly define the roles and responsibilities of stakeholders throughout the organization
- Reduce the resources (time, effort, cost) required to effectively support service delivery and operating models
- Maintain the legal admissibility of digital evidence using consistent, repeatable, reproducible, verified, and validated processes, techniques, and methodologies
- Properly align risk management strategies that deliver business value

At the end of this step, organizations will have answered the questions of "when, where, and how" their in-house digital forensics capabilities will be needed.

- Refer to Chapter 16, "Ensuring Legal Review," for further discussion about laws and regulations.
- Refer to Chapter 3, "Digital Evidence Management," for further discussion about enterprise governance framework.

Step #4: Enable Technical Execution

Far too often, figuring out how to achieve a desired outcome comes first, resulting in misaligned, insufficient, or unrelated deliverables. Like the approach followed as part of project management, it is important to clearly understand scope (why, what, when, where) before proceeding with procurement or implementation. Translating this concept over to digital forensics, before a forensics toolkit can be purchased the team needs to first understand:

- Why digital forensics is needed;
- What role it has in digital forensics;
- When digital forensics is required;
- Where digital forensics is used; and
- How digital forensics is administered.

The concept of a "forensics toolkit" is not limited to only those hardware and software technologies that will help to perform and automate digital forensics tasks, but also includes those physical and administrative components that are needed to support technologies. Within an enterprise environment, there is greater opportunity to develop the forensics toolkit to be more controlled and specific to the organization; as opposed to law enforcement that will need to have a broader toolkit.

Through this methodology, having completed the previous steps will have already addressed most administrative components that are required as part of a forensics toolkit. Next, organizations need to assess the physical components of their toolkit before they can identify those technical components that are needed.

At the end of this step, organizations will have answered the question of "how" their in-house digital forensics capabilities will be provided.

Refer to Chapter 3, "Digital Evidence Management," for further discussion about planning, designing, and building a forensics lab environment and toolkit.

Step #5: Define Service Offerings

Implementing digital forensics principles, methodologies, and techniques according to applicable business risk scenarios requires translating technical components (i.e., tools) of the discipline into a business language that can be clearly and easily understood. Achieving this is done through the creation of an enterprise service catalogue that is designed to align all technical components into the business functions that support the risk scenarios.

A service catalog provides a centralized way to see, find, invoke, and execute digital forensics services from anywhere throughout the organization. Once implemented, organizations will start seeing the benefits of having a service catalog because it:

- Positions overall digital forensics capabilities to be run like a business
- Provides a platform for better understanding and communicating the business need for digital forensics
- Helps to market the enterprise awareness and visibility into digital forensics as a means of building stronger business relationships

Most likely, a service catalog already exists within the organization and can be amended to include digital forensics services. If it has not been created, proper enterprise governance and oversight need to be in place to ensure the efficient use of resources, that is, that time and money are not wasted in creating service catalogs that are not effective. Refer to Template 5, "Service Catalog," for further discussion about the methodology for building a service catalog.

At the end of this step, organizations will have answered the question of "who" provides their in-house digital forensics capabilities.

Maintaining a Digital Forensics Program

Building an in-house digital forensics program is, to some extent, a linear process whereby many steps outlined above are performed once. However, once all steps to build the program are completed, there is the matter of ongoing care and feeding to ensure what was built is, to some degree, sustained but also goes through varying levels of continuous improvement transformation.

For a digital forensics program to not just operate at its maximum capability, but to also remain at the peak of its capabilities, there must be a systematic approach in place to make intelligent and informed decisions for improving the overall program.

Educational Roadmap

A common question posed to those in the digital forensics discipline is what type of knowledge and training is needed to get into the field, and subsequently what education is needed for career advancement. The reality is that there is no one best way for someone to gain their digital forensics education, acquire new skills, and keep current those skills they already have.

Instead of setting out a professional development plan that digital forensics practitioners should follow, a better strategy is to illustrate the building blocks needed for different types and levels of education a person can gain.

Refer to Chapter 14, "Establish Continuing Education," to find discussions on the knowledge and experience required in accordance with the scientific principles, methodologies, and techniques of the digital forensics profession.

Forensics Toolkit Maintenance

At this point, the lab environment has been built with all tools and equipment implemented to support the organization's digital forensics capabilities. Ongoing maintenance and upkeep to the lab and equipment are essential in maintaining the required standards for guaranteeing the integrity, authenticity, and legal admissibility of digital evidence. Doing so requires routine inspections to be performed to provide assurance that the lab environment continues to operate within the established level of security controls and necessary operating standards. These reviews should be performed by objective, independent parties who are not directly involved with the digital forensics team to:

- Determine if structural issues are present within the walls, doors, floor, and ceiling
- Inspect all access control mechanisms to ensure they are not damaged and continue to function as expected
- Review physical access logs for both approved individuals and visitors
- Analyze tracking logs to identify issues with continuity and integrity of evidence

With advancements in technology, tools and equipment used within the portfolio of the digital forensics toolkit also need to be maintained to ensure it continues to operate at the required level for guaranteeing the integrity, authenticity, and legal admissibility of digital evidence. Within the scope of the ongoing maintenance and support required for forensics toolkit components, the following activities should be performed regularly:

- Digital forensics workstations must operate at the required security baseline, including:
  - Operating system (OS) patches and updates applied frequently
  - Security applications, such as anti-malware technologies, updated and scheduled scans of the full system enabled
  - File systems defragmented to improve workstation performance
    - Verified data wiping tools used to securely remove temporary and cached files or files located in slack or unallocated space
- Digital forensics software and hardware upgraded and patched following appropriate validation; verification processes completed

Aside from the technology aspects of maintaining the digital forensics toolkit, there is the business side that cannot be overlooked or forgotten. With all tools and equipment, whether software or hardware based, there are ongoing maintenance support agreements with vendors and manufacturers to ensure that professional services are available when required. Paying the ongoing maintenance support, as a requirement for maintaining the digital forensics toolkit, ensures that organizations have access to upgrades and support resources (when or if needed).

Key Performance Indicators (KPI)

Once the digital forensics program is implemented and its services are being used throughout the organization, it should not be left to operate in its current state indefinitely. Relevant KPIs are the cornerstone for tracking, measuring, and reporting on how the digital forensics program is being delivered and help personnel make informed decisions about where improvements are needed.

Generally, a relevant KPI is significant and attributable to the metric it measures. However, developing relevant KPIs for the digital forensics program can be somewhat of a challenging task because many of the metrics are focused solely on the execution and operation of the digital forensics program. When developing KPIs, the following can be used as guidelines:

1. Relate measurable metrics to the purpose and priorities.
2. Link organizational goals and objectives to the services offered.
3. Use them to influence the organization's decision-making process related to digital forensics capabilities.
4. Use industry best practices and benchmarks for measuring the organization's digital forensics service offerings.
5. Ensure they are meaningful and useful to the organization's digital forensics capabilities.

Every organization operates under different contexts (e.g., industry, size) and has unique requirements for implementing in-house digital forensics capabilities, and selecting the most accurate and appropriate KPIs is unique to each organization, depending on its business profiles. Before measuring any KPI, it is important to first calculate the base formulas that will be used universally to measure multiple KPI parameters, including:

- *Full-time equivalents (FTEs)* are calculated as the total number of employees who support the organization's digital forensics investigations service.
- *Work hours (WH)* are the total number of work hours during which FTE are dedicated to supporting the organization's digital forensics investigations service. *WH* is calculated as:

$$Work\ hours\ (WH) = (t * hours)$$

where *hours* represents the number of hours in a work day and *t* represents the number of days in the evaluation period. The evaluation period applied to this ratio should be dynamic to allow for measurement adjustments over different reporting periods (e.g., monthly, quarterly, yearly).
- *Overhead time (OT)* is the total number of work hours allocated to non-investigative functions (e.g., meetings, education, support). The *OT* ratio is calculated as:

$$Overhead\ time\ (OT) = WH - (t * hours)$$

- *Investigative time (IT)* is the total number of work hours allocated to investigative functions. The *IT* ratio is calculated as:

$$Investigative\ time\ (IT) = WH - OT$$

Using the above values as input for KPIs measurements, the following is an example of a ratio that an organization should consider when measuring the effectiveness of its digital forensics program related to the organization's continuous improvement strategies.

Resource Capacity

The traditional approach to measuring resource capacity is to define and assign tasks, including estimating work effort and availability, on an individual basis. However, modern approaches to resource capacity management, such as with the Agilé perspective, are oriented toward the team as a collective rather than individuals. This current approach assumes that different types of work require different skills and, through the combined experiences and skills of the collective team, the work required to support the organization's digital forensics program can be achieved more effectively than through individual efforts.

Therefore, calculating the resource capacity ratio, represented as RC, will be done for the entire team rather than on an individual basis. *Resource capacity* should consider the following factors as components of its measurement:

- The number of workdays in the period, represented as t
- The number of team members, represented as FTE
- The total non-investigative work hours, represented as OT
- Planned time off for each team member
- The total investigative work hours, represented as IT

The approach to calculating the RC ratio is completed as:

1. Multiply the number of workdays, or t, in the time by the number of hours per day, represented by *hours*. Let's assume a one week period with five working days at eight hours per day:

$$Work\ hours\ (WH) = (t * hours)$$
$$WH = (5 * 8)$$
$$WH = 40$$

2. Subtract the total time allocated for the non-investigative activities and tasks to determine the availability for investigative activities and tasks. Let's assume that collectively the team spends one day per week in meetings:

$$Overhead\ time\ (OT) = WH - (t * hours)$$
$$OT = 40 - (4 * 8)$$
$$OT = 40 - 32$$
$$OT = 8$$
$$Investigative\ time\ (IT) = WH - OT$$
$$IT = 40 - 8$$
$$IT = 32$$

3. To calculate the RC ratio, this step involves three sub-routine calculations:
   a. Subtract availability and time off for each team member, then multiply the result by availability to get individual capacity.

Table 5.1   Resource Availability and Time Off

Team Member		% Availability	Hours Off	Hours
Individual #01		25%		8.00
Individual #02		38%		12.16
Individual #03		75%		24.00
Individual #04		75%		24.00
Individual #05		75%		24.00
Individual #06		50%	16.00	8.00
Individual #07		75%		24.00
Team Member Days Available	15.5	**Team Resources**	3.10	**Team Hours** 124.16

b. Add the individual team members' capacities to get the entire team capacity in work hours and divide by 8, the assumed work hours per day value, to get the team's capacity in workdays.

c. Divide the team's work hour capacity by the total work hours to get the team resources value.

Outlined in Table 5.1, the total work hours for team members has been added to sum 124.16 work hours, or 15.5 workdays, for the team collectively.

Challenges and Strategies

Naturally, implementing a digital forensics program into an enterprise environment comes with challenges. There is no prescriptive way that outlines exactly how enterprise digital forensics programs must be implemented because the reality is, as stated previously, every organization is unique and its own requirements for digital forensics capabilities. Below are areas where organizations need to answer questions before they can successfully implement their digital forensics program.

Team Placement

There is no right answer for to whom within any (or every) enterprise an in-house digital forensics service should hierarchically report. In some instances, for example, digital forensics could report to the information technology (IT) division, information security (IS), risk management, legal, or even compliance. Going a step further, there is a question of whether digital forensics capabilities should be centralized to a single department or should be distributed amongst different regions and business lines.

Generally, the placement of digital forensics in the enterprise goes back to the size and the business risk scenarios outlined previously. Small and medium-sized business (SMB) environments might decide to centralize their digital forensics capabilities given that their operations are limited in size and geographic diversity. However, large organizations may decide that it is more effective to have multiple teams in respective department to facilitate a specific business risk, such as support the legal team with electronic discovery (e-discovery) collections or within the incident response (IR) team to facilitate incident recovery tasks.

With a distributed approach, there will be varying degrees of responsibilities and involvement of digital forensics practitioners depending on the scope of their role, such as leadership, consultant, or advisor. While the team and functions have been decentralized, it is important that the organization establish a direct reporting relationship for the team to a common department where digital forensics governance, management, and strategies are defined and communicated outwards. This approach will ensure that even though the organization has distributed its capabilities, all teams will follow consistent principles, methodologies, and techniques when supporting digital forensics capabilities throughout the enterprise.

Industry Regulation

Different laws, standards, and regulations govern the operations of organizations conducting business in different industries. Depending on the regulations applicable to an organization's business, there might be a requirement to have specific digital forensics capabilities support throughout the enterprise. Refer to Chapter 16, "Ensuring Legal Review," for further discussion on laws, standards, and regulations.

For example, regulatory development such as the Sarbanes–Oxley (SOX) Act of 2002 requires organizations to develop and implement a series of plans and processes that specifically address how the organization handles fraud incidents using digital forensics. Additionally, the Payment Card Industry Data Security Standard (PCI DSS) has established the PCI Forensics Investigator (PFI) certification that identifies organizations and other entities that in compliance with all regulatory requirements for conducting investigations relating to the compromise of cardholder data.

The regulations applicable to any specific organization are subjective to their industry and must be known to ensure that digital forensics capabilities can be adapted accordingly. As outlined in the beginning of this chapter, regulatory compliance is not one-size-fits-all. As a business risk scenario supported by digital forensics, demonstrating compliance with regulatory requirements requires the production of factual evidence documenting that standards have been met.

Political Influences

Political jurisdictions can vary between countries and region around the world. Generally, the laws established through these countries and regions were created to bridge the gap between risk (i.e., criminal activity) and technology (i.e., fruit or tool) within the scope of the jurisdiction's perspective on digital crime and subsequent access, transmission, and storage of ESI as digital evidence.

Where organizations have a presence in multiple countries and regions, their investigations are increasingly becoming international in nature. Where digital evidence needs to be gathered and processed from many countries and regions, a decision must be made as to how respective data protection laws allow for these activities to occur. For example, the European Union Data Protection Directive 95/46/EC outlines the requirement to protect individuals with regards to the processing of personal data specific to data flow transmission across borders.

Most often, organizations that don't consider these political influences find themselves in situations where quick decisions are made, which can result in laws being circumvented or disregarded. However, political influences do not have to impede an organization's ability to conduct international investigations if the right approach is taken and many of the political considerations are addressed early on when establishing the governance framework.

Summary

Enabling digital forensics in an enterprise environment requires a systematic approach that is designed to answer "who, where, what, when, why, and how" in-house digital forensics capabilities will be successfully implemented and continuously improved. While the technical execution of digital forensics within an enterprise environment resembles that seen in other organizations and agencies, the purpose and roles it serves are somewhat unique. Before digital forensics can be readily enabled in an enterprise environment, it is important to understand the role and function it serves to the organization's business.

Enhancing Digital Forensics II

Understanding Digital Forensic Readiness

6

Introduction

Digital forensics investigations are commonly performed in reaction to an event or incident. During the post-event response activities, investigators must work quickly to gather, process, and present digital evidence. Subjective to the environment where an investigation is conducted, the evidence necessary to support the investigation may or may not exist, leading to complications with arriving at a solid conclusion of what happened.

In the business context, the opportunity to gather digital evidence in advance is more prevalent than the ability to gather evidence in a law enforcement setting. If digital evidence has not been gathered to start with, there is a greater chance that it may not be available when needed. Any organization that depends on, or utilizes, technology should have a balanced concern for information security and forensics capabilities.

Digital evidence is fundamental in helping organizations to manage the impact of business risk, such as validating or reducing the impact of an event or incident, supporting litigation matters, or demonstrating compliance. Regardless of the business risk, there are situations where a simple event or incident can escalate into something much more serious. Digital forensics readiness is the ability of an organization to proactively maximize the prospective use of electronic information to reduce the cost of the digital forensics investigative workflow.

What Is Digital Forensics Readiness?

The concept of a forensics readiness program was first published in 2001 by John Tan. Through a forensics readiness program, an organization can make appropriate and informed decisions about business risks to make the most of its ability to proactively gather digital evidence. Under a forensics readiness program, Tan outlines that the primary objectives for an organization are to:

- Maximize the ability to collect credible digital evidence; and
- Minimize the cost of forensics during an event or incident.

In the 2001 Honeynet Project, John Tan participated as a judge, and he discovered the most remarkable finding in this exercise was the cost of the incident.

During email communications with Dave Dittrich, head of the Honeynet Project, John and Dave identified that the time spent by intruders (approximately 2 hours) significantly differed from the time spent to clean up after them (between 3 and 80 hours).

This led to the conclusion that every 2 hours of intruder time resulted in 40 billable hours of forensics investigative time. However, this estimation did not include intrusion detection (human element), disk image acquisition, restoration and hardening of compromised system(s), network scanning for other vulnerable systems, and communications to stakeholders.

Forensics readiness emphasizes anticipating that an event or incident will occur by enabling an organization to make the most efficient use of digital evidence, instead of concerning itself with the traditional responsive nature of an event or incident. It is a business requirement of any organization that requires key stakeholders to serve a broad role in the overall investigative workflow, including:

- The investigative team
- Senior/executive management
- Human resources and employee relations
- Privacy and compliance
- Corporate security
- IT support staff
- Legal

By having key stakeholders involved in the overall investigative workflow, forensics readiness enables an overall organizational approach to digital evidence. As an overall strategy, the objectives of forensics readiness can be summarized as "the ability to maximize potential use of digital evidence while minimizing investigative costs," with the purpose of achieving the following goals:

- Legally gather admissible evidence without interrupting business functions
- Gather evidence required to validate the impact incidents have on business risks

- Permit investigations to proceed at a cost that is lower than the cost of an event or incident
- Minimize the disruption and impact to business functions
- Ensure evidence maintains positive outcomes for legal proceedings

Costs and Benefits of Digital Forensics Readiness

Management will be cautious of the costs related to implementing a forensics readiness program. While cost implications will be higher where organizations have immature information security programs and strategies, the cost is lessened for organizations that already have a good handle on their information security posture. In either case, the issues raised by the need for a forensics readiness program must be presented to senior management, where a decision can be made.

Cost analysis of a forensics readiness program should be weighed against the value-added benefits the organization will realize once implemented. To make an educated and informed decision about whether implementing a forensics readiness program is practical, organizations must be able to perform an apples-to-apples comparison of the tangible and intangible contributors to the program. The starting point of this task is to document the individual security controls that will be aligned to the forensics readiness program through a service catalog.

Addendum B, "Service Catalog," as found in the Addendum section of this book, further discusses the service catalog to better understand how to hierarchically align individual security controls into the forensics readiness program.

Cost Assessment

Forensics readiness consists of costs involving administrative, technical, and physical information security controls implemented throughout the organization. Through the service catalog, each of these controls is aligned to a service where all cost elements can be identified and allocated appropriately. While not all controls and services will contribute to forensics readiness, the following will directly influence the overall cost of the forensics readiness program:

- *Governance document maintenance* is the ongoing review and updating of the information security and evidence management frameworks (e.g., policies, standards, guidance, procedures).
- *Education and awareness training* provides for continued improvements to:
  - Information security awareness of staff indirectly involved with the information security discipline

- Information security training of staff directly involved with the information security discipline
- Digital forensics training of staff directly involved with the digital forensics discipline
- *Incident management* involves the activities of identifying, analyzing, and mitigating risks to reduce the likelihood of re-occurrence.
- *Data security* includes the enhanced capability to systematically gather potential evidence and securely preserve it.
- *Legal counsel* provides advice and assurance that methodologies, operating procedures, tools, and equipment used during an investigation will not impede legal proceedings.

The inclusion of a service as a cost contributor to the forensics readiness program is subject to the interpretation and/or appetite of each organization. Knowing which services, where controls are aligned, contribute to the forensics readiness program is the starting point for performing the cost assessment. From the service catalog, the breakdown of fixed and variable costs can be used as part of the cost-benefit analysis for demonstrating to management the value of implementing the program.

Benefits Analysis

With forensics readiness, it is necessary to assume that an incident will occur, even if a thorough assessment has determined that residual risk from defensive information security controls is minor. Depending on the impact from this residual risk, organizations need to implement additional layers of controls to proactively collect evidence to determine the root cause of an event.

With the realization that some type of investigative capability is required, the next step an organization must take is to address this need through efficient and competent capabilities. Forensics readiness that is designed to address the residual risk and enhance proactive investigative capabilities offers organizations the following benefits:

- *Minimizing costs*: Operating with an anticipation that an event or incident will occur, the organization will minimize disruption to business functions and support investigative capabilities that are much more efficient, quicker, and more cost effective. With digital evidence already having been collected, the investigative workflow becomes much simpler to navigate, as more focus can be placed on the processing and presentation phases.
- *Control expansion*: In response mode, the capabilities and effectiveness of information security controls provide functionality limited to notification, containment, and remediation. Where proactive

monitoring is utilized, organizations are able to expand their implementation of these information security controls to identify and mitigate a much wider range of cyber threats before they become more
serious incidents or events.

- *Crime deterrent*: Proactive evidence gathering, combined with continuous monitoring of this information, increases the opportunity to
  quickly detect malicious activity. As word of proactive evidence collection becomes more widely known, individuals will be less likely to
  commit malicious activities because the probability of being caught
  is much greater.
- *Governance and compliance*: With an information management
  framework in place, organizations can better demonstrate their
  ability to conduct incident prevention and response. Showing this
  maturity not only provides customers with a sense of security and
  protection when it comes to safeguarding their assets, but investors
  will also have more confidence in the organization's ability to minimize threats against their investments.
- *Law enforcement*: Ensuring compliance with laws and regulations
  encourages good working relationships with both law enforcement
  and regulators. When an incident or event occurs, the job of investigators is much easier because the organization has taken steps
  to gather digital evidence before, during, and after an incident or
  event.
- *Legal preparations*: International laws relating to electronic discovery (e-discovery), such as the *Federal Rules of Civil Procedure* (FRCP)
  in the United States and Canada, and *Practice Direction 31B* in the
  United Kingdom, require that digital evidence be provided quickly
  and in a forensically sound manner. Information management in
  support of e-discovery involves activities such as incident response,
  data retention, disaster recovery, and business continuity policies,
  all of which are enhanced through a forensics readiness program.
  When an organization enters into legal proceedings, the need for
  e-discovery is significantly reduced because digital evidence will
  already be preserved, increasing the probability of success when it is
  used to contribute to legal defense.
- *Disclosure costs*: Regulatory authorities and/or law enforcement
  agencies may require immediate release or disclosure of electronically stored information (ESI) at any time. An organization's failure
  to produce the requested ESI in an appropriate and timely manner
  can result in considerable financial penalties for being non-compliant
  with mandated information management regulations. A forensics
  readiness program strengthens an organization's information management strategies—including data retention, disaster recovery, and

business continuity. Having digital evidence proactively gathered in a sound manner makes it possible for organizations to easily process and present ESI when required.

In June 2005, AMD launched a lawsuit against its rival Intel, claiming that Intel engaged in unfair competition by offering rebates to PC manufacturers who agreed to eliminate or limit the purchase of AMD microprocessors.

As part of e-discovery, AMD requested the production of email evidence from Intel to demonstrate this claim. Intel failed to produce the email evidence due to (1) a fault in email retention policy and (2) failing to properly inform employees that their ESI was required as evidence through legal hold.

Due to this failure to produce evidence, in November 2009 Intel agreed to pay AMD $1.25 billion as part of a deal to settle all outstanding legal disputes between the two companies.

Addendum C, "Cost-Benefit Analysis," as found in the Addendum section of this book, further discusses how to perform a cost-benefit analysis to determine if implementing a forensics readiness program is valuable to an organization.

Implementing Forensics Readiness

Forensics readiness provides a "win-win" situation for organizations because it is complementary to, and an enhancement of, the information security program and strategies. Even if not formally acknowledged, many organizations already perform some information security activities, such as proactively gathering and preserving digital information, relative to forensics readiness.

Making progress with a forensics readiness program requires a risk-based approach that facilitates a practical implementation to manage business risk. The chapters found throughout this section of the book will examine the key activities within information security that are relevant to implementing an effective forensics readiness program. Specifically, the inclusion of certain aspects of forensics readiness as a component of information security best practices will be discussed in the following steps:

1. Define the business risks and scenarios that require digital evidence.
2. Identify available data sources and types of digital evidence.

3. Determine the requirements for gathering digital evidence.
4. Establishing capabilities for gathering digital evidence in support of evidence rules.
5. Develop an information security framework to govern digital evidence management.
6. Design security monitoring controls to deter and detect event and incidents.
7. Specify the criteria for escalating events or incidents into formal digital investigations.
8. Conduct security awareness training to educate stakeholders on their organizational role.
9. Document and present evidence-based findings and conclusions.
10. Ensure legal review to facilitate event or incident response actions.

Summary

Digital forensics readiness enables organizations to maximize their proactive investigative capabilities. By completing a proper cost-benefit analysis, the value-add of an enhanced level of readiness can be demonstrated through investigative cost reduction and operational efficiencies gains.

Defining Business Risk Scenarios 7

Introduction

As the first stage, organizations must clearly understand the "who, where, what, when, why, and how" motives for investing time, money, and resources into a digital forensics readiness program. To better gain this understanding, a risk assessment is performed to identify the potential impacts on business operation from diverse types of digital crimes, disputes, incidents, and events.

This risk assessment will be used, from the business perspective, to describe where digital evidence is required and its benefit in reducing impact to business operations, such as alleviating efforts to reactively collect digital evidence. Generally, if the identified business risks and the potential benefits of a digital forensics readiness program indicate that the organization will realize a positive return on investment (ROI), then there is a need to consider proactively gathering digital evidence to mitigate the identified business risk scenarios.

What Is Business Risk?

Generally, business risk implies a level of uncertainty due to unforeseen events happening that present a threat of impact to the organization. Business risks can directly or indirectly impact an organization but collectively can be grouped as being influenced by two major types of risk contributors:

- *Internal events* are those risks that can be controlled and take place within the boundaries of the organization, including:
  - Technology (i.e., outages, degradations)
  - Workplace health and safety (i.e., accidents, ergonomics)
  - Information/physical security (i.e., theft, data loss, fraud)
  - Staffing (human error, conflict management)
- *External events* are those risks that occur outside of the organization's control, including:
  - Natural disasters (i.e., floods, storms, and drought)
  - Global events (i.e., pandemics, climate change)
  - Regulatory and government policy (i.e., taxes, restrictions)
  - Suppliers (i.e., supply chain, business interruptions)

Internal and external events that have the potential to create an impact depend on the type of business operations offered by an organization (e.g., financial, records management) and should not be treated as universally equivalent. Putting these risks into a business context, internal and external events can be grouped into five major types of risk classifications:

- *Strategic risk* is associated with the organization's core business functions and commonly occurs because of:
  - Business interactions where goods and services are purchased and sold, varying supply and demand, adjustments to competitive structures, and the emergence of new or innovative technologies
  - Transactions resulting in asset relocation from mergers and acquisitions, spin-offs, alliances, or joint ventures
  - Strategies for investment relations management and communicating with stakeholders who have invested in the organization
- *Financial risk* is associated with the financial structure, stability, and transactions of the organization.
- *Operational risk* is associated with the organization's business, operational, and administrative procedures.
- *Legal risk* is associated with the need to comply with the rules and regulations of the governing bodies.
- *Other risks* are associated with indirect, non-business factors such as natural disasters and others as identified based on the individual characteristics of the organization.

Without knowing the assets that are most critical and equally what threats, vulnerabilities, or risks can impact the organization, it is not possible for key decision-makers to response with appropriate protection strategies. As part of the overall risk management approach, a risk assessment should be completed to evaluate:

- Vulnerabilities that exist in the environment;
- Threats targeting organizational assets;
- Likelihood of threats creating actual impact;
- Severity of the impact that could be realized; and
- Risk associated with each threat.

Addendum E, "Risk Assessment," further discusses the overall approach and process for how organizations can complete a risk assessment.

Forensics Readiness Scenarios

Like the business risk contributors noted previously, within the context of digital forensics readiness there are also a series of direct and indirect influences that organizations must identify and develop strategies to manage exposure of digital evidence. To illustrate the business risks where digital forensics readiness can demonstrate positive benefit, each risk scenario will be explained following the "who, where, what, when, why, and how" motives to justify investing time, money, and resources.

Scenario #1: Reduce the Impact of Cybercrime

Having technology play such an integral part of most core business functions increasingly exposes organizations to the potential impact of cybercrime and a constantly evolving threat landscape. Completing a risk assessment for this scenario first requires organizations to understand the security properties of their business functions that they need to safeguard. The list below describes the security properties that organizations must protect:

- *Confidentiality*: Ensuring that objects and assets are only made available to the subjects they are intended for
- *Integrity*: Validating that change to objects and assets is done following approved processes and by approved subjects
- *Availability*: Guaranteeing that objects and assets are accessible when needed and that performance is delivered to the highest possible standards
- *Continuity*: Ability to recover the loss of processing capabilities within an acceptable time
- *Authentication*: Establishing that access to objects and assets identifies the requesting subject; or alternatively a risk acceptance is approved to permit alternate means of subject access
- *Authorization*: Explicitly denying or permitting subjects access to objects and assets
- *Non-repudiation*: Protecting against falsely denying a subject ownership over an action

Reducing the impact of cybercrime should be a consideration for all security properties listed above. However, it is not enough to only consider these security properties. Further analysis needs to be done to understand exactly how individual security threats pose business risk and can potentially impact operational functions.

Using a threat modeling methodology, as discussed in Addendum F, "Threat Modeling," allows organizations to become better equipped to identify, quantify, and address security threats that present a risk. Resulting from the threat modeling, a structured representation can be created into the ways that threat actors can go about executing attacks and how their tactics, techniques, and procedures can be used to impact an organization.

Table 7.1 Threat Category to Security Property Relationship

Threat Category	Security Property
Spoofing	Authentication
Tampering	Integrity
Repudiation	Non-repudiation
Information disclosure	Confidentiality
Denial of service	Availability continuity
Elevation of privilege	Authorization

Detailed information collected from the threat modeling exercise must now be translated into a business language that aligns with strategies for reducing the impact of cybercrime. Using a series of threat categories, individual security threats can be placed into larger groupings based on commonalities in their tactics, techniques, and procedures. As discussed in Addendum F, "Threat Modeling," the STRIDE threat model describes the six threat categories into which individual security threats can be grouped. Illustrated in Table 7.1, the relationships between security properties and threat categories can be correlated to further enhance the alignment of individual security threat with focus areas for reducing the impact of cybercrime.

Scenario #2: Validate the Impact of Cybercrime or Disputes

When cybercrime occurs, organizations must be prepared to show the amount of impact the incident had on its business operations, functions, and assets. To do so requires supporting evidence to be gathered and made readily available when an incident is declared. Inadequate preparations can lead to delayed validation or insufficient results.

The total cost an incident has on an organization should not be limited to only those business operations, functions, and assets that were directly impacted. To gain a complete and accurate view of the entire cost of an incident, organizations should consider both indirect and collateral contributors as part of validating the impact of cybercrime or disputes.

Mitigating Control Logs

The constantly evolving threat landscape brings about new and/or transformed cybercrimes which must be identified and assessed to determine relevance and potential impact. Using threat tree workflows, such as the one illustrated in Addendum F, "Threat Modeling," organizations can leverage the outputs of risk mitigation controls to validate the impact of an incident. Generally, controls can be implemented as:

- *Preventive*: Stop loss, harm, or damage from occurring
- *Detective*: Monitor activity to identify errors or irregularities
- *Corrective*: Restore objects and information to a known good state

Depending on the type of control there will be distinct types of log files generated that contain relevant, meaningful, and valuable information for validating the impact of an incident. Regardless of whether the control was implemented as a component (e.g., host-based malware prevention) or standalone (e.g., network-based firewall), at a minimum the following log file types should be maintained:

- *Application*: Records actions, as predetermined by the application, taken by secondary systems components and processes
- *Security*: Records actions, as chosen by the organization, taken by non-system subjects relating to authorization and authentication activities into the system and contained objects
- *System*: Records actions, as predetermined by the system, taken by system components and processes

Refer to Chapter 3, "Digital Evidence Management," for further discussion about sources and types of log files.

Overhead Time and Effort

The time it takes to contain and remediate an incident depends on the amount of impact suffered. However, when an incident occurs, the costs associated with the overall business impact are commonly scoped down to the loss, harm, or damage of assets and operations. While these are essential considerations in determining the overall impact of an incident, the overhead cost of managing the incident can sometimes be overlooked as a contributor to the overall business impact.

Generally, as a best practice the overhead cost required to run the incident response program should be included in the overall cost of the incident. This requires that organizations maintain accurate time tracking to ensure that the total amount of time invested by resources assigned to the incident response process are recorded. Without tracking overhead costs, organizations cannot effectively demonstrate the resource time and effort required to manage the incident.

Indirect Business Loss

Generally, an incident requires a team of specialized resources to participate in one or more of the incident response stages. Additionally, it is not uncommon for resources to participate in the incident response process in addition to having daily functions and operations they perform.

Under these circumstances, the time and effort required for these resources to participate in the incident response process create a cascading effect where other business operations and functions are subsequently impacted by the incident. Using time tracking, the costs associated with the inability to perform normal duties should be taken into consideration as a contributor to the overall impact of the incident.

Recovery and Continuity Expenses

Following the threat tree workflows illustrated in Addendum F, "Threat Modeling," the progression from potential threat to business impact includes technical impact. Incidents that generate a technical impact where assets are harmed, lost, or damaged requires several steps to ensure the organization's recovery time objectives are met.

In these circumstances, the overall impact of the incident should include disaster recovery and business continuity costs. While the inclusion of these costs is different for each organization, at a minimum these costs should include:

- The overhead time and effort to restore business operations;
- Indirect productivity loss due to unavailable systems;
- New hardware to replace harmed/damaged hardware (if needed); and
- Restoration of information lost due to harmed/damaged hardware

Scenario #3: Produce Evidence to Support Organizational Disciplinary Issues

For the most part, organizations require that employees comply with their business code of conduct. The organizational goal related to having a business code of conduct is to promote a positive work environment that strengthens the confidence of employees and stakeholders alike.

By signing this document and agreeing to comply, employees are held to the organization's expectations related to ethical behavior in the work environment, when performing operational duties, or as part of their relationship with external parties. Employees who violate the guidelines set out in the business code of conduct could be subject to appropriate disciplinary actions, and in the process, supporting digital evidence may need to be gathered and processed.

With any disciplinary actions, there is the potential that the employee could decide to escalate the matter into a legal problem. To prevent this from happening, the organization must approach the situation fairly and reasonably, using consistent procedures that, at a minimum:

- Are in writing;
- Are specific and clear;
- Do not discriminate;
- Allow the matter to be dealt with quickly;
- Ensure gathered evidence is kept confidential;

- Inform the employee(s) of what disciplinary actions might be taken;
- Indicate what authority each level of management has for different disciplinary actions;
- Inform the employee(s) of the complaints against them with supporting evidence;
- Provide the employee(s) with an opportunity to appeal before a decision is made;
- Allow the employee(s) to be accompanied (e.g., by human resources);
- Ensure no employee(s) is dismissed for a first offense, except in circumstances of gross misconduct; and
- Require a complete investigation be performed before disciplinary action is taken.

Scenario #4: Demonstrating Compliance with Regulatory or Legal Requirements

The need for regulatory or legal compliance can be business-centric depending on several factors, such as the industry the organization operates within (e.g., financial) or the countries where business operations are conducted (e.g., Unites States, India, Great Britain). Laws and regulations can also be enforced by different entities having different requirements for managing compliance and non-compliance, such as:

- Self-policed by a community (i.e., "peer regulation");
- Unilaterally by those in power (i.e., "fiat regulation"); or
- Delegated to an independent third-party authority (i.e., "statutory regulation").

The importance of how these governing laws and regulations directly influence the way organizations operate must be clearly understood. Despite the grumblings of ensuring business operations follow the "red tape" of regulations, they are generally necessary to provide evidence of controls and show due care in circumstances where there is potential for negligence. While the types of regulations listed below may not be complete, the list provides an understanding of the categories that can be applicable to organizations:

- *Economic regulations* are a form of government regulation that adjusts prices and conditions of the economy (e.g., professional licenses to conduct business, telephony service fees).
- *Social regulations* are a form of government regulation that protects the interests of the public from economic activity such as health and the environment (e.g., accidental release of chemicals into air/water).

- *Arbitrary regulations* mandate the use of one out of several equally valid options (e.g., driving on the left/right side of the road).
- *Good faith regulations* establish a baseline of behavior for an area (e.g., restaurant health checks).
- *Good conflict regulations* recognize an inherent conflict between two goals and take control for the greater good (e.g., wearing seatbelts in vehicles).
- *Process regulations* dictate explicitly how tasks are to be completed (e.g., call centre scripts).

Scenario #5: Effectively Manage the Release of Court-Ordered Data

No matter how diligent an organization is, there are times when a dispute will end up before a court of law. When this happens, the organization must be able to quickly produce credible evidence that supports their case and will not be called into question during legal proceedings.

For the most part, all organizations have common types of electronically stored information (ESI) that are considered discoverable as digital evidence, such as email messages. However, the likelihood that the courts will require discovery of different ESI will vary depending on the nature of the dispute and the business performed by the organization.

With adequate preparation, routine follow-ups, and a thorough understanding of what is considered reasonable in a court of law, organizations can effectively manage this risk. The most critical aspect of managing this risk to the court's expectations is to be diligent with validating and verifying the integrity of ESI and avoid any interaction or activity that will be viewed as practicing bad faith.

As discussed in Chapter 10, "Establishing Legal Admissibility," *Federal Rules of Evidence 803(6)* describe ESI as being admissible as digital evidence in court if it demonstrates "records of regularly conducted activity" as a business record, such as an act, event, condition, opinion, or diagnosis. Ensuring compliance with this ruling requires organizations to implement a series of safeguards, precautions, and controls to ensure ESI is admissible in court and that it is authenticated to its original source.

Scenario #6: Support Contractual and Commercial Agreements

Depending on the nature of business performed, organizations can face disagreements that extend beyond disputes that commonly involve internal staff. Resulting in various actions from breach of contract terms, improper termination of contracts, or large-scale class action lawsuits, these disputes can involve external entities such as business partners, competitors, shareholders, suppliers, or customers.

The majority of the interactions involved with contractual and commercial agreements can take place electronically. With these interactions being largely electronic, organizations must ensure they capture and electronically preserve critical metadata about the agreements, such as details about the terms and conditions or the date the agreement was co-signed. Having this information available when needed can be extremely useful when it comes to preventing any type of loss (e.g., financial, productivity) or when using arbitration as an alternative resolution path.

ESI needed to support contractual and commercial disputes may require detailed documentary evidence that thoroughly describes the relationship between the organization and the external entities. To ensure information regarding contractual and commercial agreements is accurately captured, a contract management system can be used to standardize and preserve the metadata needed to provide sufficient grounds for supporting a dispute.

Scenario Assessment

Of the five forensics readiness scenarios discussed previously, not all are relevant to every organization. To determine which scenarios are applicable to a particular organization requires that an assessment of each scenario be completed.

Determination of whether a scenario applies to an organization requires that both a qualitative and quantitative assessment, discussed further in Addendum E, "Risk Assessment," be performed to ensure that a thorough understanding of the potential risks is achieved. Following the completion of these assessments, organizations will have a complete picture of all potential risks which can then be used to perform a cost-benefit analysis, discussed further in Addendum C, "Cost-Benefit Analysis," to determine the likely benefits of being able to use digital evidence.

Generally, if a risk exists in any scenario, and it has been identified that there is a return on investment for forensics readiness, then consideration of what evidence sources need to be gathered should occur.

Summary

Defining the business risk scenarios that are the primary driver for establishing proactive investigative capabilities is the most critical aspect of practicing digital forensics readiness. Although each business risk scenario contains a series of unique use cases and requirements for proactively gathering digital evidence, there remains a degree of commonality in the justifications for why these data sources need to be readily available.

Identify Potential Data Sources

8

Introduction

As the second stage, organizations work to identify sources of evidence to support the risk scenarios identified as being relevant to their business. With each risk scenario, work needs to be done to determine what sources of potential digital evidence exist, or could be generated, and what happens to the potential evidence in terms of authenticity and integrity.

Generally, the purpose of completing this stage is to create an inventory of data sources where digital evidence is readily available throughout the organization. Not only does this inventory support the proactive gathering of digital evidence to support digital forensics readiness, but it also allows the organization to identify systems and applications that are deficient in their data collection requirements.

What Is a Data Source?

The most familiar technology where potential digital evidence is located comes from traditional personal computing systems such as desktops, laptops, and servers. Typically, with these technologies digital evidence will be located directly on the internal storage medium, such as the internal hard drive(s), or indirectly on external storage medium, such as optical discs or universal serial bus (USB) devices.

However, organizations should also consider the possibility that data sources exist beyond the more traditional personal computing systems. With the widespread use of technology in business operations, every organization will have electronically stored information (ESI) that is considered potential digital evidence generated across various sources.

Careful consideration must be given when determining what potential digital evidence should be gathered from data sources. When identifying data sources, organizations should consider placing the potential digital evidence into either of the following categories.

Background Evidence

Background evidence is data that has been gathered and stored as part of normal business operations, according to the organization's policies and standards governance framework. The gathering of this type of evidence includes:

- Network devices such as routers/switches, firewalls, domain name system (DNS) servers, and dynamic host configuration protocol (DHCP) servers
- Authentication records such as directory services logs, physical access logs, and employee profile databases
- Electronic communication channels such as email, text, chat, and instant messaging
- Data management solutions such as backups, archives, classification engines, integrity checkers, and transaction registers
- Other sources such as internet service providers (ISP) and cloud service providers (CSP)

Foreground Evidence

Foreground evidence is data that has been specifically gathered and stored to support an investigation or identify perpetrators. The action of gathering this type of evidence can also be referred to as "monitoring" because it typically involves analyzing—in real time—the activities of subjects. Depending on regulations and laws concerning privacy and rights, organizations should consult with their legal teams to ensure that the active monitoring of employees is done correctly. The gathering of this type of evidence includes:

- Network monitoring systems such as intrusion prevention systems (IPS), packet sniffers, and anti-malware
- Application software such as anti-malware and data loss prevention (DLP)
- Business process systems such as fraud monitoring

While the above sample of data sources is by no means a complete representation of potential digital evidence, every organization has different requirements and will need to determine the relevance and usefulness of each data source as it is identified. Refer to Chapter 3, "Digital Evidence Management," for further discussion about types and sources of digital evidence.

Cataloguing Data Sources

Like how a service catalog provides organizations with a better understanding of how to hierarchically align individual security controls with the forensics readiness program, discussed further in Addendum B, "Service Catalog," each data source must be placed into a similar hierarchical structure. The methodology for successfully creating a data source inventory includes activities that have been completed previously and well as activities that will be completed afterward, as discussed in subsequent chapters of this book.

Specific to the scope of this chapter, creating a data source inventory includes the following phases:

Phase #1: Prepare an Action Plan

An action plan is an excellent tool for making sure the strategies used by the organization when developing the data source inventory achieve the desired final vision. The action plan consists of four steps that must be completed to deliver a complete and accurate inventory:

- What tasks and/or activities need to take place for data sources to be identified
- Who will be responsible and accountable for ensuring the tasks/ activities are completed
- When the tasks/activities will take place, in what order, and for how long
- What resources (e.g., funding, people) are needed to complete the tasks/activities

At this point, there are several questions that organizations need to answer so that when it comes time to identify and document data sources, they will be able to thoroughly and accurately collect the information they need to produce the inventory. In no order, these basic questions should include:

- *Where is the data generated?* Have the systems and/or applications that are creating this data been identified and documented in the organization's service catalog?
- *What format it is in?* Is the data in a structure that can be interpreted and processed by existing tools and/or processes; or are new tools and/or processes required?
- *How long is it stored for?* Will the data be retained for a duration that will ensure availability for investigative needs?

- *How it is controlled, secured, and managed?* Is the authenticity, integrity, and custody of the data maintained throughout its lifecycle?
- *Who has access to it?* Are adequate authentication and authorization mechanisms in place to limit access to only those who require it?
- *How much data is produced at a given interval?* What volume of relevant data is created that needs to be stored?
- *How, where, and for how long is the data archived?* Are there sufficient resources (e.g., network bandwidth, long-term storage, systems) available to store it?
- *How much data is currently being reviewed?* What percentage of the data is currently being analyzed using what tools, techniques, and resources?
- *Who is responsible for this data?* What business line within the organization manages and is responsible for each aspect of the data's lifecycle?
- *Who is the data owner?* Which specific individual is responsible for the data?
- *How can it be made available for investigations?* What processes, tools, or techniques exist that allow this data to be gathered for investigative needs?
- *What business processes does this data relate to?* What are the business and/or operational workflows where this data is created, used, and stored?
- *Does it contain any personally identifiable information (PII)?* Does the data contain any properties that can be used to reveal confidential and/or sensitive personal information?

Phase #2: Identify Data Sources

Following the direction set in the action plan, the organization will be better equipped to identify data sources—throughout their environment—where digital evidence exists. As data sources are identified, each must be catalogued and recorded in a centralized inventory matrix.

There are no pre-defined requirements indicating what specific elements must be included in the inventory matrix, leaving the decision to include or exclude elements entirely up to the subjectivity of the organization. The most common descriptive elements that organizations should use in the data source inventory matrix, as provided as a reference in the "Templates" section of this book, should include the following:

- *Overall status* provides a visual representation of the organization's maturity related to the gathering of digital evidence for the overall business scenario, including the following labels:

- Green = fully implemented
- Blue = partially implemented
- Orange = in progress
- Yellow = plan in place
- Red = not implemented

- *Business scenario* indicates which of the business scenarios, as discussed in Chapter 5, "Digital Forensics as a Business," the data source contributes to as digital evidence.
- *Operational service* aligns the data source to the operational service it is associated with as documented in the organization's service catalog, which is discussed further in Addendum B, "Service Catalog," such as digital investigations, litigation support.
- *Data format* describes the high-level grouping of how the information is arranged in this data source, such as structured or unstructured.
- *Data origin* identifies the system and/or application where the information is generated, such as email archive, end-user system, network share, or cloud service provider.
- *Data category* illustrates the exact type of information available in this data source, such as multimedia, email messages, or productivity suite documents.
- *Data location* determines how the information persists within the data source, such as at-rest, in-transit, or in-use.
- *Data owner* documents the specific individual who is responsible for the data.
- *Business use case* identifies the high-level grouping representing the motive for why this information exists, such as data loss prevention, data classification, or intrusion prevention.
- *Technology name* documents the organization that created and provides ongoing support for the solution where the data source persists.
- *Technology vendor* documents the organization that created and provides ongoing support for the solution where the data source persists.
- *Technology owner* documents the specific individual who is responsible for the solution where the data source persists.
- *Status* provides a visual representation of the organization's maturity related to the gathering of digital evidence for the specific data source, including the following labels:
  - Green = fully implemented
  - Blue = partially implemented
  - Orange = in progress
  - Yellow = plan in place
  - Red = not implemented

- *Status details* provide a justification for the status assigned to the maturity rating for the specific data source.
- *Action plan* describes the activities required for the organization to improve the maturity rating for the specific data source.

Phase #3: Document Deficiencies

As the inventory matrix is being developed, the organization might encounter instances where there is insufficient information currently available in a data source or gaps in the availability of information from unidentified data sources. Resolving these findings should be done separately because the activities that need to be performed are somewhat different in scope.

Insufficient Data Availability

Although a data source has been identified and included in the inventory matrix, this does not mean that it contains relevant and useful information to support forensics readiness. Generally, determining whether a data source provides an acceptable level of digital evidence requires that organizations ensure that the information contained within supports the investigation with either content or context.

Content Awareness   Content is the element that exists within information that describe details about an event or incident. Information that can be used as digital evidence during an investigation must provide the organization with details sufficient to allow them to arrive at evidence-based conclusions.

Commonly categorized as foreground evidence, information gathered from data sources should contain enough content to support the "who, where, what, when, and how" aspects of an investigation. This requires that, at a minimum, all information within data sources that will be used as digital evidence include the following metadata properties:

- *Timestamp* of when the event/incident occurred, including full date and time fields with time zone offset
- *Source* of where the event/incident originated, including an identifier such as hostname or IP address
- *Destination* of where the event/incident was targeted, including an identifier such as hostname or IP address
- *Description* provides an unstructured, textual description of the event or incident

In addition to these minimum requirements, organizations must recognize that every data source is different and depending on the system (or application) that created it the information contained within will provide varying types of additional details. By assessing the content of a data source, organizations will be able to determine if it contains information that is relevant and useful as digital evidence.

Contextual Awareness Context is the circumstances whereby supplemental information can be used to further describe an event or incident. Commonly categorized as background evidence, supplemental information gathered from data sources can improve the "who, where, what, when, and how" aspects of an investigation.

Consider a layered stack model, like that of the open systems interconnection (OSI) model, where each layer serves both the layer above and below it. The model for how context is used to enhance digital evidence can also be grouped into distinct categories that each provides its own supplemental benefit to the data source information.

A layered context model follows the same methodology as the OSI model where each layer brings supplemental information that can be applied as an additional layer onto existing digital evidence. As illustrated in Figure 8.1, the attributes comprised within a layered context model include:

- *Network*: Any arrangement of interconnected hardware that supports the exchange of data
- *Device*: Combination of hardware components adapted specifically to execute software-based systems
- *Operating system*: Variations of software-based systems that manage the underlying hardware components to provide a common set of processes, services, applications, etc.

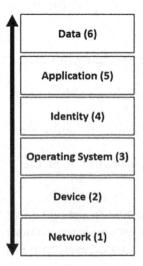

Figure 8.1 Context awareness model.

- *Identity*: Characteristics that define subjects interacting with software-based systems, processes, services, applications, etc.
- *Application*: Software-based processes, services, applications, etc. that allow subjects to interface (read, write, execute) with the data layer
- *Data*: Structured and/or unstructured content that is gathered as foreground digital evidence in support of an investigation

By applying meaningful contextual information to digital evidence, evidence-based conclusions can be reached at a much quicker rate because the team can answer the questions of "who, where, what, when, why, and how" with a much higher level of confidence.

In 2013, Target retailers were the victims of a sophisticated cyber-attack that lead to an eventual data breach where cyber criminals stole approximately 40 million credit/debit cards and approximately 70 million personal records of customers (i.e., name, address, email, phone).

In a statement made by Target's spokesperson, it was indicated that:

Like any large company, each week at Target there are a vast number of technical events that take place and are logged.

Furthermore, the Target spokesperson stated that:

Through our investigation, we learned that after these criminals entered our network, a small amount of their activity was logged and surfaced to our team. That activity was evaluated and acted upon.

However, the Target spokesperson continued to say that:

Based on their interpretation and evaluation of that activity, the team determined that it did not warrant immediate follow up... With the benefit of hindsight, we are investigating whether if different judgments had been made the outcome may have been different.

From the statements made by Target's spokesperson, it is recognized that the company was well equipped with proper information security defenses that ultimately identified and alerted their security team of the ongoing attack. However, Target indicated that the ability of their security team to make an informed decision was affected by the absence of context about the alert.

Unidentified Data Sources

Before a decision is made to include these data sources in the inventory matrix, organization must first determine the relevance and usefulness of the data during an investigation. When assessing additional data sources, the business scenarios aligned to the forensics readiness program must be used as the foundation for the final decision to include or exclude the data.

If a decision is made to include the data source into the inventory matrix, the organization will need to start back at the first phase, *Phase #1: Preparation*, to ensure that the action plan is followed and all prerequisite questions have been answered.

External Data Considerations

Retrieving digital evidence from data sources owned by the organization can be relatively straightforward. However, with the continuous growth in the use of cloud service providers (CSP) there is a new level of complexity when it comes to gathering digital evidence from this type of data source.

For the most part, with these cloud environments, organizations do not have direct access to or ownership over the physical systems where their digital evidence can persist. This requires that, to guarantee digital evidence will be readily available in an acceptable state (i.e., integrity, authenticity), organizations need to ensure that a service agreement contract is established with the CSP where service level objectives (SLO) for incident response are outlined.

Where a CSP has been contracted to manage and offer computing services, organizations must ensure that the service agreement between both parties includes terms and conditions specific to incident response and investigation support. Generally, the CSP must become an extension of the organization's incident response team and ensure that they follow forensically sound processes to preserve digital evidence in their environment(s).

Organizations must first obtain a reasonable level of assurance that the CSP will protect their data and respond to incidents and/or event within an acceptable SLO. The terms and conditions for how this assurance is achieved should be included as part of the service agreement established between both parties. Once the terms and conditions have been agreed to by both parties, the roles and responsibilities of the CSP during an incident or investigation must be defined so that the organization knows who will be involved and what roles they will play.

Having established the terms and conditions specific to incident response and investigative support, it is essential that organizations involve the CSP when practicing their computer incident response program.

Refer to Chapter 18, "Forensics Readiness in Cloud Environments," for further discussion about applying forensics readiness capabilities within cloud computing environments.

Data Exposure Concerns

The aggregation of data from multiple sources into a single repository ensures that digital evidence is proactively gathered and is readily available during an investigation. However, the security posture of the aggregated digital evidence from the multiple data sources is extremely critical and should be subject to stringent requirements for technical, administrative, and physical security controls.

Essentially, the collection of this digital evidence into a common repository has the potential to become a single point of vulnerability for the organization. Completion of a risk assessment on this common data repository, as discussed further in Addendum E, "Risk Assessment," will identify the organization's requirements for implementing necessary countermeasures to effectively secure and protect the digital evidence.

Forensic Architectures

Traditionally, investigations have been performed in response to a security event or incident to determine root cause or assess business impact. Generally, the objective for performing any investigation is to establish factual evidence-based conclusions from relevant data sources (e.g., mobile devices, computer systems) across dissimilar architectures (e.g., corporate, cloud) in varying states (i.e., volatile, persistent). Ever since the formalization of the digital forensics discipline, there have been ongoing efforts to strategically integrate its foundational principles, methodologies, and techniques throughout an organization's security capabilities so that there is a higher level of assurance that credible digital evidence will be available when required.

Within the realms of information and cyber security, the CIA triad (confidentiality, integrity, and availability) describes the fundamental components for implementing security controls to safeguard informational assets. Likewise, following this CIA methodology, security architectures contain design principles that consider relationships and dependencies between various technology architectures with the goal of protecting informational assets and systems. Naturally, this approach introduces complications for enabling digital forensics capabilities because potential evidence may be unavailable due to improper design and implementation of security architectures.

As the starting point, the design of security architectures—that proactively support digital forensics capabilities—can be accomplished through the development of reference architecture templates (or blueprints). By having these templates readily available, organizations will have a common framework with a consistent glossary of terms as reference for stakeholders (e.g., development teams) to understand digital forensics requirements.

For example, organizations can outline the following as components of their digital forensics requirements for security architectures:

- Regularly performing system and application backups and maintaining them as defined in the organization's enterprise governance framework
- Enabling audits of security information and events for corporately managed assets (i.e., end-user systems, servers, network devices) into a centralized repository
- Maintaining records of known-good and known-bad signatures for systems and applications
- Maintaining accurate and complete records of network, system, and application configurations
- Establishing an evidence management framework to address the control of evidence to guarantee authenticity and integrity throughout its lifecycle

Systems Lifecycle

Traditionally, accurately identifying and successfully implementing technical security requirements fell within the responsibility of network or system administrators. However, given the dynamic and mobile nature of today's workforce, coupled with the continuously evolving threat landscape and expanded scope of potential digital evidence, it has become apparent that assurance for adequate security standards needs to be integrated as part of the organization's overall security assurance procedures.

This doesn't mean that organizations need to re-invent the wheel by developing new processes by which they can effectively integrate digital forensics requirements into their security architectures. Rather, as a strategy they should look to incorporating reference architectures for digital forensics into existing systems'—and applications'—lifecycle processes. It is important to note that the word "development" was not included because security is concerned with not only the development phases, but also the ongoing operations and maintenance phases after the system (or application) has been developed.

Waterfall and Agile Models

Traditionally, the system (or application) lifecycle has followed a waterfall methodology where each phase of the process is performed in a steady downward sequence (non-iterative). With this approach, the next phase is only executed once the preceding phase has been completed. While there are many iterations of the waterfall methodology, each with its own variations, the following illustrates the high-level phases of the model:

- *Requirements* is the initiation point where the concept is captured and requirements are documented.
- *Design* analyzes requirements to create models and schemas resulting in the system architecture.
- *Implementation* includes product coding, proving, and testing.
- *Operations* involves the installation with ongoing support and maintenance of the completed product.

Under the waterfall model, incorporating security requirements must be systematically achieved right from the beginning of the process. This way, when it comes time to design and implement the system (or application), due diligence has been completed to minimize the attack surface and reduce risk from security flaws. However, with the velocity of technology advancements and the rate at which technology is being consumerized, it became apparent that customer expectations were that greater functionality could come at a much faster pace. Because the waterfall model is linear in nature, which can result in an extended time until a completed product is delivered, organizations began looking to the agile methodology as an alternative.

With the agile model, work products are delivered through incremental and iterative phases, otherwise known as "sprints." Unlike the waterfall, the agile model continually revisits development requirements throughout the lifecycle, which can result in the direction of a project changing suddenly. Considering how the agile model enables organizations to follow a continuous integration and development approach, security has a key place in this methodology because of the extreme risk related to original requirements and changing design. Generally, with each iteration of agile development, security needs to be incorporated by documenting and understanding:

1. The current state, including:
   - Affected systems, applications, users, etc.
   - Data flows, interchanges, and communications between systems, applications, and users
   - Review of previously documented security concerns and findings to prevent reoccurrence
   - Impact assessment of change against enterprise security program
2. What product will be delivered, including:
   - Business operations and service involved
   - Threat and risk assessment of informational assets and systems requiring protection

3. How to securely delivery the product, including:
   - Apply the principle of least access privilege
   - Incorporate proactive capabilities (as described in the sections above)

Ensuring security requirements are incorporated as a component of either methodology is easier said than done. Without security being interwoven throughout the systems' (and applications') lifecycle, the organization's digital forensics capabilities will be hindered when it comes to the availability of potential digital evidence. Also, the absence of security within the systems' (and applications') lifecycle will result in digital forensics capabilities being impeded from becoming more proactive in terms of maturity, rather than continuing to operate reactively.

Summary

Digital evidence that is beneficial in supporting proactive investigations can be identified from a broad range of data sources. As this data is being gathered, not only does it need to provide details about the incident and/or event, it must provide investigators with the contextual information to make informed conclusions. Incorporating forensics requirements during the SDLC will further enhance an organization's ability to gather digital evidence from data sources that is meaningful and relevant.

Determine Collection Requirements 9

Introduction

As the third stage, organizations must produce a collection requirements statement that effectively outlines to business risk stakeholders what their responsibilities are—throughout the enterprise—for operating and monitoring systems where digital evidence will be sourced from.

However, in addition to the need for defining business risk scenarios and identifying data sources, before an organization can establish a statement around the proactive gathering of digital evidence they should ensure that a thorough assessment is performed to ensure the requirements for collecting any digital evidence are justified and authorized.

Pre-collection Questions

Deciding on what the organization's requirements are for proactively gathering digital evidence requires some preliminary activities to be completed before work can begin on creating an overall statement describing exactly what these requirements are. The moderating factor in producing a requirements statement is a cost-benefit analysis (CBA). Refer to Addendum C, "Cost-Benefit Analysis," for further discussion about how to perform a cost-benefit analysis in support of producing the digital evidence collection requirements statement.

Similar to how a CBA is used to determine if implementing a forensics readiness program is valuable to an organization, as discussed in Chapter 1, "Understanding Digital Forensics," this time around it is used to help organizations determine factors such as how much it will cost to gather the digital evidence and what benefit there is in collecting it. To determine if creating a requirements statement to gather digital evidence is beneficial, organizations must answer several questions that focus on whether it can be done in a cost-effective manner.

Question #1: Can a forensics investigation proceed at a cost in comparison to the cost of an incident?
    To get an accurate comparison, organizations should factor in all monetary aspects associated with conducting an investigation

in reaction to an incident against the resulting impact of an incident. As a starting point organizations can pull cost elements from their service catalog, discussed further in Addendum B, "Service Catalog," to understand how administrative, technical, and physical security controls contribute to conducting a forensics investigation. Examples of cost elements that organizations must consider including as part of this comparison include ongoing maintenance of governance documentation (e.g., standard operating procedures (SOP)); resource allocation to facilitate both incident management and continuous improvement activities; and the operational costs of technologies used to manage the business risk. With this initial analysis complete, a secondary comparison must be completed, including all monetary aspects, tangible and intangible, associated with performing an investigation after proactively gathering the digital evidence versus the resulting impact of an incident. Using results from the two comparative analyses, organizations can determine the quantitative benefits of creating a requirements statement.

Question #2: Can digital evidence be gathered without interfering in business operations?

When conducted in reaction to an event, forensics investigations can require that organizations temporarily assigned several support resources to assist in the gathering of digital evidence. In some instances, the organization might realize that their ability to effectively and efficiently gather digital evidence in reaction to an incident is challenged by some type of roadblock (e.g., restoration time delay). Where potential digital evidence can be proactively gathered, organizations can benefit from having digital evidence readily available when needed and not having to allocate resources away from their day-to-day business operations to assist. This improvement in operational efficiencies can reduce the need for resources to be temporarily removed from their normal duties and avoid any lost productivity or degradation in service availability.

Question #3: Can a forensics investigation minimize the negative impact to business operations?

The potential for an incident to result in the loss or degradation of day-to-day business operations is a realistic scenario that most organizations face. In reaction to these events, the organization's ability to manage the incident directly depends on their capability to quickly gather and process digital evidence to understand the content and context of the incident. Having digital evidence gathered and made readily available, not only can the organization improve on the amount of time needed to investigate but they can also have the ability to conduct proactive investigations. In addition to supporting forensics investigations, the capability to perform proactive investigations in support of security control assessments or user behavior analytics can reduce the likelihood of an event resulting in impact or interruption to the business.

Question #4: Can digital evidence make a positive impact on the likely success of legal actions?

Whether part of a forensics investigation, contract dispute, etc., producing digital evidence in support of legal matters requires that organizations ensure that electronically stored information (ESI) is admissible to the matter at hand. As discussed in Chapter 10, "Establishing Legal Admissibility," the *Federal Rules of Evidence 803(6)* describes that ESI is admissible as digital evidence in a court of law if it demonstrates business "records of regularly conducted activity" such as an act, event, condition, opinion, or diagnosis. Determining the relevance and usefulness of ESI as digital evidence before creating a collection requirements statement ensures that organizations will not give way to over-collecting that results in unnecessary downstream processing and review expenses.

Question #5: Can digital evidence be gathered in a way that does not breach compliance with legal or regulatory requirements?

Laws and regulations can be imposed against organizations depending on several factors such as the industry they operate within (e.g., financial) or the countries where they conduct business (e.g., Unites States, India, Great Britain). Organizations must have a good understanding of how these governing laws and regulations influence the way they conduct their business operations. To provide reasonable assurance there is adherence to these requirements, organizations need to produce digital evidence of controls that demonstrates they are practicing a reasonable level of due care to ensure adherence. Consideration must be given to how background and foreground digital evidence, as discussed in Chapter 8, "Identify Potential Data Sources," will be proactively gathered and preserved in accordance with the compliance requirements.

Assessing the quantitative and qualitative implications of creating a collection requirements statement in advance helps organizations to determine if proactively gathering digital evidence will reduce investigative costs, such as selecting storage options, purchasing technologies, and developing SOPs.

Evidence Collection Factors

Traditionally, most digital evidence is gathered from sources that contain the actual data content used to describe the "who, where, what, when, and how" elements of a forensics investigation. In addition to the actual data content, there are several other factors that can be used to supplement the details about an event and influence its meaningfulness, usefulness, and relevance during a forensics investigation.

Best Evidence Rule

Originating from British law in the 18th century, the best evidence rule is a legal principle that holds the original copy of a document, including both real (or physical) and electronic evidence (or logical), as the superior evidence. In most cases, this means that the original (and verifiably authentic copy of a) document must be the one admitted into a court of law as evidence, unless it has otherwise proven to have been previously lost or destroyed. Additionally, the rule of best evidence states that secondary evidence, such as a bit-level forensics image, will not be legally admissible if an original, authentic exists and can be obtained. For example, the application of the best evidence rule can be equated to *Federal Rules of Evidence (FRE) 1003* which states that "a duplicate is admissible to the same extent as the original unless a genuine question is raised about the original's authenticity or the circumstances make it unfair to admit the duplicate."

Generally, the best evidence rule only applies when a party (e.g., the defending organization) wants to legally admit a specific document, where the original is no longer available, and wants to prove the contents as evidence. If the court rules that the producing party has demonstrated why the original document cannot be admitted, then the secondary evidence can be accepted as legally admissible.

Time

When collecting digital evidence from multiple data sources, time synchronization is a huge concern. Essentially, the higher the number of devices that are connected to a networked environment, the less chance they will all hold the exact same time, which will create increased confusion when it comes to analyzing digital evidence from across these sources.

Using a centralized logging solution, such as an enterprise data warehouse (EDW), timestamps can be generated and recorded as data is collected. Additionally, using a consistent and verifiable timestamp unanimously across all distributed data sources will ensure that digital evidence collected will be much easier to correlate, corroborate, and associate during the analysis phase.

There are several mechanisms that can be used on various platforms but are still considered a de-centralized means of establishing time synchronization across distributed data sources. Alternatively, using the network time protocol (NTP) set to Greenwich Mean Time (GMT), with time zone offsets configured on the local systems, is the best practice for establishing consistent timestamps in support of a forensics investigation. While NTP addresses the issue of centralized time synchronization, it does not account for the accuracy of time being published to connected data sources.

Originally developed for military use, Global Positioning System (GPS) provides accurate data about current position, elevation, and time. GPS receivers have a high rate of accuracy and are relatively simple to install because they only need an antenna with unobstructed line of sight to several satellites for them to work correctly. Connecting a GPS receiver to the NTP device is a cost-effective way of ensuring accurate time signals are being received.

Although organizations might only conduct business in one time zone, an incident will most often produce digital evidence on data source that span several time zones. Having a centralized solution to provide distributed data sources with accurate time synchronization is not something that has traditionally been easy to challenge in a court of law.

Metadata

On its own, the data content of digital evidence can be challenging for investigators to use because it lacks contextual awareness, a concept discussed further in Chapter 8, "Identify Potential Data Sources," Metadata, which is essentially "data about data," is used to add a supplemental layer of contextual information to data content. It gives digital evidence meaning and relevance by providing corroborating information about the data itself, revealing information that was hidden, deleted, or obscured, and helps to automate the correlation of data from various sources.

Primarily, metadata is used during an investigation to reduce the volume of digital evidence by adding meaning to information so that relevant information can be more accurately located. Additionally, metadata can also be used to provide forensics investigators with the ability to identify additional evidence, associate different pieces of evidence, distinguish different pieces of evidence, and provide location details. Some of the most common types of metadata used during a forensics investigation include:

- Date and time a file was modified, accessed, or created (MAC)
- Location a file is stored on an electronic storage medium
- Identity and profile information of user accounts

- Digital image properties such as number of colors or the originating camera model
- Document properties such as the author, last date saved, and print timestamp

Regardless of its application within digital forensics, metadata can be understood in the following distinct categories:

- *Structural metadata* is used to describe the organization and arrangement of information and objects such as database tables, columns, keys, and indexes.
- *Guide metadata* is used to assist with locating and identifying information and objects, such as a document title, author, or keywords.

However, because metadata is fundamentally just data it is also susceptible to the same evidence management requirements imposed on digital evidence, a concept that is discussed further in Chapter 3, "Digital Evidence Management." Safeguards must be taken to ensure that the authenticity and integrity of metadata is upheld so that it can be used effectively during a forensics investigation and meets the legal requirements for admissibility in a court of law.

Nevertheless, because metadata is not generally accessible or visible there is a need for greater skills and the use of specialized tools to properly gather, process, and preserve it. An organization's capability to use metadata to contextualize a forensics investigation will significantly reduce the amount of resources spent manually analyzing digital evidence by improving its meaningfulness, usefulness, and relevance.

Cause and Effect

The Pareto principle, also referred to as the "80/20 rule," states that approximately 80% of all effects come from roughly 20% of the causes. As a rule of thumb, for example, this rule can be used as a representation of the information security industry, where 80% of security risks can be effectively managed by prioritizing the implementation of 20% of available security controls, reinforcing a very powerful point that distributions are very rarely equal in any scenario.

In 2002, Microsoft announced they had made initial progress on the Trustworthy Computing initiative which focused on improving the reliability, security, and privacy of their software.

As the initiative continued to develop over the year, Microsoft quickly realized that among all the bugs reported in their software a relatively small number of them resulted in some type of error.

Through further analysis, Microsoft learned that approximately 80% of the errors and crashes in their software were caused by 20% of all bugs detected.

A common challenge with any forensics investigation is to identify the cause of an event because the effect can very well be different depending on the context, such as the type of storage media it occurred on, the user/process that generated the event, etc. For example, one of the most common scenarios is when a user/process modifies a file which results in a change to its meta-data properties, specifically, the file's timestamp. While this scenario is common across most file systems, regardless of the underlying electronic storage medium, an event where a file has been deleted has a much different effect. Depending on the file system, and the way in which the file was deleted, the activities to identify and recover the data can vary in terms of complexity and effort (e.g., soft-delete vs hard-delete.)

It is not realistic for an organization to identify and understand every possible combination of cause and effect. Instead, by referring to the business risk scenarios outlined in Chapter 7, "Defining Business Risk Scenarios," organizations can reduce the scope of which cause and effect events need to be considered based on their applicability to the organization and business risk scenarios. From narrowing the scope of cause and effect down to only those that are relevant to the organization, supplementary data sources can be identified and considered for inclusion in the collection requirements statement to enhance the analysis of digital evidence by further improving its contextual meaning and relevance.

Correlation and Association

Digital evidence, which is traditionally considered the primary records or indication of an event, gathered during a forensics investigation is used to indicate the details about what happened during an incident, including system, audit, or application logs; network traffic captures; or metadata.

For quite some time, the scope of a digital crime scene was somewhat limited to only the computer system(s) directly involved in the incident itself. However, today most organizations have environments that are made up of interconnected and distributed resource where events on one system are frequently related to events on other systems. This requires that the scope of an event be broadened outwards to include all systems that would be—in some form or another—involved in the incident.

With the expansion of the investigative scope, establishing a link between the primary evidence sources is needed so investigators can determine how, when, where, and by whom events occurred. To provide this additional layer of details, consideration needs to be given to other supporting data sources that can be used to establish the links between the content and context of digital evidence.

Under the chain-of-evidence methodology, illustrated in Figure 9.1, each set of discrete actions performed by a subject is placed into groups separated from each other based on the level of authority required to execute them. However, it is important that each group of actions in the various sources of digital evidence be linked to the adjacent action group to complete the entire chain of evidence link.

The ability to create a link between the various data sources is crucial for organizations to establish a complete chain of evidence and enhance their analytical capabilities by getting a better overall understanding of the incident. Using the chain-of-evidence model allows organizations to better plan for a complete trail of evidence across their entire environment. Following this model requires thinking in terms of gathering digital evidence in support of the entire chain of evidence instead of as individual data sources that may or may not be useful during the processing phase of the forensics investigations.

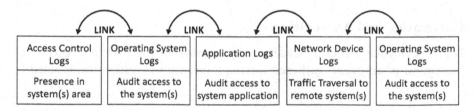

Figure 9.1 Chain-of-evidence model as applied to contextual awareness model.

Corroboration and Redundancy

Coupled together with how pervasive and distributed it has become in our personal lives, technology has also been so deeply embedded into business operations and functions that when it comes to investigating an incident, there is no shortage of digital evidence to be gathered and processed. However, when an incident does occur, organizations can be challenged with proving what happened because individual pieces of digital evidence on their own do not provide the context necessary to arrive at a conclusion.

With the aggregation of multiple data sources, there will most likely be some level of duplication in terms of information content, This duplication of information should not be viewed negatively, but should instead be taken advantage of to confirm the details of an incident during the forensics investigation.

From a digital forensics perspective, the strength of digital evidence collected will ultimately improve when it can be vetted by across data sources. Generally, the goal of every forensics investigation is to use digital evidence as a means of providing credible answers to substantiate an event and/or incident. Achieving this requires that the same or similar digital evidence from multiple sources be gathered and processed as an entire chain of evidence because there will most likely be indicators of the same incident found elsewhere.

Over time, the continued gathering of data across multiple sources can provide an amount of digital evidence sufficient to minimize the need for a complete forensic analysis of systems. By preserving digital evidence from multiple sources, it allows organizations to leverage a consistent toolset across the entire chain of evidence that can be used to support several investigative purposes such as incident response, digital forensics, and e-discovery.

Storage Duration

Retention of different digital information types, regardless of whether they are preserved as digital evidence, has unique requirements for the length of time for which an organization must preserve it. In many instances, the length of time an organization must preserve digital information is stipulated by regulators or legal entities. Where this governance applies, organizations must ensure they formally document their preservation requirements in a data retention policy, as discuss further in Chapter 3, "Digital Evidence Management."

Alternatively, if digital information is being preserved as digital evidence, organizations must ensure they safeguard it by implementing and following evidence management processes.

For example, a customary practice for many organizations is to retain in long-term storage digital information such as email messages and security logs (i.e., intrusion prevention systems (IPS), firewalls, etc.). Not only does retaining this digital information support regulatory or legal requirements, but it can also hold potential evidentiary value and might need to be recalled in support of a business risk scenario, as discussed in Chapter 7, "Defining Business Risk Scenarios."

Organizations must carefully plan which type of electronic storage media will be used to support their long-term storage requirements. As an example, backups are commonly used for long-term storage; however, organizations should be diligent to ensure that the type of backup media used is not susceptible to losing information each time they are re-used. To determine the most appropriate electronic storage media, organizations should complete a cost-benefit analysis, as discussed in Addendum C, "Cost-Benefit Analysis," to identify which solution best meets their needs.

Storage Infrastructure

The rapidly increasing size of electronic storage media is most certainly the biggest challenge facing organizations today. As storage capacity increases so does the volume of potential digital evidence that needs to be gathered, processed, and preserved in support of the business risk scenarios discussed in Chapter 7, "Defining Business Risk Scenarios."

Even though there have been significant advancements in how forensics tools and techniques have helped to reduce the time required to work with digital evidence, there remains the underlying issue of how the organization can efficiently manage the data volumes that need to be gathered and processed during a forensics investigation.

Foremost, there is a need to design a storage solution that can easily adapt to the continuously growing volumes of data that need to be accessed in both real time and near real time. Using a storage solution such as an EDW allows organizations to store both structured and unstructured data in a scalable manner that can easily and dynamically adapt to changing storage capacity requirements.

Secondly, as data volumes continue to increase organizations can start to experience inefficiencies in their potential to effectively perform data mining and analytics. Integrating into the EDW solution, the use of cataloging and indexing of metadata properties allows organizations to quickly identify data and reduce the length of time it takes for data to be retrieved. Not only does the organization benefit from data being readily accessible because of cataloging and indexing, but the ease with which data processing can be performed will improve the overall evidence-based reporting during a forensics investigation.

It is important to keep in mind when working with digital information that there is always the potential to inadvertently change the original data source. Therefore, when implementing any type of digital evidence storage solution, it is important that the principles, methodologies, and techniques of digital forensics consistently be adhered to. Organizations must always ensure that their storage solutions adhere to the best practices for maintaining the integrity and authenticity of digital evidence and not risk the data being inadmissible in a court of law.

Refer to Addendum G, "Data Warehousing Introduction," for further discussion on implementing a storage solution for proactively gathering digital evidence.

Data Security Requirements

Having such a large amount of data located in a common centralized storage solution can become a problematic if adequate security controls are not enforced. Securing the data repository depends on the organization's diligence and attention to compliance regulations, awareness of potential threats, and identification of both the risk and value of collected data.

There is a significant amount of preliminary work that needs to be completed before data gathering and storage can take place. Complementary to the architectural design work that takes place, organizations must incorporate current best practices and standards for implementing a data repository that will provide adequate security and reliability throughout the solution's lifetime. This requires that ongoing assessments of the centralized storage solution be completed to identify and understand the risks associated with each aspect of its eventual implementation, including:

- Analyzing requirements specific to:
  - The value of data being collected; and
  - The architectural design
- Interpreting security and compliance standards and guidelines
- Assessing the effectiveness of security controls and designs

Analysis of security requirements begins with understanding the business needs and desires related to building the centralized storage solution. As described in the sections throughout this chapter, the capabilities and functionalities related to the storage solution have been identified, and now security controls, countermeasures, and data protection need to be established.

Generally, security requirements are complementary to the functional requirements whereby they address the need to ensure the protection of the system, its data, and its users. They are typically addressed separately and occur after the system's functional requirements have been documented.

While security requirements can commonly be sourced from regulatory requirements, at a minimum organizations should adopt industry best practice standards as a measurement of due diligence to protect the storage solution. Understanding that there are many different controls that contribute to the protection of the system, its data, and its users, the following are examples of how industry best practices can be applied to the seven security principles:

- *Confidentiality*: Applying data classification labels as a mechanism for enforcing mandatory access control (MAC)
- *Integrity*: Generating cryptographic hash values, such as the Message Digest Algorithm family (e.g., MD5) or the Secure Hashing Algorithm family (e.g., SHA-2), for collected data stored in the centralized repository
- *Availability*: Requiring that backups be taken in support of disaster recovery capabilities
- *Continuity*: Building cold/warm/hot sites in support of business continuity capabilities
- *Authentication*: Leveraging existing centralized directory services for subject identification
- *Authorization*: Implementing role-based access controls (RBAC) to objects
- *Non-repudiation*: Using cryptographic certificates to associate the actions of or changes by a specific subject, or to establish the integrity and origin of information

Refer to Addendum H, "Requirements Analysis," for further discussion about how to perform a requirements assessment for gathering digital evidence.

Summary

Developing a requirements statement for the collection of digital evidence requires organizations to conduct thorough planning and preparation. Not only does the storage solution need to be functionally assessed in terms of its architectural design, it is critical that further security assessments be completed to ensure the collected digital evidence is safeguarded from unauthorized access.

Establishing Legal Admissibility

10

Introduction

At this stage of implementing a digital forensic program, organizations will have a grasp on the totality of digital evidence available for proactive collection and have determined which of it, based on the business risk scenarios discussed in Chapter 7, "Defining Business Risk Scenarios," can be gathered within the scope justified through the completion of a cost-benefit analysis.

With the organization's collection requirements defined, steps must now be taken to implement a series of controls to guarantee that secure preservation of digital evidence is maintained when it is gathered from relevant data sources. These steps are important for organizations to establish that data has been preserved as authentic records and will not be disputed when admitted to a court of law as digital evidence.

Legal Admissibility

Essentially, admissibility is the determination of whether information that is presented before the trier of fact (i.e., judge, jury) is worthy to be accepted in the court of law as evidence. Generally, for digital evidence to be deemed legally admissible it must be proven to have relevance (i.e., material, factual) and not be overshadowed by invalidating considerations (i.e., unfairly prejudicial, hearsay).

Within the legal system, there is a set of rules that are used as precedence for governing whether, when, how, and for what purpose digital evidence can be placed before a trier of fact. Traditionally, the legal system viewed digital evidence as being hearsay because its authenticity could not be proven, beyond a reasonable doubt, to be factual. However, exceptions do exist under the *Federal Rules of Evidence 803(6)* where digital evidence can be admitted into a legal proceeding only if it demonstrates "records of regularly conducted activity" as a business record, such as an act, event, condition, opinion, or diagnosis.

For digital evidence to qualify under this exception organizations must demonstrate that their business records are authentic, reliable, and trustworthy.

As stated in the *Federal Rules of Evidence*, to attain these qualifying properties organizations must be able to demonstrate that their business records:

- Were created as a regular practice of that activity
- Were created at or near the time by—or from information transmitted by—someone with knowledge
- Have been preserved in the course of a regularly conducted activity of a business, organization, occupation, or calling
- Are being presented by the custodian, another qualified witness, by a certification that complies with either Rule 902(11) or Rule 902(12), or with a statute granting certification
- Do not show that the source of information or method or circumstances of its preparation indicate a lack of trustworthiness

Furthermore, even if a business record qualifies under these exceptions, organizations must still determine if the business record falls within the context of being either of the following:

- *Technology-generated data* that has been created and is being maintained because of programmatic processes or algorithms (e.g., log files). These records fall within the rules of hearsay exception on the basis that the data is proven to be authentic because of properly functioning programmatic processes or algorithms.
- *Technology-stored data* that has been created and is being maintained because of user input and interactions (e.g., word processor document). These records fall within the rules of hearsay except on the basis that author of the data is reliable, is trustworthy, and has not altered it.

Even if a business record meets the criteria for being admissible as digital evidence, there is the potential that it will be challenged during legal proceedings. The basis for these contests is directed at the authenticity of the data and whether it has been altered or damaged either after it was created or because of interactions and exchanges with the data.

To reduce such opposition, the *Federal Rules of Evidence* (FRE) 1002 described the need for proving, beyond a reasonable doubt, the trustworthiness of digital evidence through the production of the authentic and original business record. Meeting this rule requires that organizations demonstrate their due diligence in preserving the authenticity of the original data source through the implementation of safeguards, precautions, and controls to guarantee that business records can be admitted as digital evidence during legal proceedings.

Preservation Challenges

Collecting business records is not as straightforward as it seems. As an example, where organizations operate in multiple jurisdictions and countries, they are bound in each location to multiple factors that determine how they can effectively preserve their business records.

First and foremost, organizations need to answer two preliminary questions before determining how they will guarantee the authenticity of their business records.

Can digital evidence be gathered without interfering with business operations and function?

The overall strategy of forensics readiness, summarized as "the ability to maximize potential use of digital evidence while minimizing investigative costs," includes an objective to gather admissible digital evidence without interrupting business operations and functions.

Typically, forensics investigations are performed in reaction to an event and require the assistance of several support resources to gather relevant digital evidence. In some instances, this reactive approach commonly results in roadblocks where business records are not readily available which requires support resources to be removed from the day-to-day business operations to assist. Where gathering business records has been identified as beneficial to forensic readiness, organizations need to assess the work effort required of resources to implement the proactive collection requirements while not impeding the day-to-day operations.

Can digital evidence be gathered legally?

Following along with the overall strategy of forensics readiness noted above, another objective of gathering admissible digital evidence is to do so in a manner that does not violate any laws or regulations. This determination should not be done without obtaining legal advice to ensure that the evidence collection requirements are met and upheld. In some countries, there are relevant laws around data protection, privacy, and human rights that will dictate what business records can be collected and, if they can be collected, where or how they are stored. For organizations to ensure that they demonstrate a reasonable assurance, the collection of all business records must adhere to all applicable laws or regulations.

Preservation Strategies

Having answered these questions and knowing the constraints around what, how, and where business records can be gathered, organizations can now implement strategies to ensure they are compliant with applicable laws and regulations. As these strategies are being identified and developed, it is important to keep in mind that they should encompass a series of complimentary administrative, physical, and technical security controls.

Administrative Controls

Before any type of technical or physical security controls can be implemented, there must first and foremost be a foundational governance structure in place. This governance structure is established in the form of administrative controls that include the creation and approval of organizational policies, standards, and guidelines that support the preservation of the authenticity and integrity of digital evidence.

Policies

These documents are created with the intent of building a formal blueprint that describes the goals for preserving digital evidence. They are designed to provide generalized direction that allows organizations to consider any subsequent physical or technical security controls that are required to safeguard their digital evidence.

Guidelines

Building off policy documentation, guidelines can now be created as documents that provide recommendations for how to implement the generalized direction set previously. The context of these documents is intended to be subjective such that organizations will use the recommendations as a way of gathering requirements for how to preserve the authenticity and integrity of their digital evidence.

Standards

Following the interpretation of the guidelines recommendations, standard documents are created to outline the minimum level of technical and physical security controls necessary to preserve digital evidence. These documents should contain the exact configurations, architectures, and specifications for implementing technical and physical security controls in support of policies and guidelines.

Procedures

The previously noted administrative controls do not have direct oversight of interactions with collected digital evidence. Through the implementation of standard operating procedures (SOP), the exchanges and interfaces between administrators, operators, and investigators and digital evidence are documented.

For further information about how these administrative controls support the overall evidence management lifecycle, including specific examples of governance documentation, refer to Chapter 3, "Digital Evidence Management."

Technical Controls

Stated previously in this chapter, even if a business record meets the criteria for being admissible during a legal proceeding, organizations will still be faced with the challenge of proving it has not been altered or damaged after it was created or because of interactions and exchanges with it.

To mitigate the potential for the authenticity of business records being challenged in a court of law, organizations should implement several technical controls to guarantee that business records can be admitted as digital evidence. Understanding that every organization's business environment is different, at a minimum the following technical controls must be in place to ensure secure preservation of business records as digital evidence.

Storage Security

Organizations can select any different type of electronic storage medium to preserve their collected digital evidence, such as hard drives or backup tapes. Regardless of how the information is being stored, organizations must consider the data-at-rest implications by ensuring the preserved digital evidence is not exposed if unauthorized access to the storage medium is gained. Using cryptography, inactive data can be protected through one of the following implementations:

- *Full-disk encryption (FDE)* applies cryptographic algorithms to the physical storage medium, regardless of its content, to encrypt all information
- *Encrypted file system (EFS)* applies cryptographic algorithms at the file system level to encrypt logical data sets

The use of disk encryption does not replace the need for file encryption in all situations. In some instances, the two can be used in conjunctions with each other to provide a more layered defense and guarantee the authenticity and integrity of digital evidence.

Integrity Monitoring

All types of digital data, whether technology-generated or technology-stored, are prone to issues of trustworthiness where the content and context of the information cannot be easily validated and is often challenged for its authenticity. These issues of data integrity and authenticity are some of the contributors that render business records inadmissible as digital evidence in a court of law.

However, organizations can get the upper hand on the matter of data integrity and authenticity using solutions such as file integrity monitoring (FIM). With these technologies, validation of both system and data integrity can be achieved by authenticating specific data properties of the current data state against the known-good state of the data. Examples of data properties that can be used in as part of this verification and validation include:

- Subject permissions and entitlements
- Actual data content of files
- Metadata attributes (e.g., size, creation date/time)
- Cryptographic values (i.e., Message Digest Algorithm family [MD5], Secure Hashing Algorithm family [SHA])

Implementation of integrity monitoring is an essential security control to guarantee the authenticity and integrity of business records as digital evidence. In addition to the use of integrity monitoring as means of maintaining integrity and proving authenticity of data, these solutions have also been established as a requirement for several regulatory compliance objectives, including:

- Payment Card Industry Data Security Standard (PCI DSS)—Requirement 11.5
- Sarbanes–Oxley Act (SOX)—Section 404
- Federal Information Security Management Act (FISMA)—National Institute of Standards and Technology (NIST) Special Publication (SP) 800-53 Rev3
- Health Insurance Portability and Accountability Act (HIPAA) of 1996—NIST SP800-66

The online reference to the above regulatory objectives can be found in the "Resources" section at the end of this book.

Cryptographic Algorithms

Every interaction with and exchange of digital information introduces the potential of that data being modified, whether knowingly or unintentionally.

Proving the authenticity of digital information to the original source and maintaining that level of integrity throughout a forensics investigation is critical for it to be admissible as digital evidence.

Cryptography supports many information security–centric services—such as authentication and non-repudiation—that are fundamental to the digital forensic science discipline and digital evidence management, as discussed in Chapter 3, "Digital Evidence Management." Examples of common cryptographic algorithms that are used in digital forensics as part of evidence management are as follows:

- The Message Digest Algorithm family (e.g., MD5) is commonly used during a forensics investigation to generate a unique cryptographic identifier of files, data streams, and other digital evidence. However, in 2010 researchers could generate collisions where the same 128 bit hexadecimal value could be generated for two distinctively different pieces of digital information.
- The Secure Hashing Algorithm family (e.g., SHA-2) is also used during forensics investigations to generate a unique cryptographic identifier for digital evidence. From the collisions identified within specific versions of the Message Digest Algorithm family, specifically MD5, the SHA family of hash functions has become popular as a means of establishing the integrity and authenticity of digital evidence.
- Cyclic redundancy checks (CRC) are commonly used during the forensic duplication of digital evidence to detect modifications to the underlying data. Using these calculations allows forensics investigators to use the duplicate data during analysis instead of risking potential contamination of the original evidence source.

When implemented, cryptography provides organizations with assurances that the integrity of collected business records can be proven when authenticated to the original data source.

Remote Logging

Technology-generated data stored on local systems, such as security or audit log files, is inevitably more vulnerable to being (1) manipulated to conceal activities or events or (2) planted to incriminate other individuals. These data integrity issues lessen the credibility of the information and render it inadmissible as evidence in a court of law.

As a best practice, remote logging capabilities should be leveraged to redirect the logging of technology-generated data off local systems and into a centralized remote logging infrastructure, such as a data warehouse discussed in discussed in Addendum C, "Cost-Benefit Analysis."

Enforcing this safeguard will reduce the likelihood of data tampering on local systems and maintain the integrity of technology-generated data as admissible digital evidence.

Secure Delivery

Where remote logging capabilities exist, organizations must consider the data-in-transit implications for collected digital evidence. Regardless of whether information is travelling across a public or private network, there is a need to ensure the secure delivery of digital evidence to maintain its authenticity and integrity.

Network communications are, in general, insecure where information travelling across them can readily be accessed or modified by unauthorized subjects if appropriate controls are not in place. Knowing this, organizations should be concerned with the confidentiality and integrity of digital evidence as it is being collected into their remote logging solution(s). As a countermeasure, organizations should implement an encrypted communication channel using, for example, internet protocol security (IPsec) to mitigate the risk of data-in-transit security concerns.

Physical Controls

Generally, physical security controls are designed to control and protect an organization's physical assets (i.e., building, systems, etc.) by reducing the risk of damage or loss. As organizations design their approach to secure preservation of digital evidence, they must consider the costs of building, operating, and maintaining physical security controls that work in conjunction with their administrative and technical security controls.

While physical security controls may not always have the same direct interaction with digital evidence that technical controls have, they provide an additional layer of defense to safeguard the physical medium (e.g., tapes, hard drives) where digital evidence is stored. Physical security controls indirectly contribute to preserving the authenticity and integrity of digital evidence as implemented in one of the following categories:

Deter

The goal of these physical security controls is to convince potential intruders/attacks that the likelihood of success if low because of strong defenses. Typically, the implementation of deterrent security controls is found in the combined use of physical barriers (e.g., walls), surveillance (e.g., Closed Caption Television [CCTV]), and lighting (e.g., spot lights).

Crime Prevention through Environmental Design (CPTED)   CPTED is an approach to planning and developing physical security controls that use natural or environmental surroundings to reduce the opportunities for crime. As part of a comprehensive approach to guaranteeing the authenticity and integrity of digital evidence, examples of CPTED controls that can be implemented include:

- Natural surveillance such as implementing lighting design to illuminate points of interest that do not generate glare or blind-spots
- Natural access controls such as multi-level fencing to control access and enhance visibility
- Natural territorial reinforcements such as restricting activities to defined areas using signage

Detect

Generally, detective controls are intended to discover and interrupt potential intruders before an incident or event occurs. Optimally, these controls should be implemented to reveal the presence of potential intruders/attacks while they are collecting information about how they can gain access to the physical medium where digital evidence is being stored.

While it also plays a part in the deterrence of potential intruders/ attacks, the use of CCTV is one of the most common physical controls for discovering an incident and/or event. Additionally, physical alarm systems and sensors can be used in combination with other types of controls (e.g., barriers, guards) to trigger a response when a breach has been detected.

Deny

Identical to the use of authentication and authorization mechanisms to control logical access to systems and data, the same type of restrictive security controls must be used to deny physical access to the organization's assets. The primary objective of these physical controls is to deny potential intruders/ attackers the ability to cause damage to systems and information.

Within the context of preserving authenticity and integrity, examples of physical controls that can be used to deny access to collected digital evidence include:

- Constructing secure storage facilities, such as lockers and restricted areas, that have true floor-to-ceiling walls
- Entrances that are constructed of material resistant to tampering and have internally facing hinges

- Mechanisms to control and restrict access to secure lockers and restricted areas, such as lock and key, biometric scanner, or card/badge readers

Delay

Where the implementation of physical security controls is unable to deter or detect potential intruders/attackers, such as having obtained a key that provides access into the secure storage area, additional controls must ensure that their ability to easily gain access to digital evidence is delayed.

Typically, these types of controls are the last line of defense when all previous implementation (deter, detect, delay) have failed to deliver the level of protection that they were intended for. Examples of how these security controls provide the last line of defense in physical protecting digital evidence include:

- Placing secure lockers inside restricted areas that are located away from the exterior of the building and require multiple checkpoints to gain access
- Requiring security guards to conduct searches and inspection of people, parcels, and vehicles as they leave buildings

Implementing physical safeguards provides organizations with a layer of security controls complementary to their administrative and technical controls. Not only do these physical security controls help to guarantee the authenticity and integrity of collected digital evidence, but they also support data protection requirements as part of the overall evidence management lifecycle.

Summary

For business records to be admissible in legal proceedings, organizations must prove their authenticity by meeting specific criteria that direct rules for digital evidence. Through a layered implementation of safeguards, precautions, and controls that encompass the administrative, technical, and physical requirements for ensuring secure evidence preservation, organizations can guarantee that their business records can be admitted as digital evidence during legal proceedings.

Establish Secure Storage and Handling 11

Introduction

Considering the safeguards and controls implemented to ensure collected digital evidence is legally admissible, organizations must now determine how they will sustain these requirements as their digital evidence is being handled by several individuals and technologies. Likewise, as digital evidence is being transferred from one storage facility to another, such as long-term or off-line storage, consideration must be given to ensure the data is securely preserved and readily available when needed for an investigation.

Establishing a governance framework over the handling and storage of digital evidence can be achieved by following the traditional approach of implementing complementary administrative, technical, and physical controls. Through the combination of these different controls in a layered fashion, organizations can ensure that their digital evidence will be handled correctly and stored securely.

Secure Storage Attributes

Storage solutions such as an enterprise data warehouse (EDW), discussed further in Addendum G, "Data Warehousing Introduction," provides a centralized repository for aggregating digital evidence from multiple data sources. While it can be complex to implement, when done correctly an EDW can generate significant benefits such as allowing digital evidence to be analyzed over a longer time for improved data mining and analytics.

However, as discussed previously in Chapter 10, there are several administrative, technical, and physical controls that must be implemented to ensure that digital evidence being collected into a storage solution, such as an EDW, will be legally admissible. Having identified safeguards required to maintain this legal admissibility, organizations must now determine how to expand these controls to ensure that their digital evidence is being handled correctly, throughout its entire lifecycle, and that its authenticity and integrity are maintained as it is transferred between different storage facilities.

Least Privilege Access

Even though the modern threat landscape has changed, the delivery channels and attack vectors used by potential threat actors continue to count on the absence or weakness in a system's or application's access control mechanism(s). In the context of legal admissibility, the deficiencies in strong access controls are a blueprint for disaster when it comes to preserving the authenticity and integrity of digital evidence in secure storage.

One of the fundamental cornerstones in the information security discipline is the concept of applying the principle of least privilege access. Generally, implementing least privilege implies that subjects have access only to the objects that are necessary as part of normal business operations and functions. However, as illustrated in Figure 11.1, when privileges are assigned they are typically granted beyond the scope of what is necessary, thus permitting access that is otherwise not required.

Exercising rigid controls over subjects that have administrative access into storage solutions housing digital evidence is critical. Without enforcing the use of least privilege access to these secure storage facilities, organizations cannot demonstrate admissibility in a court of law because the potential for unauthorized subject access puts into question the authenticity and integrity of their digital evidence.

End-to-End Cryptography

Outlined previously in Chapter 10, "Establishing Legal Admissibility," cryptography supports several information security–centric services that are fundamental to the digital forensics discipline. Supporting several use cases for preserving digital evidence, examples of how cryptography can be applied

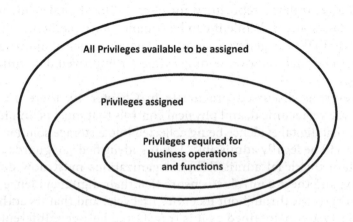

Figure 11.1 Privilege assignments.

were identified as data-at-rest controls, used to guarantee that unauthorized access to the storage medium does not expose the digital evidence (e.g., Full Disk encryption), or data-in-transit control, used for securing the transmission of digital evidence across any type of network infrastructure (e.g., internet protocol security [IPsec]).

Additionally, following along with the principles of least privilege access, digital evidence being stored should be readable only by those authorized. A simple way of achieving this is to use passcodes for protection of collected digital evidence; however, this control does not provide a guarantee that authenticity and integrity will be preserved. Alternatively, by using cryptography organizations can achieve a much stronger authentication mechanism to achieve a more effective data-in-use security control.

As digital evidence is being collected it should be encrypted using, for example, a secret key to help enforce the principle of least privilege and restrict access to only authorized subjects. As an example, while the application of an encrypted file system (EFS) contributes to the protection of data at rest, it also provides data-in-use controls where only those users in possession of the secret key can access and read the digital evidence.

Integrity Checking

Outlined previously in Chapter 10, "Establishing Legal Admissibility," integrity monitoring is an essential security control to guarantee the authenticity and integrity of digital evidence. With the known-good state of digital evidence captured, ongoing verification and validation must be implemented to ensure that no alteration to preserved digital evidence has been made.

When digital evidence is being preserved in a storage solution, such as an EDW, integrity checks should be scheduled in alignment with the organization's requirements for meeting regulatory compliance and to effectively demonstrate legal admissibility. However, if digital evidence has been transferred into off-line storage, such as backup tapes, routinely performing integrity checks cannot be easily achieved. In this situation, organizations must take an alternate approach to preserving the authenticity and integrity of their digital evidence as follows:

1. Prior to digital evidence being transferred to off-line storage, an integrity check must be completed by comparing the known-good state (set #1) to the current state of the digital evidence (set #2) through a cryptographic hash value such as the Message Digest Algorithm family (e.g., MD5) or the Secure Hashing Algorithm family (e.g., SHA-2).
2. Once the initial integrity checking is completed, set #2 of hash values must be maintained for the duration of the transfer process for use in subsequent integrity checking after digital evidence has been stored on the off-line storage.

3. After all digital evidence has been transferred to off-line storage, a new set of hash values (set #3) is produced and compared against set #2 to guarantee the authenticity and integrity of digital evidence has been preserved.

Physical Security

Outlined previously in Chapter 10, "Establishing Legal Admissibility," physical security controls are designed to control and protect an organization's physical assets (i.e., building, systems, etc.) by reducing the risk of damage or loss. While physical security controls may not always have the same direct interaction with digital evidence that technical controls have, they provide layers of defense that deter, detect, deny, and delay potential threat actors from accessing digital evidence preserved in any type of storage solution.

Where digital evidence is preserved in a storage solution such as an EDW, physical security controls are focused on reducing the risk of unauthorized access to the infrastructure housing the digital evidence. However, if digital evidence has been transferred into off-line storage, such as backup tapes, the scope of physical security controls extends beyond protecting only the infrastructure.

Digital evidence housed in off-line storage is subject to the same requirement for demonstrating authenticity and integrity for it to be admissible in a court of law. For example, the Good Practices Guide for Computer Based Electronic Evidence, developed by the Association of Chief of Police Officers (ACPO) in the United Kingdom, was created with four overarching principles that must be followed when handling evidence to maintain evidence authenticity:

- *Principle #1*: No action taken by law enforcement agencies or their agents should change data held on a computer or storage media which may subsequently be relied upon in court.
- *Principle #2*: In circumstances where a person finds it necessary to access original data held on a computer or on storage media, that person must be competent to do so and be able to give evidence explaining the relevance and the implications of their actions.
- *Principle #3*: An audit trail or other record of all processes applied to computer-based electronic evidence should be created and preserved. An independent third party should be able to examine those processes and achieve the same result.
- *Principle #4*: The person in charge of the investigation (the case officer) has overall responsibility for ensuring that the law and these principles are adhered to.

When digital evidence has been transferred to off-line storage such as backup tape, a chain of custody for this new storage medium must be established to ensure its authenticity and integrity by tracking where it came from, where it went after seizure, and who handled it for what purpose. From this point forward, the chain of custody must accompany the off-line storage and be maintained throughout the lifetime of the evidence. A chain of custody template has been provided as a reference in the "Templates" section of this book.

Furthermore, tapes should be stored using physical security controls that are intended to deny or delay potential threat actors from accessing digital evidence. Achieving these layers of defenses can be accomplished by implementing the following physical security control:

- Off-line storage medium, such as backup tape, should be placed in an evidence bag that, at a minimum, supports the following characteristics:
  - Bags contain a secure pouch to store the media and an externally accessible pouch for accompanying documentation.
  - Proper labelling is affixed to correctly and efficiently identify the contents.
  - Tamper proof tape or locking mechanism is used to seal evidence inside.
  - Chain of custody is placed in the externally accessible pouch.

Physical access to digital evidence in off-line storage must also be controlled following the same security principles of least privilege access. Once digital evidence has been properly sealed in evidence bags, these bags should be placed in a secure locker, safe, or library for long-term retention. It is important that the chain of custody be updated to demonstrate ownership and location of the digital evidence.

Administrative Governance Foundations

Forensic viability can be accomplished only when digital evidence has been tracked and protected right from the time it was created and meets the requirements for legal admissibility throughout its entire lifecycle. Although technical and physical security controls have a more direct contribution to the secure handling and storage of digital evidence, they cannot be effective unless there is an organizational requirement to adhere to. Therefore, to guarantee that digital evidence is forensically viable, organizations must have an established governance framework in place to ensure the collection, preservation, and storage of digital evidence is done properly.

Ultimately, the objective of this governance framework is to established direction on how the organization will preserve the authenticity and

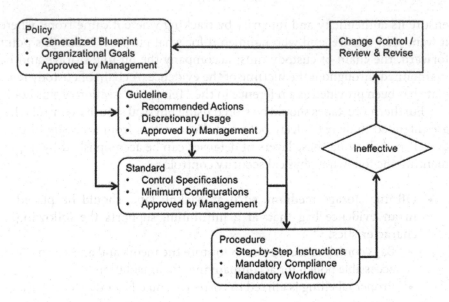

Figure 11.2 Information security management framework.

integrity of the digital evidence. Management, with involvement from key stakeholders such as legal, privacy, security, and human resources, must work together to define a series of documents that describe exactly how the organization will go about achieving these goals. Illustrated in Figure 11.2, and discussed further in Chapter 3, "Digital Evidence Management," an information security management framework consists of a hierarchy of different types of documents that have direct influence and precedence over other documents.

Within the context of guaranteeing the forensic viability of digital evidence, governance documentation should be created to address the following areas:

Personnel

- Provide continuous training and awareness regarding the governance framework to all stakeholders involved in the collection, preservation, and storage of digital evidence.
- As acknowledgement of their adherence to the governance framework, stakeholders should be required to sign the necessary document to indicate their understanding of and commitment to it. Management, legal, privacy, security, and human resources should all be involved to ensure that these signed documents can be legally enforced.
- Require enhanced background checks to be routinely conducted for personnel who have access to digital evidence.

Evidence Storage

- Document all operational aspects of the digital evidence storage solutions and facilities, including, normal operations and maintenance, scheduled backups, and error handling.
- Provide clear guidance and direction regarding the installation of or updates to hardware and software components.
- Ensure storage solutions are designed and built to meet the requirements and specifications of their intended business strategy or function.
- Enforce the principle of least privilege access and implement the use of multi-factor authentication mechanism, including:
  - Something you have (e.g., smart card)
  - Something you know (e.g., password)
  - Something you are (e.g., fingerprint)
- Apply a layered defense-in-depth approach to physical security using a combination of controls that are designed to deter, detect, deny, and delay potential threat actors.

Evidence Handling

- Apply integrity monitoring and checks to ensure digital evidence has not been tampered with or modified from its known-good and authenticated state.
- Prohibit the alteration or deletion of original sources of data.
- Restrict the storage of, transmission of, and access to digital evidence without the use of cryptographic encryption.
- Enforce the principle of least privilege access to only authorized personnel.
- Ensure that the long-term storage of digital evidence uses any form of storage medium that is write once read many (WORM).
- Seal digital evidence in appropriate containers (e.g., evidence bag, safe) to preserve authenticity and integrity during long-term storage.
- Define the long-term retention and recovery strategies for digital evidence.

Incident and Investigative Response

- Require that each incident and investigation be tracked and reported separately.
- Ensure that digital evidence used is proven to be authentic to the original source.

Assurance Controls

- *Require that routine audits or control assessments be conducted.* Essentially, the culture and structure of each organization influence how these governance documents are created. Regardless of where (throughout the world) business is conducted or the size of the organization, there are five simple principles that should be followed as generic guidance for achieving a successful governance framework:
  - *Keep it simple.* All documentation should be as clear and concise as possible. The information contained within each document should be stated as briefly as possible without omitting any critical pieces of information. Where documentation is drawn out and wordy, it is typically more difficult to understand, less likely to be read, and harder to interpret for implementation.
  - *Keep it understandable.* Documentation should be developed in a language that is commonly known throughout the organization. Leveraging a taxonomy, as discussed in Addendum D, "Building a Taxonomy," organizations can avoid the complication of using unrecognized terms and slangs.
  - *Keep it practicable.* Regardless of how precise and clear the documentation might be, if it cannot be practiced then it is useless. An example of an unrealistic documentation would be a statement indicating that incident response personnel are to be available 24 hours a day, even though there is no adequate way to contact them when they are not in the office. For this reason, documentation that is not practicable is not effective and will be quickly ignored.
  - *Keep it cooperative.* Good governance documentation is developed through the collaborative efforts of all relevant stakeholders, such as legal, privacy, security, and human resources. If key stakeholders have not been involved in the development of these documents, it is more likely that problems will arise during implementation.
  - *Keep it dynamic.* Useful governance documents should be, by design, flexible enough to adapt to organizational changes and growth. It would be impractical to develop documentation that is focused on serving the current needs and desires of the organization without considering potential future circumstances.

Backup and Restoration Strategies

Even if digital evidence is put into off-line storage for long-term retention, there might come a time when it is needed in support of a business risk scenario, as discussed previously in Chapter 3, "Digital Evidence Management."

Table 11.1 Recovery Time Objectives

RTO Value	Backup Solution Required
<1 hour	near real-time data replication
1–6 hours	data replication
6–24 hours	data restoration from on-line backup media
2–14 days	data restoration from off-line backup media

When this time comes, it is critical that in addition to the integrity of digital evidence being authenticated, the data itself must also be restored and made readily available so that there is no delay in the investigative process.

The recovery time objective (RTO) that an organization accepts for restoring digital evidence from backups is what drives the type of backup strategy that will be implemented. RTO is commonly represented in units of time as minutes, hours, days, or longer depending on the needs for restoring digital evidence. When setting the RTO targets, it is important that organizations realize that lower values will result in more expensive backup solutions. Recognizing that every organization has different RTO targets for restoring digital evidence, Table 11.1 provides an approximation of values and corresponding backup solutions required to meet the service levels.

Near Real-Time Data Replication

Meeting service levels with this type of backup solution requires that data be synchronously replicated across multiple identical and distributed instances of the storage solution, such as an EDW. Because this type of backup strategy requires multiple instances of the storage solution to be highly available for near real-time data clustering, it is considered the most expensive, complex, and resource intensive.

Data Replication

Performed on a consistent schedule, this backup solution replicates data to two or more identical and distributed instances of the storage solution. Like the requirements of the near real-time strategy, this type of solution still requires the implementation of two or more identical and distributed instances of the storage solution. However, with more moderate RTO targets, this type of backup solution is considered just as expensive but slightly less complex and resource intensive.

Data Restoration from On-line Backup Media

With data replications set to occur on a schedule, this backup solution replicates data to highly available on-line media; such as network attached storage

(NAS). Service levels for this type of strategy are reduced to allow for data to be restored to the production storage solution when required, which makes this type of backup solution less expensive, complex, and resource intensive.

Data Restoration from Off-line Backup Media

Discussed previously in this chapter, data can be transferred to off-line media, such as backup tapes, for long-term storage. This type of backup strategy is the least expensive because it does not have the complexities of implementing additional storage infrastructures; however, the RTO targets for this solution are extremely relaxed because of the time required to restore from off-line media.

Summary

Preserving the authenticity and integrity of digital evidence extends beyond the implementation of technical and physical security controls. Through the implementation of a governance framework that ensures forensic viability right from when data is created, organizations can ensure that legal admissibility of digital evidence is maintained during secure handling and storage.

Enabling Targeted Monitoring

12

Introduction

Until this point, emphasis has been placed on the requirements for organizations to ensure that the digital evidence they gather, in support of the major business risk scenarios, is done in a manner that guarantees it will be admissible in a court of law. In addition to gathering digital evidence for later use in legal proceedings, the aggregation of data sources can also be used to enhance monitoring capabilities to detect potential threats in a more effective and timely manner.

This step is not about simply gathering data for the sake of gathering data. The purpose of this step is about making sure that additional data sources being collected can be effectively used in the process of detecting potential threats. However, determining what is a potential threat is subjective to each organization, as they have their own risk tolerance levels, which begs the question, "At what point should we be suspicious?"

What Is (un)acceptable Activity?

Through the creation of governance documents, such as policies and standards, organizations will define what they consider acceptable and unacceptable activity to be within their business environment. Generally, acceptable activity includes any communication that is within the defined boundaries as stated in the organization's governance documentation. As an example, using secure email solutions for the transmission of customer information is within the boundaries of acceptable activity.

On the other hand, unacceptable activity includes any communication that is specifically prohibited outside of the defined boundaries as stated in the organization's governance documentation, such as policy violations, potentially harmful behavior, or breach of confidentiality. Essentially, unacceptable activity is any activity that is not within the confines of what the organization has defined as acceptable. As an example, uploading customer information to cloud storage is unacceptable activity.

To facilitate the monitoring of and alerting about any activity, organizations should explicitly define in their governance documentation what they deem to be acceptable activity so that everyone understands clearly which actions are acceptable and which are not.

Digital Forensics in Enterprise Security

As discussed in Chapter 1, "Understanding Digital Forensics," the evolution of cybercrime has always accompanied advancements made in technology throughout the decades. However, with the increasing pervasiveness of technology in both the personal and business context, it is extremely important for organizations to have an effective and efficient enterprise security program in place.

In today's modern threat landscape, many organizations have established an enterprise security program with applicable governance models, security architectures, and strategies to effectively manage their business risk(s). They also seek to mitigate compromising (losing, exposing) those informational assets belonging to—or entrusted to—them. Most commonly, organizations will reference and (where feasible) adopt industry best practices for developing their enterprise security program which, if not suitably tailored to their respective business risks or needs (i.e., legal, regulatory), may not consider the importance of implemented defense-in-depth—administrative, technical, and physical—controls to increase the success rate of digital forensic investigations.

Seeing how digital forensics is considered a sub-discipline of information security, it only seems natural that there is a close relationship between the two. Theoretically, if the defense-in-depth security was impenetrable, the potential for an organization's informational assets and system to be compromised would be impossible. But the reality is that security can never be completely effective and therefore digital forensics capabilities are essential when security events occur. Generally, when a security event does occur, it is critical that immediate and appropriate actions are taken to reduce impact, recover business functions, and ultimately investigate. If not, there is an increased potential that relevant evidence will be damaged, dismissed, or simply overlooked.

Although digital forensics, information security, and cyber security are viewed as different enterprise disciplines, there are commonalities amongst them that present opportunities for enhancing digital forensics capabilities across the enterprise. As part of the enterprise security program, a primary objective is to achieve assurance that the damage or loss of information assets or system is minimized to within an acceptable level of business risk. One aspect of this comes from having proactive digital forensic capabilities that are intended to maximize the use of potential electronically stored information (ESI) while reducing the cost of investigations. Supporting this, examples of controls that can be implemented throughout the enterprise include:

- Evidence management framework (i.e., policies, standards, guidance)
- Administrative, technical, and physical control mechanisms (i.e., operating procedures, tools and equipment, specialized technical skills)
- Education and training programs (i.e., knowledge, skills)
- Organizational, regulatory, and legal compliance requirements

For example, a primary objective of an enterprise security program is to achieve assurance that the damage or loss of information assets or systems is minimized to an acceptable level of risk. Alternatively, a primary goal of reactive digital forensic capabilities is to establish fact-based conclusions based on credible evidence. Examples of controls supporting both disciplines can be implemented throughout the enterprise include:

- Incident response capabilities, such as a security incident response team (SIRT) or computer (security) incident response team (CIRT|CSIRT)
- Disaster recovery planning
- Business continuity planning
- Gap analysis and recommendations
- Standard operating procedures (e.g., run books)

A proper balance needs to be reached so that where industry best practices are adopted, necessary principles, methodologies, and techniques of digital forensics are incorporated so that activities, such as containment and recovery, account for proper evidence gathering and processing requirements. As an enterprise's technology footprint changes over time, it is important that the ways in which digital forensics capabilities are integrated also evolve alongside. Naturally, it can be a constant struggle for organizations to effectively enable their required enterprise security capabilities while finding the right balance of how to continuously improve their digital forensic capabilities at the same time. Fortunately, digital forensics principles, methodologies, and techniques have been clearly defined, well-established, and scientifically proven over several decades which allows organizations to integrate them relatively seamlessly to most enterprise architectures.

Within an enterprise environment, digital forensics practitioners play a vital role in the protection of informational assets and systems. Depending on their level of knowledge and experience gained, discussed further in Chapter 14, they can often be viewed as a "jack of all trades" because of the way their role has allowed them to develop skills across many different fields, such as systems development, information technology (IT) architecture, or information and cyber security. As result of their involvement in enterprise investigations, digital forensic practitioners can become deeply immersed in the detailed inner-workings of many different aspects of an enterprise's business operations.

Information Security vs. Cyber Security

Naturally, every organization is going to speak its own language when it comes to business operations. While this is expected, it is important that every organization speak the same language related to what information security means versus what cyber security means. Contrary to common perception, whether done inadvertently or not, *information security* and *cyber security* are not the same. So, this begs the question "What is the difference between information security and cyber security?"

Since the use of computer systems back in the 1960s, as discussed in Chapter 1, information security has been a discipline focused on the security of informational assets or systems, regardless of state (e.g., physical paper, logical databases). As a means of safeguarding informational assets or systems, various technologies, processes (e.g., runbooks), and physical countermeasures (e.g., security checkpoints) are implemented in a defense-in-depth approach to protect physical and electronically stored information from unauthorized access, disruption, modification, or destruction.

With the introduction of inter-connected computer systems and the Internet, the growing need to safeguard information grew beyond standalone computer systems expanded into the digital realm. What has evolved into what is now referred to as cyber security involves the security of informational assets or systems but only in a digital state (e.g., database, financial system). Safeguarding electronically stored information (ESI) involves making use of various technologies and processes to protect networks, information systems, and data from attacks, damage, or unauthorized access.

The reality is, taking a closer look at these disciplines, it's evident that there are distinctively unique characteristics between the two. Illustrated in Figure 12.1, not only is it reasonable to say that the discipline of cyber security is a subset of information security, which is comprised of a significant overlap in control functions, except where physical security comes into play, but also

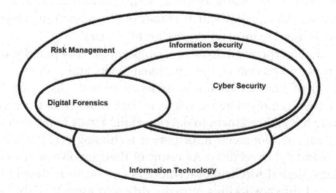

Figure 12.1 Information and cyber security.

that there are key characteristics shared across other information-centric operational functions (i.e., business continuity). What also becomes evident is that information technology encompasses only a portion of risk management. This is because complementary administrative and physical controls, not just technology, need to be in place to effectively manage business risk.

Defense-in-Depth

Organizations with effective information security programs have traditionally followed a defense-in-depth strategy that uses multiple layers of security controls. With this traditional approach, their defense-in-depth strategy has commonly focused on defining a physical perimeter as the boundary between the organization's internal network and the external Internet.

Traditionally, security controls are deployed and implemented throughout the enterprise following an overall defense-in-depth strategy. Illustrated in Figure 12.2 are the different layers found throughout a defense-in-depth strategy where security controls are implemented so that different views into information assets can be seen across the enterprise. Essentially, at the center of the defense-in-depth strategy is where data resides. Moving outwards from data through the layers is where different interactions and the need for deploying appropriate security controls comes into play.

Traditional Security Monitoring

Monitoring activity that is not within the boundaries of what has been defined as acceptable is a type of technical security control. It should be implemented to increase the possibility of positively identifying unacceptable activity, such as threats or attacks (true-positive), while decreasing the probability of alerting against acceptable activity (false-positive). Achieving this goal requires organizations to invest in efforts to understand their business

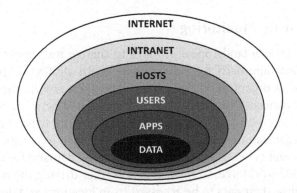

Figure 12.2 Defense-in-depth layers.

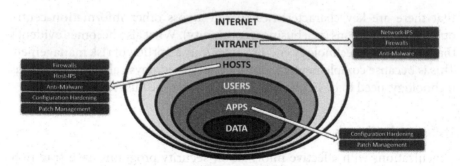

Figure 12.3 Traditional security layers.

environment so monitoring technologies can be customized to efficiently sort out the false-positives and improve visibility into the true-positive alerts.

Deploying security controls, for targeted monitoring activity, must be done as part of an organization's overall defense-in-depth strategy. Illustrated in Figure 12.3, defense-in-depth security controls implemented throughout the organization help to improve monitoring capabilities by providing different views into the information flows across assets. Most commonly, the following security controls are implemented to facilitate security monitoring:

- Network devices, such as routers/switches and firewalls, with access controls lists (ACL) to regulate data flows between different security zones (e.g., demilitarized zone (DMZ), between regional offices)
- Host-based hardening and vulnerability scanning to reduce the potential attack surface by applying configuration changes and software updates
- Subject authentication and authorization to maintain the principles of least privilege for access to objects
- Signature-based technologies to detect and mitigate risk of threat actors in both endpoint and network devices, such as anti-malware solutions or intrusion prevention systems (IPS)

Modern Security Monitoring

As the modern threat landscape continues to change and cybercrime evolves, the conventional approach to a defense-in-depth strategy is transforming. More often today, organizations are building business environments that stray away from the concept that there needs to be a defined network perimeter and that all devices are—and will always be—connected to, trusted by, and managed by the organization. The distinction of what used to constitute a defined network perimeter is being driven by the increasing demand for a more accessible and mobile workforce. In turn, this is further driving the need for organizations to allow their data to be accessed from locations and devices that are not guaranteed to be protected by traditional security monitoring strategies.

As modern technologies—such as mobile computing, desktop virtualization, or cloud infrastructures—continue to proliferate as tools for conducting business, organizations are increasingly faced with the need to expose their business records and applications beyond the borders of their traditional network perimeter controls. With this modern change in business practice, deploying security controls under the traditional methodologies will not be as effective in identifying unacceptable activity.

To ensure that security monitoring capabilities adapt to continuously evolving technology, threats, and business practices, organizations need to re-engineer their security controls to concentrate more on the actual data. This is not to say that traditional security controls used for monitoring at the network and end-point layers should be discarded; rather organizations should consider using a new layer of security controls to provide coverage for monitoring closer to the data. In addition to the security controls specified previously, Figure 12.4 illustrates examples of modern security controls that should be considered as part of data-centric security monitoring.

- Next-generation (next-gen) firewalls combine traditional deep-packet inspection capabilities with applications awareness to better detect and deny malicious or unacceptable activity.
- Data loss prevention (DLP) use classifiers to detect and prevent potential data exfiltration through data-at-rest, data-in-transit, and data-in-use scenarios.
- Mobile device management (MDM) allows remote administration and enterprise integration of mobile computing devices such as smartphones and tablets.
- Content filtering monitors activity and enforces compliance with defined acceptable use policies and standards.
- Whitelisting, which is the opposite of a known-bad signature-based approach, controls application execution by permitting only trusted and known-good applications to operate.

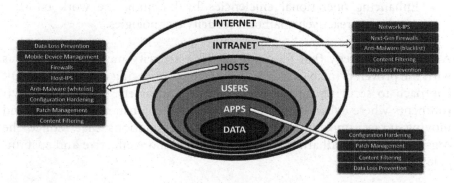

Figure 12.4 Next-gen security control layers.

Positive Security

Traditional approaches to managing information security through checklists, rules, and compliance cannot keep up with the modern threat landscape or increasing volumes of cyber-related threats and attacks. Essentially, continuing to play the "cat and mouse" game with cyber criminals is not feasible when they have invested significant effort into understanding the strengths and weaknesses of targeted security controls. For example, the current antivirus solutions, which follow a blacklisting approach, suffer from a low detection rate and, as a result, suffer from reduced effectiveness to protect information systems and assets from malicious attacks.

As the effectiveness of blacklisting solutions create greater opportunities for cyber-criminals to be successful in their attacks, attention needs to turn towards security strategies that reduce the overall attack surface(s) by following a risk-based approach. With a risk-based-approach, rather than being concerned with identifying and managing threats through specific technology functionalities, the organization's overall attack surface is reduced by implementing agnostic solutions that employ "deny by default" mechanisms in more of a whitelisting approach.

Through a risk-based methodology, or "positive security" approach, organizations will begin to realize several business benefits with respect to the protection of their information systems and assets, such as:

- Displacing security controls (such as anti-virus solutions) that are becoming less effective or are contributing little value to the organization's overall defense-in-depth strategy;
- Improving overall performance of network and information systems by eliminating (blacklist) signature databases that consume significant resources;
- Reducing the strain on supporting infrastructure(s) for deploying (blacklist) signature updates across remote locations; and
- Enhancing operational efficiencies by lessening the work effort required to reactively maintain security technologies.

Adopting a strategy that follows a positive security methodology aligns with the proven principles of least privilege by enforcing a deny-by-default approach to securing information systems and assets. In modern environments where cyber-attacks and threats are a constantly evolving and moving target, implementing attack-agnostic solutions that reduce the organization's overall attack surface is a much more effective and sustainable strategy.

Australian Signal Directorate (ASD)

First published in February 2010, the Australian Signal Directorate (ASD) developed a series of prioritized security controls that, when used strategically, help to mitigate cyber security incidents and intrusions, ransomware and external adversaries with destructive intent, malicious insiders, and breach of business records. The guidance was generated as result of the ASD's experience in operational security, incident management, vulnerability assessments, and penetration testing. With this guidance, it is important to note that there is no single security control that can be implemented to mitigate the risk of a cyber security incident. However, the ASD has proven the effectiveness of implementing the following top four strategies that are proven to be essential in mitigating approximately 85% of cyber security incidents, including:

- *Application whitelisting* to permit and trust "known-good" applications while restricting the execution of malicious or unapproved applications
- *Patch applications* to mitigate the risk of application vulnerabilities being exploited
- *Patch operating system* vulnerabilities to mitigate the risk of operating system vulnerabilities being exploited
- *Restrict administrative privileges* to the principle of least privilege access for subjects permitted access to only those objects required to perform their duties

While these top four strategies have been deemed essential security controls, and were declared mandatory for Australian government agencies as of April 2013, organizations can selectively implement any of the top thirty security controls to address specific security needs. Subsequently, in February 2017 the ASD issued a revision to the list which illustrated further break-outs of the top four mitigation strategies across multiple risk areas, including:

1. Mitigation strategies to prevent malware delivery and execution:
   - *Application whitelisting* of permitted/trusted applications to prevent the execution of malicious/unapproved applications
   - *Patch applications* to mitigate the risk of application vulnerabilities being exploited
   - *Configure Microsoft Office* macro settings to block embedded execution to "trusted locations" (i.e., digitally signed) with limited write access

- *User application hardening* to block, disable, or remove unneeded third-party applications featured in productivity suites (e.g., Microsoft Office), web browsers, and viewers (e.g., Flash)
2. Mitigation strategies to limit the extent of cyber security incidents:
    - *Restrict administrative privileges* to the principle of least privilege access for subjects permitted access to only those objects required to perform their duties
    - *Patch operating system* vulnerabilities to mitigate the risk of operating system vulnerabilities being exploited
    - *Multi-factor authentication* for remote access services (i.e., Virtual Private Networks (VPN)) and for all privileged access or actions (i.e., access to sensitive data)
3. Mitigation strategies to detect cyber security incidents and respond:
    - *Continuous incident detection and response* using automated analysis across centralized and time-synchronized log repositories; refer to Chapter 3 for further discussion on security logging
4. Mitigation strategies to recover data and system availability:
    - *Daily backups* of data, software, and configuration settings that are retained in offline repositories as per the enterprise's defined retention period(s)

Incorporating these mitigation strategies identified as "essential" is proven to be effective in preventing a wide range of cyber security risks. Additionally, while not directly related to enabling digital forensics capabilities, the technology-generated logs outputted from these security controls can be useful as potential digital evidence during an investigation.

Analytical Techniques

Approaches to how security monitoring is performed depend on several factors such as the type of security control used or how the vendor designed the functionality of their technology. Regardless, the foundation of security monitoring is based on the concept that unacceptable activity is noticeably discernable from acceptable activity and can be detected because of this difference. While there have been several security monitoring techniques suggested, the following are considered the three major categories used:

Misuse Detection
Misuse detection is a technique that applies correlation between observed activity and known unacceptable or known-bad behavior. While this technique is effective in identifying threats or attacks, successfully performing

misuse detection drives the need for organizations to define what they consider to be unacceptable or known-bad activity. Ultimately, it cannot be used to detect unacceptable behavior if such behavior has not been defined, such as through the creation of a signature within an IPS. The typical model of the misuse detection technique consists of the following components:

1. Information is gathered from different data sources.
2. Gathered information is translated and structured into a signature that can be interpreted by the applicable technologies.
3. The signature is applied to analyze activity and characterize unacceptable or known-bad behavior.
4. Activity detected as matching the signature is captured for reporting.

Within the misuse detection technique, there are five implementation classes for how organizations can apply this approach to their security monitoring:

- *Simple pattern matching* uses text-based searching, such as GREP, looking for an exact string of unacceptable or known-bad behavior within a single observed activity.
- *Stateful pattern matching* applies the text-based searching capabilities to look for an exact string of unacceptable or known-bad behavior across multiple instances of observed activities.
- *Protocol analysis* incorporates a layer of contextual intelligence where the composition of observed activity, such as the domain name system (DNS) protocol, is examined to determine if there are variations in the way it is supposed to be structured.
- *Heuristical analysis* involves varying levels of intelligence, learning, and logic about observed activity to determine if unacceptable or known-bad behavior is occurring.

Anomaly Detection

Anomaly detection assumes that all observed activity is unacceptable or known-bad behavior if it is not within the predefined scope of acceptable behavior. This technique starts by establishing a baseline of what acceptable behavior is through the process of observing activity to learn and form an opinion. The typical model of the misuse detection technique consists of the following components:

1. A baseline of acceptable behavior is established from all observed activity.
2. The baseline is translated and structured into a model that can be interpreted by the applicable technologies.

3. Observed activity is compared against the baseline model to determine if a deviation from acceptable behavior exists.
4. Unacceptable or known-bad behavior is captured for reporting.

While the main advantage of using this technique is that it applies the concept of whitelisting to detect unacceptable or known-bad behavior, versus the use of signatures in misuse detection, the activity used to establish the normal baseline must not contain abnormal activity. It is important when establishing the baseline of acceptable activity that the organization is not currently under an attack. If this is the case, when the system is in the process of learning behavior it may misinterpret unacceptable behavior as acceptable, resulting in increased false-positive or false-negative detections.

Specification-Based Detection

Specification-based detection techniques do not follow the same methodologies as misuse or anomaly detection. Rather, this technique uses behavior specifications, such as the principles of least privilege access, to detect unacceptable or known-bad behavior that does not conform to the intended execution behavior. Essentially, instead of establishing a baseline of acceptable activity through a learning process, stakeholders collectively define the threshold of acceptable behavior that is then used to capture reporting of unacceptable or known-bad behavior.

However, organizations need to consider the effort and complexity of establishing the specifications of a system's acceptable behavior. Although security monitoring technologies can help to automate the assessment of a system's behavior, organizations need to ensure that they conduct ongoing reviews to verify that the previously defined specifications for a system's acceptable behavior remain valid.

Machine Learning

As early as the 1980s, advancements in technology powered a realization that new algorithms used as part of artificial intelligence and machine learning could eventually help in decision-making processes. In the context of digital forensics, the application of machine learning is the process of applying multiple techniques and technologies to better interpret and gain knowledge about evidence from multiple data sources.

Making effective use of machine learning capabilities requires understanding which approach is best suited to the needs of the investigation, including the following:

- *Inductive machine learning* involves self-learning based on techniques such as cluster analysis, link analysis, and textual mining analytics.

- *Deductive machine learning* involves supervised learning based on rule generators and decision trees.

Generally, machine learning forensics is the capability to recognize patterns across potential digital evidence to reduce or validate the impact of cybercrime; further discussion about applying digital forensics capabilities to mitigate business risk scenarios can be found in Chapter 5. When using machine learning, digital forensics practitioners need to consider using any combination of both inductive and deductive approaches to the fact-based conclusions established during the investigation.

Extractive Forensics

Extracting data from unstructured data sources has become increasingly challenging because of the way in which technology is rapidly advancing and the volume by which data is growing. Extractive forensics involves any combination of techniques that are used to uncover relationships and associations between individuals and ESI (i.e., documents, email messages). For example, the following are techniques commonly used as part of extractive forensics techniques.

Link Analysis   Link analysis is used to understand context such as "who knew what, when, and where." Generally, link analysis assists digital forensics practitioners in discovering relationship by directing them to specific relevant evidence (and other information) of interest that requires further analysis, rather than identifying large data patterns independently.

With link analysis, entities (e.g., individuals, systems) are represented as objects (e.g., circles) and are referred to as *nodes*. Connecting the *nodes* together are lines, known as *edges*, that apply weighting to represent the strength of relationships between nodes, with stronger links having thicker connection lines. With link analysis technologies, graphs are used to visualize the relationships between nodes, their associations, and in some cases the counts and direction of the connections and relationships.

As with any technique and technology, there are limitations with the use of link analysis during a security investigation. For example, while link analysis is great for discovering associations and relationships, its main limitation becomes noticeable as the number of nodes grows too large and graphs become cluttered. Because of this, the use of link analysis during an investigation should be assessed to ensure that its application will simplify and narrow the scope of an investigation.

Text Mining   Text mining is a technique used to discover content (and context) hidden within the massive volumes of data sources. As technology continues to advance, organizations are increasingly generating and storing their informational assets in an unstructured format. This technique has become increasingly important because of how it allows digital forensic practitioners to sort and organize large volumes of unstructured ESI through tasks such as taxonomy categorization, concept clustering, and summarization.

Using technology, analyzing substantial amounts of unstructured ESI can be automated to improve pattern and concept identification. Without the use of these tools, digital forensics practitioners could potentially miss or overlook hidden patterns or concepts because of how difficult, if not impossible, it can be to discover these by applying traditional (manual) investigative techniques.

Generally, text mining applies three approaches to sort, organize, and prioritize unstructured ESI: information retrieval, information extraction, and natural language processing. By using these approaches, digital forensics practitioners can convert massive amounts of unstructured ESI into structured models that can be used to enhance analysis and correlation of digital evidence during an investigation.

Inductive Forensics

Creating visual representations and predictive models based on investigative evidence helps digital forensic practitioners establish their fact-based conclusions. Inductive forensics is a form of unsupervised learning that involves performing cluster analysis to group a set of objects into smaller groups based on some level of digital similarities, including the following:

- *Hierarchical clustering* builds multi-leveled orders using a tree structure.
- *Mean clustering* partitions data into distinct groups based on the point by which all data within a cluster intersects.
- *Gaussian mixture* models different clusters as a combination of two or more variables.
- *Self-organizing maps* use models to learn the topology and distribution of data.
- *Hidden Markov models* apply observed data to recover the sequence of data states.

For digital forensics practitioners, the use of unsupervised learning and cluster analysis provides a way of making observations that can lead to establishing evidence-based facts and conclusions about the investigation. While this type of unsupervised fact discovery can be useful for exploratory analysis, it can lead to a deductive type of analysis that can now be used to establish facts around differences and uniqueness amongst different clusters.

Deductive Forensics

In today's digital world, it is difficult to exist without having some level of digital profile existing throughout a broad range of technologies. Because of this, the information available during an investigation can allow for patterns to be captured, modeled, and used so that behaviors and the potential of impending security events or incidents can be anticipated.

In the early days of technologies, the vision of what machine learning could become was realized through tools such as decisions trees and mathematical algorithms. With the significant advancements made to technologies from the 1980s and beyond, a new generation of machine learning capabilities was realized with the evolution of clustering and link or text analysis. In this new paradigm of machine learning capabilities, where a variety of techniques are applied in different combinations, organizations are moving further away from being reactive and are increasingly customizing their targeted security monitoring capabilities based on what is learned from deductive learning.

Deductive reasoning works by making generalized information more specific, which is often referred to as a "top-down" approach. It begins by developing a theory and moves into a hypothesis that is testable or verifiable through fact-based observations and evidence. In Figure 12.5, the phases of both inductive and deductive reasoning are illustrated in how inductive and deductive reasoning work simultaneously to form a continuous cycle.

For example, consider what was traditionally used as the underlying process for enabling digital marketers to push products and services—also known as "user and entity behavior analytics" (UEBA). The same behavioral technologies are now applying a variety of extractive and inductive machine learning techniques to track and identify security events as a component of enterprise security, and digital forensics, programs. Generally, UEBA solutions are designed to identify and baseline the behavior of users and entities (i.e., systems, applications) to detect deviations from normal behavior. This is much like the concept of baselining information systems to detect deviations from that baseline with file integrity monitoring (FIM) technologies where profiles are built based on several factors, such as work hours, logical and physical access, or business role.

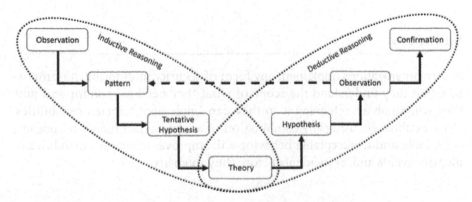

Figure 12.5 Phases of deductive and inductive reasoning.

Machine learning forensics can be strategically deployed throughout the organization to react and take appropriate action(s) to mitigate security events or incidents from happening and reduce the overall business risk posture. However, it is important that organizations remember that the use of any machine learning tool or technique during an investigation still requires interactions and involvement of digital forensics practitioners. For the time being, human guidance, experience, and contribution are the key success criteria in establishing evidence-based facts and conclusions during any digital forensics investigation.

Implementation Concerns

Before organizations begin practicing any of the analytical techniques discussed previously, it is important that decisions are made regarding the deployment of the security monitoring solution. As a starting point, the implementation of the monitoring solution must be supported through existing governance documentation and justified through a formalized risk assessment, as discussed further in Addendum E, "Risk Assessment." The following list outlines other areas of consideration that must be decided before a security monitoring solution can be implemented:

- Ensuring criticality-based deployment of monitoring capabilities to target high-value and high-risk employees, systems, networks, etc.
- Selecting the combination of analytical techniques to be used as part of the monitoring solution
- Using a monitoring solution that meets the established service level objectives (SLO) for responding
- Conducting regular reviews of signatures and detection mechanisms to ensure accurate and timely identification of unacceptable or known-bad behavior.

Summary

Before organizations implement any form of security monitoring, it is important that they understand the scope of what they need to monitor and how they will go about achieving it so they can implement targeted capabilities. Once established, using any combination of analytical techniques to monitor acceptable and unacceptable behavior will improve detection capabilities to identify events and/or incidents before they intensify.

Mapping Investigative Workflows

13

Introduction

Forensic investigations can be triggered from several types of events generated by a variety of security controls. Whether they originate because of human watchfulness, rule matching in an intrusion prevention system (IPS), or modification of data alerted on file integrity monitoring (FIM), organizations must demonstrate an acceptable level of due diligence by ensuring they review each event as it is generated.

While reviewing events, security analysts need to quickly assess the level of risk to the organization and decide whether a full forensic investigation needs to be initiated. The criteria for deciding when an event becomes an investigation should not be simply left to the judgment of the security analyst; a series of policies and procedures must be established to clearly define when this escalation is performed. At the point an investigation is initiated, the governance documentation should already include detailed information for how to proceed and who should be involved.

Incident Management Lifecycle

A forensic investigation can be initiated from several types of events or incidents. Like how the digital forensic readiness model, as illustrated in Figure 13.1, provides a consistent and repeatable workflow for conducting a forensic investigation, the way in which organizations manage their incidents should also follow a consistent, repeatable, and structured workflow framework.

Incident management consists of several phases through which specific activities are performed to mitigate the impact of the incident by containing it and ultimately recovering from it. Illustrated in Figure 13.2, there are four major phases within the incident management lifecycle, each containing a subset of activities and steps that must be performed. Typically, the phases of an incident management lifecycle are completed in sequence and, like that of the forensic readiness model, may require that preceding phases be revisited as new events or findings are detected, a situation making it very much a lifecycle.

157

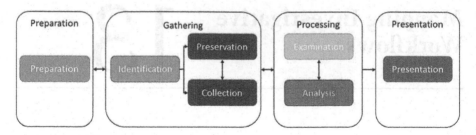

Figure 13.1 High-level digital forensic process model.

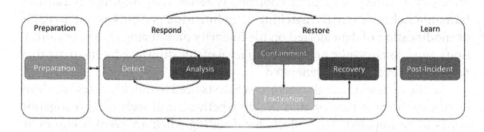

Figure 13.2 Incident management lifecycle.

Integrating the Digital Forensic Readiness Model

When an incident has been declared, organizations must consider the ramifications of their actions on potential digital evidence, with respect to its admissibility in a court of law, as they work through the incident management lifecycle. Illustrated in Figure 13.3, the activities and steps performed during incident response have a direct and collateral effect on the organization's ability to support and conduct a forensic investigation.

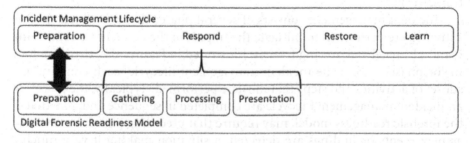

Figure 13.3 Incident response—forensic readiness integration.

Those members of the incident response team (IRT) responsible for performing forensic activities need to have knowledge of the principles, methodologies, procedures, tools, and techniques that apply throughout each phase of the incident management lifecycle. Not only does having this knowledge facilitate more efficient and effective response to incidents, it also ensures that the actions taken during incident handling and response will not interfere with the authenticity and integrity of digital evidence.

Included throughout the sections below, the integration points between each incident response phase and digital forensics have been specified.

Incident Handling and Response

There are four major phases included as part of the incident management lifecycle:

- Preparation (initiation)
- Respond (detection & analysis)
- Restore (containment, eradication, & recovery)
- Learn (post-incident)

The activities and steps performed in some of these lifecycle phases are common to all security incidents, such as when a detected incident has been validated and the IRT moves towards containment actions, while in some incidents there are activities and steps that may not be performed, such as when a detected incident has been invalidated and the IRT moves towards recovery actions.

Making effective use of the incident management lifecycle requires that organizations minimize the number of ad hoc decisions and subjective judgments being made during an incident. Not only will this facilitate reducing stress related to potentially making an incorrect decision, but it also provides organizations with a comprehensive methodology that is demonstrably consistent and repeatable when challenged in a court of law.

Phase #1: Preparation

The incident management lifecycle starts by completing activities that ultimately enable the organization to effectively respond and handle incidents. This is the most critical phase of the entire lifecycle because it establishes a foundation for how the subsequent phases will be executed within the capabilities throughout the organizations.

"Event" versus "Incident"

One of the first actions that should be to taken is to specify as part of a taxonomy, discussed further in Addendum D, "Building a Taxonomy," what the organization defines as an *event* and an *incident*. Doing this as the first step provides a clear scope so that further decisions can be made as to roles and responsibilities, team structures, and escalation workflow criteria.

An *event* is any observable occurrence. Events can be physical or technical in nature such as a user accessing a restricted area or a firewall blocking a connection attempt. Additionally, an *adverse event* is a specific type of event that results in a negative consequence such as system failures, malware execution, or data exfiltration.

An *incident* is any violation or imminent threat of violating the organization's policies, standards, or guidelines. Examples of incidents are:

- A distributed denial of service (DDoS) attack resulting in system failures
- The release of confidential or sensitive information to unauthorized parties

Policies, Plans, and Procedures

Organizing an effective incident handling and response capabilities requires organizations to establish formal incident management policies, plans, and procedures before an incident occurs.

This series of documentation must emphasize how interactions throughout the organization, as well as with external parties such as law enforcement, will be conducted.

Policies   At the highest level, policies are built as formalized blueprints used to describe the organization's goals specific to incident management. These documents address general terms and are not intended to contain the level of detail found in the plans and procedures that are created afterwards.

While the contents of these documents will be subjective to the organization's individual incident management needs, the following elements are commonly used across all policy implementations:

- Statement of management commitments to incident management
- Purpose and objective for creating the policy
- Scope of to whom, how, and when the policy applies
- Inclusion of, or reference to, the organization's taxonomy which is used to define common terms and language
- Prioritization or severity ranking of incidents
- Escalation and contact information
- Organizational structure, including roles and responsibilities, chain of command, and information sharing rules

Plans   Building off policies, plans are the documents that formally outline the focused and coordinated approach to incident management. It is important for each organization to have a plan that is implemented to meet their unique requirements and provide the roadmap for how they will implement their incident response capabilities.

In addition to describing the resources and management support required, this document should also include the following components:

- Mission, strategies, and goals for incident management
- Approach and methodology used to support incident management
- Communication and information sharing plan
- Stakeholder (e.g., management) approval of the document
- Service level objectives (SLO) used to measure performance
- Roadmap for maturing incident management capabilities

Procedures   Standard operating procedures (SOP) should be created and maintained based on the organization's implementation of governing policies, plans, and staffing models. Contained within these SOP documents should be comprehensive and detailed technical processes, checklists, and forms that will be used for handling and responding to an incident following digital forensics principles, methodologies, and techniques.

The goal for creating these SOP documents is to provide a consistently repeatable process that are relevant to all incidents and that can be accurately applied to all forensic activities throughout. Suggested components for an SOP document, including the requirements for digital forensics, are presented throughout the incident handling and response phases in the sections to follow.

Team Structure and Models

An IRT should always be readily available for anybody who identifies or suspects that an event within the organization has occurred. Beyond the availability of incident management documentation, the success of the IRT to analyze events and act appropriately depends on the involvement of key individuals through the organization. Generally, the IRT is responsible for:

- Developing appropriate incident management documentation
- Retaining resources necessary to perform incident management activities
- Investigating the root cause of detected incidents
- Managing digital evidence gathered and processed from the incident
- Recommending countermeasures and security controls (administrative, technical, or physical)

The way in which an IRT is deployed depends largely on the organization's size. In business environments where operations are centralized to a smaller geographical region, it is quite effective to have a centralized IRT. However, as business environments become more dispersed and operations are scattered across multiple geographic locations, there could be a need to deploy regional IRTs. Where there are multiple IRTs distributed across a larger business environment, it is important that all teams be part of a single coordinated unit so that policies, plans, and procedures are consistently used for incident management throughout the organization.

At the end of the day, the decision to use a centralized or distributed IRT comes down to the cost of deploying the model. Through a cost-benefit analysis, as discussed further in Addendum C, "Cost-Benefit Analysis," organizations can determine which team model works best for them.

Roles and Responsibilities   It is important that there is participation of stakeholders throughout the organization to provide their expertise, judgement, and abilities throughout the incident management lifecycle. While the duties performed by each of these stakeholders may not have direct involvement in conducting incident response or handling related activities, their cooperation is essential to ensuring that the policies, plans, and procedures are consistently followed.

Depending on the size of the organization, not all business areas specified in the list might exist. Where this is the case, it is important that the organization identify people who are experienced in these subject matters so that when an incident occurs, there will be no knowledge gap with how to proceed under certain circumstances.

- *Management* are ultimately accountable for establishing incident management documentation, budgets, and staffing. They are also held responsible for coordinating incident response and handling capabilities amongst stakeholders and dissemination of information.
- *Information security* resources provide supplementary support during distinct stages of the incident response and handling activities, such as validating security controls (e.g., firewall rules).
- *Information technology* (IT) support and administration resources have the most intimate knowledge of the technology they manage daily. This expertise is important to have when ensuring that appropriate actions are taken for affected assets; such as the proper sequence for shutting down critical systems.
- *Forensic practitioners* are knowledgeable in the scientific principles, methodologies, and techniques, and are equipped with tools to ensure that incident response activities preserve the forensic viability and admissibility of digital evidence for use in a court of law.

- *Legal experts* should review all incident management documentation to ensure the organization is compliant with applicable laws, regulations, guidance, and the right to privacy. Furthermore, their expertise should also be sought when it is believed that an incident will have some form of legal ramifications, such as prosecution of perpetrators or the creation of binding agreements for external information sharing.
- *Public and corporate affairs* will facilitate, depending on the nature and context of the incident, the communication and sharing of information with external parties (e.g., media) and the public.
- *Human resources and employee relations* mediate disciplinary proceedings when an employee is suspected of being involved with the incident.
- *Business continuity planning* ensures that all incident management documentation is aligned and consistent with the organization's business continuity practices. During an incident, their expertise can be used to help minimize operational disruptions and assist with communication. Additionally, these people should be made aware of the impact resulting from incidents so they can revise documentation accordingly, such as business impact and risk assessments.

Communication and Escalation

When an incident occurs, those individuals throughout the organization who have a vested interest in the process must be kept readily informed of what is happening. This requires that throughout each phase of the incident management lifecycle, the IRT must ensure they provide adequate and timely information about the incident.

Communication plans should account for the dissemination of information to a wide variety of audience, across many different delivery channels (e.g., in person, email, paper), and be formatted based on the intended audience (e.g., other IRTs, management, stakeholders). Not only should information be communicated on a periodic basis (e.g., hourly updates, daily summary), but it should also be made available when requested on a "need to know" basis.

Recording and distributing information about an incident should be limited to specific IRT members, sometimes referred to as scribes, whose responsibility is solely communication and escalations. These individuals work closely with other members of the IRT team(s) to document the activities, steps, and progress through the incident management lifecycle and ensure that accurate and appropriate information is provided to those need it.

External Information Sharing From time to time, organizations may need to share information with a variety of external parties such as law enforcement, media, industry experts, and so on. When required, key stakeholders throughout the organization—such as legal, executive management, and public/corporate affairs—should always be consulted prior to the dissemination of any information to external parties. Without having these teams involved to determine how and to what level of detail information can be shared, there is a risk that sensitive or confidential information could be disclosed to unauthorized individuals.

Escalation Management

When required, the IRT may need to escalate specific activities about the incident to highlight issues so that appropriate individuals can respond and provide the required level of resolution. Most commonly, escalations are used during incident response to re-prioritize, reassign, or monitor specific activities or actions so normal business operations, functions, and services can be restored as quickly as possible. Escalations can typically be grouped into one of the following categories:

Hierarchical Escalation Hierarchical escalations are used to ensure that attention is given to the necessary actions for resolving an issue. During a hierarchical escalation, the focus is placed on following the documented chain of command until a resolution is achieved.

In Figure 13.4, an example of this can be seen during security monitoring where the first-level analysts complete the initial event triage and if they are unable to resolve the issue it is escalated to the second-level analysts, and so on until it is resolved.

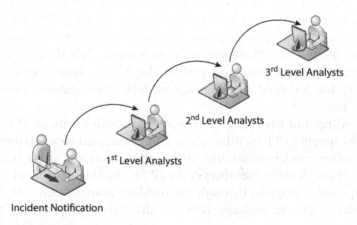

3rd Level Analysts

2nd Level Analysts

1st Level Analysts

Incident Notification

Figure 13.4 Hierarchical escalation.

Functional Escalation Functional escalations are used to ensure that issue resolution is achieved within a given SLO. During a functional escalation, the focus is placed on the priority for resolving the issue because of the combined importance and urgency.

Illustrated in Figure 13.5, a priority matrix demonstrates how priority can be determined to resolve issues within a given SLO.

Escalations should not be predominantly used as a means of deviating from established incident management processes. This typically happens when an organization incorrectly or vaguely defines when an escalation is to be used during the incident management lifecycle, and the IRT will not know under what circumstance they should initiate an escalation, with whom they should communicate, and how they are to perform the escalation. Examples of when an escalation can be triggered under both categories specified previously include the following:

- Evidence of a reportable crime exists.
- Evidence indicates a fraud, theft, or other loss.
- The estimate of possible damage exceeds a specified threshold.
- Potential for embarrassment or reputational damage exists.
- Immediate impact to customers, partners, or profitability is imminent.
- Recovery plans have been invoked or are necessary.
- The incident is reportable under legal or compliance requirements.

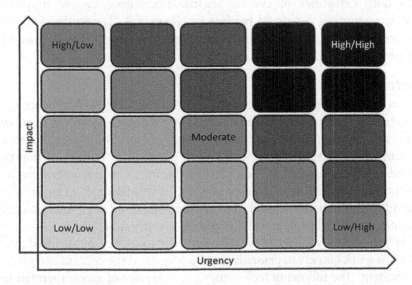

Figure 13.5 Functional escalation.

The use of escalations should be limited to specific circumstances as defined in the incident management documentation. To ensure escalations are only performed when required, the IRT should include a decision maker, such as the incident manager, who will decide whether an escalation is required.

Phase #2: Respond

One of the most challenging aspects of the incident management lifecycle is accurately detecting and assessing potential incidents, primarily because incidents can originate from many different attack vectors such as loss/theft of equipment or lack of employee awareness.

While the established SOP supports a consistent and repeatable process for responding to all incidents, the way in which organizations handle each incident varies. Contained with the scope of this phase, activities and steps performed are focused primarily on the detection and analysis of incidents as they are received.

Detection

Incidents can be detected through many sources other than the targeted security monitoring capabilities discussed previously in Chapter 12, "Enabling Targeted Monitoring." Regardless, the indicators of an incident can be grouped into one of the following categories:

- *Precursor* incidents are those events that imply that an incident may occur in the future.
- *Indicator* incidents are those events that signify that an incident has or is occurring now.

With both categories of events, organizations need to use supplemental information, as discussed further in Chapter 9, "Determine Collection Requirements," to prevent an impending incident from escalating and further impacting business operations.

Analysis

Generally, assessing incidents would be relatively simple if precursor and indicator events were guaranteed to always be accurate. However, even when events are confirmed to be accurate, it does not necessarily signify that an incident will or is about to occur. For this reason, it is important that those individual(s) responsible for completing the initial triage determine if the event(s) is true-positive or false-positive. This validation is a crucial step in determining what activities and steps will be performed next, such as whether to contain the incident or move directly into recovery activities.

Where initial validation corroborates the existence of an incident, the IRT must work quickly to prioritize and understand the context surrounding the incident. The following techniques are examples of recommended techniques that can effectively reduce the complexity of incident analysis:

- *Profiling* is characterizing activity so that unknown or abnormal activity can be more easily identified. Examples of profiling techniques that can be used during incident analysis include file integrity monitoring, discussed further in Chapter 10, "Establishing Legal Admissibility," and misuse/anomaly/specification-based detection, discussed further in Chapter 12, "Enabling Targeted Monitoring."
- *Maintaining an information knowledge base*, such as centralized incident and case management solutions, is important so that it is readily available for the IRT to reference quickly during an incident. The knowledge base should contain a variety of information that can be used to assess an incident, including the following:
  - *Observables* are the resulting outputs that might be or have been seen across an organization (e.g., service degradation).
  - *Indicators* describe one or more observable patterns that, combined with other relevant and contextual information, represent artifacts and/or behaviors of interest (e.g., file hashes).
  - *Incidents* are distinct instances of indicators that are affecting an organization accompanied by information discovered or decided upon during an investigation.
  - *Adversary tactics, techniques, and procedures* (*TTP*) are the attack patterns, tools, exploits, infrastructure, victim targeting, and other methods used by the adversary or attacker.
  - *Exploit targets* are vulnerabilities, weaknesses, or configurations that might be exploited.
  - *Courses of action* are specific countermeasures taken as corrective or preventative response actions to address an exploit target or mitigate the potential impact of an incident.
  - *Campaigns* are instances of threat actors that are performing a set of TTPs or incidents potentially seen across an organization.
  - *Threat actors* are malicious adversaries with intent and observed behaviors that represent a threat to an organization.
  - *Internet search engines* can help the IRT find information about similar incidents or perpetrators. When performing Internet research, it is important to use systems that are not directly associated or connected with the organization so that anonymity can be maintained. Additionally, by using throwaway systems, such as a virtual machine, organizations can avoid the potential of their searches being tracked or correlated by always using a system that operates within a pre-established and known condition and/or state.

Prioritization

Following the analysis and assessment of an incident, the most critical decision to be made by the IRT is establishing incident priority. As a rule of thumb, incidents that have been assessed should be handled by priority and not on a first-come-first-served basis, as in how a hospital's emergency department (ED) might operate. Prioritizing incidents can be achieved by using the following factors:

Functional Impact Incidents targeting an organization's information technology (IT) assets typically impact the organization. The IRT should consider not only the immediate negative impact to the business, but also the likelihood of future impact if the incident is not contained.

See Table 13.1 for criteria related to prioritizing incidents that have a functional impact.

Informational Impact Incidents can affect the security properties of an organization's information, including confidentiality, integrity, availability, authentication, authorizations, and nonrepudiation. The IRT must consider the implications of sensitive or confidential information potentially being exfiltrated because of the incident.

See Table 13.2 for criteria related to prioritizing incidents that have an informational impact.

Table 13.1 Functional Impact Prioritization

Category	Criteria
None	No effect to business operations, functions, or services
Low	Minimal effect to business operations, functions, or services; no critical services have been impacted
Medium	Moderate effect to business operations, functions, or services; a subset of critical services have been impacted
High	Significant effect to business operations, functions, or services; all critical services have been impacted

Table 13.2 Informational Impact Prioritization

Category	Criteria
None	No information was exfiltrated, lost, or otherwise compromised.
Privacy breach	Sensitive information was exfiltrated, lost, or otherwise compromised (e.g., personally identifiable information [PII]).
Proprietary breach	Internal information was exfiltrated, lost, or otherwise compromised (e.g., architectural diagrams).
Integrity breach	Sensitive or proprietary information was exfiltrated, lost, or otherwise compromised (e.g., financial records).

Table 13.3   Recoverability Impact Prioritization

Category	Criteria
Regular	Restoration time is predictable and can be achieve using existing resources.
Supplemented	Restoration time is predictable but requires additional resources.
Extended	Restoration time is unpredictable and requires assistance from existing, additional, and external resources.
Not recoverable	Restoration time is unpredictable and not realistically possible.

Recoverability Impact   Incidents can result in varying levels of impact to assets and operations. In some instances, it may be possible to quickly recover from an incident; however, in other incidents additional resources might be required to facilitate the restoration of business assets and operations throughout the organization. See Table 13.3 for criteria related to prioritizing incidents that have recoverability impact.

Once the criteria for prioritizing incidents have been established, the IRT needs to ensure that they notify and escalate, if required, to the appropriate stakeholders. Further details about requirements for notification and escalation have been specified in the following sections of this chapter.

Phase #3: Restore

Once an incident has been responded to, appropriate actions must be taken to mitigate any further impact on the organization and start working to recover business operations, functions, and services.

While the established SOP documentation supports a consistent and repeatable process for restoring business operations, functions, and services, the ways in which an organization contains and eradicates each incident vary.

Within the scope of this phase, activities and steps performed are focused primarily on the containment and eradication of the incident and subsequent recovery of business operations, functions, and services.

Containment

Before an incident can intensify further, organizations need to determine the appropriate strategies for controlling the impact of the incident beyond the assets and resources it has already affected. Every incident varies in context, and because of these variations there is no single containment strategy that can be used across the board. Ultimately, deciding which containment strategy works best for controlling impact beyond the currently affected assets and resources requires organizations to understand the context under which the incident occurred. Examples of criteria that can be used to select an appropriate containment strategy include the following:

- Functional, informational, and recoverability prioritization
- Potential damage to or theft of assets and resources
- Effectiveness of the containment strategy
- Time required to implement the containment strategy

Although the IRT's primary goal is to select a containment strategy that will assist in eradication of and recovery from the incident, careful consideration must be given to the need for preserving potential digital evidence for legal proceedings. Once the containment strategy has been selected, such as shutting down systems or isolating network segments, the IRT must ensure potential digital evidence is gathered and preserved in the order of the data's volatility rating.

Generally, the more volatile data within a system is, the more challenging it is to forensically gather it because it is only available for a specific amount of time. The ability to gather potential digital evidence prior to implementing a containment strategy comes with inherent risk because the longer it takes to make a decision, the greater the risk of the incident intensifying and digital evidence being lost.

When deciding to preserve volatile data, it is important to keep in mind that the more volatile the data is, the greater is a need for knowledgeable individuals and specialized tools to ensure the data is gathered and preserved in a forensically sound manner. See Table 13.4 for the order of volatility for digital evidence, ordered from most volatile to least volatile.

Eradication and Recovery

After a containment strategy has been implemented, work can begin to remove the elements of the incident from where they exist throughout the organization. Now, it is important that all affected assets and resources have been identified and remediated to ensure that, when containment measures are removed, the incident does not come back or propagate further through the organization.

Recovery efforts that follow eradication involve restoring assets and resources to their normal and fully functional state, such as changing passwords, restoring data from backups, or installing patches. Recovery should be completed following the eradication of an incident's impact from an asset or resource, not in parallel. By completing these tasks through a phased approach, organizations can prioritize removing the threats from their environment as quickly as possible, then focusing on keeping the organization as secure as possible for the long term.

Table 13.4   Order of Volatility

Lifespan	Storage Type	Data Type
As short as a single clock cycle	CPU storage	Registers
		Caches
	Video	RAM
Until host is shut down	System storage	RAM
	Kernel tables	Network connections
		Login sessions
		Running processes
		Open files
		Network configurations
		System date/time
Until overwritten or erased	Non-volatile data	Paging/swap files
		Temporary/cache files
		Configuration/log files
		Hibernation files
		Dump files
		Registry
		Account information
		Data files
		Slack space
	Removable media	Floppy disks
		Tapes
		Optical disc (read/write only)
Until physically destroyed		Optical disc (write only)
	Outputs	Paper printouts

Phase #4: Learn

Every incident varies in context and most often includes a new threat, attack vector, or threat actor that the IRT has not previously accounted for in their incident management program. However, the most commonly overlooked and disregarded phase of the incident management lifecycle involves learning from the incident.

By holding a "lessons learned" meeting with all stakeholders after an incident, the organization can identify additional controls to improve the organization's security posture and enhance the IRT's capabilities for future incidents. This meeting is the organization's opportunity to close the incident and review specific details, including:

- What happened and at what time(s)?
- How well did stakeholders and the IRT deal with the incident?

- Were incident management processes and procedures followed?
- Did incident management documentation contain adequate information?
- Did any activities, steps, or actions inhibit restoring business operations?
- How could notification, escalation, and information sharing be improved?

Following the completion of activities in this phase, the incident management lifecycle resets to the preparation phase. When this happens, the outputs from the post-incident activities must be carried forward so the incident response process and accompanying documentation can be revised accordingly to reduce the likelihood of new incidents occurring.

The Incident Response Team (IRT)

Within the incident response team (IRT), there will most likely be a combination of technical and business representatives who all have an interest in mitigating the business impact. An IRT should always be readily available to respond and work to mitigate potential business impact from an incident. Generally, the IRT is responsible for:

- Developing appropriate incident management documentation
- Retaining resources necessary to perform incident management activities
- Investigating the root cause of detected incidents
- Managing digital evidence gathered and processed from the incident
- Recommending countermeasures and security controls (administrative, technical, or physical).

The ways in which the IRT is implemented depends largely on the organization's characteristics, such as geography, size, and business functions. For example, in some enterprises the IRT might be contained to a single and centralized location where all incident response capabilities are managed. Alternatively, some organizations may decide to implement regional IRTs across separate locations to support needs in various areas while maintaining a single coordinated governance structure.

In either case, it is important that the IRT have stakeholders representing different key business environments so that the necessary expertise, skills, and decision-making capabilities can be fully utilized. For example, depending on the organization, the following expertise may be needed in the incident management lifecycle:

- *Management* personnel are responsible for establishing documentation, providing funding, and allocating resources. Ultimately, they are accountable for coordinating incident response capabilities amongst all stakeholders and for the distribution of information.
- *Information security* (*IS*) personnel provide supplementary support throughout the incident response workflow, such as validating security controls (e.g., firewall rules, intrusion prevention signatures).
- *Information technology* (*IT*) personnel have the most intimate knowledge of systems and the potential impact to them from incident response activities, such as the sequence for shutting down critical systems.
- *Legal* personnel should review all documentation to ensure the organization is compliant with applicable laws, regulations, standards, and the right to privacy. Additionally, these individuals must be engaged when there is potential for some type of legal ramifications associated with the incident, such as prosecution of perpetrators.
- *Public and corporate affairs* personnel facilitate, depending on the incident, communicate and share information with external parties (e.g., the media).
- *Human resource and employee relations* personnel mediate disciplinary proceedings where violation of corporate governance (e.g., business code of conduct) has occurred and an employee is involved.
- *Business continuity planning* personnel ensure documentation is aligned and consistent with the organization's ability to continue its business operations. Their expertise can be used to help minimize operational disruptions and assist with communication.

In addition to having stakeholder representation from key business lines, every successful IRT has clearly defined roles for critical functions during an incident. For example, every IRT should have individuals placed in the following roles:

- The *team lead* oversees all activities performed during the incident. This role is also responsible for coordinating the review of all actions taken during phase #4, which can lead to changes in documentation and how incidents are handled going forward.
- The *incident lead* has ownership over the immediate incident and oversees coordinating all incident response activities. All communication about the incident is coordinated through this role to ensure accurate and timely dissemination of information.
- *Associate members* are those individuals who form the IRT as representatives from different business lines. Their involvement and roles can vary depending on the nature of the incident.

- *Scribes* are persons who track all activities and document the actions taken throughout the entire incident. Depending on the nature of the incident, multiple scribes might be necessary to capture a complete and comprehensive register of all activities and actions taken.

The Role of Digital Forensics During an Incident

Digital forensics individuals are those with knowledge in the scientific principles, methodologies, and techniques of the discipline. They are equipped with knowledge, experience, and tools necessary to ensure that activities performed during the incident response workflow preserve the forensic viability and legal admissibility of digital evidence.

Generally, the role of digital forensics within the IRT can be two-fold: the first being that of an advisor (or consultant) to ensure the team addresses concerns of preserving digital evidence; and the second being the technical professional who leads the activities to gather and process digital evidence. Whether these roles are held by a single individual or split amongst multiple people is completely dependent on the nature of the incident, size of the organization, and overall maturity of the organization's incident response capabilities. In circumstances where the incident necessitates having the role of digital forensic resources separated, the following must be considered during the incident response workflow.

Practitioner

People in this role are technically hands-on when it comes to gathering digital evidence during an incident. These individuals must demonstrate the knowledge and skills necessary for applying the fundamental principles, methodologies, and techniques of digital forensics so that gathered evidence is forensically sound and legally admissible.

Advisor

People in an advisory role are technically hands-off all activities directly involving the gathering of digital evidence. These individuals must demonstrate a thorough understand of the fundamental principles, methodologies, and techniques so that they can correctly instruct and influence key decision making during the incident response workflow.

In circumstances where there is need to have a single digital forensic resource assigned to the incident, this individual will be responsible for switching between practitioner and advisory roles. In this situation, the role demands for these individuals to guide the IRT through decision-making processes as well become hands-on when it comes time to gather digital evidence. At times, playing both roles can be daunting and cumbersome when trying to ensure that the IRT does not make rash and uninformed decisions that could potentially impact digital evidence. To mitigate this risk, it is recommended that the advisor and practitioner roles be performed individually through any combination of internal (i.e., employees) and external (i.e., professional services) resources based on cost, skills, response time, and data sensitivity.

Further discussions about education and training relating to digital forensics can be found in Chapter 14, "Establish Continuing Education."

Investigation Workflow

The logical flow from the time when the initial event occurs requires organizations to follow a consistent and repeatable incident handling and response process that encompasses several stages of information gathering (e.g., preserving digital evidence, conducting interviewing), communication (e.g., stakeholder reporting, escalations), and documentation (e.g., SOPs, incident or case management knowledge base).

The goal of following a logical investigative process, made up of clear and concise workflows, is to reduce the potential for rushed and uninformed decisions being made during incident handling and response. However, understanding that the context of every incident is different, the investigative workflow should still provide those involved with the ability to make the best and most educated decision for what actions are performed next.

Before an incident is escalated into an investigation, the IRT should have collected sufficient information to assess the impact of this decision on the organization, including the following:

- Can an investigation proceed at a cost that is proportional to the size of the incident?
- How can an investigation reduce the impact to business operations, functions, and services?

Understanding that each organization varies in how they will build their investigative workflow, the diagrams provided in the "Templates" section of this book can be used as a reference for starting to build a logical investigative workflow process.

Types of Security Investigations

Conducting digital forensic investigations in the private sector is not much different from conducting them in the public sector. For example, in both the private and public sectors, digital evidence can be gathered and processed to support some type of criminal allegation; however, in the private sector there can also be a need for digital evidence based on corporate asset abuse or policy violations. Generally, most security events and incidents that require organizations to conduct a forensic investigation involve the misuse or abuse of informational assets or systems where potential sources of evidence can be located across many disparate technologies.

Typically, there are several business scenarios where digital forensics can be leveraged to effectively manage an organization's business risk; refer to Chapter 5, "Digital Forensics as a Business," Depending on how an organization implements and integrates their digital forensic capabilities, the following are examples of different security investigations that can be encountered:

- *Data breach* involves access to and dissemination of informational assets to unauthorized entities.
- *Email abuse* involves the transmission of content that is outside the scope of acceptable usage as defined by the organization's enterprise governance framework (i.e., acceptable use policy).
- *Inappropriate activity* involves access to and rendering of contraband content (e.g., pornography, pirated media).
- *Internet abuse* involves access to and transmission of content that is outside the scope of acceptable usage as defined by the organization's enterprise governance framework (i.e., acceptable use policy).
- *Intrusion attempts* involve efforts to gain unauthorized access to informational assets or systems.
- *Malware infections* involve the installation and execution of malicious code.
- *Unauthorized access* involves access to informational assets or systems without approval or delegated privilege.

As the investigation proceeds and evidence is processed, it is important to know how to distinguish between civil and criminal violations. Because any civil investigation can become a criminal investigation, it is critical that all digital evidence be handled following documented, repeatable, and consistent methodologies and techniques; refer to Chapter 3, "Digital Evidence Management," for further discussion.

Summary

Forensic investigations are most commonly triggered because of some type of incident, whether an event was detected through security monitoring, a subpoena was received for legal proceeding, or theft/loss of an asset occurred. Regardless, the logical investigative workflow used to handle and respond to all incidents must be well-defined to reduce incorrect decision making but flexible enough to support a variety of incidents as they occur. In any case, organizations must ensure that their governance framework supports consistent and repeatable actions that can be used throughout their entire incident management capabilities.

Establish Continuing Education

14

Introduction

Organizations cannot successfully implement digital forensics readiness without ensuring that all stakeholders involved have an adequate knowledge of how they contribute to its overall success. Once stakeholders have established how they contribute to digital forensics readiness, the level of educational training and professional knowledge required will vary for everyone.

Without proper training and education, the people factor, not technology, becomes the weakest link of a digital forensics readiness program. Knowing this, it is essential for organizations to implement a comprehensive and well-designed program to ensure that all those who have any sort of involvement with digital forensics readiness are knowledgeable and experienced.

Types of Education and Training

Much like other components of a digital forensics readiness program, a successful education and training program starts with the implementation of organizational governance that reflects the need for (1) informing stakeholders of their responsibilities, (2) providing the appropriate level of training and education, and (3) establishing processes for monitoring, reviewing, and improving their level of knowledge.

Having different education and awareness programs in place for all stakeholders, depending on their involvement with digital forensics, is an effective way of distributing information about the benefits and value of digital forensics readiness throughout the organization. Illustrated in Figure 14.1, the following sections describe the difference between awareness, training, and education curricula that organizations should consider as part of their overall continuing education for digital forensics readiness.

Within each education and training curricula illustrated above, organizations must ensure that the information is adapted according to the

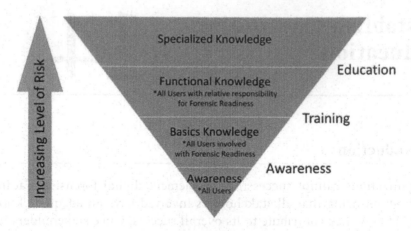

Figure 14.1 Continuing education hierarchy.

stakeholder's role (job function). As an example, a simplified concept for grouping the education and training information for applicable stakeholders has been placed into the following three categories:

- *All personnel* have a perspective that recognizes the importance of information security enough to positively contribute to the digital forensics readiness program.
- *Functional/specialized roles* emphasize the importance of performing job duties to support the organization's digital forensics readiness program.
- *Management* personnel need to understand the functional, operational, and strategic value of the digital forensics readiness program so they can communicate and reinforce it throughout the organization.

Awareness

As the first stage of education and training, general awareness is intended to change the behaviors of individuals and reinforce a culture of acceptable conduct. The objective here is not to provide users with in-depth or specialized knowledge, rather it is designed to provide stakeholders with the knowledge they need to recognize what the organization defines as unacceptable behavior and take the necessary steps to keep it from occurring.

With one of the focuses for implementing digital forensics readiness being investigating employee misconduct against the organization's policies, this type of education and training will reduce the likelihood that an incident will occur and require a formal forensic investigation.

The information provided at this level is generic enough that it can be provided to all stakeholders without being adapted according to their job function. Examples of topics and subject areas that should be included as part of general awareness education and training include the following:

- Policies, standards, guidelines
- Social engineering (e.g., phishing)
- Privileged access
- Data loss prevention (DLP)

Organizations should consider requiring all stakeholders to complete the general awareness program. At a minimum, organizations should require existing stakeholders to complete the general awareness education and training annually. Alternatively, when new stakeholders are identified they should be expected to complete the general awareness program immediately.

Basic Knowledge

As the next stage of education and training, the need for basic knowledge of digital forensics readiness provides stakeholders with the fundamental knowledge that is essential to ensuring they are competent. The distinction between basic knowledge and general awareness is that this level of education and training is designed to teach stakeholders the basic skills they will need to support a digital forensics readiness program.

The education and training provided at this level provides stakeholders with skill set(s) that continue to build off the foundations of the general awareness information. In-house training courses can, for the most part, be designed to contain the same quality of information that could be obtained by enrolling in a formal college or university course.

The information provided at this level becomes more specific, so it must be adapted to meet the knowledge required of each category of stakeholder. Examples of topics and subject areas that should be provided to each stakeholder group include the following:

- Audit logging and retention
- Development lifecycle security
- Incident handling and response
- Logical access controls

Completion of these basic knowledge courses can be positioned as either elective, where stakeholders can enrol themselves at their leisure to improve their professional development relating to digital forensics, or mandatory, where stakeholders must complete the training to maintain their supporting role of digital forensics.

Functional Knowledge

Taking education and training another level higher, there is a need for stakeholders to have a working and practical knowledge of the digital forensics discipline. Essentially, these individuals must have the skills and competencies necessary to ensure that principles, methodologies, and techniques are upheld in support of the organization's digital forensics readiness program.

Digital forensics requires individuals to have a significant amount of specialized training and skills to thoroughly understand and consistently follow the established scientific fundamentals. The information provided at this level of training is specific to the digital forensics discipline and requires stakeholders to have strong working and practical knowledge. Appendix B, "Education and Professional Certifications," provides a list of higher/post-secondary institutions that offer formal digital forensics education programs.

Professional Certification

Following completion of formalized education, there are several recognized industry associations that offer professional certifications in digital forensics. It is important to keep in mind that professional certifications are designed to test and evaluate an individual's knowledge and experience; they do not provide individuals with in-depth training on digital forensics and information technology (IT) as obtained through formalized education. Professional certifications, or professional designations, provide assurance that an individual is qualified to perform digital forensics.

Appendix B, "Education and Professional Certifications," provides a list of higher or post-secondary institutes that offer formal digital forensics education programs as well as recognized industry associations offering digital forensics professional certifications.

Specialized Knowledge

It wasn't too long ago that digital forensics was considered niche. However, these days if you practice digital forensics you are recognized as somewhat of a generalist in the discipline. With the continuing advancements in technology and how it is being used to support business operations, simply being a digital forensic generalist is no longer practical for most individuals.

Having gained the necessary functional knowledge, the next level of education and training is to become a specialist or professional in a subject area of the digital forensics profession. For this reason, it is common for individuals to expand their knowledge of digital forensics and how it can be integrated with and applied to other disciplines throughout the organization. The following are examples of areas where digital forensic specialization can be achieved:

- *Cybercrime*, which emphasizes applying investigative techniques and methodologies of digital forensics to subject areas including:
  - *Electronic discovery (e-discovery)*, which relates to the discovery, preservation, processing, and production of electronically stored information (ESI) in support of government or litigation matters
  - *Network forensics and analysis*, which relates to the monitoring and analysis of network traffic for the purposes of information gathering, gathering of digital evidence, or intrusion detection
  - *Memory forensics*, which relates to the gathering and analysis of digital information as digital evidence contained within a system's random access memory (RAM)
  - *Cloud forensics*, which, as a subset of network forensics, relates to the gathering and analysis of digital information as digital evidence from cloud computing systems
- *Information assurance*, which emphasizes applying investigative techniques and methodologies of digital forensics to subject areas, including:
  - *Incident handling and response*, which relates to reducing business impact by managing the occurrence of computer security events; this is discussed further in Chapter 13, "Mapping Investigative Workflows."
  - *Threat modeling* builds appropriate countermeasures that effectively reduce business risk impact through the identification and understanding of individual security threats that have the potential to affect business assets, operations, and functions; this is discussed further in Addendum F, "Threat Modeling."
  - *Risk management* is an examination of what, within the organization, could cause harm to assets so that an accurate decision of how to manage the risk can be made; this is discussed further in Addendum E, "Risk Assessment."
  - *Security monitoring* applies analytical techniques to identify unacceptable behavior patterns in the organization's systems and assets to detect potential threats in a more effective and timely manner; this is discussed further in Chapter 12, "Enabling Targeted Monitoring."

Organizational Roles and Responsibilities

In a corporate environment, there are many people beyond digital forensics practitioners involved with supporting their organization's digital forensics lifecycle. These people, such as system support personnel and management, all have distinct roles and responsibilities when it comes to their involvement in digital forensics. Overall, every role played is equally important in ensuring that the organization's digital forensic capabilities operate within established principles, methodologies, or techniques so that evidence will be admissible in a court of law.

The need for separate roles within the digital forensics lifecycle not only guarantees admissibility of evidence, but also helps to support and maintain a separation of duty. Fundamentally, the ability to create distinct roles with respect to digital forensics is subjective to factors such as the size or structure of the organization. Depending on the ability to create these distinct roles, there will be individuals located throughout the organization who will play distinct roles and have varying involvement throughout the digital forensics lifecycle.

Naturally, the responsibilities carried with each role differ because of how the individuals in them will interact and are (in)directly involved in the digital forensics lifecycle. For example, the following are distinct types of roles whose support in an organization's environment is a necessity for the digital forensics lifecycle:

- *Executive sponsor* is an individual within the executive management team, such as a vice president (VP) or senior vice president (SVP), who is ultimately responsible for the organization's digital forensics program.
- *Director* is an individual responsible for directly overseeing the funding and resourcing, including people and technology, of the digital forensics program.
- *Team* is the group directly responsible for the digital forensics program. Within the team, there can be a series of sub-roles depending on the size and arrangement of the organization, including:
  - *Manager or team lead* is an individual responsible for providing task delegation and leadership to team members.
  - *Members* are individuals who are responsible for the execution and delivery of activities and tasks specific to the organization's digital forensics program.
  - *Stakeholders* are business lines, other teams, individuals, or organizations, both internal or external to your organization, that are impacted or have an impact on the digital forensics program.

The Digital Forensics Team

In the example roles identified above, roles on the digital forensics team are played by several individuals who are the core individuals responsible for executing the activities and tasks of a digital forensics program. Titles used to describe distinct roles—specific to the digital forensics team—can be subjective and are commonly used interchangeably.

Roles

Regardless of the title used, individuals who have a direct role on the digital forensics team, in contrast to the organizational roles outlined above, are much more involved in applying and adhering to the scientific principles, methodologies, and techniques of the profession. For example, the following are titles commonly used for the distinct roles within a digital forensics team:

- *Technician* is a role that is responsible for identification, collection, and preservation of evidence at a crime scene, as outlined in the *gathering* phase of the investigative process workflow. In some cases, this role is responsible for gathering and processing volatile data from live systems as evidence. These individuals must be adequately trained in proper evidence handling techniques to establish the chain of custody and guarantee the integrity and authenticity of evidence is preserved. Additionally, it's critical that these individuals have the knowledge and expertise necessary to make informed decision about the order in which volatile data should be gathered and processed.
- *Examiner and analyst* are titles commonly used interchangeably to describe individuals who are responsible for the examination and analysis of evidence after it has been gathered, as illustrated in the *processing* phase of the investigative process workflow. In cases where the role of a technician does not exist, this role will also be responsible for gathering, processing, and handling evidence as described above. In addition to the knowledge and experience required for a technician's role, individuals in this role must also be educated and trained in the use of tools and techniques to interpret the context and content of evidence to determine its relevancy to an investigation. Not only do these individuals need to be strong technically, so that they can accurately decipher the meaning of evidence, they also need to have a sharp analytical mindset that allows them to establish links between evidence and draw factual conclusions.
- *Investigator* is another example of a title that is used. Most often, this title is used in place of analyst or examiner and inherits the scope of responsibilities. However, the responsibilities of this role go beyond just processing evidence and include duties such as working with

internal (e.g., IT support teams) and external (e.g., law enforcement) entities to identify new pieces of evidence relevant to the investigation. Depending on the organization, individuals who occupy this role might also assume the responsibilities of technician and analyst or examiner as noted above. It is important to note that in some jurisdictions the use of the investigator title requires those individuals to have a private investigator license to validate they meet the minimum requirements for maintaining their education and experience in the field of practice.

- *Team lead* is any individual who provides members of the digital forensics team with direction, instruction, and guidance on how to execute their responsibilities. In some cases, this role may not exist because the size of the digital forensics team—or organization—does not warrant having it. Where this role does exist, even though the scope of responsibility for these individuals does not directly include gathering or processing evidence, they can be used to assist in performing an investigation when needed. Because there is this possibility, the team lead needs to be educated and have experience in performing the activities and tasks across all roles of the digital forensics team.

- *Managers*, like team leads, also provide the digital forensics team with direction, instruction, and guidance on how to execute their responsibilities. Also, like the role of team lead, a manager role may not exist in an organization because it is not warranted due to the size of the team. However, a notable difference in comparison to the team lead is that the manager role has expanded leadership responsibilities for the overall success of the digital forensics team, including resourcing and funding. While these individuals do not have direct involvement with the day-to-day execution of the digital forensics program, it is expected that they be educated and knowledgeable about how to consistently uphold the scientific principles, methodologies, and techniques of digital forensics.

Refer to Chapter 2, "Investigative Process Methodology," for more details about the investigative workflow and the order of volatility.

Titles

Just as some of the roles above are interchangeably used to illustrate the separate roles within the digital forensics team, the following titles were not referenced in the above list because of the subtle differences in how they represent an individual's achievement in (non-)technical skills, as discussed in the section below:

- *Practitioner* is an individual who is actively engaged and occupied in the field of digital forensics. These individuals are recognized as a result of their documented qualifications (i.e., diploma or degree) and possess both the technical and non-technical skills to directly support an organization's digital forensics program.

- *Specialist* is any individual who is highly skilled and concentrates on one (or more) focus areas of digital forensics. An argument could be made that the digital forensic discipline can be viewed as a focus area, but given how broad it has become (e.g., computer systems, gaming consoles, mobile devices), using this title is better suited to describe a specific area of digital forensics, such as malware forensics, cloud computing, or e-discovery.
- *Professional* is an individual who has a paid occupation in the digital forensics discipline. Not only are these individuals highly skilled and possess formal education in the technical execution of digital forensics, but in some occupations (e.g., enterprise environment) also have significant non-technical business skills as described later in this chapter.
- *Expert* is an individual who has been authoritatively recognized for knowledge and experience in digital forensics. Applying the word "authoritative" to this title suggests that this title is held by those individuals who have established themselves in a court of law.

As noted above, these three titles do not articulate a function or responsibility; therefore, they are not used to illustrate a role on the digital forensics team. Generally, they are more often used to describe individuals who have gained extensive knowledge and experience in digital forensics.

An Educational Roadmap

Ask around and most likely you'll get unique perspectives about what education means. To some, it means graduating from college or university to earn a degree, diploma, or certificate. To others, it means attending training sessions put on by some third party such as a vendor. And yet, there are those who prefer the self-taught methods using resources at their fingertips (e.g., books, webinars).

A common question posed to those people already in the field of digital forensics is "What type of knowledge and training is needed to get into the field?" The reality is that there is one best way for someone to gain their digital forensics education, acquire new skills, or keep current those skills they already have. Rather than setting out a development plan that people should follow on their educational roadmap, the following sections provide building blocks for several types and levels of education a person can gain.

The intention of the following sections is to provide people with the generalized subject areas for which continuous education and training will provide a catalyst for growing themselves within the digital forensics profession. While the below subject areas contribute to understanding digital forensics principles, methodologies, and techniques, it is important to remember that these topics are pertinent in organizational settings and do not necessarily reflect the knowledge or experience required in law enforcement or other industries.

Technical Knowledge

When developing a digital forensics skill set, the most common type of training provided through education programs (i.e., academic institutions, books) are the technical components. Within this context, the word "technical" isn't used to reference specific information technology, but rather to the practical execution of digital forensics which includes putting into practice its principles, methodologies, and techniques.

Introductory

Entering the field of digital forensics means starting out somewhere. There are volumes of resources, such as books, that provide people with an excellent way of building a foundation for their educational roadmap. As a sample, the following subject areas are essential knowledge for all digital forensics practitioners to have:

- *Investigation principles* are the values that a digital forensics practitioner must consistently follow and apply throughout the investigative process, including forensic soundness, evidence authenticity and integrity, and chain of custody. Refer to Chapter 1, "Understanding Digital Forensics," for further details about the principles of digital forensics.
- *Evidence management* includes the technical, administrative, and physical controls necessary to safeguard digital evidence before, during, and after a digital forensics investigation.
- *Computer systems* are made up of interconnected hardware components that share a central storage system and any number of peripheral devices, such as printers and scanners.
- *Operating systems (OS)* are software programs that are perhaps one of the most important components of a computer systems. Essentially, an OS is a collection of software that manages hardware and performs basic tasks, such as controlling peripheral devices, managing input devices (e.g., keyboards), and scheduling tasks. Recognizing that there are several types of OS software available in the market today (i.e., Microsoft Windows, Apple MacOS, Linux, Unix), at a

minimum a digital forensic practitioner should understand the more popular platforms that are commonly used by consumers and those that are present throughout their organization.

- *File systems* are the methods and structures used by an OS to organize, track, and retrieve data. Recognizing that there are several types of file systems used today (i.e., FAT12/16/32, NTFS, ext2/3/4, iOS), at a minimum a practitioner should understand the more popular platforms that are commonly used by consumers and those that are present throughout their organization.
- *Networking protocols* are the mechanisms by which devices, such as systems, define rules and conventions for communicating with each other.
- *Scripting* is an interpreted programming language designed for integrating and communicating with other programming languages in support of task automation. Recognizing that there are several scripting languages (i.e., BATCH, Visual Basic [VB] Script, Perl, Python), a practitioner should understand at least one scripting language.
- *Legal studies* includes knowledge of the precedence set forth by the rules, standards, and directives of legal systems. Refer to Chapter 16, "Ensuring Legal Review," for further details about the application of law to forensic science.

As a practitioner, these subject areas are considered foundational knowledge required for the technical execution of digital forensic principles, methodologies, and techniques throughout the investigative process workflow, which is discussed further in Chapter 2, "Investigative Process Methodology."

Intermediate

With foundational knowledge acquired, practitioners can decide to further their education by expanding the scope of knowledge beyond those topics directly linked to the execution of digital forensics. The following are examples of subject areas where knowledge gained will enhance a digital forensics practitioner's educational roadmap:

- *Cryptography*: While one of its purposes is to protect the confidentiality of information, it has also been used as a means of hiding—or concealing—data and communications. Knowledge of cryptography's use for security and anti-forensics is valuable when examining and analyzing digital evidence.
- *Mobile devices* have proliferated in the past decade, which has allowed for growth in the mobile workforce community and supported the concept of "always connected, always available." Recognizing that there

are countless manufacturers that have their own proprietary devices (e.g., Apple, Blackberry, Samsung), at a minimum a practitioner should understand the platforms used predominantly throughout the organization.

- *Cyber and security investigations* can encompass a broad scope of digital evidence that must be gathered and processed from systems and applications located throughout the Internet. Also, understanding the different laws, standards, and regulations that govern accessing and gathering evidence is important; refer to Chapter 16, "Ensuring Legal Review," for further details about the application of law to forensic science.
- *Incident response* is the structured approach by which organizations address and manage computer security events. Digital forensics practitioners are key stakeholders throughout the entire methodology.
- *Electronic discovery*, or e-discovery, refers to the use of a structured approach by which organizations identify, gather, and process ESI for producing evidence per legal or compliance requests.
- *Cloud computing* is changing the landscape of how business operations are conducted and how digital evidence is gathered and processed. It is important to be proactive in developing strategies for adapting and expanding their organization's digital forensics capabilities into these environments.
- *Network forensics*, a sub-discipline of digital forensics, consists of monitoring and analyzing the network traffic and communications of computer systems and devices for the purpose of gathering evidence. Like RAM, network forensics largely involves volatile data that is only available for a brief period. The ability to forensically gather digital evidence from networks can help to corroborate and correlate digital evidence from other devices and computer systems.
- *Malware reverse engineering*, as it relates to digital forensics, is the process of analyzing computer systems to (1) identify malicious software, (2) establish conclusions for how it got there, and (3) what changes it caused on the host system. Building this skill requires learning and using a variety of systems and network tools designed to isolate, disassemble, and analyze the properties of malware.

Advanced

Leveraging what was learned previously, this level of education further expands subject areas of other disciplines and professions into the application of digital forensics. The following are subject areas that can elevate a digital forensics practitioner's education to the highest level of technical and practical execution:

- *Systems development,* also referred to as application development, describes the process for planning, creating, testing, and deploying information systems. Knowledge about the system development life cycle (SDLC) is important for practitioners to understand the ways in which systems and applications interact with data.
- *Security architecture* complements enterprise architecture, focusing on the necessities and potential risk involved in certain scenarios or environments throughout the organization. Knowing how and where the implementation of administrative, technical, and physical security control can create greater capabilities for digital forensics is valuable knowledge for a practitioner to have.

Non-Technical Knowledge

For the most part, academic institutions focus more on the technical aspects of digital forensics to provide practitioners with the knowledge and skills necessary to directly support their role and responsibilities. However, it is equally important to balance these technical skills with non-technical (soft) skills. Within this complementary set of non-technical skills come varying levels of knowledge that, depending on a particular educational roadmap, can elevate someone's career to the next level.

Introductory

We already know that getting into the digital forensics profession means starting out somewhere. While there are resources available to provide people with knowledge about these non-technical (soft) skills, perfecting them comes with practice and experience over time. For example, the following subject areas are foundational knowledge for all digital forensic practitioners to have:

- *Time management* is about planning and controlling time spent to effectively accomplish a task or goal. With respect to digital forensics, this means being able to prioritize the tasks and activities required to work through the investigative process methodology and establishing fact-based conclusions.
- *Analytical skills* involve the ability to extract meaning and relevance from masses of data to find hidden patterns and unexpected correlations so that fact-based conclusions can be established. While

learning about analytical styles can be gained academically, perfecting these skills requires practitioners to continuously refine and improve their capabilities.

- *Technical writing* is any form of writing that is used to communicate in a clear and concise manner the findings and conclusions of a digital forensics investigation. It is important to avoid the over-use of technical jargon or slang that can create confusion amongst non-technical readers.
- *Communication skills* are essential to have in any career and are complementary to technical writing skills. This means being able to illustrate complex technical information in a natural, logical business language that is simple to understand.
- *Critical thinking* is a person's ability to remain objective when analyzing digital evidence during an investigation. Possessing this skill is essential for upholding a standard of professional conduct and ethics; refer to Chapter 4, "Ethics and Conduct," for further discussion.

Intermediate

Continuing to build and develop the foundational non-technical skills outlined above, practitioners determined to enhance their educational roadmap can seek to expand skills into new subject areas. As mentioned previously, acquiring a new skill is not a "one and done" process but more of a continuous development plan. In addition to refining and improving existing skills, the following are examples of subject areas where knowledge gained will enhance a digital forensics practitioner's educational roadmap:

- *Interrogation* is a form of interviewing used to obtain information from people during an investigation. This is a skill that can range from simple techniques, such as building rapport, to more advanced techniques, such as deciphering (non-)verbal cues. Being another skill that requires ongoing development, it can elevate a person to the next level of their non-technical career.
- *Interpersonal skills* are used when a person interacts with other people. This skill can be viewed as beneficial in a few ways: the first is in demonstrating leadership and professionalism when getting along with others as a means of getting the job done, and the second is complementary to interrogation (i.e., rapport building) to obtain useful information.
- *Leadership* within an organization could be viewed as either taking on any form of leadership role, such as a team lead or manager, or being able to effectively communicate the importance of digital forensics throughout the organization. Learning how to lead both people and the future of a digital forensics program is essential

knowledge if the education roadmap is to elevate into a director or executive sponsor role.

- *Project management* involves the application of knowledge, skills, methodologies, and techniques to complete defined activities to meet pre-defined requirements. Project management is related to time management, and possessing this skill expands a practitioner's ability to effectively execute (multiple) investigations by consistently following the same investigative process methodology.

Advanced

When an educational roadmap is intended to grow someone into the role of director, or eventually into executive sponsorship, the focus turns from skills directly related to digital forensics and moves into subject areas that are intended to bring about heightened business-centric proficiencies. In addition to refining and improving existing skills, the following are examples of subject areas where knowledge gained can move a digital forensics practitioner into a management role:

- *Conflict resolution* is how two or more parties find a solution to a disagreement between them. For the most part, this skill is better suited for a leadership role (e.g., team lead or director), and other skills such as negotiation and interrogation are more beneficial to other digital forensics roles (e.g., investigator).
- *Budget management* involves adhering to corporate protocols to analyze, organize, and provide oversight to the costs and expenditures of the digital forensics program. Knowledge in this subject area is critical for ensuring sustained delivery of operations and continued growth.
- *Resource management* involves the deployment and allocation of people when and where required. In the context of a digital forensics program, this skill builds upon the previous leadership knowledge to move into more of a management role.
- *strategic mindset* demonstrates that you are aware of the importance of digital forensics capabilities for an organization. This proactive approach includes an aptitude for establishing and maintaining strategic relationships, building and nurturing strategic relationships, and applying previous skills towards strategic influencing.

The subject areas outlined above, both technical and non-technical (soft), are building blocks of the knowledge and experience someone would need to have as part of their educational roadmap. However, one should recognize that all organizations are different and that some of the intermediate or advanced topics may or may not be applicable in that specific environment. But this doesn't mean these items shouldn't be considered for someone's educational roadmap. Progressing through the educational roadmap is not a simple task; it requires people to invest themselves by dedicating their time and effort into furthering their career.

Piecing it all together, as new knowledge and experience are gained as people progress through their educational roadmap, naturally they will be better equipped to evolve their role within digital forensics into something greater, such as from analyst to investigator. Using the map illustrated in Figure 14.2, the relationships between the multiple elements of the education roadmap have been laid out in a manner that shows how an individual's competencies, both technical and non-technical, represent the roles and titles within the digital forensics profession.

Portrayed in the map above, the following methodology was applied as criteria for representing both the role and title of individuals as they increase their technical and non-technical competencies throughout the educational roadmap.

- The x-axis represents the technical knowledge of an individual starting with the introductory skills (left) and progressing into the advanced skills (right). Progressing on this axis, as characterized by the increase in technical skills, is depicted by the alphabetic representation of the digital forensics role found in the accompanying legend.
- The y-axis represents the non-technical knowledge of an individual starting with the introductory skills (bottom) and progressing into the advanced skills (top). Progressing on this axis, as characterized by the increase in non-technical skills, is depicted by the color scheme representing the digital forensic titles.

Digital Forensics Experts

Absent from the map above is the use of the title *expert*. As discussed previously, we understand that an *expert* is any individual who has been authoritatively recognized for knowledge and experience in digital forensics. The need to be authoritatively recognized implies that the use of the *expert* title is then respectively held by individuals who have established themselves in the digital forensics profession and have been granted use of the title by a person or group qualified to do so. In turn, this begs the question of "Who is qualified to decide whether an expert is really an expert?"

For the longest time, there was an ongoing debate about whether it makes sense that the legal system, judges and juries, is the authoritative body

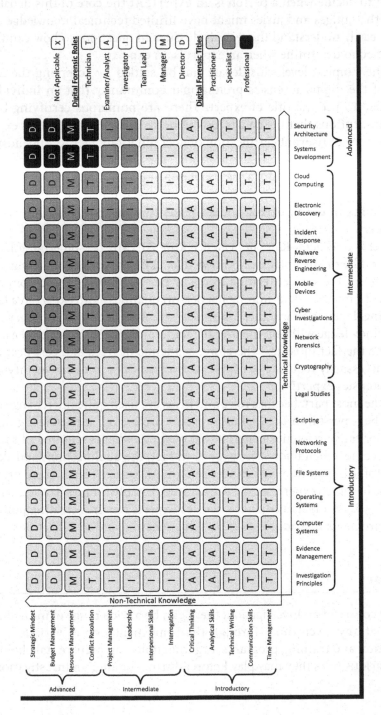

Figure 14.2 Educational roadmap.

qualified to decide when a person is an expert. At the core of this debate is the fact that judges and juries might have limited technical knowledge and may not easily understand the technical issues in question; so how can they be qualified to determine when an expert is an expert?

At the simplest level, this debate can be settled by accepting the consensus of the digital forensics professional community that an individual is qualified to use the title of expert. There are numerous certifying bodies and institutions that the courts look upon to demonstrate that an expert has some type of relevant certification or accreditation; refer to Appendix B, "Education and Professional Certifications," for a list of digital forensics certifications. Yet, doubt can still arise about holding a credential as a qualifying means of being an expert because the courts are simply placing their trust and reliability in the certifying bodies or institutions to qualify individuals as an expert.

Under *U.S. Federal Rules of Evidence Rule 702*, any person is qualified as an expert if he or she possesses "knowledge, skill, experience, training, and education" on the subject relating to his or her testimony beyond common experience. However, determining if a person qualifies as an expert in a legal proceeding depends on whether his or her "scientific, technical, or other specialized knowledge will help the trier of fact to understand the evidence or to determine the fact in issue." Therefore, academic degrees and certifications are not necessarily requisite to expertise. So how does someone qualify as a digital forensics expert?

For the most part, because roles and titles are used quite interchangeably to describe a person in the digital forensics profession, it is challenging to find authoritative reference material that outlines what is required of someone to become a digital forensics expert. In fact, the qualifications and skills required of a digital forensics expert remain an issue because there are no standards by which expertise can be measured. Establishing a set of standards that qualify individuals as digital forensics experts requires creating policies and requirements that addresses expected education and qualifications.

Summary

Over the course of an investigation, there can be a wide range of individuals involved at any given time. Through the implementation of various levels of education and training programs, organizations can prepare stakeholders for the various roles they may play before, during, or after an investigation.

Maintaining Evidence-Based Reporting   15

Introduction

Conducting an investigation is more than simply supporting the business risk scenarios discussed in Chapter 7. From conducting an investigation, organizations must also be able to provide answers to questions—of who, where, what, when, why, and how—and demonstrate how their digital evidence supports the credibility of these answers.

Achieving these goals requires that forensic viability of digital evidence, including the authenticity and integrity of the data, is maintained by following the steps outlined throughout this book, such as the need for governance over the collection, handling, and storage of digital evidence. Furthermore, by applying an evidence-based methodology for managing an investigation, organizations will be in a better position to establish the credibility of the answers to questions as they arise.

Importance of Factual Reports

Having processed all digital evidence, a formal report must be created to communicate the results of the investigation. However, one of the biggest downfalls of any investigation is deficiencies in the final report. Ultimately, if decision makers cannot understand and interpret the information detailed within the report, the entire investigation could result in failure.

As with any investigation, organizations should always conduct themselves while keeping in mind that the matter will continue on to legal proceedings. Therefore, creating a formal report should be done not only to share information within the context of the organization, but also with the intention of presenting evidence as testimony in a court of law.

Required under Rule 26 of the *U.S. Federal Rules of Civil Procedure*, any person(s) who will be presenting evidence as testimony has a duty to disclose a written report.

These reports must disclose all "facts or data" considered by the person(s) during the investigation, the basis of how they established these "facts or data," and the information that was used in order to arrive at these "facts or data."

It is important to understand that Rule 26 defines the intent to exclude theories or opinions and the need for creating a credible investigative report that limits the disclosure of "facts or data" to only information that is "material of a factual nature."

Types of Reports

Completed during the presentation stage of the digital forensics readiness model, discussed further in Chapter 2, investigative reports are essential in communicating facts about the information analyzed to various stakeholders, such as presenting evidence as legal testimony. As the first step to creating a report, it is important that the authors identify the target audience and the purpose for creating the report.

Identifying the target audience is particularly important. Authors need to ensure that the content of the report is structured to be clear, concise, easy to follow, and understandable to the target audience. For example, where a report is being provided to management, the authors should consider accompanying any technical content with reference or educational materials to clarify or further elaborate this information so as not to alienate the reader.

With the audience determined, the next step is to decide which type of report is required. Typically, investigative reports can be grouped into one of the following categories:

- *Verbal formal* reports are typically quite structured and are commonly used to present information to management or in front of a jury without producing any form of document. An important consideration when using this presentation style is the amount of time available to communicate the facts. If the pace is quick, there is a chance that the audience will not clearly understand the information; alternatively, if the pace of delivering the report is too slow, the author may not have enough time to share important pieces of information contained within the report. Authors must ensure that they organize the presentation of information in a way that clearly and concisely focuses on the facts of the investigation.

- *Verbal informal* reports are typically less structured and are commonly used to present information to management or in an attorney's office without producing any form of document. With respect to using this style for management communication, it is commonly done as an "elevator speech" where the facts of the investigation need to be shared quickly. Alternatively, this presentation style can also be used when communicating with attorneys where there is a need to reduce the amount of written information that can later be discovered as part of a legal proceeding. Authors must ensure that they are prepared to deliver this style of report by focusing on key relevant and meaningful facts of the investigation to avoid confusion or misinterpretation.

- *Written formal* reports are typically quite structured and result in the creation of a document that will be used to present information to management or as part of legal proceedings. Regardless of who the audience is, this style of report is considered legally discoverable and can be used in a court of law. These reports require authors to pay a great deal of attention to detail and ensure that the report is focused specifically on communicating credible and factual information only. When writing these reports, it is recommended that the authors use natural language, as discussed below, and not use words or grammar that are difficult for readers to understand. The arrangement of these reports is discussed in the section below.

- *Written informal* reports are considered high-risk because the information being documented might not yet be proven as factual to the investigation. If this style of report must be produced, it is important for organizations to understand that these documents are discoverable in a court of law. Instead of making preliminary statements about information that may not be factual, authors should include the same level of information provided in the verbal informal report discussed above.

Creating Understandable Reports

A written report should flow just as naturally and logically as we think or speak. Each related fact and piece of information should be grouped together into a single paragraph and build upon each other from beginning to end.

The use of jargon and slang should be avoided at all times. Where technical terms need to be used, they must be defined using natural language as part of a taxonomy, which is discussed further in Addendum D,

"Building a Taxonomy." Additionally, when using acronyms or abbreviations, they should be written in full expression upon first use or defined as part of the taxonomy.

Events being communicated occurred before the report was written, which means the authors should primarily write in the past tense but can decide to change tense to use either present or future where appropriate.

Arranging Written Reports

Regardless of whether the investigation will proceed to a court of law, all investigative reports should be structured to communicate relevant and factual information. At a minimum, authors should ensure that the following components are consistently found in every type of report that is being presented:

- Accurate description of all events/incident details is provided
- Report content is clear, concise, and understandable to relevant decision makers
- Content is deemed admissible and credible in a court of law
- Does not portray opinions or information that are open to misinterpretation
- Contains sufficient information to establish factual relevance of conclusions
- Is completed and presented in a timely manner

With verbal reports, whether formal or informal, the intention is to speak about the facts of the investigation. Alternatively, when using a written report the authors should ensure that they follow a consistent approach in the layout and presentation of the facts. In addition to ensuring the above noted goals are achieved, a standardized template should be used to establish a repeatable standard for how facts and information will be presented.

Understanding that the inclusion of information in a written formal report is subjective to the organization's needs, the required components of a standardized report template should include the following:

- *Executive summary*: The sub-sections included within the executive summary are intended to provide readers with a high-level summary of the investigation. Most commonly, this section might be all that management reads to get an understanding of the investigation. For this reason, it is important that the information contained in these sub-sections be written in a natural and business language that does not include unnecessary technical details.

- *Background*: Describes the event(s) and/or incident(s) that brought about the need for the investigation, the objectives of performing the investigation, as well as who authorized the investigation to be conducted.
- *Summary of findings*: Summarizes the significant findings as a result of the investigation.
- *Conclusions*: Establishes credible answers to questions that came about from the investigation.
- *Investigative details*: The sub-sections included within the investigative details are intended to provide readers with detailed information about the investigation. While the information contained within places emphasis on the digital evidence, it must be focused on detailing the credibility of facts as experienced during the investigation.
- *Chain of evidence*: Describes the continuity of all digital evidence related to where it was identified, the techniques used to seize it, and methods used to transport it.
- *Gathering of evidence*: Specifies the methodologies, tools, and equipment used to collect and preserve digital evidence.
- *Processing of evidence*: Specifies the methodologies, tools, and equipment used to examine digital evidence.
- *Analysis of evidence*: Details the meaningful, relevant, and factual findings from analyzing digital evidence.
- *Addendums*: The sub-sections included within the investigative details are intended to provide readers with in-depth supplementary information that supports the findings outlined in the previous section. Examples of supplementary information that can be included are:
  - Tables listing full pathnames of significant digital evidence
  - The total amount of digital evidence reviewed during the investigation
  - Keywords and terms used and results of string searching

A template for creating written formal reports has been provided as a reference in the "Templates" section of this book.

Inculpatory and Exculpatory Evidence

While the objective of performing an investigation is to determine the root cause or identify a culprit, all conclusions derived from the analysis of evidence must be factual and credible. However as conclusions are being drawn, it may become clear that there is inculpatory (indication of guilt) and exculpatory (indication of innocence) evidence that needs to be considered further before any factual and credible conclusions can be established.

The totality of all digital evidence, whether inculpatory or exculpatory, is an important consideration when establishing credible facts. The suppression of exculpatory evidence, which indicates innocence, is a violation of U.S. Supreme Court rules and can result in implausible facts. Organizations must ensure that they have clearly defined in their governance documentation, such as standard operating procedures (SOP), how to handle exculpatory evidence when it is encountered.

Brady v. Maryland 373 U.S. 83 (1963), is a milestone in court rulings that has set precedence for establishing the requirement to disclose all exculpatory evidence.

The state of Maryland prosecuted Brady for murder, an accusation to which he claimed a companion had committed the actual crime. The prosecution willfully withheld from the defendant the companion's written statement by which he confessed to committing the murder.

Under the Brady rule, named after this matter, the Supreme Court ruled that suppression of evidence that is favorable to a defendant is a violation of due process and established that evidence of information that proves innocence must be disclosed.

Summary

When communicating the findings of an investigation, it is important that reports are created to focus specifically on the credible facts that have been established during the investigation. Regardless of whether findings from digital evidence demonstrate guilt or innocence, as long as reports are an accurate representation of the event(s), they are considered relevant and credible.

Ensuring Legal Review 16

Introduction

At any time during the forensic investigation workflow, as discussed in Chapter 2, "Investigative Process Methodology," it may be necessary to obtain legal advice regarding the current state of the case. This advice will provide the investigative team with a level of assurance that either (1) there is credible digital evidence to support legal proceedings or (2) the collected digital evidence does not support factual conclusions about the event(s) or incident(s).

Where the legal team determines that the strength of existing digital evidence is adequate, the investigation has met the criteria for progressing into formal legal proceedings. However, where the legal team determines that strength of existing digital evidence is deficient, the investigative team must work with the legal advisors to identify what additional actions and activities are required to progress into formal legal proceedings.

The Role of Technology in Crime

In relation to crime, technology can play multiple roles that can then be used to gather and process several types of evidence. Depending on how much digital evidence is contained within any given piece of technology, it may or may not be authorized for seizure and subsequent collection as evidence as part of an investigation. When technology plays a significant role in criminal activity, it is much easier to justify its seizure so evidence can be processed.

Through the years, several authors have tried to develop a standard classification scheme for the distinct roles technology can play in crime. In the 1970s, Donn Parker was one of the first individuals to recognize the potential seriousness of technology-related crimes, which led him to create the following four categories, which remain relevant today:

1. *Object of crime* applies when technology is affected by the crime (e.g., when a device is stolen or damaged).
2. *Subject of crime* applies when technology is in the environment in which the crime was committed (e.g., system infected by malware).

3. *Tool of crime* applies when technology is used to conduct or plan crime (e.g., illegally forged documents).
4. *Symbol of crime* applies when technology is used to deceive or intimidate (e.g., falsified investment profits).

Distinguishing when technology plays one role or another is important on many levels. For example, knowing when technology is an object or subject is important because, from the perspective of the practitioner, this demonstrates intent of the perpetrator. Also, when technology is a tool, like a gun or other weapon, this could lead to additional charges or increased punishment. However, although technology as a symbol may seem irrelevant because no actual system is involved in the crime, when categorized under this role technology is represented as an idea, a belief, or any entity that can be useful in understanding motivations for committing the crime. As an example, the chief executive officer (CEO) is a symbol of her organization and as such can become either the victim or target of crime because of what she symbolizes.

In 1994, the U.S. Department of Justice (USDOJ) developed its own categorization scheme that made a clear distinction between hardware, being physical components, and information, being data and programs that are stored or transmitted. It is important to note that with a single crime there is the potential to fall into one or more of these categories, for example, when a system is used as the instrument of crime, it may also contain information as evidence. The categories proposed by the USDOJ include:

- *Hardware as contraband or fruits of* crime, that is, any item that is illegal to be possessed or was obtained illegally
- *Hardware as an instrumentality*, that is, when technology played a role in committing the crime, such as a gun or weapon
- *Hardware as evidence* (i.e., scanners with unique characteristics that can be used and linked to the creation of digitized content)
- *Information as contraband or fruits of crime*, that is, computer programs that can encrypt content to conceal evidence
- *Information as an instrumentality*, that is, programs used to break into other systems
- *Information as evidence*, that is, digital artifacts revealing a user's activities on a system

In 2002, the USDOJ updated the categorization scheme as part of the publication titled "Searching and Seizing Computers and Obtaining Electronic Evidence in Criminal Investigations." The most notable difference in the updated categorization was the realization that data and program content, not the hardware, is usually the target of the crime; but even when information is the target, collecting the hardware may be required.

Laws and Regulations

In many geographic regions, there are laws and regulations that dictate how technology can be used, such as information privacy, anti-spamming, and data exporting. Designed to connect technology with risk, these laws and regulations can be generally grouped into one of the following categories. Online references related to the following types of laws and regulations can be found in the *Resources* section at the end of this book.

Information Technology (IT) Law

Unbeknownst to some, most activities on the Internet, whether for business or personal use, are governed by some type of law. *Information technology law*, otherwise referred to as *technology law* or *IT law*, are those laws that allow legal systems to regulate the collection, storage, and transmission of digital information within the boundaries of their jurisdictions, such as:

- *Payment Card Industry Data Security Standard (PCI DSS)*: Originally introduced in 2008, and last revised in 2016, these standards cover both technical and operational system components included in or connected to cardholder data (i.e., credit cards).
- *Sarbanes–Oxley Act (SOX)*: Introduced in 2002, this legislation is mandatory for all organizations to follow. It regulates financial practice and corporate governance.
- *Health Insurance Portability and Accountability Act (HIPAA)*: Passed by the U.S. Congress in 1996, this legislation mandates industry-wide standards for the protection and confidential handling of protected health information to reduce fraud and abuse.
- *General Data Protection Regulation (GDPR)*: Passed by the European Parliament in 2016, this legislation addresses the unified protection of personal data outside of the European Union with the primary objectives of (1) giving control over their personal information back to citizens and residents and (2) simplifying the regulatory environment for businesses to operate internationally.

In 2014, the U.S. Securities and Exchange Commission (SEC) laid charges against the chief executive officer (CEO) and chief financial officer (CFO) of a Florida-based computer equipment company for misrepresenting to external auditors and shareholders the state of its internal controls over financial reporting.

As required through SOX, a management report describing the internal controls over financial reporting is required and must be included in the annual report. This management report must be signed by both the CEO and CFO as a means of confirming they have disclosed all significant deficiencies and certifying the information in the management report is accurate.

Through an administrative proceeding, it was discovered that the CEO and CFO withheld information about deficiencies, the circumvention of inventory controls, and improper handling of accounts receivable and inventory recognition.

"Corporate executives have an obligation to take the Sarbanes–Oxley disclosure and certification requirements very seriously," said Scott W. Friestad, associate director in the SEC's Enforcement Division.

Cyberlaw or Internet Law

Internet law, or *cyberlaw*, refers to those laws and regulations that govern issues involving the use of the Internet. Claiming that there are laws that can achieve this form of regulation is somewhat of a stretch today because such laws would struggle to keep the international and volatile nature of the Internet in check. While a few international laws and regulation exist, the Internet is one of the most complex landscapes because it is not geographically bound and national laws do not apply globally across all countries and regions, such as:

- *U.S. Electronic Communications Privacy Act*: Originally introduced in 1986, this act applies to email, telephone conversations, and data stored electronically to protect communications when they are being created, when they are in transit, and when they are stored on computer systems. This act has since been amended by the Communications Assistance for Law Enforcement Act (CALEA) of 1994, the USA PATRIOT Act (2001), the USA PATRIOT reauthorization acts (2006), and the Foreign Intelligence Surveillance Act (FISA) Amendments Act (2008).

- *EU ePrivacy Act*: Also known as Directive 2002/68/EC, this 2002 act defines rules to ensure security in the processing of personal data, the notification of personal data breaches, and the confidentiality of communications. It also bans unsolicited communications where the user has not given consent.
- *Philippine (PH) Cybercrime Prevention Act*: Officially recorded as Republic Act No. 10175 in 2012, this legislation addresses legal issues concerning online interactions and the Internet, such as cybersquatting, cybersex, identity theft, and illegal access to data.

In 2006, law enforcement conducted a series of raids throughout central Sweden where they seized several servers and other computer equipment involved in operating the file-sharing site known as The Pirate Bay (TPB).

In 2009, four individuals involved with operating TPB were put on trial for allowing its users to download copyrighted materials through their services and software offerings. The defense argued that the activities of these four individuals are legal under Swedish copyright laws because TPB did not host copyrighted content; it simply acted as a search engine to direct its users to locations where they could download music and films.

As part of the ruling, it was ordered that TPB's site be shut down.

Computer Law

Perhaps the most common type of technology-related law, *computer law* is an ever-evolving area of the legal system that has grown mostly as result of increased use of technology to commit crimes. Areas of interest for *computer laws* include legalities such as file sharing, intellectual property, privacy, and electronic signatures, such as:

- *United Kingdom (UK) Computer Misuse Act*: Enacted in 1990, this law introduced three criminal offenses related to computer crimes:
  1. Unauthorized access to computer material
  2. Unauthorized access with intent to commit or facilitate commission of further offenses
  3. Unauthorized acts with intent to impair, or with recklessness as to impairing, operation of computers and other related equipment
- *Australian (AU) Cybercrime Act*: Enacted in 2001, this law introduced criminal offenses related to computer crimes:

477.1: Unauthorized access, modification, or impairment with intent to commit a serious offense

477.2: Unauthorized modification of data to cause impairment

477.3: Unauthorized impairment of electronic communication

478.1: Unauthorized access to, or modification of, restricted data

478.2: Unauthorized impairment of data held on a computer disk or similar equipment

478.3: Possession or control of data with intent to commit a computer offense

478.4: Producing, supplying, or obtaining data with intent to commit a computer offense

Between 1999 and 2000, at least forty large U.S. companies—such as Online Information Bureau (OIB), eBay, and Speakeasy—experienced similar attacks where perpetrators hacked into their networks and then attempted to extort money. From a digital forensics investigation, it was determined that Internet traffic for all of these attacks originated from a single internet protocol (IP) address in Russia. Through further investigation, the Federal Bureau of Investigation (FBI) identified Alexey Ivanov as the perpetrator of these activities.

In 2000, the FBI constructed a false company called Invita Security which they used as a front for inviting Ivanov to interview for a job. He was accompanied by his companion Vasiliy Gorshkov, and the pair was interviewed by Invita, where it was explained that the company was looking for hackers that could break into the network of potential customers in an effort to persuade those companies to hire Invita.

Ivanov and Gorshkov were charged with several crimes, including computer fraud, conspiracy, hacking, and extortion. A move was made to dismiss the indictment, claiming that the court lacked jurisdiction because the pair was physically in Russia when the offenses were committed, so they could not be charged with violations under U.S. law. The U.S. court denied the motion on the basis that the intended and actual effects of the criminals' actions occurred within the United States and because the statutes under which charges were laid already extended extraterritorially; the U.S. Patriot Act increased the scope of the Computer Fraud and Abuse Act to expressly cover systems outside of the United States.

Both Ivanov and Gorshkov pled guilty to the charges and were sentenced to a U.S. prison.

Legal Precedence

Within the legal system, a precedent is any legal case that establishes a rule subsequently used when deciding a similar issue of fact. Within some legal systems, decisions made within the higher courts (e.g., Supreme Court) are mandatory and must be followed by lower courts; this is also known as *binding precedent*. On the opposite end of the spectrum, decisions made in lower-level courts are not binding to higher courts. However, there are times when higher courts will adopt these decisions because of their importance; this is known as *persuasive precedent*. Every once and a while, a decision made by the courts will be so significant that it establishes a new legal principle or changes an existing law; this is referred to as a *landmark decision*. When a decision is made by courts at the same level, while it should be carefully considered, it is not mandatory that it be followed.

Brady Rule: Inculpatory and Exculpatory Evidence

One of the main goals of conducting an investigation is to establish factual conclusions that are based on credible evidence. With the totality of evidence taken into consideration, practitioners may encounter specific findings that need to be assessed further before factual conclusions can be drawn. Of importance, practitioners need to pay special attention when either of the following types of evidence exists:

- *Inculpatory evidence* is any evidence that demonstrates, or tends to show, a person's involvement in an act that establishes an indication of guilt. For example, a person uses his corporate email account to send confidential customer data to his friend, and that act is flagged in security monitoring technologies; this could be considered inculpatory evidence.
- *Exculpatory evidence* is any evidence that is favorable to a person and that exonerates, or tends to exonerate, involvement in an act that establishes an indication of innocence. Following the example above, through the analysis of electronically stored information (ESI) it was identified that unauthorized access to the person's email was gained to send the confidential customer data through email; this could be considered exculpatory evidence.

It is important to know that the suppression of exculpatory evidence is a violation of court rules and can lead to implausible facts. In 1963, U.S. court rulings in the matter of *Brady v. Maryland 373 U.S. 83* were a milestone in setting a precedence for disclosing exculpatory evidence. In a statement, Brady went on record claiming that he was innocent and that his friend had committed the crime. However, the state of Maryland intentionally suppressed a written statement from the friend that contained a confession to committing the murder. As result, the *Brady rule* was created: suppression of evidence favorable to a person is a violation of due process, and evidence that proves innocence must be disclosed.

Frye versus Daubert Standard: General Acceptance Testing

The advancements in and adoption of technology over the past fifty years has allowed for increased capabilities to apply new scientific techniques for gathering, processing, and presenting digital evidence. However, use of these techniques can provide opportunity to challenge the results and raise concern around its effect on the judicial process.

Within the context of criminal law, there is a need for the admissibility of evidence submitted during trial to be scientifically demonstrated as result of proper validation and verification testing. Traditionally, courts have resolved the need for general acceptance testing by applying rulings of the matter involving *U.S. v. Frye, 293 F. 1013 (D.C. Cir. 1923)*. During this trial, a lie detector test was used to support the defendant's claim that he was telling the truth when he denied committing murder. However, the court ruled that evidence was inadmissible because the scientific principles upon which the lie detector test was based were not "sufficiently established to have gained general acceptance in the particular field in which it belongs." As a result, the *Frye standard, Frye test,* or *general acceptance test* became the standard by which scientific evidence and the expert opinion of scientific technique is legally admissible only where it has been generally accepted in the relevant scientific community. The Frye standard had precedence for many years, until it was superseded by the *Daubert standard*.

The Daubert standard came about in 1993 as result of a U.S. Supreme Court decision in the matter of *Daubert v. Merrell Dow Pharmaceuticals, 509 U.S. 579*. Through this ruling, it was identified that *Federal Rules of Evidence 702* did not incorporate a general acceptance test for assessing whether the testimony of scientific experts was based on reasoning or scientific methodology that was properly applied to facts. Furthermore, the court outlined that evidence based on innovative or unusual knowledge is only admissible after it has been established as reliable and scientifically valid. To meet the requirements under this ruling, the Daubert standard was created where specific criteria were established for determining the reliability of scientific techniques as follows:

1. Has the theory or technique in question undergone empirical testing?
2. Has the theory or technique been subjected to peer review and publication?

3. Does the theory or technique have any known or potential error rate?
4. Do standards exist, and are they maintained, for the control of the theory or technique's operation?
5. Has the theory or technique received general acceptance in the relevant scientific community?

Under the Daubert standard, for ESI to be legally admissible as evidence, documented testing and experimentation must be completed to demonstrate repeatable and reproducible results. Achieving this legal standard means that organizations must ensure that all tools and equipment used while investigators are interacting with the evidence meet the above criteria as demonstrated through proper validation and verification testing.

Jurisdiction

Jurisdiction is the power, or right, of a legal system (i.e., court, law enforcement) to exercise its authority in deciding over a (1) person, relating to the authority for trying individuals as a defendant; (2) subject matter, relating to authority originating from the country's laws and regulations; or (3) territory, relating to the geographic area where a court has authority to decide. In some cases, depending on the crime committed, concurrent jurisdiction can exist where two different legal systems have simultaneous authority over the same case.

In the simplest of scenarios, a legal matter can be tried in the location (i.e., country, region, district) where the crime took place. However, with the ways in which technology, such as the Internet, has an extensive global reach and crimes are committed using this delivery channel spanning several countries, it has become somewhat challenging to determine where to prosecute. In cases when there is contention over where a case should be tried, the jurisdiction needs to be assessed and alternatives considered.

Although modern technology adds an additional layer of complexity to issues of jurisdiction, international courts are becoming more familiar with laws and regulations relating to technology and are making more informed decisions about which legal system has jurisdiction.

Technology Counselling

For the legal team to provide educated and accurate advisement on the current state of an investigation, not only will they need to know laws around evidence admissibility, they will also need to be knowledgeable in applicable information technology (IT), cyberlaws, and computing laws. This requires that legal advisors be trained and are experienced so that they are readily equipped to provide appropriate counsel in response to digital evidence being presented as part of an investigation report, as discussed in Chapter 15, "Maintaining Evidence-Based Reporting."

As an example, an information technology (IT) attorney is an individual who is educated and knowledgeable in legal matters as they relate to technology. In addition to having a law degree, these attorneys should be trained and knowledgeable in several areas of technology to provide the organization with support in terms of:

- Drafting, negotiating, interpreting, and maintaining (where needed) technology-related documentation (e.g., agreements, contracts, reports)
- Ensuring digital evidence is gathered, stored, and handled in compliance with applicable privacy policies, regulations, and laws
- Providing high quality, specialized, and practical advice for how to proceed with investigative matters

Obtaining Legal Advice

With legal resources trained and educated in appropriate cyberlaws, organizations are equipped to determine if the findings of an investigation are credible enough to be upheld in a court of law or if additional actions are required. Throughout the investigation, legal advice could be required to facilitate decision making related to the following issues:

Constraints

Laws and regulations exist that impose controls over the proper and effective use of digital evidence during an investigation. Generally, the three areas where legal advice can be provided are:

- Security controls resulting from laws and/or regulations that set a precedent to restrict the necessary identification and disclosure of information protected as privileged or confidential
- Practices governing the identification and disclosure of information within a reasonable timeframe when formal legal proceedings have been filed
- Rules of evidence on the admissibility of information for legal proceedings

Disputes

Depending on the nature of business performed, organizations can face commercial disputes over contractual commitments and obligations.

When these disputes involve external entities such as business partners, competitors, shareholders, suppliers, or customers, consultation with the legal team is required to advise and guide the organization towards resolution.

Employees

The purpose of conducting a forensic investigation is not to find fault or blame in the actions of an employee. However, where an investigation reveals credible facts about the involvement of an employee, based on the nature of the employee's actions a decision must be made on the most appropriate course of action to deal with the employee. Through consultation with the legal team, organizations can ensure that when it comes time to take action and deal with the employee, they do not go beyond the boundaries of their authority or violate any legal rights that could result in unwanted liabilities.

Liabilities

At any point during the investigation an action, circumstance, or event might be identified which could reasonably be expected to result in some form of legal action against the organization, such as a breach of customer information. When this occurs, the investigative team should involve legal resources to determine how to properly manage the situation and the best course of action to take (e.g., engaging public and corporate affairs to formally manage information sharing, contacting law enforcement due to the involvement of criminal actions).

Prosecution

As digital evidence is being analyzed, investigators work to correlate and corroborate different sources of digital evidence that might lead to credible findings where prosecution and/or punishment, both internal and external, are possible. In these circumstances, involving the legal team could improve the likelihood of the organization getting restitution for any losses they experienced or ensure that claims (i.e., insurance) are proper substantiated.

Communication

One possible outcome of a successful cyber-attack could be the unintentional or malicious exfiltration of sensitive and/or confidential information (e.g., personally identifiable information [PII]). In conjunction with other teams within the organization (e.g., privacy, public and corporate affairs), legal can assist in assessing the severity of the information disclosure, as well as the impact it has on partners, customers, and/or investors, and establish when/if the notification of the data exposure must be distributed.

Involving Law Enforcement

Depending on the severity and impact to the organization, a decision could be made to contact appropriate law enforcement agencies to further assist with the investigation. While a decision to involve law enforcement could help to identify whether organized crime is involved, or to engage law enforcement personnel in other jurisdictions, it is important that organizations understand that they could be required to surrender control of the investigation.

Summary

At any point during an investigation, it may be necessary to obtain legal advice regarding the current state of the case. Making these decisions requires that attorneys who will be involved throughout the forensics investigation be trained and educated in applicable laws and regulations to ensure that accurate and timely legal counsel is provided to determine if sufficient credible facts exist or if additional evidence is required to make an informed decision about the investigative findings.

Accomplishing Digital Forensic Readiness

17

Introduction

For the most part, digital forensics investigations are still being performed in reaction to an event or incident where organizations must work quickly to gather and process digital evidence. Ultimately, the availability of relevant and meaningful digital evidence is a critical requirement to effectively manage business risk.

When conducting investigations in reactive mode, there is increased risk that the evidence necessary to establish credible facts and conclusions may not exist. Where organizations have identified opportunities to proactively gather digital evidence in anticipation of an event or incident, they will be better equipped to manage the impact of an event or incident, support litigation matters, or demonstrate regulatory compliance.

Digital forensics readiness is the ability of an organization to proactively maximize their prospective use of electronically stored information (ESI). By following a systematic and proactive approach to gather and preserve potential digital evidence, the added value of a digital forensics readiness program will be realized through reduced investigative cost and gains in operational efficiencies.

Maintain a Business-Centric Focus

One of the most significant barriers to implementing digital forensics readiness is that organizations don't effectively communicate their business risks to those who work with their IT systems. Essentially, making progress towards a successful implementation means following an approach established from a risk-based methodology.

As discussed in Chapter 1 cybercrime continues to evolve as technology increasingly becomes more deeply entrenched in both our business and personal lives. In response to this evolution, the traditional "wall-and-fortress" approach continues to focus on technology aspects where each specific threat is addressed as it emerges. A successful digital forensics readiness implementation requires organizations to ensure their approach is adequately balanced to understand the business reasons (who should be involved under what circumstances) for executing this program to properly and sufficiently support its technical elements (how do go about performing forensics).

Don't Reinvent the Wheel

Even if not formally acknowledged, many organizations already perform some activities, such as proactively gathering and preserving ESI, relative to a digital forensics readiness program. The systematic and proactive approach achieved from digital forensic readiness is complementary to many business operations and functions within an organization, such as:

- Enhancing the overall effectiveness of managing business risk;
- Demonstrating the organization's due diligence in meeting legal and/or regulatory requirements;
- Determining the need for preserving digital evidence in support of business functions such as incident response and business continuity; and
- Improving identification and detection of security events to mitigate potential impact.

Integrating the elements of digital forensic readiness should not have to be a process that is started from the ground up. Included throughout this book is a collection of industry best practices, references, methodologies, and techniques that can be used to achieve digital forensic readiness. The investment in time, effort, and resources to accomplish digital forensic readiness must be focused on what is required for its successful implementation, and not on re-creating materials that are available for use.

Understand Costs and Benefits

Implementing a digital forensics readiness program requires organizations to follow the systematic methodology outlined throughout this book. Decisions to skip, substitute, or not invest the required amount of time, effort, and resources into the digital forensics readiness methodology will most certainly result in a failed, incomplete, or misaligned digital forensics readiness program.

For these reasons, it is extremely important that organizations take their time to fully understand how digital forensics readiness creates value in mitigating business risks and what bearing it will have on their budgetary needs.

As found throughout this book, the assessment of costs versus benefits is not limited to just one aspect of digital forensics readiness and should be a recurring process to ensure that the goals of the program are achieved at a reasonable cost.

Summary

Like how organizations understand the importance and need for having proper disaster recovery and business continuity plans in place, it is equally important to have understand the need to have proper digital forensic readiness planning. The continuing trend to take a reactive approach to dealing with security events or incidents is both disruptive and riskier to business operations in terms of digital evidence being altered, lost, or incorrectly handled.

Digital forensic readiness is an organization's capability to proactively maximize use of digital evidence while minimizing investigative costs. Organizations that understand the importance of establishing proactive controls to maintain the forensic viability and admissibility of digital evidence have a better chance of ultimately surviving and prospering in the evolving threat landscape.

As stated previously, the intention of this book is to provide readers with a business perspective of the digital forensics discipline. This book was written from a non-technical business perspective and is intended as an implementation guide for preparing your organization to enhance its digital forensic readiness by becoming more proactive with investigations and moving away from the traditional reactive approach to events and/or incidents. The methodology discussed throughout this book is also an effective way for organizations to demonstrate their due diligence and good corporate governance over their assets and business operations.

Integrating
Digital Forensics

III

Forensics Readiness in Cloud Environments

18

Introduction

As discussed previously in this book, the concept of digital forensics readiness is focused primarily on reducing costs and minimizing business interruptions when performing investigations. In a cloud environment, achieving a state of digital forensics readiness is important because of the volatile nature in which cloud computing environment operate and the increased potential for service disruptions to gather evidence during an investigation.

Through the combination of several major technology concepts, cloud computing has evolved over several decades to become the next generation of computing models. As cloud computing continues to mature, providing organizations with an inexpensive means of deploying computing resources, it is driving a fundamental change in the ways technology is becoming a common layer of service-oriented architectures.

Cloud computing presents unique challenges to an organization's digital forensics capabilities because of the dynamic nature in which information exists and a shift where organizations have less control over physical infrastructure assets. This leads to the inherent challenge of maintaining best practices for cloud computing while continuing to enable digital forensics capabilities.

Brief History of Cloud Computing

When thinking of cloud computing, commonly we think of historical milestone when ideas and solutions started to arise throughout the twenty-first century; however, cloud computing is not a new concept. The reality is that the concepts that eventually led to cloud computing have existed for several decades, building out an infrastructure path that eventually led to formalizing the computing models.

Dating back to the 1950s, the fundamental concepts of cloud computing emerged with the introduction of mainframe systems. When organizations started to prioritize the efficiency of their large-scale computing resources, where multiple users could simultaneously access a central computer system using terminals, the gradual evolution towards cloud began. Because technology was rather costly to buy and maintain at this time, providing shared access to a single resource was an economical solution that made sense for organizations who used it.

Move forward to the 1970s, when the concept of virtual machines (VM) emerged where it was now possible to execute one or more operating systems (OS) simultaneously inside one single physical piece of hardware. This technology advancement was an important catalyst in taking shared computing to the next level and further evolving communication and information sharing capabilities.

During the 1990s, the World Wide Web (WWW) exploded onto the scene, allowing Internet-based computing to really take off. Before the Internet, telecommunication providers could only offer single and dedicated point-to-point connections. Now, the concept of virtual private network connections was introduced, so instead of building out physical infrastructure for each connection, organizations could leverage shared access using the same physical infrastructures. At this time, cloud computing was in its infancy; it was enabling electronic business (eBusiness) such as online shopping, streaming content, and managing bank accounts.

Following the dot-com explosion in the early 2000s, several organizations played key roles in the further development of cloud computing services where the availability of high-capacity networks and low-cost computing resource was introduced, together with pervasive adoption of virtualization and service-oriented architectures. During this time, cloud computing was maturing to a point at which it was providing expanded information technology (IT) as a service capability, for example, virtualized environments for storage and computing capacity.

Today, most cloud-based service attention focuses on enterprises that focus on using it as an alternative for sourcing technology resources and capacity. As cloud computing evolves into its next level of maturity, the concept of "everything as a service" will enable most enterprise infrastructures and applications to be sourced through on-demand service models.

What Is Cloud Computing?

The origin of the term "cloud" in relation to digital forensics stems back to the telecommunications world where networks and the Internet were commonly visualized on diagrams depicted as clouds. Generally, the use of cloud in these diagrams signified areas where information was moving and being processed without persons needing to know what was happening. This philosophy is still central to cloud computing today where the customer requests and receives information and services without knowing where they resides or how they are transmitted.

Generally, cloud computing is a model for enabling convenient and on-demand delivery of computing resources (i.e., systems, storage, applications) over a network (i.e., Internet) that can be rapidly provisioned and released with minimal effort or interaction. From all advancements made throughout history, the major technology concepts that ultimately explain the evolution and creation of cloud computing are:

- *Grid computing* to solve large problems using parallel computing systems
- *Utility computing* to offer computing resources as a metered service
- *Software as a service (SaaS)* to allow for network-based subscriptions to applications
- *Cloud computing* to provide anywhere and anytime access to computing resources that are delivered dynamically as a service

Characteristics

Within all cloud computing infrastructures, there are five essential characteristics as follows:

- *Rapid elasticity*: With cloud computing, it is challenging for cloud service providers (CSP) to anticipate usage volumes or demands. Therefore, cloud capabilities need to provide dynamic scalability, in some cases automatically, to rapidly meet the customer's computing resourcing demands.
- *On-demand self-service*: This offers the ability to utilize a self-service model via which consumers can automatically provision and release computing resources, such as systems or storage, as needed without requiring human interaction with the CSP.
- *Broad network access*: In a society that is always connected from anywhere, cloud computing services need to be available over networks through standard interfaces that promote use by a wide variety of platforms (e.g., mobile devices, laptops).
- *Measured service*: Cloud systems have metering capabilities that have a level of abstraction appropriate to the type of service (i.e., bandwidth, storage, users) so that resources can be monitored, controlled, and report transparently.
- *Resource pooling*: Providing cloud computing under a multi-tenant model, both physical and virtual resources are dynamically assigned, and reassigned based on demand, without consumers having control or knowledge over where resource are located (i.e., country, data center).

Service Models

Within all cloud computing infrastructures, there are three distinct service models as follows:

- *Software as a service (SaaS)*: Consumers are provided the capability to use the provider's applications running within the cloud infrastructure. These applications are commonly accessible from a variety of client devices (e.g., web browser, program interface). Consumers do not manage or control the underlying cloud infrastructure (i.e., network, systems, storage, applications), except where user-specific application configurations are permitted.
- *Platform as a service (PaaS)*: Consumers are provided with capabilities to deploy, onto the cloud infrastructure, any applications they have created or acquired using the programming tools (i.e., languages, libraries, services) supported by the CSP. Consumers do not manage or control the underlying cloud infrastructure (i.e., network, systems, storage) but have control over deployed applications and the user-specific configurations.
- *Infrastructure as a service (Iaas)*: Consumers are provided with capabilities to provision and release computing resources (i.e., processing, storage, networks) where operating systems (OS) and applications can be used. Consumers do not manage or control the underlying cloud infrastructure (i.e., network, systems) but have control over the operating systems, applications, storage, and select network components (e.g., host-based firewalls).

Delivery Models

Within all cloud computing infrastructures, there four types of deployment models as follows:

- *Private cloud*: This model is provisioned exclusively for use by a single organization. It may exist either on or off the organization's premises, where it can be owned, managed, and operated by the organization or by the CSP.
- *Community cloud*: This model is provisioned for use by a specific community of consumers that have a shared interest (e.g., security requirements, compliance needs). It may exist either on or off the organization's premises, where it can be owned, managed, and operated by the organization or by the CSP.

- *Public cloud*: This model is provisioned for open use by the public. It exists exclusively within the CSP premises and can be owned, managed, and operated by either the CSP or another entity (i.e., organization, academic, managed service provider [MSP]).
- *Hybrid cloud*: This model is provisioned as any combination of two or more other cloud models (i.e., private, community, public) bound together by technologies that enable data and application portability (i.e., load balancing).

Isolation Models

Within all cloud computing infrastructures, there two types of isolation models as follows:

- *Dedicated*: Where infrastructure is reserved, and isolated, for specific users or customers
- *Multi-tenant*: Where infrastructure is shared amongst several groups of users or customers

Illustrated in Figure 18.1, each of the three models discussed above are shown to be complementary building blocks to the others and form the basis for which cloud computing environments are created.

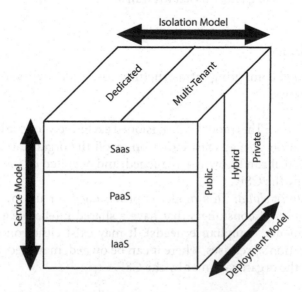

Figure 18.1 Cloud computing model dimensions.

Challenges with Cloud Environments

Cloud computing has transformed the ways in which electronically stored information (ESI) is stored, processed, and transmitted. From the information security perspective, corporate information being stored in these services is, for the most part, beyond the boundaries of IT control and is increasingly vulnerable because the controls may (or may not) meet their security requirements (i.e., encryption, data residency, logical access).

Challenges often faced when conducting a forensics investigation in a cloud environment primarily revolve around the control of ESI, especially when it comes to gathering and processing it in a forensically sound manner. These broadly categorized technical, legal, and organizational challenges can impede or ultimately prevent the ability to conduct digital forensics. While cloud computing possesses similarities to its predecessor technologies, the introduction of this new model presents significant challenges when applying traditional digital forensics methodologies and techniques.

Outlined in the following sections, challenges within cloud computing environments cannot be solved solely based on technology, law, or organizational principles. Rather, overcoming these difficulties requires an approach combining technology, law, and organizational principles to develop mitigation strategies based on people, processes, and technology.

Mobility

Mobile devices—as a business tool—have changed the "where and how" aspects of the data-centric security approach when it comes to the storage of an organization's informational assets. For example, informational assets that have been entrusted to an organization—by customers or employees—can be configured to synchronize across multiple devices, or other cloud-based services, which aggravates issues of data residency and increases the possibility of this ESI being compromised, lost, or stolen. Refer to Chapter 9, "Determine Collection Requirements," for further discussion on the data-centric security methodology.

Hyper-Scaling

Generally, hyper-scale environments are distributed computing infrastructures where ESI volumes, and demand for certain processing types, can increase exponentially and be accommodated quickly in a cost-effective manner. Virtual resources used are extremely short-lived and can also use container orchestrations, discussed below, to manage thousands of instances.

These "containers" are often associated with cloud computing because they help organizations become more efficient, use less power, and respond quickly to customer demands. The non-persistent and volatile nature of ESI within these environments can leave little, if any, digital evidence for gathering and processing.

Containerization

For the longest time, a traditional means of deploying software applications was as much a science as it was a systematic process. Similarly, the modern use of container orchestrations to deploy software applications allows for standardization of the underlying computing environment and takes away the need to depend on operating system version and hardware specifications. As the use of containers grew, there was a need to better manage the extraction of containers much in the same way as that used with data centers with traditional computing systems. The reality is that many of the existing digital forensics tools and processes are not aware of or capable of analyzing containers, so alternatives must be explored.

First Responders

When responding to a security incident where infrastructure is not owned or directly managed by the organization, such as when cloud-based services are managed by a CSP, there is a need to rely on others to perform initial triage tasks and functions. The reality is that most organizations are often faced with concerns related to the competence and trustworthiness of incident first responders. While contractual service level objectives (SLO) and service level agreements (SLA) can be defined to ensure CSPs respond accordingly, a joint incident response plan needs to be developed with the CSPs to outline how to manage several types of security incidents.

Evidence Gathering and Processing

With cloud-based systems managed by CSPs, organizations don't have direct access to the technologies to gather and process evidence following traditional methodologies and techniques. As result, collection and preservation of cloud-based evidence that is relevant to a specific organization's investigation can be challenging where factors such as multi-tenancy, distributed resourcing (cross-borders), or volatile data are persistent. Furthermore, organizations may encounter issues where correlation and reconstruction of events are not easily achieved because artifacts exist within multiple CSPs or across several virtual images.

Forensics Readiness Methodology

Following traditional methodologies, as illustrated in Figure 18.2 and discussed further in Chapter 2, "Investigative Process Methodology," digital forensics investigations normally follow an approach whereby evidence is searched for (identified), seized (collected and preserved), and analyzed (processed). However, traditional investigative methodologies were not designed with cloud computing in mind and, given the dynamic and volatile nature of cloud computing, following this traditional approach to digital forensics investigations is not suitable.

As an alternative, organizations need to optimize their investigative process by taking proactive steps to guarantee that evidence will be readily available if (and when) needed from their cloud computing environments. Throughout the sections below, each step outlined for implementing digital forensics readiness will be discussed vis a vis improving investigative capabilities within cloud computing environments.

Step #1: Define Business Risk Scenarios

Digital forensics investigations in a cloud environment require organizations to follow a proactive approach whereby controls and measures have been implemented to guarantee digital evidence will be available when (and if) needed.

Whether within an organization's control (i.e., internal network) or located in a CSP, the business risk scenarios where digital forensics readiness demonstrates positive benefits are similar and include:

1. Reducing the impact of cybercrime
2. Validating the impact of cybercrime
3. Producing evidence to support organizational disciplinary issues
4. Demonstrating compliance with regulatory or legal requirements
5. Effectively managing the release of court-ordered data
6. Supporting contractual and commercial agreements

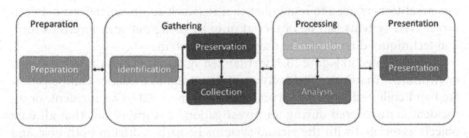

Figure 18.2 High-level digital forensics process model.

Rather than assuming the use of a cloud environment will limit the span of business risk scenarios, it is recommended to ensure all six scenarios are included right from the outset of the cloud engagement. By doing so, organizations have established a wide scope of risk that allows them to be better positioned for focusing on specifics, rather than establishing a narrow scope and having to expand after identifying missed evidence.

Refer to Chapter 7, "Defining Business Risk Scenarios," for further discussion on the six business risk scenarios applied to digital forensics readiness.

Step #2: Identify Potential Data Sources

Cloud computing presents a unique challenge because of the dynamic nature in which information exists as well as a shift landscape in which organizations have less control over physical infrastructure assets. This leads to the inherent challenge of maintaining best practices for cloud computing while continuing to enable digital forensics capabilities.

Cloud computing has revolutionized the ways in which ESI is stored, processed, and transmitted. There are numerous challenges facing the digital forensics community when it comes to gathering and processing digital evidence in cloud computing environments. While cloud computing possesses similarities to its predecessor technologies, the introduction of this operating model presents challenges to digital forensics, as illustrated in Figure 18.1.

Virtualization is the foundational technology for cloud computing environments because it is a cost-effective means of quickly provisioning technology resources. For the most part, systems hosted in these virtual environments produce digital artifacts similar to those found in traditional computer systems with physical hardware. However, within these rapidly elastic virtual environments exists a networking backplane of system communications that do travel beyond the physical host system where virtualization is being run.

Because of how this internal backplane operates, all indicators that an attack is moving between virtualized systems are not going to be available in typical technology-generated log files because of the way in which virtualization works. Where this type of internal communication exists, digital forensics practitioners need to remember that network communications between virtualized systems can be observed only by using network forensics tools and techniques directly on the physical host system.

As illustrated in Figure 18.3, virtualized systems have an underlying host environment (hardware and software) where digital evidence can be generated and collected. When a virtual system is involved in an incident, or an incident is discovered during an investigation, it is important that all data objects associated with the virtual systems be gathered from both host and guess systems. These data objects may include the following:

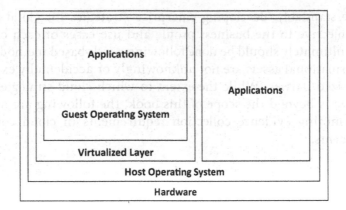

Figure 18.3 Virtualization architecture.

- Virtual machine images, which are files that contain a guest operating system, file system, and data objects
- Log files containing information such as virtual disk partitioning, virtual networking settings, or state configurations
- Dump files from random access memory (RAM) or paging files

Refer to Chapter 8, "Identify Potential Data Sources," for further discussion on creating an inventory of digital evidence data sources as applies to digital forensics readiness.

Step #3: Determine Collection Requirements

In cloud environments, gathering and processing evidence is not as straightforward as it is with ESI located within an organization's traditional computer systems and technologies. For example, a common challenge with cloud computing is that in most cases, physical access to hardware running cloud instances is often unfeasible, making search and seizure quite impossible. Alternatively, organizations can proactively collect ESI from cloud environments that could be required during a digital forensics investigation.

Where direct access to the hardware is not permitted, gathering and processing digital evidence needs to follow traditional forensics principles, methodologies and techniques. As a result, collection and preservation of cloud-based evidence that is relevant to a specific organization's investigation can be challenging where factors such as multi-tenancy, distributed resourcing (cross-borders), or volatile data are persistent. This can be an overwhelming task to undertake, as cloud computing environment are quite dynamic in nature and the rate at which ESI changes can't be kept up with through manual processes.

Understandably, developing enterprise strategies for cloud computing is subjective to the business profile and use cases of each organization and ultimately should be done following a risk-based methodology so that informational assets are not unknowingly or accidentally exposed to unauthorized parties. While the extent to which cloud strategies should be develop is beyond the scope of this book, the following are necessary for determining evidence collection requirements in cloud computing environments.

Enterprise Management Strategies

Preparing the underlying infrastructure to holistically and practically support digital forensics capabilities; however, every variation of cloud models being used will have several types and forms of ESI that can be used as digital evidence. A key factor with enabling any digital forensics capability within an organization is to ensure that a comprehensive approach to designing the architectural and technical models that make up cloud environments is done by applying complimentary administrative, technical, and physical controls that are given equal treatment.

Developing enterprise strategies for cloud computing is subjective to each organization and their respective business requirements; and should be done following a risk-based methodology so that informational assets are not unknowingly or accidentally expose to unauthorized parties. For example, the following are two significant components for enabling cloud computing as it pertains to enhancing digital forensics capabilities.

Cloud Computing Governance

Implementing technology to secure cloud computing, as a precursor to enabling digital forensics capabilities, is only one piece of an organization's broader strategy to govern use of and access to these technologies. Before digital forensics capabilities can be realized, there needs to be documentation approved that establishes the requirements for using cloud-based services to secure data storage and access, as well as what is considered acceptable and unacceptable conduct. Combined with the documentation created through the organization's information security governance framework, standard operating procedures (SOP) are the backbone for performing digital forensics within cloud computing environments.

Within the information security governance framework, there needs to be a series of documents that specifically addresses the use of and access to the cloud computing environment with respect to the organization's data. These documents provide the organization with a foundation for planning the eventual enablement of cloud computing capabilities, guidelines for user behavior and conduct, as well as a driver for enabling digital forensics capabilities.

For example, the following corporate governance needs to be implemented before cloud computing should be enabled:

- A *code of conduct* is a high-level governance document that sets out the organization's values, responsibilities, and ethical obligations. This governance document provides the organization with guidance for handling different situations related to employee behaviors and actions.
- An *acceptable use policy* is designed to govern the use of cloud computing environments so that employees know what the organization considers to be acceptable and unacceptable behavior and activity.

Security and Configuration Standards

Largely, security controls within cloud computing environments are no different than those found within traditional IT environments. However, there is a difference in the models that cloud computing employs, which may present slightly different risk profiles than traditional IT environments have.

With cloud computing environments, the scope of security responsibilities for the CSP and consumer differ based on the models used. Understanding the difference in how security controls are deployed between cloud service models is critical for organizations as they seek to manage the business risk of using cloud computing environments, for example:

- In *SaaS* environments, the scope of security controls—such as SLO, privacy, and compliance—are negotiated as part of the terms and conditions outlined in formal contractual agreements.
- In *IaaS* environments, CSPs are responsible for implementing security controls for the underlying infrastructure and abstraction layers, while the consumer is responsible for the remainder of the stack (i.e., OS, applications, etc.).
- In *PaaS* environments, securing the platform is the responsibility of the CSP, while securing applications (either developed or purchased) belongs to the consumer.

Reference Architectures

Knowing that there are different methods, services, and responsibilities for securing different cloud computing models, organizations are faced with significant challenges when it comes to properly assessing risk and determining the level of security controls needed to protect their informational assets.

Reference architectures (RA) provide a comprehensive and formal means to overlay security within cloud infrastructures. Using an RA to secure cloud-based services lays out a risk-based approach for organizations to determine CSP responsibilities for implementing specific controls throughout a cloud ecosystem. Generally, the RA framework provides a high-level summary to:

- Identify the core security components that can be implemented in a cloud ecosystem;
- Provide the core set of security components, based on deployment and service model, that are within the responsibility of the CSP; and
- Define the formal architectures that add security-centric layers to cloud computing environments.

Illustrated in Figure 18.4, there are multiple layers of interactions found throughout enterprise technology stacks where security controls can be deployed and implemented. As modern technologies—such as mobile devices, virtualization, and cloud computing—continue to proliferate as tools for conducting business, organizations are increasingly faced with the need to expose their business records and applications beyond the borders of their traditional network perimeter.

Addressing security requirements in cloud computing environments should follow the traditional risk-based approach that focuses on agnostic controls—that can be applied to most systems or software development methodologies—to reduce their attack surface. Alternatively, instead of managing the security of cloud-based solutions through specific technology components, organizations should manage their attack surfaces using security control families based on the type of cloud models deployed. Examples of security control families relevant to cloud computing environments include:

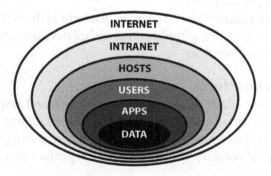

Figure 18.4 Security controls layers.

- Access controls
- Awareness and training
- Audit and accountability
- Security assessment and authorization
- Configuration management
- Identification and authentication
- Incident response
- Media protection
- Physical and environmental protection
- Risk assessment
- System and information integrity

With cloud computing environments based on a standardized multi-tier architecture, security control families should be implemented based on the security concerns found throughout each layer. Generally, there are four technology solution domains within cloud-based solutions that describe security concerns and can be used to map security control families appropriately:

- *Presentation services* is the interface between end users and the cloud-based solution. The requirements for security controls within this domain will vary given the type of cloud service model provided (i.e., PaaS, IaaS, or SaaS) and the interface with the user (i.e., mobile device, web site, etc.). Examples of security control families within this domain include access controls, identification, and authentication.
- *Application services* are the rules and processes behind the *presentation services* that interact with and manipulate information on behalf of end users. The requirement for security controls within this domain is to ensure that the development processes used to build services within this tier maintain the integrity of the information. Examples of security control families within this domain include configuration management, system, and information integrity.
- *Information services* prioritize, simplify, and manage the risk associated with the storage of information. The requirements for security controls within this domain are to properly manage the extraction, transformation, normalization, and loading of information within the technology solution. Examples of security control families within this domain include risk assessment, system, and information integrity.
- *Infrastructure services* provide the core technology capabilities required to support the higher-level tiers of a cloud-based solution architecture. The requirement for security controls within this domain is to provide physical security capabilities that match the risk characteristics found throughout the higher-level cloud technology

solution domains. Examples of security control families within this domain include media protection, physical, and environmental protection.

Providing a detailed mapping of security control families to the cloud technology solution domain is beyond the scope of this book. Alternatively, the following security reference architectures can be used as guidance for securing cloud computing environments and have also been provided in the *Resources* chapter at the end of this book:

- *NIST Cloud Computing Security Reference Architecture* contains detailed guidance for organizations to adopt best practices and security requirements for cloud service contracts, SLOs, SLAs, and deployment of cloud computing environments.
- *Trusted Cloud Initiative (TRI) SRI* provides a comprehensive approach to securing identity-aware cloud ecosystems that combine the best of breed architecture models (i.e., Information Technology Infrastructure Library [ITIL]).

Refer to Chapter 5, "Digital Forensics as a Business," for further discussion about policies, processes, procedures, and how an organization's governance framework complements digital forensics.

Refer to Chapter 9, "Determine Collection Requirements," for further discussion on the administrative, technical, and physical controls requirements for gathering relevant and meaningful digital evidence.

Step #4: Establish Legal Admissibility

As stated previously, some cloud deployments don't allow customers to have direct access to backend systems and infrastructure. For example, every component of the virtualization architecture—illustrated in Figure 18.2— that the organization does not own or manage introduces various levels of uncertainty around the integrity and authenticity of evidence not within their span of control.

Layers of Trust

Before determining what can be used as an evidential data source, it is important to first understand the layers of trust within the cloud computing environments. Keeping in mind that a rule of thumb of digital forensics is that all investigations will end up in a court of law. And while a judge or jury will ultimately decide whether presented evidence is admissible and will be accepted, there can be varying degrees of confidence about whether cloud-based evidence is accurate and reliable.

For example, in traditional computer forensics where a hard drive has been removed from a standalone computer system for imaging, digital forensics practitioners must trust that their forensics hardware and software are operating as expected; refer to Appendix A, "Tool and Equipment Validation Program," for further discussion about validation and verification of forensics tools. However, where a computer system exists within a cloud environment, there are new layers of trust introduced that digital forensics practitioners need to consider when collecting digital evidence.

Generally, there are six layers of trust within cloud environments where techniques used to gather digital evidence will differ (see Table 18.1). Working down through the architectural layers of a cloud environment, there are distinct levels of trust in the information within being secure and trustworthy. Ultimately, this means that if there are concerns about the integrity of information at any layer, the courts can render a legal decision not to admit the evidence. As a strategy for addressing these issues, digital forensics practitioners should follow scientifically proven and documented techniques to verify and validate the integrity and authenticity of evidence.

Depending on the nature of the investigation, organizations need to determine which layer of evidence outlined above needs to be collected and preserved. Ultimately, making this assessment involves two key decision criteria: the first being the organization's technical capability to forensically gather evidence at that layer and the second being the level of trust in the data at that layer. Where cloud environments are located within the organization's boundaries of control, technical probability and level of trust will be relatively higher because network forensics tools and techniques can be used to gather evidence from known and managed infrastructures.

However, when there is no physical infrastructure present within the enterprise, digital forensics practitioner need to turn to their suite of enterprise security controls to gather network traffic data relevant to the incident or investigation. Doing so requires that a well-defined SOP be in place to gather the maximum amount of evidence possible, while causing minimal impact to the business that maintains both forensics viability and legal

Table 18.1 Cloud Layers of Trust

Cloud Layer	Acquisition Technique	Trust Level
(6) Applications/Data	Subjective to application/data	Guest OS, Hypervisor, Host OS, Hardware, Network
(5) Guest OS	Digital Forensics Tools	Guest OS, Hypervisor, Host OS, Hardware, Network
(4) Virtualization	Introspection	Hypervisor, Host OS, Hardware, Network
(3) Host OS	Access to Virtual Disk	Host OS, Hardware, Network
(2) Physical Hardware	Access to Physical Disk	Hardware, Network
(1) Network	Network Forensics Tools	Network

admissibility. Chain of custody must be strictly enforced to guarantee there is no potential for the integrity or authenticity of this data to be questioned.

Gathering evidence that is located beyond the organization's network perimeter is the point where contractual agreements with CSPs are factored in to gather evidence. Where CSPs are involved with service offerings, access to evidence might be limited because organizations might have little to no control over the physical infrastructure involved in the incident or investigation.

For the most part, many CSPs do not provide customers with options or the interfaces necessary to gather evidence from these cloud environments, leaving organizations faced with no option but to collect evidence at a high level of abstraction. Given that most cloud ecosystems are implemented using virtualization technologies, the most common form of evidence gathered from cloud environments is in the form of an object or container, such as virtual hard drive images.

Where concerns about trust do exist within cloud-based systems, it is important that the system's architecture is designed in a way so as to increase the organization's forensics capabilities and minimize potential matters about evidence integrity and authenticity. Like the multiple layers of interactions found throughout enterprise technology stacks where security controls can be deployed and implemented, as illustrated in Figure 18.3, these security controls can also be leveraged to enhance forensics capabilities in cloud environments by placing controls closer to the actual data as a means of protection.

Refer to Chapter 3, "Digital Evidence Management," for further discussion about data-centric security.

Refer to Chapter 10, "Establishing Legal Admissibility," for further discussion about strategies for establishing and maintaining legal admissibility.

Step #5: Establish Secure Storage and Handling

Generally, cloud computing environments are extremely volatile by design, largely due to their dynamic nature and varying levels of trust. Considering the layers of trust illustrated previously in Table 18.1, there can be concerns about the integrity of information at any layer, requiring organizations to implement strategies for addressing these potential issues. Because of this, unlike traditional computing environments, all ESI that would be deemed relevant and meaningful as potential digital evidence needs to have an elevated degree of security controls implemented to safeguard its integrity and authenticity.

For example, hyper-scaling introduces a layer of complexity where data can be accessed and transmitted across virtual resources that are often only available for short-lived periods and are distributed across dynamic infrastructures. Given the potentially volatile conditions of cloud-based systems, it is important that all ESI serving as relevant digital evidence be secured while in use, in transit, and at rest. At a minimum, the following control mechanisms should be implemented (where possible) to guarantee the secure storage and handling of potential evidence in a cloud environment:

- Real-time logging of technology-generated (i.e., log files) and technology-stored (i.e., word productivity document) data to a remote and centralized repository
- One-way cryptographic hash algorithm, such as the Message Digest Algorithm family (i.e., MD5, MD6) or the Secure Hashing Algorithm family (i.e., SHA-1, SHA-2, SHA-3), to establish and maintain both the integrity and authenticity of ESI

Refer to Chapter 3, "Digital Evidence Management," for further discussion about data-centric security, technology-generated data, and technology-stored data.

Refer to Chapter 11, "Establish Secure Storage and Handling," for further discussion about strategies for establishing and maintaining evidence integrity during handling and storage.

Step #6: Enable Targeted Monitoring

Traditionally, digital evidence was primarily gathered from computer systems such as desktops, laptops, and servers. However, with the widespread use of technology in business operations, every organization will have ESI that is considered potential digital evidence generated across various sources, including cloud infrastructures.

With cloud computing environments, evidence can be located across many distributed systems and devices where, for the most part, access will be outside the organization's scope of control. Knowing that cloud forensics is a sub-discipline of network forensics, which largely involves post-incident analysis of systems and devices, it is important that network-based evidence sources are included within the scope of investigation involving cloud environments.

Because of this, when conducting a forensics investigation where cloud systems are within scope, it is important that organizations consider that to establish facts and conclusions, they will need to gather and process digital evidence from network-based data sources that cannot be seized without generating some type of business outage or disruption. *Background evidence* is any ESI that has been created as part of normal business operations that are used during cloud forensics investigation. Examples of this type of evidence include:

- Network devices such as routers, switches, or firewalls;
- Application programming interface (API) service calls between cloud systems and applications;
- Internal calls within the virtual machine (VM) system; or
- Audit information such as system, application/software, or security logs.

Refer to the Chapter 3, "Digital Evidence Management," for further discussion about common sources of evidence.

Step #7: Map Investigative Workflows

Gathering and processing digital evidence from cloud environments differs from the traditional approaches of digital forensics where organizations do not, in some cases, own the infrastructural components. With cloud computing based on requirements for broad network access, the application of cloud forensics is therefore a subset of and adaptation of network forensics principles, methodologies, and techniques.

However, knowing that there are potential limitations in conducting cloud forensics, it is necessary to implement guidelines and processes by which the digital forensics practitioner can gather and process potential digital evidence. The high-level digital forensics process model, illustrated previously in Figure 18.2, will be applied to the activities and tasks involved in conducting cloud forensics.

Phase #1: Preparation

As discussed in Chapter 2, "Investigative Process Methodology," the activities and tasks performed in this first phase are essential in successfully executing all subsequent phases of the investigative workflow. As a component of the preparation phase, organizations can proactively align their people, processes, and technologies to support their cloud forensics capabilities.

Processes and Procedures   With cloud forensics being a sub-discipline of network forensics, which is a sub-discipline of digital forensics, the existing baseline of standards, guidelines, and techniques discussed in Chapter 5, "Digital Forensics as a Business," become the foundation for documentation specific to cloud forensics.

For the most part, the standard operating procedures (SOP) created for digital forensics still apply to cloud forensics. However, given that cloud infrastructure may not be owned by the organization, there is a need to develop specific SOPs so that digital forensics practitioners know how to engage CSPs to facilitate gathering evidence.

Education, Training, and Awareness   Like digital forensics, depending on an individual's role with respect to cloud forensics determines the level of knowledge they are provided. Further discussion about the different levels of education, training, and awareness is found in the section below.

Technology and Toolsets   Within the dedicated forensics lab environment, discussed in Chapter 5, "Digital Forensics as a Business," organizations will need to acquire specific software and hardware to support their cloud forensics capabilities. However, the extent to which an organization invests in such a "toolkit" is dependent on their business environment and the degree to which they need to gather and process digital evidence from cloud environments.

As a subset of network forensics, tools and techniques used for cloud forensics will include a suite of network monitoring and collection utilities that allow digital forensics practitioners to replay and analyze traffic patterns. It is important that all tools used can process large datasets, given the potential volume of traffic on any given network segment, and subsequently pinpoint—with accuracy—where each piece of information was derived from.

Further discussion about digital forensics tools and technologies can be found in Chapter 5, "Digital Forensics as a Business."

Phase #2: Gathering

As discussed in Chapter 2, "Investigative Process Methodology," this second phase of the investigative workflow consists of the activities and tasks involved in the identification, collection, and preservation of digital evidence. The same requirements for establishing the integrity, authenticity, and legal admissibility of digital evidence applies for cloud computing. However, given the predominant use of virtualization for cloud-based services and that an investigation might also involve multiple entities (the organization and the CSP), there are additional activities and tasks that need to be performed for cloud forensics.

Identification   Largely, the activities and tasks performed here are no different than those discussed in the Chapter 2, "Investigative Process Methodology." Regardless of the evidence that has been identified, both physical and logical, digital forensics practitioners must follow consistent and repeatable methodologies and techniques to secure, document, and search a crime scene. Sample templates that can be used when securing, documenting, and searching crime scenes have been provided in the *Templates* section of this book.

Where cloud environments have been identified as relevant to an investigation, and there is some component of the cloud-based service being provided by a CSP, the scope of an investigation widens significantly to include identification of evidence located in sources that are indirectly owned and managed by the organization. Further complicating the scope of an investigation, although organizations have a contractual agreement in place with their direct CSP, most cloud applications often have dependencies on other CSPs that need to be considered.

To establish cloud forensics capabilities that ensure digital evidence will maintain legal admissibility, each CSP must be equipped with educated and experienced resources (people) to assist in all forensics activities, as discussed in the *Phase #1: Preparation* section above. Establishing where potential digital evidence exists involves working through the order of volatility, discussed in Chapter 2, "Investigative Process Methodology," subjective to the technology infrastructure involved in the incident or investigation.

Collection and Preservation   Referring back to the layers of trust illustrated in Table 18.1, organizations need to determine the order in which the different layers of evidence need to be collected and preserved. Ultimately, making this assessment involves two key decision criteria, the first being the organization's technical capability to forensically gather evidence at that layer and the second being the level of trust in the data at that layer.

When gathering evidence that is located beyond the organization's network perimeter, contractual agreements with CSPs are factored in to gather evidence. Where CSPs are involved with service offerings, access to evidence might be limited because organizations might have little to no control over the physical infrastructure involved in the incident or investigation.

Phase #3: Processing

As result of network forensics activities, there will most likely be various datasets from the different network forensics tools that can prove to be valuable for the investigation. As disparate evidence, processing logs can be challenging because, on their own, these datasets cannot be used to establish factual conclusions. This means that all gathered evidence needs to be aggregated into a single dataset so the investigation team can better correlate and establish a chronology so that relevant and meaningful evidence is not lost, skipped, or misunderstood.

Beyond analyzing the network forensics datasets, the tools and equipment used to process virtual hard drive images are for the most part the same as those used for traditional digital forensics, with the exception that there will most likely be only logical evidence, nothing physical (e.g., hard drive). At this stage of the investigation, the traditional methodologies and techniques used to analyze and examine digital evidence should follow SOPs to ensure consistent and repeatable processes are being followed to establish fact-based conclusions.

Phase #4: Presentation

As discussed in Chapter 2, "Investigative Process Methodology," documentation is a critical element of every investigation and needs to start at the beginning of the investigation and carry on to the end. In this last phase of the investigative workflow, the final investigative report will be created to communicate factual conclusions by demonstrating the processes, techniques, tools, equipment, and interactions used to maintain the authenticity, reliability, and trustworthiness of digital evidence.

Refer to the following section for further discussion about maintaining evidence-based presentation and reporting.

Step #8: Establish Continuing Education

Like digital forensics, depending on an individual's role with respect to cloud forensics determines the level of knowledge they are provided. Detailed discussion about the diverse levels of education, training, and awareness an organization should require of their people in support of digital forensics can be found in Chapter 14, "Establish Continuing Education."

General Awareness

As the lowest type of education, this is a generalized level of training and awareness that is designed to provide people with foundational knowledge without getting too deep into cloud computing or cloud forensics. Leveraging the education and training that has already been put in place for digital forensics, this education provides people with the competencies they need about organizational policies, standards, and guidelines so that they indirectly contribute, through some form of behavior or action, to the organization's digital forensics program.

Examples of topics and subjects that should be included as part of a mobile device forensics awareness program include the following:

- Business code of conduct
- Cloud computing acceptable use policy
- Data protection and privacy

Basic Training

Essentially, the difference between this training and the previous awareness is that the knowledge gained here is intended to teach people the skills necessary to directly support the organization's digital forensics program as it relates to how, where, and to what extent cloud devices are used for business purposes.

Information communicated at this level is more detailed than the previous type of education because it must provide people with the knowledge required to support a specific role or function, such as managing cloud computing ecosystems.

For example, as part of basic mobile device forensics training, information about audit logging and retention should be covered. Generally, this topic relates to the practice of recording events and preserving them, as per the organizational governance framework, to facilitate digital forensics investigations.

Formal Education

A working and practical knowledge of cloud forensics requires people to first and foremost have the skills and competencies necessary to ensure that all network forensics—as a sub-discipline of digital forensics principles, methodologies, and techniques—is understood. Once the fundamental knowledge is gained, practitioners can then start pursuing knowledge of cloud computing and work towards a specialization in cloud forensics.

However, unlike digital forensics education programs the availability of curriculum dedicated entirely to cloud computing environments is still limited. Most commonly, cloud forensics is taught as a specific course in either higher or post-secondary institutes, or as a professional education module led by an industry-recognized training institute.

Refer to Appendix B, "Education and Professional Certifications," for a list of higher/post-secondary institutions that offer formal education programs.

Step #9: Maintain Evidence-Based Presentations

Whether hosted internally or with a CSP, the systems and ESI present can be used to commit or be the target of criminal activity. However, perhaps the biggest challenge to a digital forensics investigation where cloud environments are within scope is to determine the "who, where, what, when, why, and how" of cloud-based criminal activity. Some things to consider when writing a final investigative report include:

- Structure and layout should flow naturally and logically; like how we speak.
- Content should be clear and concise to accurately demonstrate a chronology of events.
- Use of jargon, slang, and technical terminology should be limited or avoided. Where used, a glossary should be included to define terms in natural language.
- Where acronyms and abbreviations are used, they must be written out in full expression on the first use.
- Because final reports are written after the fact, that is, after an investigation, content should be communicated in the past tense; but the tense can change where conclusions or recommendations are being made.
- Format the final report not only for distribution within the organization, but also with the mindset that it may be used as testimony in a court of law.

A template for creating written formal reports has been provided as a reference in the *Templates* section of this book.

Step #10: Ensure Legal Review

The growth of cloud computing has heightened concerns about who has custody over data and where it is located. Before making a strategic decision to move business operations into a cloud computing environment, it is important to answer the question "What data residency concerns do I need to address?" In many countries, there are strict laws and regulations around data residency that prescribe the extent to which data can be stored in other geographical locations.

With this increased utilization of cloud environments, CSPs are opening facilities across multiple regions and countries where several laws and regulations govern the use, transmission, and storage of different types of ESI. For example, the General Data Protection Regulation (GDPR) of the European Union (EU), also known as EU Directive 95/46/EC, was issued to strengthen and unify data protection requirements by giving EU citizens back control of their personal data. Likewise, the Personal Information Protection and Electronic Documents Act (PIPEDA) sets out rules for how private-sector organizations collect, use, and disclose personal information—of customers and employees—as part of their business activities.

Organizations are constantly faced with concerns of data residency and the ways in which the geographically distributed infrastructures may violate various laws and regulations. Where a legal or regulatory violation of data residency has occurred, whether done intentionally or accidentally, the consequences organizations can face include:

- Financial penalties as result of legal or regulatory fines, compensation to victims, or the cost of remedying the violation
- Legal ramifications of lawsuits by those whose data was in violation, or law enforcement—and governing—agencies
- Operational impact due to loss of reputation, customer (client) base, or right to conduct business in certain geographical regions

The reality is that if the data can be accessed, and you demonstrate control over it, local jurisdictions will most likely demand that the data be produced as evidence even if it is stored in another jurisdiction. As a means of mitigating this, and guaranteeing that data is secure in cloud environments, organizations are implementing data-at-rest encryption following a bring your own key (also referred to as bring your own encryption) approach.

Contractual Agreements

When data is transferred to a cloud-based service, the responsibility for protecting and securing the data against loss, damage, or misuse commonly remains the responsibility of the data custodian, that is, the organization. In deployments where the organization relies on a CSP to host or process its data, it is essential (and in most cases legally required) that a written legal agreement be drafted to ensure all parties involved in the cloud-based service offerings will fulfill their responsibilities.

The cornerstone of enabling cloud computing within any enterprise is having a master service agreement (MSA) in place to function as the legal framework under which all parties will operate throughout the course of their relationship. This MSA must contain clauses whereby due diligence (before execution) is defined and continuous audits (during execution) are performed. In addition, it should contain terms and conditions, including the:

- Objective for having the MSA in place;
- Duration for which the MSA will govern the relationship;
- Reason(s) for which termination of the contract can occur—and subsequently the consequences for all parties involved;
- Structure and system of governance that will be applied—such as monitoring the service (i.e., SLO, SLA) or the rights and responsibilities of all parties involved; and
- Requirements for supplying, managing, and reporting administrative, technical, and (where feasible) physical security control implementations

Entering a legal agreement with another party should not be done blindly. This means that organizations need to demonstrate due diligence in assessing their business practices, needs, and restrictions so that they have a clear and concise understanding of what is required of them—such as from a compliance standpoint—or what (legal) barriers they may encounter. In some cases, due diligence on the CSP may be necessary to determine whether the provider is fully capable of fulfilling its continued obligations outlined in the agreement.

Most commonly, a formal and complex contract agreement, tailored to meet specific requirements, is negotiated between an organization and the CSP. However, where CSPs provide organizations with a "click-wrap agreement," careful assessment of risks against benefits needs to be completed to ensure that the provisions of this contract meet the needs and obligations of all parties throughout its lifecycle. If a contractual agreement is entered into such that needs and obligations cannot be addressed, organizations must consider alternatives and not willingly accept the faults of the potential relationship, such as seeking out a CSP who is willing to enter a mutually agreeable contract relationship.

Refer to Chapter 16, "Ensuring Legal Review," for further discussion about laws, standards, and regulations.

Summary

Cloud computing introduces a unique set of challenges to the digital forensics community because of the shift away from traditional technology architectures, and organizations now have less control over physical infrastructure assets. As a subset of network forensics, and ultimately of digital forensics, organizations must address these concerns head-on by understanding and identifying how (and where) their digital forensics capabilities must adapt to support cloud-based service offerings.

Forensics Readiness with Mobile Devices 19

Introduction

As discussed previously in this book, the concept of digital forensics readiness is focused primarily on reducing costs and minimizing business interruptions when performing investigations. From significant technology advancements made over the last decade, business has transformed into a much more dynamic and mobile workforce.

Since its inception, the world of mobile technologies has evolved quickly where new devices, operating systems, and threats are emerging every day. With mobile devices, achieving a state of digital forensics readiness is important because of the dynamic and portable nature by which these devices are used to interconnect and interface both business and personal information.

Mobile devices present unique challenges to an organization's digital forensics capabilities because of how quickly these technologies are changing and the shifting of traditional concepts, such as establishing a perimeter around systems and data. This leads to the inherent challenge of maintaining best practices for mobile device usage while continuing to enable digital forensics capabilities.

Brief History of Mobile Devices

Possibly the first documented existence of a mobile phone was a device released by Motorola in the early 1970s. Being the 1970s, these mobile devices were quite basic in that they only provided users with simple telephony features and did not support the multi-purpose "smartphone" features that are currently available in today's marketplace. And, to users' delight, these devices only allowed for thirty minutes of talk time and took around ten hours to charge.

Moving forward to 1983, the first mobile phone was released with the intended audience being business users who could afford them, not the everyday consumer. In the early 1990s, manufacturers started to change the design and portability of mobile phones to draw the attention of consumers so that, by the late-1990s, these devices started to become commonplace. However, mobile phones were still limited to simple telephony features and did not offer much to the digital forensics community in terms of gathering or processing digital evidence. Early efforts to examine mobile devices involved analyzing content directly via the display screen and photographing important content.

1999 saw a major advancement for mobile devices when the first Blackberry handset was released, providing consumers with more features than simple telephony, such as email and messaging. This technology was a breakthrough that established a foundation for future mobile devices that would be released through into the early-2000s. By this time, not only could these mobile devices be used to make telephone calls, but they could contain email, web browsing information, location data, contacts, and messaging records. It was during this time that organizations started to pay attention to the mobile device market and began leveraging them to provide their workforce with the flexibility of shifting between personal and work use from anywhere at any time.

Now that mobile devices were blurring the lines between business and personal use, these devices started to be used as part of criminal activities and the digital forensics community recognized the potential for digital evidence to exist in these technologies. As the number of mobile devices began to increase, it was quickly discovered that gathering and processing digital evidence from these devices could not be done using existing methodologies and techniques. At first, like the early days of computer forensics, digital forensics practitioners used common system administration tools, such as synchronization tools, to gather and process electronically stored information (ESI). Following suit, commercial solutions providing mobile forensics capabilities started emerging which allowed digital forensics practitioners to consistently apply the same methodologies and technique to gathering and processing digital evidence from mobile devices.

Perhaps the most significant advancement in mobile device technology came in 2008 when Apple releases the iPhone device which proved to be a momentous evolution in changing the face of the mobile device marketplace forever. Not only did this device provide consumers with the features found in early "smart" devices, but the iPhone's expanded capability that allowed uses to install and use applications of all sorts meant that ESI could move beyond the commonly referenced evidence sources, such as phone logs, email messages, and instant messaging records.

When organizations came to the realization that their data could be—and most likely was already being—accessed and stored on mobile devices that they (potentially) had little to no control over, manufacturers and vendors capitalized on the opportunity and mobile device management (MDM) solutions were brought to market. Since 2008, other manufacturers have released their own versions of mobile devices that also provide organizations with challenges related to controlling how, when, why, with whom, and under what circumstance their data can(not) be used on mobile devices.

Challenges with Mobile Devices

Before mobile devices became a technology for conducting business, there was a definitive perimeter around their networks and systems, and security best practices and methodologies were traditionally within this boundary. However, knowing that today's workforce is increasingly mobile, organizations must accept the reality that it is commonplace for mobile devices to allow for multiple connections to different networks simultaneously. This means that the idea that there was once a logical perimeter that protected corporate networks and systems from outsiders has eroded, introducing a certain level of unknown hostility into what was previously a controlled and managed environment.

Furthermore, with a workforce that is always connected from any place at any time, it is quite common for mobile devices to be used for both personal and business purposes. Staying ahead of the curve in an ever-evolving landscape, the digital forensics community is constantly faced with challenges of gathering and processing evidence from all sorts of technology.

Loss

With some exception, most mobile devices have smaller form factors, making them more prone to being lost. The probability of losing a mobile device—as compared to a traditional computer system—is higher considering how easy it is for these small devices to accidentally slide out of a pocket or unintentionally be left somewhere.

When lost, mobile devices are like ticking time bombs until they have been wiped or deactivated to mitigate any risk of other persons accessing applications and data on the device. Fortunately, most mobile device manufacturers and vendors provide capabilities to locate and deactivate their technologies, but this is still essentially a race to the finish line in terms of who gets access to the device first. Within an enterprise environment, there are solutions that allow for remote management of mobile devices, a topic that is discussed later in this chapter.

Theft

Mobile devices have quite an appeal about them because of their popularity amongst consumers and the potential resale value they have. Understandably, there are people who wouldn't think twice about getting their hands on your device if you turn your head for a minute or happen to misplace it.

As when a device is lost, they are like landmines in the hands of the wrong person, and it's a race to have the device wiped or deactivated to mitigate the potential for unauthorized access to the device and content. As stated above, most mobile device manufacturers and vendors provide capabilities to locate and deactivate their technologies, and third-party solutions are available to organizations.

Replacement

Mobile devices are constantly in a state of technology advancement. Because of this, these technologies are frequently being upgraded because newer technologies are released with new features and capabilities which come with a certain appeal. When this happens, there can be times when standard operating procedures (SOP) are not followed, resulting in the old mobile devices not being wiped or deactivated. Much like being lost or stolen, until the potential for unauthorized access to the organization's data and applications on the device has been mitigated, in the wrong hands this can lead to data loss or exposure.

Local Storage

One technology advancement made with mobile devices was to allow for increased storage capacity that rivaled that of traditional computer systems. The expanded storage on these devices presents a growing possibility for an organization's—confidential or sensitive—data to persistent beyond the scope of control an organization commonly employs. An organization's capability to manage data when in use, in transit, or at rest is essential in mitigating data loss or exposure when these devices have been lost or stolen, or are being replaced.

Cloud Storage

Realistically, the local storage capacity available on mobile devices is limited. Alternatively, mobile device manufacturers and vendors have turned to cloud computing as a means of addressing storage capacity limitations because of the ways in which the cloud environment can quickly increase to accommodate growing volumes of information, and be readily accessible to users across multiple device types. Unsurprisingly, this creates increased concerns about data security when it is further beyond the scope of an organization's control.

Encryption

Perhaps the biggest desire of any digital forensics practitioner when encountering a mobile device is that is has no passcodes. However, after the National Security Agency (NSA) breach in 2013 mobile device manufacturers and vendors implemented stronger and more stringent encryption standards that rendered most bypass techniques obsolete. Subsequently, using digital forensics technologies to gather and process digital evidence became more difficult.

Within an enterprise environment, there are third-party solutions available that allow for remote management of mobile devices so that organizations can remotely reset the passcodes to allow digital forensics practitioner access. However, it is important to note that performing a remote passcode change can result in potential evidence on the mobile device being modified, deleted, or lost and should be done with caution and performed only by knowledgeable individuals with direct supervision of the digital forensics practitioner.

"Burner" Phones

The term "burner" refers to a low-cost mobile device that is either used for a short time or for a specific purpose and is then disposed of. For the most part, the data ports present on these devices are disabled and they do not come with application programming interface (API) support, both of which are required for digital forensics technologies to gather and process digital evidence.

Burners are extremely troublesome for the digital forensics community because there is almost no potential for accessing the content on these devices. The only option that exists is using advanced techniques such as the following:

- *Joint Test Action Group (JTAG) analysis* is the common name given to the technique of connecting to the standard test access port (TAP) on a mobile device and instructing the processor to transfer raw data. Using this technique requires both a high level of knowledge and training as well as specialized equipment, which makes it somewhat of a difficult and time-consuming technique to gather and process digital evidence from mobile devices. This technique has been standardized as the Institute of Electrical and Electronics Engineers (IEEE) 1149.1 Standard Test Access Port and Boundary-Scan Architecture.
- *Chip-off analysis* involves physically removing the flash memory chip(s) from a mobile device and gathering raw data using specialized equipment. While this technique allows digital forensics practitioners to gather a complete physical image of a mobile device, it is destructive and can render the device inoperable. Much like the JTAG technique above, chip-off analysis also requires a high level of knowledge and training that makes it a difficult and time-consuming technique.

Refer to Chapter 3, "Digital Evidence Management," for further discussion about data-centric security.

Refer to Chapter 18, "Forensics Readiness in Cloud Environments," for further details about enabling proactive digital forensics capabilities within cloud computing environments.

Forensics Readiness Methodology

Following traditional methodologies, as illustrated in Figure 19.1 and discussed further in Chapter 2, "Investigative Process Methodology," digital forensics investigations normally follow an approach whereby evidence is searched for (identified), seized (collected and preserved), and analyzed (processed). However, traditional investigative methodologies were not designed with mobile devices in mind and, given the dynamic nature and portability of these devices, following this traditional approach to digital forensics investigations may not be suitable.

Thus, organizations need to optimize their investigative process by taking proactive steps to guarantee that evidence will be readily available if (and when) needed from mobile devices. Throughout the sections below, each step outlined for implementing digital forensics readiness will be discussed as it relates to improving investigative capabilities with mobile devices.

As a reference, several publications on the technical execution of mobile device forensics have been provided in the *Resources* chapter at the end of this book.

Step #1: Define Business Risk Scenarios

Digital forensics investigations of mobile devices require organizations to follow a proactive approach whereby controls and measures have been implemented to guarantee digital evidence will be available if (and when) needed.

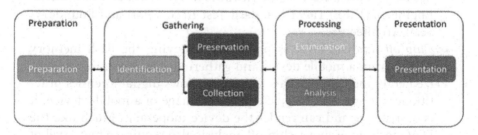

Figure 19.1 High-level digital forensics process model.

Regardless of how an organization decides to enable mobile devices for enterprise use, the business risk scenarios where digital forensics readiness demonstrates positive benefits are similar, including:

1. Reducing the impact of cybercrime
2. Validating the impact of cybercrime
3. Producing evidence to support organizational disciplinary issues
4. Demonstrate compliance with regulatory or legal requirements
5. Effectively managing the release of court-ordered data
6. Supporting contractual and commercial agreements

Rather than assuming the use of mobile devices will limit the span of business risk scenarios, it is recommended to ensure all six scenarios are included right from the offset of enabling mobile device technologies. By doing so, organizations will have established a wide scope of risk that allows them to be better positioned for focusing on specifics, rather than establishing a narrow scope and having to expand after having identified missed evidence.

Refer to Chapter 7, "Defining Business Risk Scenarios," for further discussion on the six business risk scenarios as they apply to digital forensics readiness.

Step #2: Identify Potential Data Sources

Mobile devices contain types of ESI that are similar to ESI found on other devices and that can be used as potential digital evidence. Primarily, evidence sources from mobile devices are extracted from contact data, call data, text messaging, multimedia, application-related logs, and OS information. Additionally, the following are examples of other data sources where digital evidence can be found on mobile devices:

- SIM data objects:
  - Service provider name (SPN)
  - Integrated circuit card identifier (ICCID)
  - Location information (LOCI)
  - Short message service (SMS)
  - General packet radio service (GPRS)
- Internal memory data objects:
  - International mobile equipment identifier (IMEI)
  - Personal information management (PIM) data (e.g., address book, calendar entries, to-do list, memos)
  - Call logs
  - SMS text messages

- Electronic mail
- Web browsing information
- Unstructured documents (e.g., word processing)
- Multimedia content (i.e., images, videos, graphics)

Like traditional computer systems, the order of volatility, as discussed in Chapter 2, "Investigative Process Methodology," also applies to mobile devices. Therefore, it is important that gathering volatile evidence from mobile devices follows the same methodology as for traditional computer systems. For example, in today's smartphones there can be three types of memory storage used:

- *NAND* flash memory is non-volatile and offers higher storage capacity but is less stable and only allows for sequential access to data. Types of data located in NAND memory include:
  - PIM data
  - Multimedia (video, audio, images)
  - User files
- *NOR* flash memory is non-volatile and has faster read times but slower write times than NAND, and this memory is nearly immune to data corruption. Types of data located in NOR memory include:
  - Operating system (OS) code
  - Kernel and device drivers
  - OS and user application execution instructions
- *Random access memory (RAM)* is volatile and typically used to temporarily store program execution data. Types of data located in RAM include:
  - OS and user credentials (username and passcodes)
  - OS and application configuration files

It is important to remember that with every mobile device there are different features, capabilities, applications, etc. available which determine the nature to which potential digital evidence will exist. Having completed preliminary work to prepare for mobile device examination, consideration should be given to prioritizing the order in which tools will be used to process digital evidence. In doing so, digital forensics practitioners will benefit by applying a consistent and repeatable methodology to their investigative technique.

Also, depending on the device management methodology used, such as COBO or CYOD, the scope of potential data sources for digital evidence can vary. For example, where mobile devices are personally owned by a person

(BYOD), the ability to gather and process potential evidence is challenging because the organization does not own the device and is not legally entitled to seize it—without the involvement of law enforcement—to facilitate investigations.

Step #3: Determine Collection Requirements

With mobile devices, gathering and processing evidence is not as straightforward as it is with ESI located within an organization's traditional computer systems and technologies. For example, a common challenge occurs when the organization's mobile device management strategy permits employees to use their personal devices (i.e., BYOD). This introduces a potential "grey area" wherein the boundaries of what is considered reasonable in terms of personal privacy and what is business/personal use rights can be complicated.

Understandably, BYOD is becoming a top strategy of many organizations because of the financial and operational benefits it provides. However, BYOD gets complicated when digital evidence from a mobile device (belonging to the employee) needs to be gathered and processed for an investigation. Generally, the organization does not legally own the mobile device and can't seize it as they would for any other technology considered their property (e.g., laptop, desktop). In this case, the organization must request permission to access any information that falls outside of the scope of business-enabled data, which in some instances could require the involvement of law enforcement.

Enterprise Management Strategies

Even if a mobile device is personally owned, the organization's data is still being accessed and potentially stored on it. The reality is that many organizations still struggle to define how, when, why, with whom, and under what circumstance mobile devices access and use their data. Also, there are some organizations that are not adequately equipped to ensure that when an incident happens, they have the capabilities to gather and process digital evidence.

Organizations providing their employees with the flexibility of conducting business using mobile devices must have strategies in place to manage not only the device and business content, but also the expectations of the employees in terms of usage. Developing and implementing a mobile device management strategy is a topic unto itself that requires organizations to have a strong understanding of the administrative, technical, and physical requirements that make it successful. The intention of this section is not to provide readers with a comprehensive guide so that they go and implement a mobile device management strategy; rather this chapter is designed to provide readers with the components of mobile device management that should be generally known to digital forensics practitioners.

Mobile Device Governance   Before digital forensics capabilities can be realized, there needs to be approved documentation that establishes the requirements for (un)acceptable use of mobile devices to securely access corporate networks and data. Combined with the documentation created via the organization's overall enterprise governance framework, standard operating procedures (SOP) are the backbone for performing digital forensics on mobile devices.

Acceptable Use Policy (AUP)   As mobile devices continue to become more prominent as the technology of choice for an ever-growing mobile workforce, authorized (and unauthorized) use to conduct business continues to expand. Following the same approach of establishing governance for compliance purposes, best practices call for the same establishment and enforcement of formalized policies to minimize business risk and maximize compliance.

Not considering size, geographic location, or industry, all organizations need to enforce an AUP that governs the use of mobile devices to conduct business on their behalf. Regardless of whether a mobile device is personally or corporately owned, it is being used to access and store the organization's data and as such must comply with the requirements set forth in the AUP.

If there are no rules in place, employees will not have a clear understanding of what the organization deems acceptable, which could result in activities such as transmitting confidential customer data that violate specific laws or regulations. Given the potential risk that exists for both acceptable and unacceptable use of mobile devices, it is essential that organizations formally establish and enforce an AUP that defines how, when, why, with whom, and under what circumstance employees can—and cannot—use mobile devices.

User acknowledgment and agreement: As a supplementary to the AUP, as part of the onboarding process before employees are permitted to use mobile devices for business purposes, they must be required to sign an agreement that acknowledges their responsibilities for doing so.

Generally, the purpose of these documents is to set forth the terms and conditions by which organizations make available, to their employees, information technology (IT) resources that have been deemed authorized. These IT resources may include software, networks, email services, and data storage capabilities accessible using mobile devices that have met the required security and configuration standards. It is important for employees understand that their use of mobile devices for business purposes is a privilege,

not a right, and that their acknowledgement makes them responsible for the
following terms and conditions found in these agreements:

- Abide by all organizational policies, standards, and guidelines relating to IT.
- Agree to have mobile device security and configuration settings
  pushed to this mobile device(s).
- Make appropriate backups of personal information to mitigate loss
  of information should the device be lost, stolen, or replaced.
- Do not make backups of any data belonging to the organization on
  any storage medium that has not been authorized for use.
- Allow the organization to wipe the device at their decision for the
  purposes of securing data belonging to the organization.
- Report the device lost or stolen immediately to the organization's IT
  support helpdesk.

Also, it must be clearly defined that employees' failure to follow these terms
and conditions will be handled as a disciplinary action with results such as:

- Suspension, blocking, or restriction of access to the organization's
  IT resources
- Financial liability for costs incurred due to data breach, loss, or ille-
  gal disclosure

Security and Configuration Standards As discussed in Chapter 5,
"Digital Forensics as a Business," standards are used as the drivers for policies by defining a baseline by which it is necessary to meet applicable policy
requirements. When it comes to mobile devices, these standards can be used
to establish a minimum level of configuration or specification that must be
achieved to meet the boundaries of acceptable action, behavior, or communication when using mobile devices.

See Table 19.1 for examples of recommended safeguards and controls for
mobile devices, both personally and corporately owned, that can help organizations establish baseline security and configuration standards.

Device Management Methodologies   Generally, there are four approaches
organizations can follow when deciding what level of freedom they will allow
their employees to have when using mobile devices for business purposes,
including *corporate-owned business only (COBO)*, *corporate-owned personally enabled (COPE)*, *bring your own device (BYOD)*, and *choose your own
device (CYOD)*. Each of these deployment models comes with its own benefits
and drawbacks with respect to enabling digital forensics capabilities.

Table 19.1   Safeguards and Controls for Mobile Devices

Required Controls (Minimum Level)	Recommended Controls
Mobile Device Management (MDM) Third-party solutions that enforce configuration and security policies. Refer to section below for additional details.	**Mobile Application Management (MAM)** Third-party solutions that control the installation and execution of applications. Refer to section below for additional details.
Encryption Implemented to maintain confidentiality of data at rest, in transit, and in use. Commonly enforced through third-party MDM solutions.	**Data Loss Prevention (DLP)** Monitors, filters, and protects the loss or exposure of data at rest, in transit, and in use. Availability of these solutions depends on supported capabilities on different types of devices.
Virtual Private Networking (VPN) Establish secure communication channels for transmitting data. Commonly applied on an application-by-application basis through third-party MDM solutions.	**Network Access Control (NAC)** Permits only trusted and authorized devices to gain access to networks, systems, applications, and data. Availability of these solutions depends on supported capabilities on different types of devices.
Authentication Enforcement of acceptable passcodes to mitigate unauthorized access. Commonly enforced through third-party MDM solutions.	**Multi-Factor Authentication (MFA)** Use of two or more types of authentication mechanisms (i.e., passcode, biometric, token) to access devices.
Anti-Malware Restrict known malicious applications from being installed or executed. Availability of these solutions depends on supported capabilities on different types of devices.	**Application Whitelisting** Permit known trusted and authorized applications to be installed or executed. Some mobile device manufacturers and vendors natively provide this capability. Otherwise, availability of these solutions depends on supported capabilities on different types of devices.
Remote Wipe Permits remote wiping or resetting of devices to mitigate data loss or exposure if the device has been lost, stolen, or replaced. Commonly enforced through third-party MDM solutions.	**Compliance Monitoring** Supervising usage trends, device configurations, and the user's overall compliance with the organization's governance framework. This information can be used to facilitate investigative capabilities. Refer to section below for additional details.
Audit Logs Provide information to facilitate investigative capabilities. Refer to section below for additional details.	**Web Browsing** Filtering Internet browsing activity through dynamic content analysis. Use of proxy server commonly enforced through third-party MDM solutions.

- *Corporate-owned, business only (COBO)* is one of the traditional methods of mobile device deployment where organizations choose and pay for the device then apply their most restrictive security policies. Essentially, mobile devices provisioned following COBO are limited to business use only and do not permit any personal use. In the digital forensics community, COBO is the preferred model because it eliminates the potential for interactions between personal and business activities, thus reducing the scope of digital evidence to sources under control by the organization.
- *Corporate-owned, personally enabled (COPE)* is where employees are supplied with mobile devices, chosen and paid for by the organization, but can also use these devices for personal activities. Under this model, organizations control how much freedom employees have in terms of what actions, behaviors, or communications they can perform. With COPE, this means digital forensics practitioners have a broader scope of potential digital evidence at their disposal—in comparison to COBO— as well as increased concerns over privacy related to what visibility they have into the employee's "personally enabled" components.
- *Bring your own device (BYOD)* is where employees are granted full responsibility for choosing and supporting the mobile device they use because it is their personal device. While this model is most popular in small and medium business environment, largely because of the cost savings, more enterprise environments are exploring it as an option because it reduces the technology overhead and expenditures associated with lost, stolen, or replaced devices. Even though BYOD is considered a way of pleasing employees, because they get to use their device of choice, it can become a disaster because of the extent to which there is no control over security, reliability, or compatibility with the organization. In terms of digital forensics, BYOD further complicates gathering and processing potential digital evidence because the organization does not own the device and is not legally entitled to seize it—without the involvement of law enforcement—to facilitate investigations.
- *Choose your own device (CYOD)* provides organizations with a solution in terms of getting the best of both COPE and BYOD. With this model, employees are offered a suite of technology choices but the organization retains control over security, reliability, and durability. This means that organizations maintain a list of pre-approved mobile devices and do not have to deal with variability while still allowing employees to have some degree of flexibility and privacy. For digital forensics practitioners, depending on the restriction enforced by the organization, there is potential for this flexibility to allow "personally enabled" components to be available and a broad scope of digital evidence along with complications over privacy.

Within the enterprise governance framework, there needs to be a series of documents that specifically addresses mobile device use and access with respect to the organization's network, systems, and data. These documents provide the organization with a foundation for planning the eventual implementation of mobile device management capabilities, guidelines for user behavior and conduct, as well as a driver for enabling digital forensics capabilities. Detailed discussion about digital forensics processes, procedures, and how an organization's enterprise governance framework complements digital forensics can be found in Chapter 5, "Digital Forensics as a Business."

Step #4: Establish Legal Admissibility

As with all digital evidence, maintaining authenticity and integrity is essential to guaranteeing a forensically sound and legally admissible investigation. Largely, the tools and equipment used to investigate mobile devices provide capabilities to generate, validate, and verify the authenticity and integrity of evidence using a one-way cryptographic hash algorithm.

Generally, electronic evidence has been legally admissible based on the inherent reliability of computer systems, such as within U.S. *Federal Rules of Evidence* (FRE) section 901(a). Now, with mobile devices, digital evidence is quite different from traditional computer systems where the creation and transmission of substantial amounts of information occur through a variety of devices (e.g., laptops, smartphones, tablets) so quickly and, in a lot of cases, without the verification of who did so.

Although the legal requirement for establishing the admissibility of evidence is well-established, the widespread use of mobile devices has created challenges in legal proceedings because most judicial systems have yet to decide how to authenticate ESI under current rules and procedures. Ultimately, the admissibility of mobile forensics evidence comes down to the ability to guarantee that the digital forensics practitioner has used a forensically sound and scientifically proven methodology that encompasses the following:

- Forensics tools and equipment are verified and validated to be forensically sound.
- Processes followed can be repeated by objective parties.
- Integrity and authenticity of evidence can be demonstrated through the creation and validation of one-way hash algorithms.

For further discussion about validation and verifying the tools and equipment used to gather and process digital evidence, refer to Addendum A, "Tool and Equipment Validation Program."

Step #5: Establish Secure Storage and Handling

Generally, the same forensics principles that apply to traditional computer systems also apply to mobile devices to guarantee the authenticity and integrity of potential evidence. However, with mobile devices, it is important to remember that some devices can receive data through wireless networks, which can introduce new evidence and tamper with, destroy, or alter existing evidence.

As discussed in Chapter 1, "Understanding Digital Forensics," the purpose of a forensically sound process is to document that evidence is what practitioners claim it to be and that it has not been altered or replaced since its collection. The same requirement for establishing the meaningfulness, relevancy, and legal admissibility of digital evidence applies for mobile devices; however, given the use of cellular hardware with this technology, there are additional activities and tasks that need to be performed.

As a best practice, when an inactive mobile device is encountered at a crime scene, meaning that it is powered off, it is important that it be left powered off and seized following documented SOPs. Also, all associated cables and media must also be seized with the mobile device, such as subscriber identity module (SIM) cards or secure digital (SD) cards.

Alternatively, when encountering an active mobile device at a crime scene, meaning that it is still powered on, it is important to take the necessary steps to isolate the device from other devices and technologies to mitigate the potential for digital evidence to be contaminated. As a best practice, digital forensics practitioners can use the following three basic methods for isolating mobile devices that are active:

- *Place the device in airplane mode.* This method requires interaction with the mobile device's keyboard, which poses potential risk whereby if the individual is not familiar with the device, or the device has been pre-configured with a logic bomb, this can result in potential contamination or loss of digital evidence. It is important to note that with some devices, enabling airplane mode does not disable all cellular communications (e.g., Global Positioning System [GPS]).
- *Turn the device off.* This method may also require interaction with the mobile device's keyboard and can activate authentication mechanisms (e.g., passcodes) to gain access later. In addition to risks that are similar to those posed to digital evidence, this method introduces complications and delays when it comes to acquiring and processing evidence from the mobile device.
- *Keep the device on.* This method does not require interaction with the mobile device but does require consideration of the need to prolong battery life. With this method, mobile devices are placed in a

Faraday bag to reduce cellular and wireless communications. It is important to note that Faraday bags do not completely eliminate the potential for cellular and wireless communications to occur. Also, if the Faraday bag is not properly sealed, mobile devices may unknowingly be allowed to access cellular or wireless networks. Several techniques exist to support this method and can be found in the *Resources* chapter at the end of this book.

Step #6: Enable Targeted Monitoring

Because mobile devices are portable, organizations cannot always guarantee the level of security will be equivalent to the security of those technologies that have connections that are hard-wired to their controlled network environment(s). Therefore, to ensure that both background and foreground evidence on mobile devices is available if (or when) needed, as discussed further in Chapter 3, "Digital Evidence Management," organizations need to employ a strategy that follows a defense-in-depth methodology.

Depending on which device management methodology is used, there will be varying degrees of monitoring that can be enforced on a mobile device. For example, COBO implementations provide organizations with the authority necessary to enforce monitoring on any combination of device or application components, in addition to user activity, of the mobile devices. However, BYOD implementations introduce a level of complexity because there are boundaries around what an organization can and cannot legally monitor, as these devices are not their assets.

As illustrated previously in Table 19.1, examples of recommended safeguards and controls for mobile devices, both personally and corporately owned, can help organizations establish a baseline of security and configuration standards. Additionally, the following are examples of software-based solutions that can be implemented to enhance targeted monitoring with mobile device management capabilities:

- *Mobile device management (MDM)*, sometimes referred to as mobile security management (MSM), is designed to manage a mobile device, or a segregated part of it, by enforcing security and configuration policies. Generally, these solutions don't increase the security of a mobile device, but instead facilitate security with device-level controls by allowing organizations to determine what amount of control they want to enforce. Examples of settings and configurations that can be applied include the following:
  - *Security settings* are made to improve device-level security that helps to mitigate unauthorized access (e.g., passcodes specifications).

- *Encryption settings* are made to require the use of encryption standards to mitigate exposure or loss of data when in use, in transit, or at rest.
- *Malware settings* are made to restrict known malicious applications from being installed or executed. The availability of these solutions depends on supported capabilities on different types of devices (i.e., Android, iOS, Windows).
- *System settings* are made to control specific features available throughout the operating system (e.g., screen capture, user account control).
- *Cloud settings* are made to restrict the use and transmission of data within a cloud computing environment.
- *Email settings* are made to control the transmission and use of email-based resources.
- *Application settings* are made to enforce the feature availability of native system applications (e.g., web browser, application store).
- *Device capability settings* are made to enforce the feature availability of device-level components (e.g., camera, Bluetooth)

- *Mobile application management (MAM)* is designed to provision, secure, and manage the access and actions of mobile applications rather than the entire device. Generally, while MAM solutions can be bundled together as a complementary capability to MDM solutions, they are used where organizations are exploring more flexibility and a relaxed approach to mobile device management. MAM solutions provide organizations with a way of getting a handle on which applications are being installed and run on the mobile devices that use and access their corporate networks and resources. However, MAM solutions don't provide the same level of security offered through MDM solutions, which allow organizations to lock down or limit features or capabilities of actual mobile devices.
- *Mobile content management (MCM)* is designed to securely grant access and manage the access to and use of data through the enforcement of multi-factor authentication, authorization, and access controls, such as usernames, passcodes, internet protocol (IP) addresses, or tokens. MCM focuses primarily on securing corporate data without placing restrictions on the mobile device or applications. These solutions differ from MDM and MAM, where a single specific application is delivered to mobile devices and functions as a "container" to securely grant and manage access to and use of data. While MCM solutions are perhaps the least intrusive form of mobile device management capabilities, because they don't impose any device or application restrictions, they follow a data-centric security model that enforces elevated levels of protection to the organization's data.

Refer to Chapter 3,"Digital Evidence Management," for further discussion about data-centric security.

Step #7: Map Investigative Workflows

The process of gathering and processing digital evidence from mobile devices can differ depending on manufacturer and vendors. With these potential variations, it is understandable that there is not a well-established methodology by which mobile device forensics is performed. However, with the intricacy involved in performing mobile device forensics, it is necessary for organizations to implement guidelines and process by which their digital forensics practitioners can gather and process potential digital evidence.

Knowing that there are potential limitations on conducting mobile forensics, it is necessary to implement guidelines and processes by which the digital forensics practitioner can gather and process potential digital evidence. The high-level digital forensics process model, as illustrated previously in Table 19.1, will be applied to the activities and tasks involved in conducting mobile forensics.

Phase #1: Preparation

As discussed in Chapter 2, "Investigative Process Methodology," the activities and tasks performed in this first phase are essential in successfully executing all subsequent phases of the investigative workflow. As a component of the preparation phase, organizations can proactively align their people, processes, and technologies to support their cloud forensics capabilities.

Processes and Procedures   With mobile device forensics being a sub-discipline of digital forensics, the existing baseline of standards, guidelines, and techniques discussed in Chapter 5, "Digital Forensics as a Business," become the foundation for creating new documentation specific to mobile devices.

Largely, digital forensics standard operating procedures (SOP) still apply to mobile device forensics when gathering and processing digital evidence. However, given that mobile devices differ in that they use cellular technology, there is a need to develop specific SOPs so that digital forensics practitioners know how to handle them. These considerations related to gathering and processing digital evidence from mobile devices will be discussed further in the phase below.

Education, Training, and Awareness   Like digital forensics, an individual's role with respect to mobile device forensics determines the level of knowledge they are provided. Further discussion about the different levels of education, training, and awareness is found in the section below.

Technology and Toolsets   Within the dedicated lab environment, organizations will need to acquire specific software and hardware to support their mobile device forensics capabilities. However, the extent to which an organization invests in their "toolkit" is entirely subjective to their environment and the degree to which they want to gather and process digital evidence from these mobile devices.

Considerations related to technologies and tools used to gather and process digital evidence from mobile devices will be discussed further in the phase below where applicable to the investigative workflow.

Further discussion about digital forensics tools and technologies can be found in Chapter 5, "Digital Forensics as a Business."

Phase #2: Gathering

As discussed in Chapter 2, "Investigative Process Methodology," the second phase of the investigative workflow consists of the activities and tasks involved in the identification, collection, and preservation of digital evidence. The same requirement for establishing the meaningfulness, relevancy, and legal admissibility of digital evidence applies to mobile devices; however, given the use of cellular hardware with this technology, there are additional activities and tasks that need to be performed.

Identification   Regardless of the evidence that has been identified, both physical and logical, digital forensics practitioners must follow consistent and repeatable processes to secure, document, and search the crime scene. Sample templates that can be used in the process of securing, documenting, and searching crime scenes have been provided in the *Templates* section of this book.

As a best practice, organizations should develop a scoring mechanism that can be used to decide whether on-site triage is required. Illustrated in Figure 19.2 is a decision tree that can be used by organizations as a guide when deciding whether on-site triage is required. The following list describes the decision points contained within the decision tree:

- *Urgent*: Do the circumstances warrant on-site triage and extraction of evidence?
- *Unlocked or undamaged*: Is the device in an unlocked and functional state for evidence to be extracted?
- *Battery life*: Does the device show more than 50% battery life remaining?
- *Lab distance*: Can the device be transported to the forensics lab in less than 2 hours?
- *Tools*: Does the forensics "toolkit" support on-site triage and extraction of evidence?

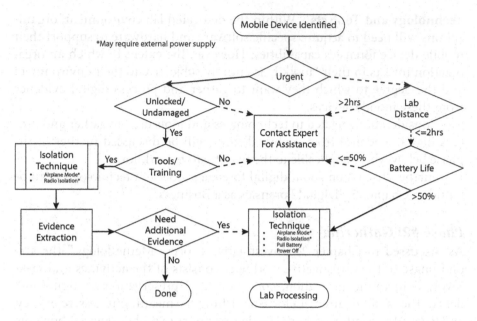

Figure 19.2 On-site triage decision tree.

- *Training*: Are trained individuals available to conduct on-site triage and extraction of evidence?
- *Need additional evidence*: After on-site triage is completed, is additional evidence required?

When the path taken through the decision tree results in on-site triage, forensics acquisition of the mobile device is the most common technique performed. Performing an acquisition during on-site triage does have an advantage whereby the potential loss of volatile data can be avoided. However, unlike a lab environment, performing acquisitions during on-site triage may be challenging vis a vis finding a controlled environment in which the work can be completed. Tools used to perform forensics acquisitions of mobile devices will be discussed in the next section of the investigative workflow.

Collection and Preservation   Where activities and tasks differ is when it comes time to collect and preserve digital evidence from a mobile device. As previously outlined in *Step #2: Identify Potential Data Sources*, the order of volatility also applies to mobile devices. Therefore, it is important that gathering volatile evidence from mobile devices follows the same methodology as for traditional computer systems.

Where possible, mobile devices that support data-at-rest encryption capabilities should be triaged at the crime scene, as volatile data may no longer exist if the screen is locked or power is lost. Depending on the context of the investigation, it may be required to conduct an on-site triage to collect and preserve volatile data. When determining whether to conduct on-site triage, organizations should consider the following benefits to the overall investigation:

- Work being performed in a digital forensics lab may be reduced because potential evidence sources can be ruled out beforehand.
- Investigative activities and tasks can be focused or prioritized based on the immediate results of findings.
- Existing resources, including people and technologies, can be enhanced by intelligence gained from the results.
- Triage tools are typically designed to require less knowledge and experience as compared to in-depth analysis tools.
- Triage tools typically are more affordable as compared to in-depth analysis tools.

Phase #3: Processing

Within this third phase is the examination and analysis of gathered evidence for relevancy. Throughout, maintaining the authenticity and integrity of evidence is essential to guaranteeing a forensically sound and legally admissible investigation. For the most part, the tools and equipment used provide automated capabilities to validate and verify the one-way cryptographic hash algorithm created when the digital evidence was seized, allowing practitioners to prove beyond a doubt that their interactions did not impact the integrity and authenticity of evidence.

The selection of appropriate tools for examining and analyzing mobile devices depends on several factors, such as the goal(s) of the investigation, the type of mobile device, and practitioner knowledge and experience. Ultimately, there is no one single tool that can process all data from every make and model of mobile device, largely because of the difference in the way digital evidence needs to be extracted from each technology. As a strategy, the following set of criteria can be used as guidance when considering which tool is best suited to a particular situation:

- *Usability*: The presentation of data is in a format that is easy for users to navigate and understand.
- *Comprehensive*: All available data is presented so factual conclusions can be drawn.
- *Deterministic*: The output of data from the tool is reproducible when provided with identical instructions and input data.

- *Accuracy*: The quality of outputted data from the tool has been verified.
- *Verifiable*: The accuracy of outputted data through presentation of results is ensured.
- *Tested*: A determination is made as to whether the data contained within mobile devices remains authentic and is accurately reported by the tool.

After leveraging the above criteria to identify the appropriate tools, consideration now needs to be given to the potential digital evidence sources that exist within mobile devices. The data present on any mobile device depends not only on its features and capabilities, but also on the cellular (voice and data) services used by the device. As previous outlined in *Step #2: Identify Potential Data Sources*, there are many data sources where digital evidence can be extracted from mobile devices.

Phase #4: Presentation

As discussed in Chapter 2, "Investigative Process Methodology," documentation is a critical element of every investigation and needs to start at the beginning of the investigation and be carried out to the end. In this last phase of the investigative workflow, the final investigative report will be created to communicate factual conclusions by demonstrating the processes, techniques, tools, equipment, and interactions used to maintain the authenticity, reliability, and trustworthiness of the digital evidence. Some things to consider when writing a final investigative report include:

- The structure and layout should flow naturally and logically; like how we speak.
- The content should be clear and concise to accurately demonstrate a chronology of events.
- Use of jargon, slang, and technical terminology should be limited or avoided, and where used a glossary should be included to define terms in natural language.
- Where acronyms and abbreviations are used, they must be written out in full expression on first use.
- Because final reports are written after the fact, that is, after an investigation, content should be communicated in the past tense. However, tenses can change where conclusions or recommendations are being made.
- Format the final report not only for distribution within the organization, but also with the mindset that it may be used as testimony in a court of law.

A template for creating written formal reports has been provided as a reference in the *Templates* section of this book.

Step #8: Establish Continuing Education

Like digital forensics, an individual's role with respect to mobile forensics determines the level of knowledge they are provided. Detailed discussion about the diverse levels of education, training, and awareness an organization should require of their people in support of digital forensics can be found in Chapter 14, "Establish Continuing Education."

General Awareness

As the lowest type of education, this is a generalized level of training and awareness that is intended to provide people with foundational knowledge without getting too specialized related to mobile device forensics. Leveraging the education and training that has already been put in place for digital forensics, this education provides people with the competencies they need related to organizational policies, standards, and guidelines so that they indirectly contribute, through some form of behavior or action, to the organization's digital forensics program.

Examples of topics and subjects that should be included as part of a mobile device forensics awareness program include:

- Business code of conduct
- Mobile device acceptable use policy
- Data protection and privacy

Basic Training

Essentially, the difference between this training and the previous awareness is that the knowledge gained here is intended to teach people the skills necessary to directly support the organization's digital forensics program as relates to how, where, and to what extent mobile devices are used for business purposes.

Information communicated at this level is more detailed than the previous type of education because it must provide people with the knowledge required to support a specific role or function, such as administering the MDM solution.

For example, as part of basic mobile device forensics training, information about audit logging and retention should be covered. Generally, this topic relates to the practice of recording events and preserving them, as per the organizational governance framework, to facilitate digital forensics investigations.

Formal Education

A working and practical knowledge of mobile device forensics requires people to first and foremost have the skills and competencies necessary to ensure that all digital forensics principles, methodologies, and techniques are understood. Once the fundamental knowledge is gained, practitioners can then start pursuing a specialization in mobile device forensics.

However, unlike digital forensics education programs, the availability of curriculum dedicated entirely to mobile devices is still limited. Most commonly, mobile device forensics is taught as a specific course in higher/post-secondary institutions or as a professional education module led by an industry-recognized training institute.

Refer to Appendix B, "Education and Professional Certifications," for a list of higher/post-secondary institutions that offer formal education programs.

Step #9: Maintain Evidence-Based Presentation

Regardless of how mobile devices are deployed in an enterprise, the systems and ESI present can be used to commit or be the target of criminal activity. However, perhaps the biggest challenge to a digital forensics investigation where mobile device technologies are within scope is the dynamic nature of determining the "who, where, what, when, why, and how" of criminal activity. Some things to consider when writing a final investigative report include:

- The structure and layout should flow naturally and logically; like how we speak.
- The content should be clear and concise to accurately demonstrate a chronology of events.
- Use of jargon, slang, and technical terminology should be limited or avoided. Where used, a glossary should be included to define terms in natural language.
- Where acronyms and abbreviations are used, they must be written out in full expression on first use.
- Because final reports are written after the fact, that is, after an investigation, content should be communicated in the past tense; but tenses can change where conclusions or recommendations are being made.
- Format the final report not only for distribution within the organization, but also with the mindset that it may be used as testimony in a court of law.

A template for creating written formal reports has been provided as a reference in the *Templates* section of this book.

Step #10: Ensure Legal Review

There are different laws and regulations around the world that govern the types of information that can be accessed on mobile devices. Although these different jurisdictions and regulators try to address matters of what access and control must be imposed to protect information, they do not address— from a corporate perspective—what access and control organizations should not have. This can lead to somewhat of a gray area in that there is no definitive boundary in place, allowing for subjectivity and best judgment to determine what is believed to be reasonable.

Establishing a governance framework that contains clear and concise language that is easy to understand and readily accessible to all parties— employer and employees—is extremely important. Not only does this help organizations to secure and manage their data regardless of the selected mobile device management strategy, it also guarantees employees' consent and co-operation when an incident involving their personal technology occurs. Equally important is ensuring employees who will be using these devices to access corporate data have read, fully understand, and agreed (in writing) with what is expected of them.

Further discussion about laws, standards, and regulations can be referenced in Chapter 16, "Ensuring Legal Review."

Summary

Mobile device technology really started to proliferate, both for business and personal use, in the 1990s. With the way we conduct business continuing to evolve into a more dynamic and mobile workforce, the appropriate use of mobile devices to conduct business needs to be clearly articulated and controlled to mitigate any potential data security risks. However, when an incident involving mobile devices occurs, it is important that organizations have adopted an investigative process methodology to support the work of digital forensics practitioners.

Forensics Readiness and the Internet of Things

20

Introduction

Since the inception of networked computing, technologies have increasingly been created with network capabilities allowing them to communicate and exchange data much like the traditional client-server model. Today, technology is being embedded in almost everything that is manufactured, from smartphones, coffee makers, and televisions to automobiles, wearable devices, and more.

The modern development of technology has brought about a new era and there are now millions of devices connected to and that communicate through the Internet. While this development has made our personal and business lives more comfortable and convenient, the Internet of Things (IoT) era raises concerns of security and privacy while presenting challenges of applying existing principles, methodologies, and techniques to gather and process potential evidence when needed.

Brief History of the Internet of Things (IoT)

Ever since the inception of technology, visionaries have imagined a day when machines can communicate with one another without human intervention. Like cloud computing, discussed in Chapter 18, "Forensics Readiness in Cloud Environments," there were several technological advancements that created the concept of the Internet of Things (IoT) and that have made it what it is today.

One of the first examples of the IoT concept being actualized was in the early 1980s. Developers at Carnegie Melon University developed a program that allowed them to connect—over the Internet—to a refrigerated Coca Cola machine. The software checked the inventory of the appliance to see if there was a drink available and if it was cold.

What could be considered the starting point for IoT dates to the 1830s, when machines were developed for direct communication (i.e., telegraphy). Subsequently, the development and advancement of both computer systems and networking capabilities throughout the 1900s was a major evolution towards the concept of IoT. Formally, the Internet of Things (IoT) as a concept was officially named in 1999 when Kevin Ashton, who was the executive director of Auto-ID Labs at the Massachusetts Institute of Technology (MIT), in a presentation given for Proctor & Gamble, stated that:

> Today computers, and, therefore, the Internet, are almost wholly dependent on human beings for information... If we had computer[s] that knew everything there was to know about things, using data they gathered without any help from us, we would be able to t[r]ack and count everything and greatly reduce waste, loss and cost.

By the year 2013, the IoT concept had evolved into a revolutionary concept that enabled most any device with an on/off switch to operate and communicate intelligently with other devices. Now, IoT applies the concept of being always connected, from anywhere and at any time, which has now allowed for people-people, people-things, and things-things connections. These potential relationships introduce new avenues by which personal and business information can be exchanged, new attack vectors (i.e., hacking a toaster to gain access into a network environment), and how or where digital evidence can persist.

What Is the Internet of Things (IoT)?

Smart devices falling within the concept of IoT have been in use for some time now in areas such as healthcare, transportation, and home automation. Knowing what classifies any technology device as an IoT device requires understanding the distinguishing characteristic that these technologies possess in comparison to traditional technologies. Illustrated in Figure 20.1, all IoT devices have the following five main modules:

1. *Sensor module* detects and reacts to:
   a. Requests made by a user or other sensor (controlled sensors); or
   b. Changes in the local environment (event-driven sensors).
2. *Processing module* processes information received from sensors and transmits it as needed.
3. *Actuation module* triggers the physical device to execute the processed results.
4. *Communication module* transmits data to other devices across networked environments.
5. *Energy module* manages the availability of power and its consumption for all other IoT modules.

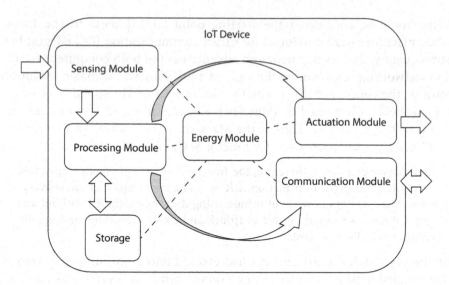

Figure 20.1 IoT module relationships.

Additionally, all IoT devices have the following five main characteristics:

1. *Existence*: Physical things can be embedded with specific (IoT) technology.
2. *Sense of self*: Physical things have a sense of identity and can handle data, make decisions, and act autonomously.
3. *Connectivity*: Physical things can connect openly with other things.
4. *Interactivity*: Physical things can interoperate and work together regardless of whether human intervention is present.
5. *Dynamicity*: Physical things can communicate with different things at any time, in any place, and in any capacity.
6. *Scalability*: Physical things can be expanding and associated across a global network.
7. *Computational limitations*: The processing unit is not designed to perform specific functions or to perform complex operations.
8. *Resource limitations*: There is limited onboard capacity to provide an operating environment (i.e., storage, power).

Challenges with the Internet of Things (IoT)

Generally, the goal of IoT is to make our lives more convenient and dynamic by allowing disparate devices to exchange information with each other to provide useful services to the owner. However, it was not necessarily designed with concerns of security or privacy in mind. As result, IoT has created new opportunities for cybercrime to capitalize on these devices as new attack vectors.

Form Factor

Predominantly, IoT devices come in many different form factors that offer varying amounts of onboard storage, primarily only for its operating system (OS). Because of storage limitations, IoT devices are exceptionally volatile in the lifespan to which they keep information, resulting in potential evidence being overwritten quickly. While a simple solution would be to leverage remote logging capabilities for IoT devices, concerns arise about guaranteeing the integrity and authenticity of evidence. Additionally, because IoT devices may not come in the form of traditional computer systems, digital forensics practitioners are faced with complexities of having to gather and process evidence from unusual sources where existing techniques are difficult to apply, such as coffee makers or televisions.

Security

With traditional computer systems, security controls are implemented as a means of safeguarding informational assets. As stated previously, the growth of IoT has raised significant concerns of security because any device can be interconnected and their form factors aren't designed for security capabilities. For example, IoT introduces new attack vectors whereby threat actors could use an IoT device (e.g., light bulb). Considering this, businesses are faced with storing massive amounts of technology-generated data, and they need to develop strategies for securely storing it to serve as potential digital evidence if (or when) required.

Privacy

Sensors and camera have become quite commonplace, allowing for information to be gathered and in some cases, without knowledge or ways to avoid it. This makes people uncomfortable knowing that information about them is being collected and, once it's been collected, they have little to no control over who has access to it.

Evidence Gathering and Processing

With IoT, devices can be widespread and located outside the organization's span of control, such as in the cloud, in a third-party facility, or at a person's residence. Because of this, the collection and preservation of IoT evidence can prove challenging when digital content is created, transferred, stored, and accessed across an interconnected and geographically distributed network of devices.

Forensics Toolkits

Technology-generated data generated from one IoT device or another may not be created or stored in a consistent structure or format. As result, digital forensics practitioners are experiencing difficulties when using existing digital forensics equipment and tools to gather and process digital evidence from IoT devices.

Forensics Readiness Methodology

Digital forensics investigations involving IoT devices require organizations to be proactive and develop strategies so that they are prepared to respond when required to. Pre-investigative readiness components are essential to ensure investigative techniques are prepared before an incident involving IoT devices occurs.

Following traditional methodologies, as illustrated in Figure 20.2 and discussed further in Chapter 2, "Investigative Process Methodology," digital forensics investigations normally follow an approach whereby evidence is searched for (identified), seized (collected and preserved), and analyzed (processed). However, traditional investigative methodologies were not designed with IoT in mind and, given the variety and (potential) location of these devices, following this traditional approach to digital forensics investigations may not be suitable.

Alternatively, organizations need to optimize their investigative process by taking proactive steps to guarantee that evidence will be readily available if (and when) needed from IoT devices. Throughout the sections below, each step outlined for implementing digital forensics readiness will be discussed as it relates to improving investigative capabilities with IoT devices.

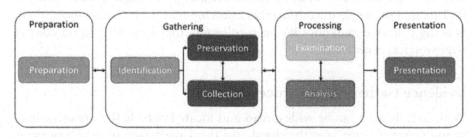

Figure 20.2 High-level digital forensics process model.

Step #1: Define Business Risk Scenarios

Digital forensics investigations involving IoT devices require organizations to follow a proactive approach whereby controls and measures have been implemented to guarantee digital evidence will be available if (and when) needed.

However, IoT devices are equipped with limited onboard hardware and scoped user interfaces such that technology-stored data cannot exist. Because technology-stored data is not created or stored on IoT devices, it is likely that all six business risk scenarios will not apply. For example, civil litigation matters are primarily concerned with producing electronically stored information (ESI) in the form of technology-stored data, with the understanding that some litigation matters will require technology-generated data to be produced.

Rather than assuming the use of IoT devices will limit the span of business risk scenarios, it is recommended to ensure all six scenarios are included right from the outset of enabling mobile device technologies. By doing so, organizations establish a wide scope of risk that allows them to be better positioned for focusing on specifics rather than establishing a narrow scope and having to expand after having identified missed evidence.

1. Reducing the impact of cybercrime
2. Validating the impact of cybercrime
3. Producing evidence to support organizational disciplinary issues
4. Demonstrating compliance with regulatory or legal requirements
5. Effectively managing the release of court-ordered data
6. Supporting contractual and commercial agreements

Refer to Chapter 7, "Defining Business Risk Scenarios," for further discussion on the six business risk scenarios as they apply to digital forensics readiness.

Step #2: Identify Potential Data Sources

Knowing that IoT devices differ from traditional computer systems in design and capabilities, the potential for evidence to exist from one device to the next can vary. However, it is still important to keep in mind that evidence can exist on these devices, and it could be relevant to an investigation.

Generally, there are two classifications of IoT devices in use today: *informational* and *special-purpose*. Interactive devices—such as vehicle consoles and smart watches—are primarily considered informational devices because, from a systems perspective, they act as proxies for humans to suggest actions and provide sensors for input. Special-purpose devices have scoped interfaces to provide specific functionality, such as temperature sensors. When an informational device is identified as an evidential data source, there is potential for both technology-stored and technology-generated data to exist. However, when a special-purpose device is identified as an evidential data source, there is no capability for human interactions that allow for data to be created, thus limiting the potential that technology-generated data will exist and that only technology-generated will be available.

With both classifications of IoT devices, the following are three types of data that can be sourced from IoT devices:

- *Passive data* is any technology-generated data that requires IoT sensors to be activated, such as through an application programming interface (API), before the data is created.
- *Active data* is any technology-generated data that is created by persistently active IoT sensors in real time.
- *Dynamic data* is any technology-generated data that is created by IoT sensors, in real time, as result of communications with other modules or IoT applications and devices.

It is common to encounter any combination of data types (passive, active, or dynamic) from one classification of IoT device to the next. Understanding what evidence can be gathered from IoT devices requires the organization to (1) have control over what IoT devices can exist within their environment and (2) be able to routinely and proactively discover IoT devices.

Step #3: Determine Collection Requirements

With IoT devices, gathering and processing evidence is not as straightforward as it is with ESI located within an organization's traditional computer systems and technologies. For example, because IoT devices have limited onboard storage, cloud computing environments are used to store data. This means that with IoT forensics, organizations need to consider the collection of digital evidence from one of the following three generic groups where ESI is located on:

- IoT devices and sensors
- Hardware and software that connect IoT devices within the scope of the organization's control
- Hardware and software that connect IoT devices outside the scope of the organization's control

With each of the above generic groups, there are three requirements that organizations should adopt to ensure digital evidence being gathered is done in a way that guarantees legal admissibility:

- *Time synchronization* is a big concern given the potential for latency or jitter than can result from the network connectivity and communications provided in most IoT devices today. Where technology permits, and the IoT device is under the organization's span of control, it is recommended that a managed and centralized time service solution be used (e.g., network time protocol [NTP]).

- *Memory and storage* resources must be available for digital forensics practitioners to gather and process the potentially large volumes of technology-generated data created by IoT devices. Careful planning of storage and processing requirements for IoT forensics must be done to accommodate both short-term and long-term storage requirements.
- *Communication* within the organization's networked environment is critical to ensure that potential evidence from technology-generated data being created by IoT devices can be extracted quickly. Organizations should develop a centralized storage facility, such as an enterprise data warehouse (EDW), as a solution for storing IoT device data.

Refer to Chapter 9, "Determine Collection Requirements," for further discussion about requirements for gathering digital evidence.

Step #4: Establish Legal Admissibility

As discussed previously throughout this book, we know that evidence, whether physical or digital, is fragile and is subject to tampering, modification, or erasure. With all (physical or digital) evidence, maintaining a chain of custody is required to guarantee authenticity and integrity as a means of establishing legal admissibility.

Zones of Trust

Like the layers of trust with cloud computing environments, as discussed in Chapter 18, "Forensics Readiness in Cloud Environments," there are several technology zones where digital evidence can exist for IoT. Each of these trust zones was designed to provide a broad segmentation of its own data, along with its own authentication and authorization requirements, that can be used to isolate damage and restrict impact to lower trust zones. Generally, zones of trust found within IoT include the following:

- *Device zone* is the immediate physical space located around the device where access can be gained.
- *Local network zone* is any system that enables and controls communication to directly connected devices in a private network environment.
- *Wide area network zone* is any system that enables and controls communication to devices located across public network environments.

- *Service zone* is any software component or module that interfaces with devices through a networked environment.
- *Application zone* is any software component or module that provisions, develops, stores, or manages service and associated datasets.
- *System zone* is any technology infrastructure used to support the software components or modules.
- *External zone* is any subject or object that remotely interacts with the system but is not under the control of the application.

Because each zone is logically separated by a trust boundary, as illustrated in Figure 20.3, information transitioning between neighboring adjoining zones can be susceptible to malicious or unwanted access, interference, or disclosure. Understanding these risks and developing appropriate countermeasures requires completing both a threat model and risk assessment following proven and documented frameworks.

Where concerns about trust do exist with IoT devices, it is important that organizations have developed solutions to identify and secure IoT located throughout their (managed) network environment so that when an incident involving IoT does occur, required evidence will be available. Like the multiple layers of interactions found throughout enterprise technology stacks where security controls can be deployed and implemented, as illustrated in Figure 20.3, these security controls can also be leveraged to enhance forensics capabilities with IoT devices by placing controls closer to the actual data as a means of protection.

Refer to Chapter 3, "Digital Evidence Management," for further discussion about data-centric security.

Refer to Chapter 10, "Establishing Legal Admissibility," for further discussion about strategies for establishing and maintaining legal admissibility.

Refer to Addendums E and F, "Risk Assessment" and "Threat Modeling," for further discussion on the framework and methodologies to follow.

Step #5: Establish Secure Storage and Handling

Generally, IoT devices are extremely volatile by design, largely due to the dynamic nature of the technologies and the varying levels of trust that exist. Considering the zones of trust illustrated previously in Figure 20.3, there can

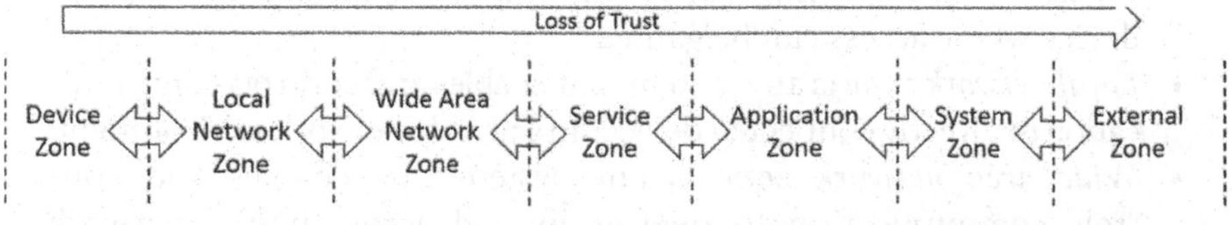

Figure 20.3 IoT trust zones.

be concerns about the integrity of information at any layer, requiring organizations to implement strategies for addressing these potential issues. Because of this, unlike traditional computing environments, all ESI deemed relevant and meaningful as potential digital evidence needs to have an elevated degree of security controls implemented to safeguard its integrity and authenticity.

For example, considering that IoT devices have limited onboard resources (i.e., storage capacity), the technology-generated data they create is often only available for short-lived periods. Given the potential volatile conditions of these devices, it is important that ESI serving as relevant digital evidence be secured while in use, in transit, and at rest. At a minimum, the following control mechanisms should be implemented (where possible) to guarantee the secure storage and handling of potential evidence in a cloud environment:

- Real-time logging of technology-generated data (i.e., log files) to a remote and centralized repository, such as an enterprise data warehouse (EDW), to address concerns of data volatility on IoT devices
- One-way cryptographic hash algorithm, such as the Message Digest Algorithm family (i.e., MD5, MD6)or the Secure Hashing Algorithm family (i.e., SHA-1, SHA-2, SHA-3), to establish and maintain both the integrity and authenticity of ESI

Refer to Chapter 3, "Digital Evidence Management," for further discussion about data-centric security, technology-generated data, and technology-stored data.

Refer to Chapter 11, "Establish Secure Storage and Handling," for further discussion about strategies for establishing and maintaining evidence integrity during handling and storage.

Step #6: Enable Targeted Monitoring

IoT devices are increasing being targeted by threat actors in large part because these technologies have weak or no security features or controls. As result, IoT devices can be a significant risk to organizations because of the increased attack surface that can be compromised as a means of gaining access to a controlled and secure network environment.

As with any traditional computer system, enabling an appropriate level of monitoring and detection is necessary for targeting (potentially) malicious activity on IoT devices. Achieving a state of digital forensics readiness within a corporate environment by enabling continuous security monitoring of IoT devices can be achieved through a variety of techniques, such as:

- *Asset management and discovery* to identify and inventory the presence of IoT devices located through the corporate network environment

- *Intrusion detection and prevention systems (IDS/IPS)* to inspect and provide alerts about potentially unwanted or malicious network communications associated with IoT devices
- *Analytical techniques* are approaches to continuous monitoring of an IoT device's use and operation, such as anomaly detection or machine learning
- *Remote logging* of technology-generated data to a centralized data repository, such as an EDW, for correlation with other events for improved security intelligence
- *Orchestration and automation solutions* to programmatically execute playbooks and workflows required to alert and notify of potentially unwanted or malicious activity with IoT devices

Refer to Addendum G, "Data Warehousing Introduction," for further discussions on the unique designs, capabilities, and purposes of these eco-systems.

Refer to Chapter 12, "Enabling Targeted Monitoring," for further discussion about analytical techniques that can be utilized for continuous security monitoring.

Step #7: Map Investigative Workflows

With existing digital forensics methodologies, as discussed in Chapter 2, "Investigative Process Methodology," the devices that can be encountered cannot be switched off at the risk of losing critical volatile data that could be used as evidence. However, following the traditional methodology with IoT devices may not be applicable because of how the unique characteristics (i.e., formats, protocols, interfaces) can complicate the techniques applied for gathering and processing evidence.

Knowing that there are additional considerations in conducting IoT forensics, it is necessary to implement guidelines and processes by which the digital forensics practitioner can gather and process potential digital evidence. The high-level digital forensics process model, as illustrated previously in Figure 20.1, will be applied to the activities and tasks involved in conducting IoT forensics.

Phase #1: Preparation

As discussed in Chapter 2, "Investigative Process Methodology," the activities and tasks performed in this first phase are essential in successfully executing all subsequent phases of the investigative workflow. As a component of the preparation phase, organizations can proactively align their people, processes, and technologies to support their IoT forensics capabilities.

Steps taken to prepare for IoT device are essential for every organization. This requires support from (top-level) management so that appropriate controls can be implemented to ensure the investigative process is holistic and well thought out. For example, the following administrative, physical, and technical controls contribute to an organization's ability to conduct IoT forensics:

- Establishing which IoT devices are approved to be connected throughout the organization's network
- Developing a strategy for what standard operating procedures (SOP) are required to gather and process evidence
- Validating that the tools and techniques used are forensically sound and can support investigative requirements
- Maturing digital forensics practitioners who can appropriately gather and process evidence from IoT devices

Refer to Addendum A, "Tool and Equipment Validation Program," for further discussion on the methodology required for validating and verifying the forensics readiness of digital forensics tools and technologies.

Phase #2: Gathering

As discussed in Chapter 2, "Investigative Process Methodology," the second phase of the investigative workflow consists of the activities and tasks involved in the identification, collection, and preservation of digital evidence. The same requirement for establishing the meaningfulness, relevancy, and legal admissibility of digital evidence applies for IoT devices; however, given the unique characteristics of each type of IoT technology, there are additional activities and tasks that need to be performed.

Identification   Regardless of the evidence that has been identified, both physical and logical, digital forensics practitioners must follow consistent and repeatable processes to secure, document, and search a crime scene. Sample templates that can be used in the process of securing, documenting, and searching crime scenes have been provided in the *Templates* section of this book.

Within the vast IoT marketplace, new types of devices are being created with multiple form factors, operating systems (OS), and (wired and wireless) networking capabilities. Because IoT devices can be found in a variety of technologies (e.g., televisions, light bulbs, and heating, ventilation, and air conditioning [HVAC] systems), it is important that organizations have the technical capabilities to scan their entire network environment to detect the presence of IoT devices so that appropriate administrative, physical, and technical controls can be implemented.

The following approaches can be used to identify IoT devices:

- *Network discovery* to identify the presence of IoT devices located throughout the corporate network environment
- *Asset management* to maintain an accurate inventory of IoT devices connected to the corporate network environment

- *Network access control* to isolate connected IoT devices in specific areas of the corporate network environment
- *Firewalls and proxies* to control how IoT devices connect to the corporate network environment

As discussed previously, IoT devices are not designed with reduced form factors where technology-generated data is extremely volatile, requiring it to be stored in a remote facility to facilitate investigations. By documenting and amalgamating all technical specifications about IoT devices, organizations will be better positioned to answer questions about associated technology-generated data, such as "Where has the ESI come from?" "Where is the ESI stored?" and "What format is the ESI forwarded and stored in?" By building a profile of identified IoT devices, organizations are better equipped to substantiate the authenticity of the ESI and to also narrow the scope of an investigation when IoT devices are involved.

Collection and Preservation   IoT devices are different from traditional computer systems because they typically have a limited power supply, lightweight computational resources, minimal storage capability, and extensive networking functionality. When encountering an IoT device, digital forensics practitioners must think about how leaving the device running at the crime scene can risk a potential loss of power or loss of potential evidence.

As a first responder, and considering the order of volatility, a decision needs to be made about whether to leave the device running—and allow data transfers from the scene to continue—or to power it off—and sever existing connections. From previous sections in this chapter we know that evidence volatility with IoT devices is more complex because the lifespan of data is extremely short. Facilitating this decision-making process requires referring to the previous phase of the investigative workflow whereby the technical specifications of the IoT device are documented and relevance can be established. Once relevance has been established via the phases outlined in the overall forensics investigation workflow, the device can be seized and secured as evidence.

Additionally, knowing that IoT devices are resource limited and need to leverage remote repositories for long-term storage of technology-generated data, there is the potential that relevant evidence will need to be sourced from cloud service providers (CSP). This presents challenges when gathering relevant evidence, as organizations may not have established contractual terms and conditions for the CSP to comply with investigative needs, and such situations may require the involvement of law enforcement.

Refer to Chapter 13, "Mapping Investigative Workflows," for further discussion on this phase of the investigation workflow.

Refer to Chapter 18, "Forensics Readiness in Cloud Environments," for further discussion on gathering evidence from cloud computing environments.

Phase #3: Processing

The forensics analysis and examination of IoT devices continues to be a challenge for the digital forensics community. Generally, these challenges are the result of several barriers associated with IoT devices, such as reduced form factors and the absence of available interfaces. Technically, current digital forensics techniques and tools have not reached a level of maturity within the IoT domain that allows for forensics acquisitions to be performed.

However, the digital forensics community continues to invest efforts in developing methodologies and techniques for processing evidence from IoT environments to address the current state of maturity. Refer to Chapter 1, "Understanding Digital Forensics," for further discussion on the evolutionary cycle of digital forensics.

From this research, the proposed forensics-aware IoT (FAIoT) model has been drafted to reduce the challenges in IoT forensics capabilities by providing methodologies and techniques for securing volatile data and establishing higher levels of evidence-based trust. Illustrated in Figure 20.4, the FAIoT model consists of the following three parts:

- The *secure evidence preservation module* monitors known IoT devices and stores associated ESI in a secure repository.
- The *secure provenance module* guarantees a complete chain of custody of IoT evidence by maintaining records of access.
- *Access to evidence through API* provides a secure and read-only connection to IoT devices to gather evidence and access information.

In addition to the FAIoT model, new techniques and methodologies have been proposed to conduct digital forensics investigations in IoT environments. Notably, the following approaches have been proposed for IoT forensics.

1-2-3 Zones *1-2-3 zones* is an approach that segregates IoT environments into the following three zones to reduce challenges and to help digital forensics practitioners focus on clearly identified areas when executing their investigative process methodology:

- *Zone 01* includes all IoT devices that can contain potential evidence.
- *Zone 02* includes all intermediate components located between internal and external networks that support IoT communications.
- *Zone 03* includes all hardware and software components that reside beyond the external networks, such as CSPs.

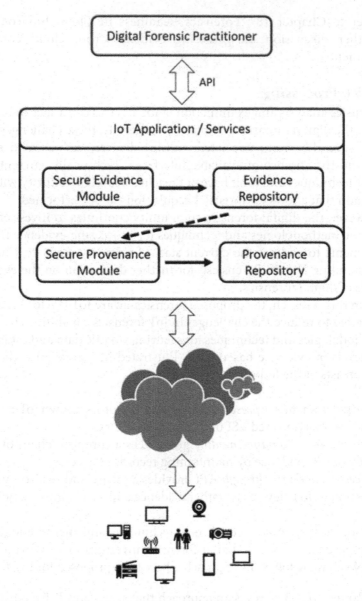

Figure 20.4 Forensics-aware IoT (FAIoT) model.

Illustrated in Figure 20.5, the three investigative zones above have been mapped against the seven trust zones discussed previously.

Next-Best-Thing (NBT) Triage Next-best-thing (NBT) triage is an approach used to identify an alternative source of evidence, within the crime scene, if the original IoT source is unavailable. In conjunction with the *1-2-3 zones* approach, the NBT approach can be used to determine what other

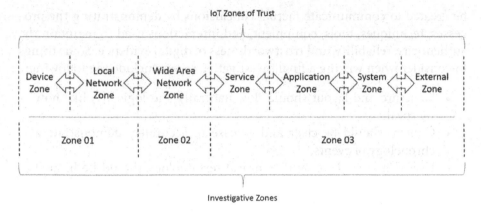

Figure 20.5 Investigative zones versus trust zones.

devices were connected to the device of interest, and subsequently identify any evidence left behind after being removed from the IoT environment.

Therefore, in such situations, digital forensics practitioners have the option of identifying and considering the next best source of relevant evidence for seizure. However, the NBT approach does not establish a systematic means by which digital forensics practitioners decide what the next best thing might be in different scenarios and situations, which can raise concerns when it comes to the relevance and meaningfulness of next best evidence sources.

While there may be constraints related to gaining access to and processing of physical IoT devices as evidence, as was discussed previously, the technology-generated data on these technologies is short lived and for investigative needs must be sent to a remote repository for long-term retention. The analysis and examination of evidence gathered from IoT devices, as with other technology-generated data, must consider the data source to effectively demonstrate authenticity and integrity.

From what has been previously covered in this chapter, it can be seen that IoT devices can transmit potentially relevant evidence to CSP environments. It is important that organizations consider the totality of potential evidence that can exist in these locations within the scope of an IoT investigation. Refer to Chapter 18, "Forensics Readiness in Cloud Environments," for further discussion on processing evidence from cloud computing environments.

Phase #4: Presentation

As discussed in Chapter 2, "Investigative Process Methodology," documentation is a critical element of every investigation that needs to start at the beginning of an investigation and be carried out to the end. In this last phase of the investigative workflow, the final investigative report will be created to communicate factual conclusions by demonstrating the processes, techniques, tools, equipment, and interactions used to maintain the authenticity, reliability, and trustworthiness of digital evidence. Some things to consider when writing a final investigative report include the following:

- Structure and layout should flow naturally and logically; like how we speak.
- Content should be clear and concise to accurately demonstrate a chronology of events.
- Use of jargon, slang, and technical terminology should be limited or avoided, and where used, a glossary should be included to define terms in natural language.
- Where acronyms and abbreviations are used, they must be written out in full expression on first use.
- Because final reports are written after the fact, that is, after an investigation, content should be communicated in the past tense; but tenses can change where conclusions or recommendations are being made.
- Format the final report not only for distribution within the organization, but also with the mindset that it may be used as testimony in a court of law.

A template for creating written formal reports has been provided as a reference in the *Templates* section of this book.

Step #8: Establish Continuing Education

Like digital forensics, depending on an individual's role with respect to IoT forensics determines the level of knowledge they are provided. Detailed discussion about the diverse levels of education, training, and awareness an organization should require of their people in support of digital forensics can be found in Chapter 14, "Establish Continuing Education."

General Awareness

As the lowest type of education, this is a generalized level of training and awareness that is intended to provide people with foundational knowledge without getting too specialized vis a vis IoT forensics. Leveraging the education and training that has already been put in place for digital forensics, this education provides people with the competencies they need related to organizational policies, standards, and guidelines so that they indirectly contribute, through some form of behavior or action, to the organization's digital forensics program.

Examples of topics and subjects that should be included as part of a mobile device forensics awareness program include the following:

- Business code of conduct
- Data protection and privacy

Basic Training

Essentially, the difference between this training and the previous awareness is that the knowledge gained here is intended to teach people the skills necessary to directly support the organization's digital forensics program vis a vis how, where, and to what extent IoT devices are used for business purposes.

Information communicated at this level is more detailed than the previous type of education because it must provide people with the knowledge required to support a specific role or function, such as managing IoT device sensors.

For example, as part of basic IoT forensics training, information about audit logging and retention should be covered. Generally, this topic relates to the practice of recording events and preserving them, as per the organizational governance framework, to facilitate digital forensics investigations.

Formal Education

A working and practical knowledge of IoT forensics requires people to first and foremost have the skills and competencies necessary to ensure that all digital forensics principles, methodologies, and techniques are understood. Once the fundamental knowledge is gained, practitioners can then start pursuing a specialization into mobile device forensics.

However, unlike digital forensics education programs, the availability of curriculum dedicated entirely to IoT devices is still limited. Most commonly, IoT forensics is taught as a specific course in higher/post-secondary institutions or as a professional education module led by an industry-recognized training institute.

Refer to the appendix *Education and Professional Certifications* for a list of higher/post-secondary institutions that offer formal education programs.

Step #9: Maintain Evidence-Based Presentation

Regardless of how mobile devices are deployed in an enterprise, the systems and ESI present can be used to commit or be the target of criminal activity. However, perhaps the biggest challenge to a digital forensics investigation where mobile device technologies are within scope is the dynamic nature of determining the "who, where, what, when, why, and how" of criminal activity. Some things to consider when writing a final investigative report include:

- Structure and layout should flow naturally and logically; like how we speak.
- Content should be clear and concise to accurately demonstrate a chronology of events.
- Use of jargon, slang, and technical terminology should be limited or avoided, and where used, a glossary should be included to define terms in natural language.

- Where acronyms and abbreviations are used, they must be written out in full expression on first use.
- Because final reports are written after the fact, that is, after an investigation, content should be communicated in the past tense; but tenses can change where conclusions or recommendations are being made.
- Format the final report not only for distribution within the organization, but also with the mindset that it may be used as testimony in a court of law.

A template for creating written formal reports has been provided as a reference in the *Templates* section of this book.

Step #10: Ensure Legal Review

Presently, there are few government or other regulatory bodies that have implemented legislation and requirements over the use of IoT devices. In large part, IoT devices continue to fall within the applicability of existing laws, standards, and regulations pertaining to the use of technology. As with other technologies, and discussed previously in this chapter, there continue to be key challenges involving the privacy of both information and users, the security of IoT devices, and the protection of ESI created, transmitted, and accessed.

Additionally, with respect to legal jurisdiction or ownership (i.e., custody, control, or possession), there is no difference between IoT devices and traditional computer systems when other organizations, service providers, etc. could be involved. In situations involving IoT devices and third parties, it is necessary to have contractual agreements in place (between all parties) to guarantee cooperation in the event of an incident or investigation involving an IoT environment.

While it is evident that IoT devices have generated significant value, in both business and personal contexts, the fact remains that legal and regulatory governance of IoT devices requires additional focus to address key problem areas. While challenges were identified previously in this chapter, the following are four key legal problem faced today:

Discrimination
While the widespread deployment of IoT devices, sensors can be used beneficially, but they also allow data to be used by organizations for discriminatory purposes, such as to draw inferences about misconduct or establish guilt. Although conclusions derived from fact-based evidence can establish guilt or innocence, the use of IoT data raises concerns about the possibility of indiscriminate exposure of information, for example, will IoT devices lead to new forms of discrimination against protected information classes such as race, age, or gender?

Privacy

Generally, the concept of privacy is invoked to respect personally identifiable information (PII) and the right to determine how such data is used. However, IoT devices generate enormous amounts of data that can be used to learn about people's activities, habits, personalities, preferences, and attributes. Accountability, a key principle of privacy, is difficult to maintain with IoT data because multiple third-party entities (i.e., organizations, vendors, service providers) collect, use, and (potentially) expose PII. Although IoT devices can be beneficial in providing relevant evidence, they can also be used in a manner that exploits or violates privacy rights.

Security

Aside from the security challenges expressed previously in this chapter, IoT devices create liabilities related to cross-border data flows. Depending on the designed purpose and functionality, IoT devices can collect data that is private or sensitive and is subject to legal or regulatory scrutiny. This can raise concerns, as the data created by IoT devices may not be restricted from being transmitted across jurisdictional boundaries where different data protection laws, standards, and regulations are enacted. Uncontrolled data flows between IoT devices raise questions about legal scope, and it can be difficult to isolate which governing body the device collecting the data falls under. Generally, this becomes a matter of whether a jurisdiction with greater data protection laws can enforce increased protection requirements on other jurisdictions.

Consent

Further complicating matters of privacy, IoT device sensors also raise concerns about whether data was collected, transmitted, and accessed with the consent of its user(s). Furthermore, IoT devices complicate matters of consent largely because protection laws are not equipped to address matters of how such data can be shared with or sold to third parties. Additionally, where organizations have deployed IoT devices that can collect data that includes PII, access to and storage of this data can bring about legal and regulatory concerns related to whether employees have agreed.

Refer to Chapter 18, "Forensics Readiness in Cloud Environments," for further discussion on legal considerations related to cloud computing environments.

Refer to Chapter 16, "Ensuring Legal Review," for further discussion about laws, standards, regulations, jurisdiction, and ownership.

Summary

Although IoT devices continue to proliferate, there is currently little research focused on incorporating digital forensics readiness into IoT environments.

Addendums

Addendum A: Tool and Equipment Validation Program

Introduction

Digital forensics tools and equipment can work differently, and may behave differently, when used on different evidence sources. Before using any tools or equipment to gather or process evidence, investigators must be familiar with how they operate by practicing on a variety of evidence sources.

This testing must demonstrate that these tools and equipment follow the scientifically proven principles, methodologies, and techniques used throughout the digital forensics discipline. This process of testing has established a level of assurance that the tools and equipment being used by digital forensics practitioners are forensically sound and introduce no doubt into the authenticity or integrity of digital evidence.

Standards and Baselines

For data to be legally admissible as digital evidence in a court of law, testing and experimentation must be completed that generates repeatable and reproducible results. This means that results must consistently produce the same results under different conditions.

In 1993, the U.S. Supreme Court decided in *Daubert v. Merrell Dow Pharmaceuticals, 509 U.S. 579* that Rule 702 of the *Federal Rules of Evidence* (1975) did not incorporate a "general acceptance" test as the basis for assessing whether scientific expert testimony is based on reasoning or methodology that is scientifically valid and can properly be applied to facts.

The Court stated that evidence based on innovative or unusual scientific knowledge may be admitted only after it has been established that the evidence is reliable and scientifically valid. Under this ruling, the *Daubert standard* was established with the following criteria applied for determining the reliability of scientific techniques:

1. Has the theory or technique in question undergone empirical testing?
2. Has the theory or technique been subjected to peer review and publication?
3. Does the theory or technique have any known or potential error rate?
4. Do standards exist, and are they maintained, for the control of the theory or technique's operation?
5. Has the theory or technique received general acceptance in the relevant scientific community?

These criteria require scientific theory or techniques to be subjected to hypotheses and experimentation—based on gathering, observing, and demonstrating repeatable and reproducible results—to prove or falsify the theory or techniques.

Because of the Daubert standard, as discussed in Chapter 16, "Ensuring Legal Review," all digital forensics tools and equipment must be validated and verified to meet specific evidentiary and scientific criteria for evidence to be legally admissible. In the context of applying the Daubert standard to software testing, there is a clear distinction between the activities and steps performed as part of validation and verification.

Building a Program

The ability to design, implement, and maintain a defensible validation and verification program is an essential characteristic that digital forensics practitioners should have. With this type of program in place, the digital forensics team will be able to provide a level of assurance related to what the capabilities of their tools and equipment are as well as to identify what, if any, limitations exist so compensating actions can be applied, such as acquiring other tools and equipment or creating additional procedures.

The methodology for performing testing of tools and equipment consists of several distinct activities and steps that must be completed in a linear workflow. To formalize this workflow, a process model must be implemented to govern the completion of each activity and the steps in the sequence that must be executed. Illustrated in Figure A.1, the phases proposed in Chapter 2, "Investigative Process Methodology," for both the high-level digital forensics process model and digital forensics readiness process model are consistently applied to the activities and steps performed in tool and equipment testing. Consisting of four phases, the digital forensics tool testing process model focuses on the basic categories of tools and equipment testing.

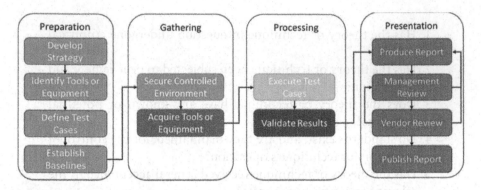

Figure A.1 Digital forensics tool testing process model.

Preparation

Like how a project charter establishes scope, schedule, and cost, the testing plan for digital forensics tools or equipment must follow identical format and structure. The starting point is to define and capture the objectives and expectations of the testing specific to how the tool or equipment is supposed to behave. Following this objective setting, further details of the testing plan must be documented using a formalized structure to include, at a minimum, the following sections:

- *Introduction*: A summary of the objectives and goals of the testing
- *Background*: Description of why the testing is being performed
- *Purpose/Scope*: Specifications of technical and business functionality the testing is expected to generate
- *Approach*: Procedures, activities, and steps that will be followed throughout the testing
- *Deliverables*: Definition of test cases and the success criteria for testing documented functionality
- *Assumptions*: Identification of circumstances and outcomes that are taken for granted in the absence of concrete information
- *Constraints*: Administrative, technical, or physical activities or steps that directly or indirectly restrict the testing
- *Dependencies*: Administrative, technical, or physical activities or steps that must be completed prior to testing
- *Project Team*: Visualization of the testing team structure and governing bodies

Gathering

This phase of the testing program is either the longest and most time consuming, or the easiest and fastest. Determining the amount of time needed depends on how well the plan's objectives, scope, and schedule were documented during the preparation phase previously. In this phase, the tactical approaches outlined in the plan's strategy are completed to acquire the tool or equipment that will be subject to the testing. Prior to purchasing any tool or equipment, it is essential that both parties enter into contractual agreement with each other, such as a non-disclosure agreement (NDA) and statement of work (SOW):

- An NDA formalizes a mutual relationship between parties to protect non-public, confidential, or proprietary information and specifies the materials, knowledge, or information that will be shared but must remain restricted from disclosure to other entities.
- An SOW is a formal document that contains details often viewed as legally equivalent to a contract to capture and address details of the testing.

Both documents contain terms and conditions that are considered legally binding between all parties involved. These documents must be reviewed and approved by appropriate legal representatives before each party commits to them by signing. In the absence of providing wording for how the content within these documents should be structured, at a minimum the following sections should be included:

- *Introduction*: A statement referring to NDA as the governing agreement for terms and provisions incorporated in the SOW
- *Description/purpose*: Summarizes the objectives and goals of the testing and provides information pertaining to the tool or equipment being tested, including technology name, version, release date, and creator
- *Location of work*: Describes where people will perform the work and the location of tools or equipment
- *Deliverables schedule*: A listing of the items that will be produced, the start and finish times, and the individuals responsible for providing results
- *Success criteria*: Baselines that will be used for measuring the success criteria against each test case, including the criteria for measuring success or failure, scenario for how the test will be executed, tools or equipment subject to the test, and the business value for conducting the test case
- *Assumptions*: Identification of circumstances and outcomes that are taken for granted in the absence of concrete information
- *Key personnel*: Provides contact information for the individuals, from all parties, who will be involved in the testing

- *Payment schedule*: A breakdown of the fees, if any, that will be paid—up front, in phases, or upon completion—to cover expenses for individuals and tools or equipment involved in the testing
- *Miscellaneous*: Items that are not part of the terms or provisions but must be listed because they are relevant to the testing and should not overlooked

Following the creation of these documents, the tools or equipment that are subject to testing can now be procured. In parallel, the team can begin securing and building a controlled environment where the test cases, as defined in the SOW, will be executed. This controlled environment must be built following previously defined baselines as well as the SOW deliverables. Once the controlled environment is created, and before it is used for the testing, the environment itself must be tested and validated to ensure it matches the specifications of the baselines and test cases. By documenting the validity of the controlled environment, it can easily be reused in future testing because a level of assurance has been established.

Processing

Software testing is one of many activities used as part of the system development life cycle (SDLC) to determine if the output results meet the input requirements. This phase is where the documented test cases are executed and success criteria are measured to verify and validate the functionality and capabilities of the tool or equipment. Before starting the activities and steps involved in executing test cases, it is important to understand the differences between verification and validation.

Verification

In general terms, a verification process answers the question "Did you build the right thing?" by objectively assessing if the tool or equipment was built according to the requirements and specifications. Verification focuses on determining if the vendor's documentation consistently, accurately, and thoroughly describes the design and functionality of the tool or equipment being tested. Techniques used during the process of verifying tools or equipment can be split into two distinct categories:

- *Dynamic analysis* involves executing test cases against the tool or equipment using a controlled data set to assess the tool's or equipment's documented functionality. This category applies a combination of black box and white box testing methodologies to support:
  - Functional assessments of documented features to identify and determine actual capabilities

- Structural review of individual components to further assess specific functionalities
- Random evaluation to detect faults or unexpected output from documented features
- *Static analysis* involves performing a series of test cases using the tool or equipment following manual or automated techniques to assess the non-functional components. This category applies a series of programmatic testing methodologies to support:
  - Consistency of internal coding properties such as syntax, typing, parameters matching between procedures, and translation of specifications
  - Measurement of internal coding properties such as structure, logic, and probability for error

Validation

In general terms, a validation process confirms through objective examination and provisioning if "you built it right" to prove that requirements and specifications have been implemented correctly and completely. Validation activities rely on the application of an all-inclusive testing methodology that happens both during and after the SDLC. Techniques used during the validation of tools or equipment can be performed by:

- Intentionally initiating faults into different components (e.g., hardware, software, memory) to observe the response
- Determining what the probability of re-occurrence is for a weakness identified in different components (e.g., hardware, software, memory), and subsequently selecting countermeasures as a means of reducing or mitigating exposures

Completing test cases can be a lengthy and time-consuming process. Completing test cases should be thorough because it is fundamental in proving that digital forensic tools or equipment maintain and protect the integrity of evidence, ultimately protecting the credibility of forensic professionals. While there are indirect factors such as caseload or other work responsibilities that impact the amount of time spent on testing, the following direct influences cannot be overlooked and must be maintained during testing:

- Regulating testing processes within secure and controlled lab environments
- Following proven, repeatable, reproducible, and consistent scientific methodologies

- Limiting the duplication of test results from others without subsequent validation
- Preventing the use of generalized processes or technologies that suggest arbitrary use

As the test cases are being executed, it is important to keep a record of all actions taken and the outputted results. Using a formalized document to track test case execution provides a level of assurance that the tests have been completed as specified in the strategy plan and SOW.

A formalized test case report template has been provided in the *Templates* section of this book, which includes a matrix for recording and tracking execution of each test case.

Presentation

Once testing has concluded, a summary of all activities, test results, conclusions, etc. must be prepared using a formalized test case report, as seen in the template provided in the *Templates* section of this book. While the initial draft of the final report might be performed by a single person, it should be reviewed for accuracy and authenticity by peers and management before being finalized. This review process will ensure that, as illustrated in the test case report template, the scope and results of the testing meet the specific business objectives so that when it comes time to obtain approvals to finalize, the testing process will not be challenged.

Having obtained final authorizations and approvals on the test case report, it can now be published and distributed to stakeholders who will be influenced because of the testing outcomes. Using the testing results, these stakeholders can now develop standard operating procedures to use the tools or equipment for gathering and processing digital evidence.

Summary

Maintaining the integrity of digital evidence throughout its lifetime is an essential requirement of every digital forensics investigation. Organizations must consistently demonstrate their due diligence by providing a level of assurance that the principles, methodologies, and techniques used during a digital forensics investigation are forensically sound.

Addendum B: Service Catalog

Introduction

Security controls can be administrative, technical, or physical in implementation and every security control that exists must deliver positive business value. Unfortunately, with the inner workings of information security typically not made common knowledge, the business value being delivered and the role it plays in achieving successful business outcomes is not usually recognized. This leaves the overall information security program vulnerable to not being strategically relevant to the organization's business functions. To be successful in demonstrating value, information security needs to be strategically aligned to business functions and positioned as an empowering contributor to the organization's success.

As part of the overall service management lifecycle, a service portfolio is the complete set of servicesmanaged and offered by the provider. The service catalog, also referred to as an information technology (IT) service catalog, is a subset of the service portfolio that acts as a centralized register and entry point for details about the organization's available services. Through the creation of a service catalog, the value of information security can be demonstrated more effectively by aligning the delivered outcomes to business functions in a format that is easily understood.

Business Benefits

At a minimum, a service catalog provides organizations with a centralized way to see, find, invoke, and execute services regardless of where the service exists within the organization. Organizations utilize this service catalog to eliminate the need for developing and/or supporting localized implementations that may be otherwise redundant.

Implementing a service catalog demonstrates a positive return on investment (ROI) for the organization in the form of direct financial savings or through maximizing effectiveness and efficiencies within the organization. From the strategic alignment of information security to business functions, organization can realize ROI through the following positive effects of a service catalog:

- Provides a platform for better understanding and communicate business requirements
- Positions the overall information security program to be run like a business
- Reduces operational costs by identifying essential services and eliminating/consolidating redundant/unnecessary services
- Enhances operational efficiencies through the strategic structuring of resources and funding
- Helps market the awareness and visibility of the information security program to build stronger business relationships

Inevitably, if a service catalog does not already exist, somebody within the organization will understand the benefits of having it in place and what it provides in terms of visibility to the information security program. Once identified, creating a service catalog should not be viewed as a straightforward task. By taking a laid-back approach to creating a service catalog, the organization may not realize true ROI and will most likely be wasting its resources, time, effort, and money. Guidance and oversight should be in place right from the start to create the service catalog to make sure the organization properly utilizes its assets throughout the entire process.

Design Considerations

The creation of services that deliver business value will differ from one organization to the next. Before starting the work of designing services, every organization should consider including four consistent elements to support the service in delivering value:

- *People*: Human resources and the organization's structure(s)
- *Processes*: Service management documentation
- *Products*: Technology and infrastructure
- *Partners*: Dependencies on external entities

Service catalogs include descriptive elements so users within the organization can easily find and request the desired service. There are no pre-defined requirements indicating what specific elements must be included in a service catalog, leaving the decision to include or exclude elements entirely up to the subjectivity of the organization. The most common descriptive elements that organizations should use in any service catalog implementation are:

Service name: The service name should clearly illustrate, in both business and IT terminology, how the service is commonly referred to throughout the organization. Structuring the name in such a way eliminates any confusion that may exist about the service.

Service description: The description should be written at a very high level, with no more than 2–3 lines, in a non-technical, business language that is simple and easy to understand.

Service family/group/category: Illustrated in Figure B.1, the hierarchical use of families, groups, and categories allows for individual services to be classified and aligned into the organization's common fields of functionality. The purpose of classifying individual services into the larger areas is to simplify resource management and cost analysis.

Service family: In the first level of the service catalog hierarchy, the purpose of a service family is to translate services into core business driven functions, such as *IT services* or *business services*.

Service group: In the second level of the service catalog hierarchy, the purpose of a service group is to expand the individual business functions contained within the service family, such as *security services* or *compliance*.

Service category: In the third level of the service catalog hierarchy, the purpose of a service category is to specify the individual service functions, such as *security operations* or *investigations*.

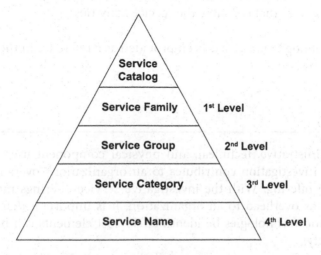

Figure B.1 Operational service catalog hierarchy.

Service owner: The owner is the person within the organization who provides funding for the service; commonly assigned to the executive management person where the service is offered.

Key contact(s): The key contact(s) of the service are those within the organization who function as the focal point for all communication between IT departments and the business communities. These individuals are responsible for understanding and supporting the level of service being delivered in line with established service level objectives (SLO).

Service costs: Documenting all services as quantifiable provides organizations with a better understanding of where funding is allocated across the total cost for operating the service. Having identified all of the contributors to the total service cost, organizations can then implement a chargeback model for performing cost allocations based on the services' activities costs.

Cost elements: The fixed (e.g., software licensing, capital) and variable (e.g., remuneration, outside data processing) costs associated with operating the service.

Cost driver: The specific fixed (e.g., software licenses) or variable (e.g., billable work hours) unit(s) of service activity that results in a change in cost to the requestor.

Cost per unit: The measurement used to identify the cost of delivering one unit of service activity.

(Total fixed costs + Total variable costs)/Total units produced

Cost allocation: The distribution of service costs through the organization to areas that consume the service activities.

A service catalog template has been provided as a reference in the *Templates* section of this book.

Summary

Every administrative, technical, and physical component used as part of a forensics investigation contributes to an organization's overall investigative service offering. With the investigative service offerings mostly being considered as overhead to an organization, it is important that associated resources and technologies be identified so cost elements can be allocated appropriately.

Addendum C: Cost-Benefit Analysis

Introduction

Completing a cost-benefit analysis is a critical step for successful project management execution. It details the potential risks and gains of the proposed solution(s) through a comparative assessment of the program's benefits against the costs associated with implementing it. If the results of this assessment identify that the benefits of the program outweigh the costs incurred to operating it, then the organization will be able to demonstrably agree to follow through with the implementation.

While completing a cost-benefit analysis requires those involved to maintain a quantitative perspective on the outcome, the activities involved are more of an art form than a science. Although performing a cost-benefit analysis can be a challenging task to complete, organizations that are willing to invest resources, effort, and time into brainstorming, researching, and analyzing data can generate an assessment that is thorough, accurate, and relevant.

What Is Cost-Benefit Analysis?

Cost-benefit analysis involves the estimation and evaluation of the benefits associated with alternative courses of action. This assessment involves identifying and comparing the net present value (NPV) of benefits against projected benefits to identify the best solution according to specified criteria. The goal of the cost-benefit analysis is for organizations to make an educated decision on whether implementing a solution is worth investing their resources, time, and effort.

All activities and steps performed in the cost-benefit analysis can be grouped into four major phases, as illustrated in Figure C.1, including:

- *Problem statement* documents an in-depth analysis of the current situation
- *Quantitative assessment* assigns monetary value to all known cost and projected benefits

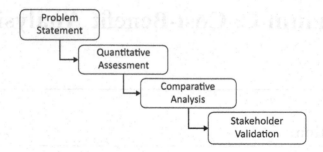

Figure C.1 Cost-benefit analysis workflow.

- *Comparative analysis* assesses if projected benefits outweigh known costs, and identifies what alternate solutions exist
- *Stakeholder validation* determines the reliability of the decision generated from the analysis

Problem Statement

The first phase of the cost-benefit analysis workflow is extremely important in any decision-making process. Documenting the problem statement is the only way an organization can identify alternate and appropriate solutions. This task involves analyzing and having a good understanding of the issues, risks, and baseline scenarios for why the cost-benefit analysis is required.

Contained within the problem statement, organizations should include specifications of the objectives they are setting for this analysis and the plan they will follow to achieving these objectives. It is important that when defining these specifications, the outputs are precise and concrete as possible so the desired future state stands alone and successful achievements can be measured. By setting these specifications too broad, focus on the original problem statement will be lost and the cost-benefit analysis will lead to inappropriate assumptions and/or incorrect results.

This phase of the workflow involves generating all possible alternative solutions and, if required, narrowing down the list by removing options that are not feasible, including solutions that do not align with basic budgetary, legal, or organizational restrictions. As a means of narrowing down the list of alternatives, organizations should answer the following questions:

- How will performing this analysis meet our objectives?
- Will this analysis involve new capital expenditures?
- Will there be a need to replace existing tangible assets?
- Will there be a need to enhance existing tangible assets?
- What are the constraints of this analysis?

- What stakeholders will be affected by this analysis?
- How will stakeholders be affected by this analysis?

Ideally, organizations should limit the list of alternatives that they will assess further to a minimum of two and a maximum of five. Reducing the list of alternatives before performing quantitative analysis allows organizations to better manage resources, time, and costs.

Quantitative Assessment

With the problem statement documented and alternatives identified, the second phase of the cost-benefit analysis workflow is to quantify all relevant costs and benefits. Completing a detailed and accurate quantitative assessment of costs and benefits, for each alternative, should not be taken lightly. This phase requires that organizations invest resources, time, and effort into identifying all relevant effects of the solution, both positive and negative, and assign a monetary value to it.

Identifying Costs

Dismissing, overlooking, or assuming any cost or benefit relating to an alternative can significantly impact the organization's ability to accurately determine which alternative should be recommended as the final solution. To mitigate this, organizations must ensure they are comparing "apples-to-apples" by categorizing costs as either tangible or intangible and categorizing benefits based on commonalities.

Tangible Costs   Using the service catalog as the source, a thorough and itemized list of quantifiable costs must be made. Where actual costs cannot be taken from the service catalog, factual research should be completed to determine estimates. Types of tangible costs include:

- Capital expenditures, or physical assets, such as property or equipment;
- Software expenses such as licensing;
- Shipping, handling, and transportation fees;
- Remuneration overhead such as employee salary or training expenses;
- Premises payments such as utilities, insurance, and taxes; or
- Outside data processing such as professional services and contingent workforce.

Most likely, there could be a span of several years before an alternative has been fully implemented where ongoing costs will need to be carried forward and incurred until completion.

Intangible Costs Associated costs can also include those that are not quantifiable. Even though these costs do not have any directly quantifiable value and cannot be bought or sold, based on factual evidence organizations are able to arrive at a hypothetical monetary value for these items. Types of intangible costs include:

- Change in customer dissatisfaction;
- Drop in employee morale; or
- Decline in quality of product or service.

Projecting Benefits

Benefits are positive effects that are realized from implementing a solution in response to issues or risks. They are achieved through any means of enhancement to the way an organization performs a business function.

Benefits can also be presented as being either tangible or intangible. Identifying benefits is done in the same way that cost contributors are documented in the previous step, although projecting them relies more on educated estimates than direct facts. Generally, benefits can be grouped into one of the following categories:

- Cost savings or avoidance
- Error reduction
- Operational efficiencies
- Increased flexibility
- Improved planning and control

Tangible Benefits Like costs, tangible benefits are the components of business or information technology that can be measured directly through known valuation. Referring to the service catalog as the definitive source for measuring tangible value, these types of benefits can be realized as one of the following potentials:

- Increased operational efficiencies
- Decreased operational funding
- Reduced workforce overhead
- Reduced rate of budgetary increase
- Lower software costs and maintenance
- Lower physical equipment costs and maintenance
- Lower outside data processing fees
- Lower internal development costs

Intangible Benefits   Also, like costs, intangible benefits do not have any directly quantifiable value and organizations will have to assign a hypothetical monetary value to these types of benefits. As indicated previously, making assumptions on the monetary values can be challenging to determine the value of intangible benefits as one of the following potentials:

- Improved asset utilization
- Improved resource control
- Improved business planning
- Improved organizational flexibility
- Quicker access to information
- Higher quality of information
- Enhanced organizational training, awareness, and learning
- Increased goodwill within workforce
- Increased job satisfaction
- Enhanced decision-making capabilities
- Quicker decision-making process
- Reduce error rates
- Improved organizational image
- Improved customer satisfaction
- Increased customer loyalty

Projecting the quantitative value of intangible benefits has the potential to significantly impact the organization's ability to accurately determine which alternative should be recommended as the final solution. Alternatively, organizations can approach the valuation of intangible benefits in any of the following manners:

- An organization may decide that it would be acceptable to leave intangible benefits entirely out of the cost-benefit analysis. This decision can be related to the degree of difficulty in assigning monetary values or that intangible benefits do not demonstrate significant improvements to business functions.
- Leave intangible benefits out of the cost-benefit analysis but their potential effects to business functions in an appendix. This way, they do not have direct influence on the assessment but can be presented as an additional consideration for selection of an alternative solution.
- Identify a stand-in measurement that can be used to include the intangible benefit valuation in the cost-benefit analysis. In this case, a stand-in measurement could be taken as the value of a similar benefit or cost that is more easily assigned a monetary value. Caution must be given when selecting a stand-in measurement to ensure that it provides an accurate and equivalent approximation of the actual benefit or cost.

- By conducting a survey of key stakeholders, the valuation of the intangible benefits can be determined. This survey is designed to ask stakeholders to assign a monetary value to the intangible benefit which can then be used for inclusion in the cost-benefit analysis.
- Use of a shadow price[4] to function as the unit of measurement to generate estimates on the monetary value of the intangible benefit. No rules or procedures exist for determining a shadow price, requiring that organizations employ an experienced matter expert to generate the valuation. The use of this option should only be explored when none of the preceding approaches will provide an accurate and equivalent approximation of the intangible benefit.

Comparative Assessment

With all identified costs and benefits assigned a common unit of measurement, each alternative solution documented in the problem statement can now be accurately assessed.

Discounting Future Value   Before starting the comparative assessment, organizations should take special consideration where there are either costs or benefits that span across several years. In these cases, it is important that organizations take note that the immediate and present value of an alternative will diminish over its lifespan.

The process of discounting can be applied to reduce the monetary value of future costs and benefits back to a common time dimension that will be used for the assessment. Discounting allows organizations to realize the immediate value of an alternative, over the future value, and provides a way of reflecting the opportunity costs. In preparation, the organization should document the following series of parameters to be used in the baseline for discounting:

- The total evaluation period[5] for the alternative
- Which year is to be used as the base discount year
- What discount rate will be used for the evaluation period
- Which price year is appropriate to use for cost estimates
- Which price year is appropriate to use for the level of inflation
- If analysis of relative prices is needed for specific cost items

Discounting is performed on the finance principle of time value of money (TVM), which assumes that value or monies or cash flow depends on the period in which they are received. In other terms, this principle suggests that monies received in the future are worth less than monies received today because monies received today can be invested and begin to accrue interest immediately. This allows organizations to determine the economic worth of the alternatives under assessment.

Present Value Assessment   The present value (PV) of costs or benefits is the representation of costs and benefits received in the future, discounted back into today's current value. The PV of each cost and benefit should be calculated for each alternative being considered as a solution. The resulting PV can then be used for selecting criteria to identify which alternative is most valuable to the organization. The PV of costs and benefits is calculated as:

$$Present\ value\ (PV) = V_t/(1 + d)^t$$

where V is the cost or benefit represented in the evaluation period t, and d is represented as the discount rate. At a minimum, the PV should be calculated and used as the primary decision criteria for identifying which alternative provides the best return on investment (ROI).

Tables C.1 and C.2 show examples of estimated costs and benefits for two alternatives identified through defining the problem statement. For the purposes of this example, an assumption is made that the discount rate r has been set at 3 percent. The final NPV calculations for these two alternatives, presented in Tables C.3 and C.4, clearly demonstrates that the benefits of both alternatives outweigh the present value of costs, with the second alternative being larger.

Table C.1   Cost-Benefit Analysis for Alternative #1

	V_0	V_1	V_2	V_3
Costs:				
Capital	$10,000	$2,000	$1,000	$1,000
Expenses	$9,000	$1,000	$1,000	$1,000
Workdays	$2,000	$1,000	$1,000	$0
Benefits:				
Process Automation	$0	$6,000	$4,000	$3,000
Increased Productivity	$0	$12,000	$9,000	$9,000

Table C.2   Cost-Benefit Analysis for Alternative #2

	V_0	V_1	V_2	V_3
Costs:				
Capital	$8,000	$1,000	$1,000	$1,000
Expenses	$9,000	$2,000	$2,000	$1,000
Workdays	$2,000	$1,000	$0	$0
Benefits:				
Increased Productivity	$0	$8,000	$5,000	$3,000
Reduced Workforce	$0	$6,000	$9,000	$9,000

Table C.3   Present Values for Alternative #1

Costs:

$$PV = [(10,000 + 9,000 + 2,000)/ \qquad\qquad\qquad = 29,542$$
$$(1 + 0.03)^0] + [(2,000 + 1,000 + 1,000)/$$
$$(1 + 0.03)^1] + [(1,000 + 1,000 + 1,000)/$$
$$(1 + 0.03)^2] + [(1,000 + 1,000 + 0)/(1 + 0.03)^3]$$

Benefits:

$$PV = [(6,000 + 12,000)/(1 + 0.03)^1] + [(4,000 + 9,000)/ \quad = 40,711$$
$$(1 + 0.03)^2] + [(3,000 + 9,000)/(1 + 0.03)^3]$$

Table C.4   Present Values for Alternative #2

Costs:

$$PV = [(8,000 + 9,000 + 2,000)/ \qquad\qquad\qquad = 27,542$$
$$(1 + 0.03)^0] + [(1,000 + 2,000 + 1,000)/$$
$$(1 + 0.03)^1] + [(1,000 + 2,000 + 0)/$$
$$(1 + .03)^2] + [(1,000 + 1,000 + 0)/(1 + 0.03)^3]$$

Benefits:

$$PV = [(8,000 + 6,000)/(1 + 0.03)^1] + [(5,000 + 9,000)/ \quad = 37,770$$
$$(1 + 0.03)^2] + [(3,000 + 9,000)/(1 + 0.03)^3]$$

The values illustrated in Tables C.1 and C.2 are high-level representations of individual costs and benefits. An NPV template has been provided as a reference in the *Templates* section of this book.

Having arrived at the final NPV calculations for each alternative, organizations can elect to use additional criteria for determining which alternative is the best solution. These additional criteria should be used as a supplemental assessment and not as a replacement of the NPV.

Benefit-Cost Ratio (BCR)   Organizations can use these criteria to select the alternative that provides the maximum ratio of benefits in comparison to costs and is calculated as the present value of identified benefits divided by the present value of known costs. This calculation is presented as follows:

$$\text{Benefit-cost ratio (BCR)} = B/C$$

where B is the total value of identified benefits and C is the total value of known costs.

The BCR calculation for the alternatives noted in Tables C.1 and C.2 are presented in Table C.5.

NPV of Net Benefits   Organizations can use these criteria to select the alternative that provides the largest NPV of net benefits and is calculated as the present value of identified benefits minus the present value of known

Table C.5   Benefit/Cost Ratios

Alternative #1	BCR = 40,711/29,542	= 1.378072
Alternative #2	BCR = 37,770/27,542	= 1.37136

costs that have been discounted back to the present. This calculation is presented as follows:

$$\text{NPV of net benefits} = (B_t - C_t)/(1 + r)^t$$

where B the value of identified benefits, C is the value of known costs, r is the discount rate, and t is the number of evaluation periods that the benefits and costs occur in.

The calculation for the alternatives noted in Tables C.1 and C.2 are presented in Tables C.6 and C.7.

Internal Rate of Return (IRR)   Organizations can use these criteria to evaluate the rate of growth a project is expected to generate. Determining the rate of growth is most commonly performed through trial and error until a discount rate resulting in a zero value NPV is found.

To help in the identification of this rate, financial calculators should be used.

Payback Period   Organizations can use these criteria to select the alternative that recovers its costs in the shortest amount of time. The major concern with using this calculation is that it does not take into consideration the TVM, potentially leading to inconsistent results when cash flows occur in later time periods. However, the advantage of this calculation is that organizations can arrive at a value quickly because it requires no knowledge of the present value of costs or benefits.

The calculation for the alternatives noted in Tables C.1 and C.2 are presented in Tables C.8 and C.9.

Table C.6   NPV of Net Benefits for Alternative #1

NPV =	$[(0 - 21,000)/(1 +$ $0.03)^0] + [(18,000 - 4,000)/$ $(1 + 0.03)^1] + [(13,000 - 3,000)/$ $(1 + 0.03)^2] + [(12,000 - 2,000)/$ $(1 + 0.03)^3]$	= 11,170

Table C.7   NPV of Net Benefits for Alternative #2

NPV =	$[(0 - 19,000)/$ $(1 + 0.03)^0] + [(14,000 - 4,000)/$ $(1 + .03)^1] + [(14,000 - 2,000)/$ $(1 + 0.03)^2] + [(12,000 - 2.000)/$ $(1 + 0.03)^3]$	= 10,229

Table C.8   Payback Period for Alternative #1

	Cash Flows (In & Out)	Cumulative Cash Flow
Year 0 (Base)	21,000	
Year 1	14,000	14,000
Year 2	10,000	24,000
Year 3	10,000	34,000

Table C.9   Payback Period for Alternative #2

	Cash Flows (In & Out)	Cumulative Cash Flow
Year 0 (Base)	19,000	
Year 1	10,000	10,000
Year 2	12,000	22,000
Year 3	10,000	32,000

An NPV is a recommended part of cost-benefit analysis that supports business decision making. The overall ranking of all alternatives to ultimately identify a preferred solution demands that the NPV, and supplemental criteria (i.e., BCR, IRR, etc.), is completed as thoroughly as possible. However, while the NPV ranking allows organizations to see which alternative will provide the best value, each alternative must be subjected to robust validation under different scenarios.

Sensitivity Analysis   Obtaining a unique figure is not always the simplest of tasks when there are so many positive and negative influences on the final NPV calculation. Having finally arrived at an NPV for each alternative, these results must be subjected to further analysis with the purpose of determining how sensitive the NPV is to changes in key variables, such as resource overhead.

The sensitivity analysis performed here allows decision makers within the organization to test the robustness of the results to collect information about how the solution will perform under different scenarios. Keep in mind that the analysis performed here does not reduce the project risk, but instead better illustrates the actual feasibility of a successful solution implementation to the organization's decision makers.

Creating a series of scenarios, most of which will be subjective to every organization, should focus on worst-cases where assumptions, estimates, are scrutinized. While there are many ways of performing sensitivity analysis, the most commonly used method is to validate the degree of error and reliability of costs, benefits, and other parameters (i.e., discount rate) recorded in the final NPV and supplemental criteria.

By creating additional NPV and criteria documents that illustrate both high and low values, the degree to which these documents differ identifies how susceptible alternatives will be to changing values or parameters. By modifying a single value or parameter, the ranking of preferred alternatives could change, leading to a different solution being identified as the most valuable.

Organizations must be cautious when performing sensitivity analysis where there are many values and parameters included in the NPV and supplemental criteria. Where a value or parameter will be subjected to this sensitivity analysis, a degree of error must be completed using both high and low comparisons, resulting in $(X)^2$ for the number of outputted documents.

Gap Analysis   Graphic aids, such as a gap analysis, are excellent tools for helping stakeholders to clearly understand the differences between continuing to operate with the current risks and issues in comparison with implementing the highest ranked alternative. Working from the baseline and future scenarios created while documenting the problem statement, the costs and benefits of each identified solution can be used to visually demonstrate the value of implementing an alternative as illustrated in Figure C.2.

To ensure that the gap analysis accurately captures the differences between current and future state scenarios, the baseline must be properly defined and relevant. Having a baseline scenario does not mean that nothing will happen to the current situation over time. The reality is that business moves on as usual and in the current situation, the risks and issues identified in the problem statement could still be subjected to legal, regulatory, or corporate policies, regardless of the future state scenario.

On this account, the impact of changes in the current situation must be properly reflected in the baseline scenario. Organizations must make a distinction between what they consider as "do nothing" and "do minimum" when it comes to the level of interactions that will happen in the current situation that do not consider the future state scenario.

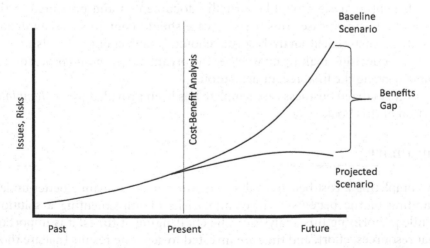

Figure C.2 Baseline-future scenario gap analysis.

Investing in an alternative that demonstrates the highest ranked value can be misleading; not because cost, benefits, or parameters have been inaccurately recorded, but because the NPV could be hiding the fact that even without implementing an alternative the current situation might not remain constant. Using an optimized baselines scenario that accounts for changes in the current situation, a more accurate comparison to the future state scenario can be performed.

Stakeholder Validation

There are usually several different stakeholders that will be affected when the selected alternative is implemented. Each group of stakeholders should be identified and assessment of whether they will gain (i.e., operational efficiencies) or lose (i.e., private costs) because of the implemented solution. Communication to stakeholders on their involvement should contain detailed information so it is clearly understood who will be the beneficiaries, who will be the losers, and by what amount.

Whether positive and negative, different types of impact that should be communicated to stakeholders as part of the overall communication plan include:

- Determining the ability to remain profitable when a reduction in workforce from enhanced operational efficiencies influences economic opportunities
- Identifying change, whether an increase or decrease, in operational (e.g., processes), regulatory (e.g., taxes), and individual (e.g., consumer) costs because of changes in the way core business functions are performed

In addition to impact assessment, the final recommendations from the cost-benefit analysis should be formally documented and presented in the form of a business case. This business case should contain sufficient details about the cost-benefit analysis so stakeholders have enough details to support their decision making on whether the organization should proceed with implementing the final recommendation.

A formalized business case template has been provided in the *Templates* section of this book.

Summary

By completing a cost-benefit analysis, organizations can gain a better understanding of the benefits and potential risks of implementing a solution. While performing this analysis can be challenging at times, it is important that resources, effort, and time are invested to generate results that are thorough, accurate, and relevant.

Addendum D: Building a Taxonomy

Introduction

A taxonomy is the name given to describe a controlled grouping of terms and language used to find and provide consistency within a specific subject field. It's a living document that might never be considered finished because it is constantly evolving alongside of changes to business operations and functions. A good taxonomy should be flexible enough to adapt to any changes so it does not have to be re-created.

Through a taxonomy, organizations can provide their stakeholders (i.e., employees, investors, etc.) with a set of categories that are:

- Common and support the aggregation of common information across the organization;
- Comprehensive and thoroughly identify components of the subject field; and
- Stable and help the comparative analysis of the subject field over time.

Development Methodology

Creating a taxonomy is a demanding task that requires the co-ordination of resources, tools, and processes to optimally implement it. In the sections to follow, the process of creating a taxonomy is performed in three stages as illustrated in Figure D.1.

Stage 1: Research & Assess

In this stage of the methodology, a team of key individuals is assembled to manage the entire development process. Once established, the team focuses on gathering information—throughout the organization—relevant to the taxonomy, the role it will have, and where there is existing information that can be consumed.

313

Figure D.1 Taxonomy development methodology.

Selecting a Team

Creating a taxonomy cannot be achieved successfully by a single individual. Rather, it requires an approach where key stakeholders with specific or specialized knowledge of the subject field must be involved. While the inclusion of team members can be based on the subject field in which the taxonomy is being developed, at a minimum, resources from the following teams should be included throughout the development process.

- *Information technology (IT)* support staff has a good understanding of the current technology environments. These resources can provide the team with insight into planned technology changes, help to discover opportunities for other technology, or identify limitation that should be addressed.
- *Legal* staff knows of current legal and litigation matters facing the organization and how they will impact the subject field.
- *Compliance* staff can advise the team of current or potential regulatory impacts that must be considered for the subject field.
- *Records management* staff has a good understanding of end-user computing practices and can advise on how to maintain good business practice by avoiding compliance gaps within the subject field.

Establish Its Role within the Organization

The incentive for an organization to create a taxonomy can be either tactical (i.e., provide guidance during daily operations) or strategic (i.e., contribute to improvement of operational efficiencies). Generally, a taxonomy is both a tool and an opportunity to establish a foundation for all activities relating to a specific subject field:

- *Tool*: The taxonomy can be used as an incentive to address organizational objectives such as:
  - Improving efficiencies by making employees more effective at performing their duties

- Protecting intellectual property by identifying assets and documenting where/how they interact
- Providing a foundation for determining the subject field's relevant components
- *Opportunity*: The taxonomy can be used to assign responsibility and accountability for a subject field such as:
  - Developing a high expectation about roles and responsibilities
  - Creating a self-reinforcing sense of morale and assurance

Define Business Requirements and Value Proposition

At this stage of the development process, the team should hold meetings with different business lines—if the organization is large enough to have more than one business line—to determine what (if any) challenges exist that require the creation of a taxonomy. In preparation for these meetings, a survey should be used to initiate conversation in the subsequent meetings about subject fields that could benefit from a taxonomy.

First and foremost, the team must clearly articulate the strategy for how the taxonomy will function throughout the organization and the issues (i.e., legal, IT, compliance) it will address. In doing so, the survey can be designed to deal with these aspects using terms and language that are simple, direct, and translatable through the organization. As the survey is being built, each question included should be structured in this way so that the surveyed individual(s) are not led into a specific response. As an example, the question "What is the most challenging task facing your business line?" allows the reader to objectively identify any subject field they consider needs attention.

Approximately one to two weeks following the distribution of the survey, all responses should be collected. These responses should be thoroughly reviewed to get an appreciation of the subject fields that have elevated urgency for the creation of a taxonomy. From here, a prioritized list of subject fields can be drafted and used to prepare questions as part of the interviews with the surveyed individuals or various business lines.

Interviews are intended to serve two purposes, the first being a tool for gathering information to further develop the business requirements for the taxonomy and the second being an opportunity to educate on what value the taxonomy will bring to the organization. During these interviews, it is important that the interviewee be permitted to do most of the talking so that as much information as possible can be captured.

Having completed all interview sessions, the team should now combine all results and prepare a list, sorted by interviewee, of the challenges and concerns identified during the sessions. With the aggregated interview results, the team will have a clear and holistic perspective into the subject fields where that should be prioritized for creating a taxonomy. The prioritized listing should be reviewed with each interviewee to ensure they understand the findings and how they align with the organizational strategy.

Assess Existing Data

Input into the taxonomy should not have to be entirely recreated from scratch. For the most part, there is a good chance that there is existing information throughout the organization that can be used as source material for the taxonomy. Gathering relevant information can happen from such data sources as the survey and interview results or pre-existing documentation such as organizational polices documentation or IT system architectures.

After reviewing the compiled information, the team will have a clear indication of how prepared the organization is for the taxonomy. The gap between readiness expectations and completeness of the pre-existing materials will determine which business lines will have difficulty with implementing the taxonomy. Identifying the degree of readiness for each business line will allow the team to focus on getting additional clarity by conducting subsequent rounds of surveys and interviews.

Stage 2: Build & Implement

In this stage of the methodology, the team conducts a series of interviews and surveys with subject matter experts to gather more information necessary to build the taxonomy. Using the aggregated results, the hierarchical classification scheme is built, evaluated, and implemented throughout the organization.

Conduct Surveys and Interviews

Most of the content in the taxonomy will be drawn from surveying and interviewing people in business lines throughout the organization. Quite often, interviewing or surveying a group of individuals with a high-level understanding of how things should be done will be ineffective in gathering relevant information.

Alternatively, individuals with a detailed understanding of their job(s), or those who pay attention to detail, can bring more value to the creation of the taxonomy. The reality is that there are "go-to" people in the organization that can provide the best information for developing the taxonomy. This is because they are the best at describing what it is they do every day, what resources they need to do their job(s), and can directly identify any challenges or issues in performing their job(s).

At this point, there are plenty of source materials that can be drawn from to create the survey targeting the individuals who can provide the most value to creating the taxonomy. The process of surveying and interviewing is the organization's best opportunity to educate and help business lines better understand the scope, value, and relevance of a taxonomy.

This round of surveys and interviews is designed so interviewees can further elaborate and provide greater details on the operations and functions they are involved in that are relevant to the taxonomy's subject field. To facilitate the level of discussion held during the interview sessions, the team should consider distributing the survey beforehand to allow people additional time to review and absorb information such as the survey's context, definitions, purpose of the project, and goals of the survey.

As interviews are completed and the associated surveys are received, the team must thoroughly review the collective results. This time around, the goal of reviewing results is to ensure the responses align with the business line interviews and survey so that the team can identify any unresolved challenges that stand in the way of completing the taxonomy. To do so, the team must ensure they have a complete view of the business line from the interviewee's perspective which requires that, where needed, unfinished survey submissions must be returned for completion with an explanation of the deficiencies needing resolution.

Processing the aggregated results, the team will begin to realize challenges that will affect how the taxonomy will be created. For example, individual employees may not know how their job(s) relate to or impact operations or processes in other business lines. This gap is where the team must note the exception and, depending on how severe the effect is to the taxonomy, determine the best course of action.

At a minimum, the team may need to re-interview individuals to gain additional details on the gap or conduct a new set of interviews and surveys with additional business lines. Alternatively, the team might determine that there is an absence of policies, procedures, or governance that needs to be implemented throughout the organization to address the gap.

Create Inventories

The collective information from interviews and survey with each business line must now be consolidated into a single repository. Whether a single table or series of tables is needed to track the inventory, the team will need to ensure the information has been normalized and standardized in a format that it can be examined for consistencies and inconsistencies.

Once the information has been arranged into a record set, the team must review the complete inventory to ensure all aspects of the organization's security, privacy, and confidentiality have been dealt with. During the inventory review, the team might identify inconsistencies in the record set that could also affect how the taxonomy is created. Like the resolution of gaps in the previous stage, the team must document the inconsistencies and potentially re-interview individuals to clarify the information before proceeding.

With the inventory confirmed to be consistent, the team will then provide each business line with the consolidated information to allow them an opportunity to provide their feedback and modifications. Quite often a business line will identify a record, such as a procedure of function, that is no longer relevant and request that it be removed from the inventory. The team should note these findings but not remove it until it has been confirmed that there are no other business lines that have procedures or functions depending on it.

Feedback from each business line must be reviewed by the team and a determination made as to whether modifications are consistent with the scope of the taxonomy. In some cases, the team may come across feedback where a business line has noted the need for modification that is specific to their operation or functions. For the taxonomy to be effective throughout the organization, the team must ensure that while feedback from each business line is considered for inclusion in the taxonomy, it must be consistent and realistic for the entire organization.

Justify a Classification Scheme

All the information collected from interviews, surveys, inventories, and business line feedback should provide the team with a good idea of how the classification scheme and associated categories within the taxonomy will be structured. The classification scheme should be structured hierarchically using generic terms and language that clearly illustrate how it will be commonly referred to, so underlying categories can be aggregated from across the organization.

Like the service catalog hierarchy discussed in Addendum B, "Service Catalog," the taxonomy must also use a consistent and relevant series of categories to aggregate information. There should be a reasonable number of categories to simplify the classification scheme hierarchy, but not too few so that the purpose of the scheme becomes meaningless. Taxonomies should be personalized to meet the specific needs of each organization.

For example, organizations should customize the categories to better reflect the taxonomy's mandate, accurately align with existing structures or classification schemes, or to introduce sub-categories that are relevant to corresponding parents. In some instances, there could be existing taxonomies throughout the organization that serve a purpose for a specific business operation or function. As mentioned previously, these taxonomies should be considered as reference or source data when developing an organizational taxonomy, as they may be existing categories that are applicable and can be re-used.

After the classification scheme has been rationalized, the team must distribute it to stakeholders and business lines affected by its implementation. Where feedback is received questioning the scheme, such as terminology or hierarchy, the team may need to re-interview individuals to ensure they understood information was captured accurately. When the team has resolved the issues and modifications to the classification scheme have been actioned, where and if needed, the first draft of the taxonomy can be developed.

Finalize the Taxonomy

Each draft of the taxonomy should be reviewed by stakeholders and business lines affected by its implementation. At this stage of the taxonomy development, most modifications should be focused on addressing issues with terminology and clarity and could potentially span multiple rounds of review.

With the final revision completed, the team must perform one last check for defects and ensure what is being delivered aligns with the original scope and purpose. Additionally, the team will also need to ensure that the final revision is an accurate representation of the organization's current state in terms of security, privacy, confidentiality, legal and regulatory compliance, and technology management.

Stage 3: Govern & Grow

In this stage of the methodology, the team is focused on planning the long-term stability and sustainability of the taxonomy. With the final revision implemented, the team must develop a governance structure focused on the continued lifecycle, including:

- Creation of policies and procedures to support its implementation and ongoing maintenance
- Definition of the roles, responsibilities, and accountabilities throughout the organization
- Establishment of training and awareness programs for support resources and employees

With the governance structure in place, the taxonomy should now be communicated and made available to employees throughout the organization so the terminology, classification scheme, and categorized of the subject field can be commonly and consistently used.

Summary

Creating a grouping of terms and language that are commonly and consistently used can drastically improve communication between individuals throughout an organization. It is important that as the organization changes, the terms and language also adapt to accommodate business operations and functions.

Addendum E: Risk Assessment

Introduction

Risk management is the process of implementing countermeasures to achieve an acceptable level of risk; at an acceptable cost. By examining (in-depth) the potential threats faced by an organization, a better understanding of business risk can be gained that will lead to identifying strategies, techniques, approaches, or countermeasures that reduce or mitigate impact. Generally, this can be achieved by asking three basic questions:

- What can go wrong?
- What will we do?
- If something happens, how will we pay for it?

Thinking about these questions in context of an organization, it might become clear that there are some areas where risk management could be applied, such as weaknesses in the software development lifecycle or manual processes that are prone to human error. Because potential damage or loss to an asset exists, the perceived level of risk is based on the value assigned by its owner and the consequential impact. Additionally, the probability and likelihood of a vulnerability to be exploited must also be taken into consideration. Therefore, as illustrated in Figure E.1, risk cannot exist without the intersection of three variables: assets, threats, and vulnerabilities.

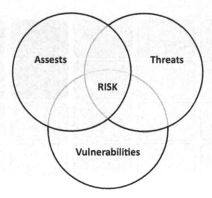

Figure E.1 Risk management variables.

What Is a Risk assessment?

A risk assessment is simply a thorough examination of what can cause harm or impact so that an accurate decision of how to manage the risk can be made. Risk assessments do not require an over-engineered approach of new processes, methodologies, or loads of paperwork. There are several industry-recognized methodologies available to use during the analysis stage of the risk management program.

Depending on the type of business offered, there will likely be one risk management methodology that is preferred over others; while others may be mandated through regulations to use a particular methodology or a decision is made to develop one that meets their specific business needs. Generally, organizations have the option of conducting a risk assessment by following one of the following two approaches.

Qualitative Assessments

Qualitative assessments are focused on results that are descriptive as opposed to measurable; where there is no direct monetary value assigned to the assets and its importance is based on a hypothetical value. Organizations should typically look to conduct a qualitative assessment when the:

- Assessors have limited expertise;
- Time frame allocated for the assessment is short; or
- Data is not readily available to accommodate trending.

Analysis commonly performed in this type of assessment can include several layers of determining how assets are susceptible to risks. This includes

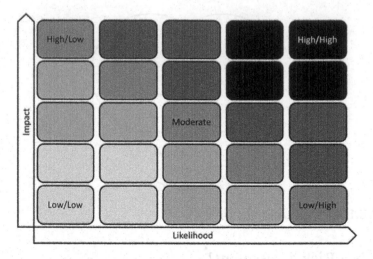

Figure E.2 Risk likelihood-severity heat map.

the correlation of both assets to threats and threats to vulnerabilities, as described further in Addendum F, "Threat Modeling," as well as the determination of likelihood and the level of impact that an exploited vulnerability will create, illustrated in Figure E.2.

In a qualitative assessment, the output generated from the comparison of likelihood and the level of impact is the severity the risk has on assets. Generally, the higher the risk level the greater the priority for the organization to manage the risk and protect its assets from potential harm.

Quantitative Assessments

The primary characteristic of a quantitative assessment is its numerical nature. Use of variables like frequency, probability, impact, or other aspects of a risk assessment are not easily measured against mathematical properties like monetary value. Quantitative assessments allow organizations to determine whether the cost of a risk outweighs the cost of managing a risk based on mathematics instead of descriptive terms.

Organizations that have invested in gathering and preserving information, combined with the enhanced knowledge and experience of staff, are better equipped to conduct this type of assessment. For this reason, getting to the end of a job requires a larger investment in resource knowledge and experience, time, and effort.

Knowing that quantitative assessments follow a mathematical basis, organizations that decide to conduct this type of analysis should consider performing the following series of calculations.

Single Loss Expectancy (SLE)

The first calculation to be completed is the single loss expectancy (SLE). The SLE is the difference between the original and remaining monetary value of an asset that is expected after a single occurrence of a risk against an asset. The SLE is calculated as

Single loss expectancy (SLE) = Asset value (AV) × Exposure factor (EF)

where AV is the monetary value assigned to an asset, and EF is an average percentage representing the amount of loss to an asset.

For example, if the AV has been identified as $5,000 and the EF is 40%, then the SLE would be calculated as

Single loss expectancy (SLE) = $5,000 × 0.40 = $2,000

Annual Rate of Occurrence (ARO)

Following the SLE, the next calculation to be completed is the annual rate of occurrence (ARO). The ARO is a representation of how often an identified threat will successfully exploit a vulnerability and generate some level of business impact within the period of a year. The ARO is calculated as

Annual rate of occurrence (ARO) = # Impact/Time period

For example, if trending data suggest that a specific threat is likely to generate business impact one time over a four-year period, then the ARO would be calculated as

Annual rate of occurrence (ARO) = 1/4 = 0.25

Annualized Loss Expectancy (ALE)

Having values for both SLE and ARO, the next calculation to be completed is the annualized loss expectancy (ALE). The ALE is the expected monetary loss of an asset that can be realized as a result of actual business impact over a one-year period. The ALE is calculated as

Annual loss expectancy (ALE) = SLE * ARO

For example, if the ARO is 0.25 and the SLE is 2,000, then the ALE would be calculated as

Annual loss expectancy (ALE) = 2,000 * 0.25 = 500

With the ALE completed, organizations can use the resulting value directly in a cost-benefit analysis as described in Addendum C, "Cost-Benefit Analysis."

For example, where a threat or risk has ALE of $500, then the cost-benefit analysis would identify that investing $5,000 per year on a countermeasure would not be beneficial.

Advantages and Disadvantages

Depending on the goals for performing an assessment, both the qualitative and quantitative approaches present benefits. Neither approach should be overlooked as a tool for performing risk assessment because each is unique in how it demonstrates risk to stakeholders.

With qualitative assessments, the approach is simpler because it does not require the in-depth analysis of numerical values through formulas and calculations. Generally, results are simpler for stakeholders to understand because the approach leverages business terms to communicate the level of risk involved. However, there is no escaping the fact that qualitative assessments are more subjective because they are based on the organization's experience and judgment which makes it more difficult to defend. The ability to monitor the implementation of countermeasures using labels and terms is difficult because they cannot be measured.

On the other hand, a quantitative assessment is considered objective because it is not influenced by subjective experiences or judgment. It relies on predetermined formulas and calculations to arrive at a risk valuation decision based on numerical measurements. However, this approach requires organizations to have existing data, have more experience, and be willing to invest more time because it is based on factual numbers and predetermined formulas.

Methodologies, Tools, and Techniques

Organizations will select their risk assessment methodology, tools, and techniques based on what works best for their specific needs, capabilities, budget, and timelines.

Tools

Given the availability of industry resources, completing a risk assessment does not need to be an overly complicated process. Several tools are readily accessible to make the risk assessment tasks easier, including software, checklists, and templates.

Depending on volume, gathering and processing data can be demanding and require significant efforts. Organizations should look to invest in automated tools that can alleviate the time needed to complete these tasks. Regardless of whether the organization plans on purchasing or building tools, this decision should be based on aspects such as appropriate timelines, skill sets, and the need to follow a proper system development life cycle (SDLC).

As organizations perform more risk assessments, they will begin to identify patterns where there are similarities in tasks being completed, such as cataloging threat agents and threats. In these situations, the use of checklists may be beneficial to ensure that the risk assessment considers all relevant information even if it may not apply in each instance.

Reviewing existing policies and procedures for relevant security gaps can be a complex and time-consuming task. When used properly, templates can be effective in improving operational efficiencies and accuracy of the risk assessment results.

Methodologies and Techniques

Generally, all risk assessments follow a similar methodology consisting of techniques used to arrive at a final risk decision, including analyzing threats and vulnerabilities, asset valuation, and risk evaluation.

However, there is no single risk assessment methodology that meets the needs of every organization because they were not designed to be "one-size-fits-all." Ultimately, each organization is unique in its own respect and has its own reasons for completing risk assessments. Therefore, a variety of industry-recognized risk assessment methodologies have been developed to address varying needs and requirements.

Contained in the *Resources* section of this chapter, a series of different risk assessment methodologies have been provided as references. It is important to note that inclusion of a methodology in this chapter does not suggest that these are better or recommended over other models that were not included.

Risk Lifecycle Workflow

An assessment of risk at any given time will naturally evolve over time and the exposure to the organization will increase or decrease accordingly. Supporting constant changes in business risk requires that the risk management process is performed regularly, not as a one-time exercise.

Effectively managing risk should be shared between multiple stakeholders because the responsibility and accountability of doing so cannot generally be placed on a single party. For example, while information security is responsible for providing guidance and oversight, accountability for implementing recommendations is with the business line that owns the risk.

Several well-established risk management frameworks are available. While slight differences exist in terminology and stages, they all use a very similar approach to the risk management lifecycle. Described in the sections to follow, Figure E.3 illustrates the four-stage workflow involved in the risk management lifecycle.

Figure E.3 Risk management lifecycle workflow.

Visualizing Risk

Challenges with demonstrating risk are largely attributed to delivering information in a format that is difficult to interpret. As illustrated in Figure E.4, a mind map is an excellent tool for conceptually representing risk in a non-linear format to build out the framework for assessing and managing the risk.

Mind maps are diagrams based on a centralized concept or subject, such as risk management, with the components revolving around it like a spider-web. Not only does the use of a mind map enhance communications using categorized groupings, it also allows the risk management team to quickly record and capture ideas being discussed during meetings.

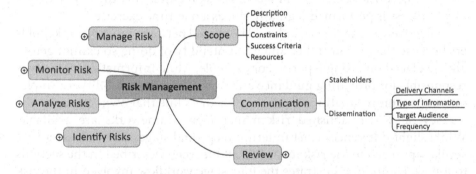

Figure E.4 Risk management mind map—communication.

Communication

Communication is an integral component of risk management. It is essential that the key stakeholders responsible for managing risk throughout the organization, such as upper management, understand the reasons why decisions are made and why the selected strategies, techniques, approaches, and countermeasures are required. For this reason, the communication activities performed as part of the risk management process should not be viewed as a sequential stage, but instead represented as a continuous activity across all stages.

With consistent communication, risk information can be more effectively re-used throughout the organization, reducing the need to conduct more than one risk assessment on the same area for different purposes (i.e., planning, auditing, resource allocations). When defining communication activities, organizations might include details that provide direction on the:

- Types of information that needs to be communicated at various stages (i.e., what information do stakeholders need or want);
- Target audience for the distinct types of information (i.e., management); or
- Means used to distribute communication to the target audiences.

Stage #1: Identify

Risk cannot be managed without first recognizing, describing, and having a solid understanding of its (potential) impact. To start, stakeholders (i.e., employees, investors, etc.) should be provided with clear direction on what the organization's expectations are when it comes to identifying risk. Once informed, all stakeholders should be provided with the appropriate tools and techniques—such as training, workshops, checklists—that will be used to accurately identify risk.

To facilitate stakeholder involvement in the process of identifying risk, organizations should create a taxonomy to ensure the use of consistent and common risk management terminology and classifications throughout the entire process. Further details about how to build a taxonomy can be found in Addendum D, "Building a Taxonomy."

Through a series of face-to-face or virtual sessions, stakeholders should contribute to the identification of risks as both collaborative and individual participation. After the collective results have been reviewed, the risk management mind map can be expanded further to include the specific components of the identification stage as illustrated in Figure E.5.

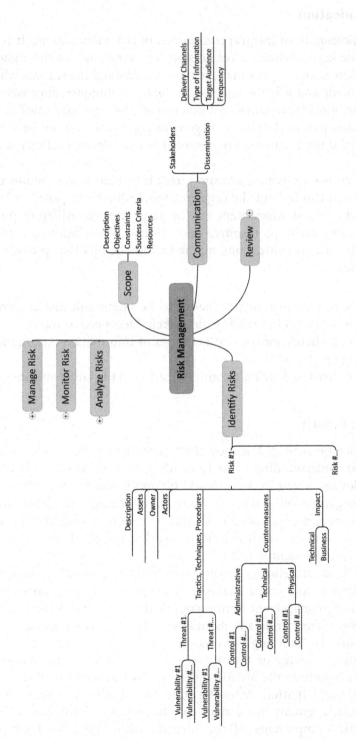

Figure E.5 Risk management mind map—identifying.

Stage #2: Analyze

Having identified all relevant assets, threats, and vulnerabilities that constitute risk, the next step is to individually analyze and prioritize all risks that have any potential of generating business impact. Analyzing each risk individually helps to prioritize them so that organizations can focus resources and efforts to managing the most appropriate risk first. When defining assessment activities, organizations might include details that provide direction on:

- Who should be involved;
- The level of detail required;
- What type of information needs to be gathered; and
- How the risk assessment should be documented to deal, for example, with planning activities.

As each risk is analyzed, organizations should consider their risk tolerance as a factor in the final risk scoring. By doing so, organizations will get a better representation of risk by being able to identify the delta between the assessed risk level and what they consider to be an acceptable risk level. Generally, there are several tools and techniques available to analyze and prioritize risks. As illustrated previously in Figure E.2, at a minimum performing a risk assessment involves determining the likelihood of a risk occurring and the level of impact it will generate, ultimately achieving the severity valuation of the risk.

Output from the risk assessment will create an understanding of the nature of the risk and its potential to affect business operations and functions. After determining the impact of each risk, which is the combination of likelihood and severity, the risk management mind map can be expanded further to include the specific components of the identification stage as illustrated in Figure E.6.

Stage #3: Manage

Completion of the preceding assessment has resulted in each risk being assigned a ranking in terms of the level of impact it has on business operations and functions. With this knowledge, the organization must determine how to minimize the probability of negative risks while improving its

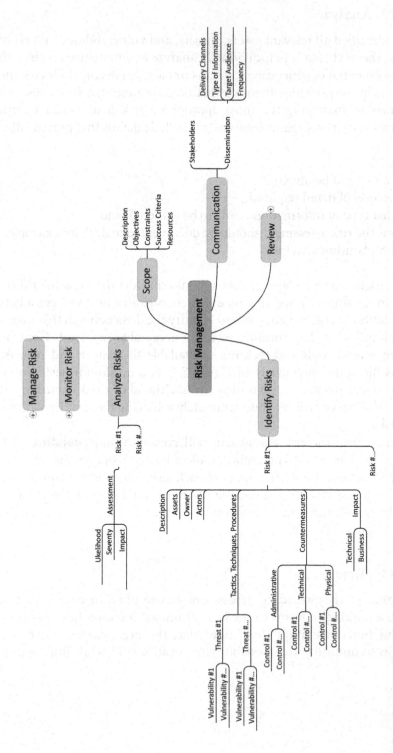

Figure E.6 Risk management mind map—analyzing.

security posture. This requires that, for each risk, a decision be made on how best to respond and manage the level of impact. Illustrated in Figure E.7, the four responses to risk include:

- *Mitigating* risk, where likelihood is high but severity is low, through the implementation of countermeasures to reduce the potential for impact
- *Avoiding* risk, where likelihood and severity are high, by keeping clear of activities that will generate the potential for impact
- *Transferring* risk, where likelihood is low but severity is high, by shifting all—or a portion of—the risk to a third party through insurance, outsourcing, or entering into partnerships
- *Accepting* risk, where likelihood and severity are low, if the result of a cost-benefit analysis determines that the cost of mitigating the risk is greater than the cost to implement the necessary countermeasures; in this scenario, the best response is to accept the risk and continuously monitor it
- Details on how to perform a cost-benefit analysis can be found in Addendum C, "Cost-Benefit Analysis"

Where the organization has determined that the best response to a risk is implementing countermeasures, it is important to remember that these controls can be applied in the form of administrative, physical, or technical

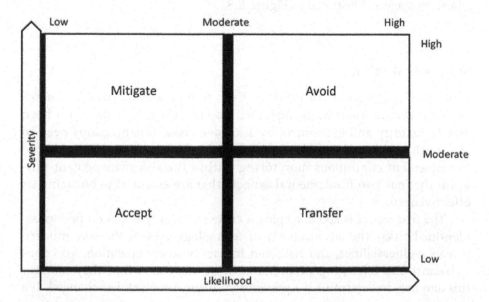

Figure E.7 Risk management responses.

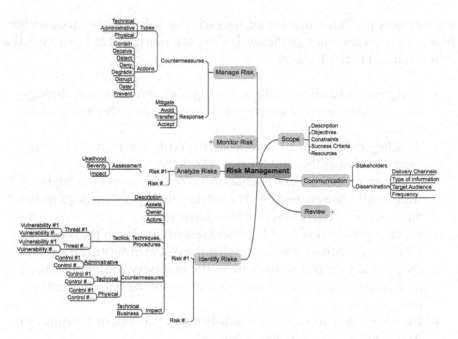

Figure E.8 Risk management mind map—managing.

controls. After determining the best response, the risk management mind map can be expanded further to include the specific components of the identification stage as illustrated in Figure E.8.

Stage #4: Monitor

Generally, risk is about uncertainty. Even though a formalized risk management program has been implemented, and up to this stage has been able to identify and get control over known risks, organizations need to ensure that it is not performed as a singular activity. Instead, they need to implement continuous monitoring within the risk management program that has two fundamental aspects that are essential to ensuring its effectiveness.

The first aspect is about keeping a close and steady watch on previously identified risks. The advancement in technology evolves the way modern threats, vulnerabilities, and risks can impact business operation. To counterbalance this effect, organizations must be vigilant in how they monitor this anomaly to determine if a previously documented risk has changed. If a change has been detected, the organization should re-assess the original risk to determine if their risk response also needs to be changed.

The second aspect is about identifying any new risks that have emerged. The advancement in technology also introduces new threats, vulnerabilities, and risks that have the potential to generate new kinds of business impact. To counterbalance this effect, organizations must implement and diligently follow a proactive management program to identify when new risks surface. Through a proactive approach, there will be greater opportunities to manage risks before they materialize and avoid impulsive risk response decisions.

The best method of risk monitoring comes from the combined implementation of administrative, physical, and technical solutions. After selecting the most appropriate risk monitoring solution(s), the risk management mind map can be expanded further to include the specific components of the monitoring stage as illustrated in Figure E.9.

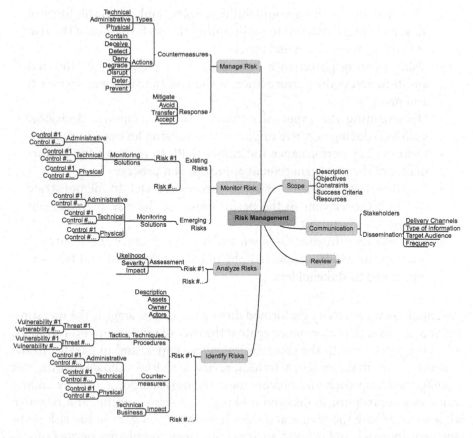

Figure E.9 Risk management mind map—monitoring.

Review

Activities performed while reviewing the risk management program are an important aspect of continuous process improvement. Reviewing the collective risk management approach and process is essential to providing stakeholders (i.e., management, investors, etc.) with awareness and assurance that the organization's overall risk management approach is performing effectively, efficiently, and is still relevant. For this reason, the review activities performed in this workflow should not be viewed as a sequential stage, but instead represented as a continuous activity.

Information gathered during review activities helps organizations to identify opportunities to improve their risk management approach and process to ensure its overall performance remains consistent. To support the activities performed during the review stage, organizations should consider the following:

- Clearly defining the accountabilities, roles, and responsibilities of all stakeholders involved in maintaining the performance of the risk management approach and process
- Using existing governance and assurance functions (i.e., internal audit) to assess the performance of the risk management approach and process
- Documenting the expected outcomes of risk response decisions, such as reducing negative impact or capitalizing on opportunities
- Defining key performance indicators (KPI) to measure the performance of the risk management approach and process
- Building the necessary systems, processes, etc. to demonstrate the findings relevant to the performance of the risk management approach and process
- Establishing a timeline for when and how governance and assurance assessments will be conducted; the outcomes decisions will be communicated to stakeholders

Essential to every activity performed during the review stage is the measurement of the overall performance against the overall implementation strategy. Working together with the communication activities, and in parallel to the remaining risk management activities, review activities validate that the risk management approach and process meet the organization's need by adding value as a contributor to decision making, business planning, and resource allocation. Where the review activities have identified gaps in the risk management approach and process, such as regulatory compliance or operational efficiencies, actions can be taken to identify opportunities to use more effective approaches, improve processes, or leverage new tools and ideas.

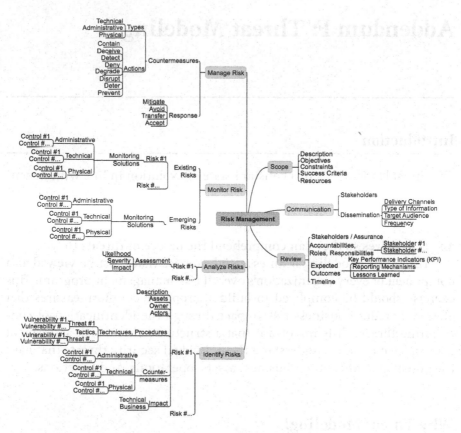

Figure E.10 Risk management mind map—reviewing.

Generally, the documentation and communication of review activities support the organization's capability to improve its risk management performance through dissemination of best practices and lessons learned. After building the review activities, the risk management mind map can be expanded further to include the specific components of the review stage as illustrated in Figure E.10.

Summary

While there is no one-size-fits-all approach to performing a risk assessment, the overall goal is to gain a better understanding of the business risk so organizations can identify appropriate strategies, techniques, approaches, or countermeasures to manage the impact. Using any industry-recognized risk assessment methodology, organizations can avoid an over-engineered approach of establishing new processes, approaches, or generating loads of paperwork.

Addendum F: Threat Modeling

Introduction

The threat landscape is in a constant state of evolution in line with dependencies placed on complex technology infrastructures. Building—and sustaining—an effective defense-in-depth strategy to manage threats requires organizations to have a balanced understanding of both their adversaries and themselves so they can comprehend the nature of threats they face.

Threat risk modeling is an essential exercise that must be viewed as a component of every organization's overall risk management program. This exercise should be completed to build appropriate countermeasures that effectively reduce business risk impact through the identification of contributing threats. It is important that a structured threat risk assessment is completed to better understand the individual security threats that have the potential to affect their business assets, operations, and functions.

Why Threat Modeling?

In relation to information security, a threat is considered any intentional (e.g., criminal activity) or accidental (e.g., natural disaster) course of action with potential to adversely impact people, processes, or technology. Like business risk, threats can be classified according to their types, such as:

- Physical damage (e.g., fire, water);
- Service impact (e.g., electrical, telecommunication);
- Information compromise (e.g., eavesdropping, media theft);
- Technical failures (e.g., software defects, performance and capacity); or
- Operational compromise (e.g., abuse of rights, denial of service [DoS])

It is important to recognize that even though the resulting impact(s) of individual security threats can be different, there are commonalities in how all threats are structured and work. For example, the Structured Threat Information Expression (STIX) framework, illustrated in Figure F.1, is designed to improve the overall management and understanding of threat information so that organizations can better develop mitigation strategies and countermeasures that are meaningful, adaptable, extensible, and automated.

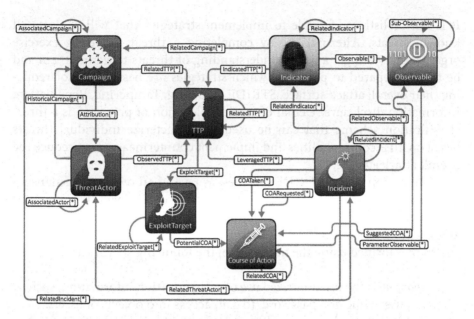

Figure F.1 Structured threat information expression (STIX) framework.

Within the STIX framework, organizations can utilize a common language for representing the following nine constructs of how threats work:

- *Observables* are the resulting outputs that might be or have been seen across an organization (i.e., service degradation).
- *Indicators* describe one or more observable patterns that, combined with other relevant and contextual information, represent artifacts and/or behaviors of interest (i.e., file hashes).
- *Incidents* are distinct instances of indicators that are affecting an organization accompanied by information discovered or decided upon during an investigation.
- *Adversary tactics, techniques, and procedures (TTP)* describe the attack patterns, tools, exploits, infrastructure, victim targeting, and other methods used by the adversary or attacker.
- *Exploit targets* are vulnerabilities, weaknesses, or configurations that can be exploited.
- *Courses of action* are specific countermeasures taken as corrective or preventative response actions to protect an exploit target or mitigate the potential impact of an incident.
- *Campaigns* are occurrences where threat actors perform a set of TTPs or incidents that could be experienced throughout an organization.
- *Threat actors* identify and/or characterize the malicious adversary with intent and observed behaviors that represent a threat to an organization.

It is not realistic or feasible to implement strategies that will mitigate all known threats. Alternatively, by completing a threat modeling exercise organizations can get a better understanding of threats targeting them and be better prepared to prioritize which strategies are best suited for reducing their overall attack surface. STRIDE (Spoofing, Tampering, Repudiation, Information disclosure, Denial of service, Elevation of privilege) is a threat classification scheme that can be used to characterize individual threats based on TTP commonalities and implement countermeasures to reduce the overall attack surface.

Application of the STRIDE scheme—as part of an overall risk management program—allows organizations to meet the requirements for maintaining security properties of confidentiality, integrity, and availability (CIA), along with authorization, authentication and non-repudiation. The STRIDE acronym is formed using the first letter of the following six threat categories:

- *Spoofing* is the unauthorized use of authentication information, such as a username and password, to gain access into objects or assets.
- *Tampering* involves the malicious and unauthorized (1) alteration of data communication between subjects such as business workflows or (2) modification of persistent objects or assets such as database content.
- *Repudiation* is the explicit denial of performing actions where proof cannot be otherwise obtained, such as executing unauthorized acts against an object or asset. Non-repudiation is the mitigating control where a record of actions is maintained such as generating an audit log event for specific acts against an object or asset.
- *Information disclosure* involves exposure of information to subjects that are, under normal circumstances, not authorized to gain access, such as an intruder reading data communications between two systems.
- *Denial of service* attacks decrease the availability and reliability of objects or assets by making them temporarily unavailable or unusable, such as overwhelming a system with access requests.
- *Elevation of privilege* occurs when unprivileged subjects obtain privileged access and are subsequently authorized to gain access to objects or assets, such as exploiting defenses and impersonating a trusted system.

Business Risk Association

As business operations and functions become much more inter-related with complex technologies, it is crucial that organizations do not continue to manage threats on a case-by-case basis as they are identified. Instead of managing threats through specific technology functionalities, organizations

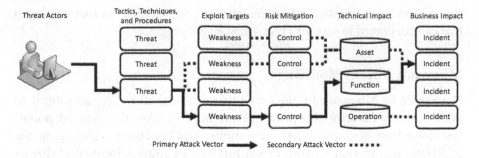

Figure F.2 Threat tree workflow.

should manage their attack surface with the goal of reducing a much larger number of threats without getting into the specifics.

To manage threats from a risk-based approach, organizations should focus on assessing threats as part of their overall risk management program. The relationship between threats and business risk is illustrated in Figure F.2, whereby threats are represented as direct contributors and drivers for impact to business operations and functions.

Threat Modeling Methodologies

Threat modeling is the process used to identify objectives and vulnerabilities, quantify exposure, and develop strategies to mitigate and countermeasure threats. Through the creation of a structured representation of collected information, organizations are better informed and can prioritize decision making to improve their risk posture.

Organizations should ensure that threat modeling is performed as an iterative process and not as a one-time exercise. Threat modeling should be performed consistently throughout each phase of the system and software development to:

- Ensure threats that are not identified during initial assessments are subsequently discovered; and
- Adapt to changes in system or software designs and evolving business requirements.

Several threat models have been published to enable the classification and categorization of individual threats; each follows a different approach. In some instances, organizations might find that adopting one threat model over another may not be appropriate for them because it does not meet their business requirements. In all cases, a functional run-through of threat models should be performed so organizations can determine which one aligns best to their specific needs. While not all threat models are specified below, the following are examples of methodologies that can be adopted to support a risk management program.

Microsoft Threat Modeling

Developed by Microsoft in 2003, this threat model allows organizations to systematically identify and prioritize threats that have the greatest potential impact on business assets, operations, and functions. Leveraging the STRIDE classification scheme, organizations can address individual threats by executing the following six stages:

- *Identify assets*: Documents all systems and objects that need to be protected
- *Create an architecture overview*: Uses dataflow and workflow diagrams to illustrate the relationships and connectivity between systems and objects
- *Decompose the application*: Provides further details about the architecture to uncover weaknesses and vulnerabilities in design, implementation, or configuration
- *Identify the threats*: Discovers the exact weaknesses and vulnerabilities that could affect the systems and objects
- *Document the threats*: Records the attributes of each weakness and vulnerability using a common classification scheme
- *Rate the threats*: Scores threats to determine the priority for implementing mitigating countermeasures

Microsoft's threat modeling methodology is designed to address the unique challenges faced by organizations when it comes to reducing the attack surface and improving security of systems and software. Those involved in performing threat modeling using Microsoft's methodology will find that while it focuses more on the technical aspects of business risk, it is easy to learn and adopt throughout any organization.

PASTA (Process for Attack Simulation and Threat Analysis)

Developed by Marco Morana and Tony "UV", this is a threat model that is platform agnostic and can be applied to most systems and software development methodologies. This model is focused on aligning business objectives with technical requirements through the completion of the following seven steps:

- *Define the business and security objectives*: Documents functional capabilities by completing a business impact analysis from a security and regulatory compliance requirements perspective

- *Define the technical scope*: Describes the inclusion of technical assets and components that will be enumerated for threats
- *Decompose the application*: Identifies the individual component data flows from which threat and vulnerability assessments are performed
- *Threat analysis*: Extracts detailed threat intelligence and assesses the likelihood of attack scenarios occurring
- *Weakness and vulnerabilities analysis*: Involves mapping threat analysis results with enumerated weaknesses to develop use/abuse cases and vulnerabilities scoring systems
- *Attack/exploits enumeration and modeling*: Establishes an attacker's perspective of the attack surface including exploit targets or TTPs
- *Risk and impact analysis*: Provides qualitative and quantitative assessments of the business risk and impact along with mitigation strategy options

PASTA was designed by combining several threat modeling approaches to give organizations an attacker's perspective of threats so they can identify mitigation strategies that follow an asset-centric approach. While there are technical aspects included in this methodology, the inclusion of business-relevant aspects changes it from a purely technical exercise into a process that requires the involvement of key organizational stakeholders.

Trike

Developed by Eleanor Saitta, Brenda Larcom, and Michael Eddington, version 1.0 of the TRIKE threat model was published in 2005 as a way of providing organizations with a unified framework for security auditing from a risk management perspective. The intention of using this methodology was to enable communication between multiple stakeholders to describe security characteristics of a system or software from the high-level architecture to the low-level implementation details.

TRIKE follows a risk-based approach where organizations sequentially complete four models to determine the impact threats should assets, operations, and functions:

- *Requirements* focuses on obtaining an understanding of the target system or software, including the intended operations, all subject interactions, the actions that trigger what functionality, and rules that constrain actions.
- *Implementation* focuses on gathering information about the implementation. From previously documenting what operation(s) the system or software is intended to perform, the following assessments can be made:
  - Identifying the actions that do not align within the scope of the intended actions for the system or software
  - Examining the individual components and develop data flow diagrams for how they are interconnected

- Creating a workflow illustrating the relationship between subjects, actions, triggers, and operations
- *Threat* focuses on identifying the threats against the implementation model. By developing an attack graph for a specific component or against the entire system or software, weaknesses can be identified and subsequently mitigation strategies created.
- *Risk* focuses on the understanding the risk factors that are in and out of scope for each component of the system or software. Risks identified can be assumed resulting in changing the prioritization of weaknesses and vulnerabilities documented during the threat model. It is important to note that this risk model is still considered experimental within the TRIKE methodology and is subject to change.

Under version 1.0, organizations may experience performance issues after reaching a certain threshold of actors and assets that are included in a single system assessment. Since the initial release there have been subsequent versions of the methodology, both versions 1.5 and 2.0, which are only partially documented and are still currently experimental. Organizations must exercise caution when considering the use of the latter versions of this methodology, as they have not been fully tested against real systems or software.

Threat Risk Matrix

From the threat modeling exercise, a formalized report should be created to document the security aspects of the system or software architecture including additional attributes that link the identified threat to a business risk mitigation strategy. Publishing a threat report helps to prioritize, manage, and align potential threats across the organization with communication to key stakeholders such as:

- Designers who can use secure software engineering principles relating to technologies and functionality;
- Developers who author systems or software following recommended mitigation strategies; or
- Testers and auditors who can verify and validate that the application security components were built as designed.

As a supplement to the overall risk assessment report provided in the *Templates* section of this book, a dedicated threat risk assessment (TRA) report can be included to illustrate how the assessed threats contribute to the overall business risk. Even though this additional report is included as part of the larger risk report, it should still contain sufficient information so that it can be used as a stand-alone report. At a minimum the TRA report, as provided in the *Templates* section of this book, should include:

- *Executive summary* provides a high-level summary of the threat assessment and findings
- *Overall risk statement* presents justification for the final risk score of each security principle specified in the assessment matrix
- *Methodology* provides an explanation of how the threat modeling exercise was conducted
- *Assumptions* identifies circumstances and outcomes taken for granted during the assessment
- *Threat tree workflows* demonstrating how each threat can lead to business impact
- *Threat assessment matrix* addresses, in sections, each security principle (i.e., confidentiality, integrity, availability, etc.) with details about each individual threat including the:
  - Unique identifier for recognizing a specific threat
  - Name and description of the threat that was assessed
  - Risk score that was assigned to the threat
  - Description of countermeasures identified to mitigate the threat
  - Description of residual risk remaining after countermeasures are implemented

Threat Modeling Next Steps

Organizations must acknowledge that over time, threats evolve resulting in changes to the business risk and impact. While countermeasures can be implemented to reduce an attack surface, it is important to remember that threats exist—regardless of the mitigation strategies previously implemented—and cannot be (entirely) eliminated as a business risk.

Threat modeling should not be treated as a program that is executed as a one-time exercise. It must be performed as an iterative and adaptable process that is constantly evolving alongside the threat landscape, changes to systems and software designs, and shifting business requirements.

Summary

As part of an overall risk management strategy, threat modeling focuses specifically on security threats that have potential to affect their business assets, operations, and functions. By performing threat modeling, organizations will gain a better understanding of the threats they face so more effective defense-in-depth strategies can be implemented.

Addendum G: Data Warehousing Introduction

Introduction

Data warehousing is first and foremost a business discipline that leverages technical infrastructures to deliver the final product. Achieving a successful data warehouse implementation requires a strategic approach that consists of picking the right project team members, is focused on both business and technical requirements, and has a sound and thorough project plan.

At the core of every successful data warehouse implementation comes proper planning. As part of this planning, it is critical that organizations do not underestimate the importance and complexity of completing their requirements analysis.

What Is a Data Warehouse?

An enterprise data warehouse (EDW) provides a centralized repository of integrated data from multiple disparate sources to allow for quicker and better-informed decision-making capabilities. Collected data is commonly maintained historically within the EDW to provide organizations with the ability to trend data over a longer period for improved data mining, analytics, and reporting.

The four common characteristics of every EDW, as first defined by William Inmon, are:

- *Subject-oriented data*: All relevant data is gathered, stored, and organized as a set of information that can be used for a specific subject area.
- *Integrated*: All data contained within the EDW is in a consistent structure that allows it to always be integrated to all other data without exception.
- *Non-volatile*: All data is loaded and accessible in the EDW in a read-only presentation.
- *Time variant*: All data is accurate as of some point in time and is represented over an extended period, such as 5–10 years.

Development Concepts

Traditionally, an EDW's functionality was scoped to provide functionality specific to analyzing an organization's business data. Supporting business reporting, the data contained within the EDW is classified as:

- *Operational data* that is commonly stored, retrieved, and updated by an online transaction processing (OLTP) system for running the business; such as an order-entry application.
- *Informational data* that is created from operational data sources and is typically:
  - Summarized operational data
  - De-normalized and replicated
  - Optimized for decision making
  - Accessible in read-only formats

Illustrated in Table G.1, the difference between operational databases and data warehouses has been identified.

To analyze and report on business trends, organizations need to have a large amount of different data sources available over an extended time. In the case of OLTP systems, they are designed to complete online transactions and query processing that requires historical data to be archived so performance demands can be met. Alternatively, an EDW serves as a solution for organizations to mine and analyze data trends over time, which makes it an online analytical processing (OLAP) system.

Illustrated in Table G.2, the major features of OLTP and OLAP systems have been identified.

Table G.1   OLTP and OLAP Differences

Operational Databases	Data Warehouses
Lack of integration	Integrated data sources
Focused on database and process design	Focused on data modeling and database design
Data is accurate as if the last time it was accessed	Data is accurate in the period of time
Data can be updated	Data cannot be modified
Current data available 60–90 days	Historical data available 50–60 yrs
Operations performed on database are: changes, insert, delete, and replace	Operations performed on database are: load and access
Regular updates made record-by-record	Once data is loaded into the database, no updates are made
Data is very fresh	Data is very old
Database contains detailed information	Database contains summarized data

Table G.2 OLTP and OLAP Features

Feature	OLTP	OLAP
User/system orientation	Custom-oriented for real-time transactions and querying	Market-oriented for historical trending and reporting
Data contents	Small amount of current and up-to-date data	Large amount of historical and accurate data
Database design	Entity-Relationship (ER) model and application-oriented	Star or Snowflake model and subject-oriented
View	Current data	Historical data
Unit of work	Short and simple transactions	Complex operations
Characteristic	Operational processing	Informational processing
Orientation	Transaction	Analysis
User	Clerical, DBA	Analyst, manager
Function	Day-to-day operations	Long-term decision making
Summarization	Highly details and flat relationships	Summarized and consolidated
Access patterns	Read/Write	Read only
Focus	Data in	Information out
Number of records	Tens of thousands	Hundreds of millions
Number of users	Thousands	Hundreds
Database size	Less than 1 GB	Greater than 100GB
Priority	High performance and availability	Highly flexible

Architectural Models

From the previous comparisons, the purpose of the EDW is better understood by knowing what role it plays within the organization. However, as EDWs become more common, organizations are constantly evolving their capabilities by finding innovative ways to use these infrastructures to collect, analyze, and process data for other business purposes.

Essentially every EDW is considered a living eco-system that is developed using both business and technical architectural components. Without a sound architecture, the solution cannot support the organization's strategic direction because the system will not function effectively as a complete and integrated solution.

The best way to approach developing the EDW architecture is to use the analogy of constructing a real building. Although the components of an EDW are different from those in a real building, the fundamentals of how they are both architected are identical whereas they both require a set of models, specifications, and structures that integrate several key components into a complete and final working solution.

Designing both the business and technical components of the EDW involves the following three distinct layers of functionality that seamlessly work together in support of the overall solution capabilities.

- *Extract* identifies and retrieves the disparate data from its distributed repository.
- *Transform* reconstructs data into structured sets that can be used for mining and analysis.
- *Load* writes structured data sets into target storage for mining, analytics, and reporting.

The methods for how the extraction, transformation, and loading (ETL) functionality of collected data is implemented depends on the organization's requirements for developing the EDW. As an example, the following architectural reference models are commonly used when developing EDW deployments.

Basic Architecture

Illustrated in Figure G.1, this is the simplest type of architecture where users are permitted direct access to data through the EDW. This architecture requires that organizations pre-process their data outside of the solution before being placed into the EDW. The components of this architecture include:

- Repositories of data located in the multiple disparate sources
- Warehouse containing the centralized repository of collected data sources
- Entities that interact with centralized data sets

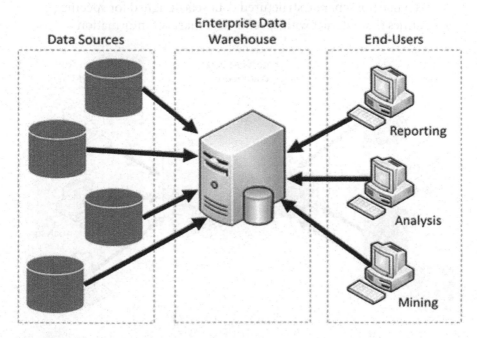

Figure G.1 Basic data warehouse architecture.

Architecture with Staging

Illustrated in Figure G.2, this type of architecture includes an intermediate staging area where ETL functions automate the pre-processing of data into a structured format before being placed into the EDW. The components of this architecture include:

- Repositories of data located in the multiple disparate sources
- Staging area where collected data sources are transformed into relevant structures
- Warehouse containing the centralized repository of structured data sets
- Entities that interact with centralized and structured data sets

Architecture with Data Marts

Illustrated in Figure G.3, this type of architecture is like the basic deployment; however, it includes data marts that contain specific structured data sets designed for a particular use case, such as compliance or governance. The components of this architecture include:

- Repositories of data located in the multiple disparate sources
- Warehouse containing the centralized repository of structured data sets
- Data mart of separate structured data sets designed for specific uses
- Entities that interact with specific data marts of information

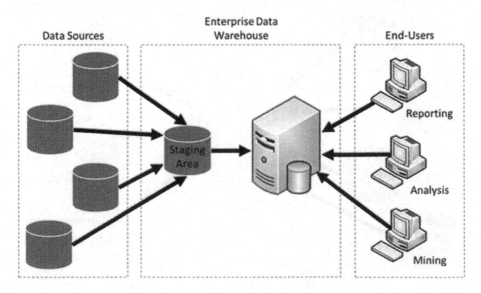

Figure G.2 Data warehouse architecture with staging.

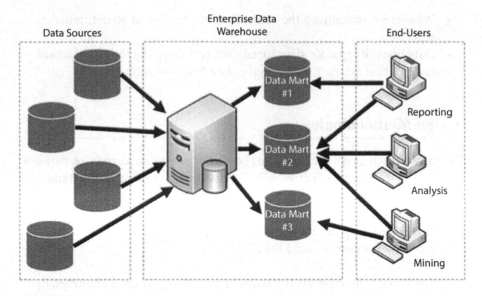

Figure G.3 Data warehouse architecture with data marts.

Architecture with Staging and Data Marts

Illustrated in Figure G.4, this type of architecture is a combination of all previous architectures where it includes both a staging area and several data marts. The components of this architecture include:

- Repositories of data located in the multiple disparate sources
- Staging area where collected data sources are transformed into relevant structures

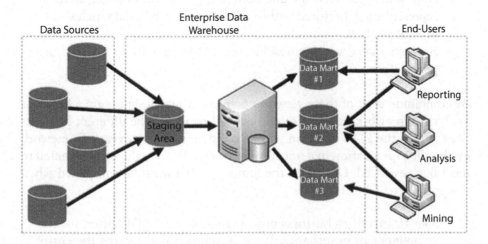

Figure G.4 Data warehouse architecture with staging and data marts.

- Warehouse containing the centralized repository of structured data sets
- Data mart of separate structured data sets designed for specific uses
- Entities that interact with specific data marts of information

Design Methodologies

No matter which EDW architectures best fit organizational requirements, to successfully design an effective EDW, organizations must understand and analyze their business need for why the system is being developed. Referring to the analogy of constructing a real building, the EDW owner, architect, and engineer will all have different views on how to achieve a final solution. The different views on how to build the EDW are:

- *Top-down view* supports the selection of relevant data, as identified by current and ongoing business needs, which is necessary for the EDW. This viewpoint provides organizations with a systematic solution with minimal integration issues; however, it can be more expensive because it takes longer to develop and does not provide a great deal of flexibility.
- *Bottom-up view* supports the creation of data marts to provide reporting and analytical capabilities for a specific business process. This viewpoint provides organizations with more flexibility and quicker implementation of the data marts; however, it is problematic when having to integrate the individual data marts into the larger EDW.
- *Data source view* depicts the data being gathered, stored, and managed by the system.
- *Data warehouse view* include both fact tables and dimension tables representing data stored within the EDW as well as data included to provide context.
- *Business query view* represents the EDW data from the end-use perspective.

By combining each of these viewpoints into a single design plan, a business analysis framework can be created that will represent the different perspectives of how the EDW solution will be constructed. This overall framework guides the organization in determining how the EDW will be constructed to meet business need. Generally, the four steps that must be completed when designing the EDW are:

- *Step #1*: Identify a business process to model the EDW after, such as compliance or governance. If the business process spans the entire organization and involves several complex data collections, the suggested EDW architecture is either a basic deployment or one with a staging area, depending on the need to pre-process collected data. If the analysis is focused on a single business process and is limited to a department, the suggested EDW architectures are those that contain data marts, where implementing a staging area depends on the need to pre-process collected data.

- *Step #2*: Determine the level of granularity for how much detail about the business process will be represented in fact tables. For example, a decision must be made as to whether each individual record with metadata will be recorded, whether individual record summaries will be recorded, and so on.
- *Step #3*: Select the dimensions, values such as timestamps, that will be stored inside of dimension tables and how/where they are associated with records stored inside fact tables.
- *Step #4*: Select the measures, values that are represented as numerical units, which will be stored inside each fact table record.

Store in the Warehouse and Toss in the Lake

A major challenge faced by all organizations today is the ability to—holistically and comprehensively—manage electronically stored information (ESI). Largely, organizations turn to strategies such as data warehouses to store cleansed and packaged structured ESI for easy consumption. However, as the types and forms of ESI continue to grow and evolve, it is not so simple to transform and load ESI in structured formats that easily fit into a data warehouse.

Generally, data warehouses and data lakes are two distinct types of repositories that provide organizations with different storage capabilities. For example, data warehouses are solutions that provide a centralized repository—of already integrated ESI from one or more disparate data sources—used for reporting and analysis. Alternatively, data lakes are solutions that provide a storage repository that holds a sizeable amount of ESI in its native and raw format until needed. Some of the key differences between a data warehouse and a data lake have been illustrated in Table G.3.

Table G.3   Data Warehouse and Data Lake Differences

	Warehouse	Lake
Format	Structured	Unstructured
Integration	Joined	Detached
Retention	Select ESI	All ESI
Purpose	Business professionals	Data scientists
Changes	Waterfall methodology	Agile methodology
Security	Mature	Developing

Deciding whether to implement a data warehouse or a data lake can be a challenging if the business purpose for implementing a solution has not been defined. With an understanding of some of the key difference between the two solutions, organizations need to thoroughly document their business requirements so they can ensure the solution they will implement is the most strategic and meets the needs of their business use. Refer to the section below for further discussion about project planning.

Implementation Factors

Amongst many other factors, the most common reason why organizations experience implementation failures is because of improper planning and inadequate project management. Before work begins on developing the EDW, thorough consideration needs to be given to some key areas that are essential to the successful implementation of the system.

Business-Driven, Not Technology-Centric

Business requirements are the primary driver for the use of all technology within an organization. While this should be common knowledge, there continue to be projects that are overshadowed by exploiting the capabilities of a technology instead of focusing on what the business need for using the technology really is. It is important that the designing and planning aspects of the EDW system are completed only after the business requirements have been well established.

With an understanding of the overall requirements, focus can be turned towards planning the development and eventual implementation of the EDW system. Regardless of which architecture model has been selected, it is recommended that the implementation of the EDW be carefully planned and executed in incremental stages as the system grows and evolves within the organization.

Value and Expectation

In some instances, organizations could implement their EDW solution without having a thorough understanding of the value that will be gained from the system. While the thought of having an EDW is appealing, first and foremost there needs to be a requirement analysis completed, as discussed further in Addendum H, "Requirements Analysis," to determine if implementing an EDW system is a worthwhile initiative.

If this assessment identifies that there is a value proposition with an EDW, the benefits need to be measured against the cost for implementing the system. This can be completed through a cost-benefit analysis, as discussed in Addendum C, "Cost-Benefit Analysis,"

Risk Assessment

Every project has risks that need to be acknowledged and accompanied by mitigation strategies to ensure that those risks do not significantly impact the successful EDW implementation. Completing a risk assessment, as discussed in Addendum E, "Risk Assessment," an organization can identify and get a better understanding of what factors have the potential to impact the project.

Buy or Build

A common sticking point for organizations is whether they should invest resources into building their EDW system in-house or buy a commercial-off-the-shelf (COTS) solution. Realistically, a wide range of solutions are available today that put into question why organizations would invest resources to reinvent the wheel and build an in-house solution from the ground up. However, it is important to keep in mind that there is no silver bullet in terms of finding a COTS solution that will meet all business requirements.

EDWs provide a wide range of functionality and, for the most part, COTS solutions allow for customizations to be made so organizations can configure the look, feel, and functionality to meet their specific business needs. Performing these customizations is where leveraging internal resources comes into use to further enhance the COTS solutions or to build out elements such as data marts. Organizations need to evaluate their options and find the right balance between in-house development and COTS solutions.

"Eggs-in-One-Basket" or "Best-of-Breed"

There are a wide range of COTS solutions catering to varying levels of EDW functionality. If a decision is made to purchase a COTS solution, the next option to consider is whether to invest in a complete EDW solution from a single vendor or to use the best COTS solution for the individual EDW functionalities (i.e., OLAP, database, repository, etc.). On one side of the coin, some considerations that should be noted when selecting a single vendor include:

- A higher level of integration throughout the EDW system
- Centralized management and support interface exchanges
- Lower total cost of ownership (TCO)
- Common look and feel
- Limited vendor offerings of fully integrated EDW solutions

Alternatively, selecting multiple vendors for specific EDW functionality also comes with its own considerations, such as:

- Increased EDW customization to fit business requirements
- Minimal compromises made on technology components

- Acquisition of solutions that are best suited to your organization
- Compatibility between different vendors can be troublesome
- Assurance of cross-vendor support for the overall system

Project Planning

At the end of the day, a project is a project and the approach used to implement an EDW system follows much the same methodology as any other technology-based initiative. However, EDW projects are slightly different where they have a much broader project scope, can have more complex architectural designs, and involve many different technologies.

Creating a project charter, as found in the *Templates* section of this book, is an excellent way of communicating the business value of implementing the system. This document should include, at a minimum, the following sections:

- *Introduction*: Describes the problem statement to be addressed, the purpose of the project, scope of the project's deliverables, and defines the intended audience
- *Business justification*: Illustrates the business need for the project and the strategic alignment to the organization's goals
- *Impact and constraints*: Highlights the risks, assumptions, and constraints that are contributors that have the potential to impact the success of the project, mitigating strategies for containing the impact and dependencies prior to project execution
- *Timing/schedule*: Demonstrates the sequence of tasks that will be completed and highlights the key milestones throughout the timeline
- *Financial statements*: Details both one-time and ongoing funding sources and financial assumptions
- *Project structure*: Details the executive sponsorship, roles and responsibilities, and both internal and external stakeholders

Summary

An enterprise data warehouse (EDW) is a solution that provides data mining, analytical, and reporting benefits throughout an organization when it is first and foremost driven by business requirements. Although its construction can be complex and involve a proportionate number of moving parts, taking the time to develop a thorough plan to identify and mitigate the risk of failure leads to resources well spent.

Addendum H:
Requirements Analysis

Introduction

Generally, requirements must be actionable, measurable, testable, related to a business need or desire, and defined at a level of detail that is sufficient for design criteria. They are commonly driven by some type of business need or desire where organizations are looking to improve a specific set of functions or processes.

Requirements analysis is a critical process toward achieving success in a project. Also referred to as requirements gathering or requirements specifications, it involves a series of steps and activities that allow organizations to determine what conditions must be met during the system design.

The Importance of Requirements

Organizations must ensure that the process of requirements analysis is not confused or mistaken for the system design process. Essentially, analysis is concerned with what needs to be done, such as studying the current state of a process and determining how it works. On the other hand, design is focused on how it needs to be done, such as implementing a technology to improve the process.

Knowing the scope of what requirements analysis is, the process is essential in translating business need or desires into an architectural view than can be used as the basis for systems design. Within the context of the system development life cycle (SDLC), requirements analysis focuses on identifying gaps within an area within the organization and is performed:

- After the organization's strategies are thoroughly understood; and
- Before developing architectural design specifications.

The process of defining requirements involves considering how they are built. When organizations do not allow sufficient time to ensure that requirements are accurate and complete, the resulting consequence will be a finalized set of requirements that are ambiguous, untestable, and not capable of satisfying business needs or desires. Ultimately, the effects of these downfalls will lead to an unsuccessful project due to collateral damage such as:

- Higher development costs
- Schedule slippage
- Scope creep
- System defects
- Customer dissatisfaction

It is important that organizations define their requirements to be clear, meaningful, effective, and aligned with business needs and desires.

Defining Requirements

Requirements analysis is centered on addressing the needs and desires of business strategies. From this, the requirements analysis process is performed to translate these business needs and desires into a comprehensive architectural model that can be used throughout the organization.

As described in the sections to follow, requirements analysis encompasses several phases to interpret business language and ultimately arrive at a deliverable solution. Understanding that the methodology used is subjective to the needs of each organization, the approach illustrated below is intended to provide a simplified workflow to performing requirements analysis.

Phase #1: Defining Scope

Similar to how any business project is initiated, boundaries must be set around what business strategy will be assessed. Without determining the scope for which requirements will be identified, the architecture model that will be delivered will not address the business needs and desires, resulting in an unsuccessful project as explained previously in this chapter.

Contributing to the scope definition, the following elements must be captured in terms of the specifics that will play a factor in the architectural model:

- *Data*: What facts of significance are used to describe the organization and what they mean?
- *Activities*: What processes, functions, etc. need to be included in this assessment?
- *Locations*: Where in the organization will the activities be addressed?

- *People and organizations*: What resources are involved in the activities that need to be included in this assessment?
- *Timing*: Which business events are drivers that are included in this assessment?
- *Motivation*: What objectives, goals, policies, etc. affect the activities included in this assessment?

There are no predefined rules or guidelines that dictate how to define scope; it is subject to every organization's interpretation. Organizations must rely on their experience and common sense when determining the width and depth of where to set the scope boundaries. At the completion of this phase, a detailed scope statement is produced and will be used as the basis for executing the remaining phases.

Phase #2: Preparing Assessments

Although the scope has already been defined, there has yet to be a plan put together to outline the activities, people, and schedule that will be needed to complete this assessment. In establishing these components, it is important to keep in mind that there is traditionally a trade-off where only two out of three can be maximized.

To avoid unexpected surprises later in the process, it is important that organizations decide what the priorities for this assessment are. Figure H.1 illustrates the three scenarios that will occur based on deciding which components are priorities:

- If the goal is to have a shorter schedule and maintain higher quality through increased activities, then there will be increased cost.
- If the goal is to have a shorter schedule and reduce cost, there will be fewer activities, resulting in lower quality.
- If the goal is to reduce cost and maintain higher quality through increased activities, then there will be a longer schedule.

Figure H.1 Priority triad.

Phase #3: Gathering Requirements

Identifying and capturing a baseline set of requirements must be done in a clear and concise business language. To arrive at a model that encompasses a complete set of business needs and desires, this baseline set of requirements needs to be drawn from various sources throughout the organization, including:

- Operational support documentation
- Stakeholder interviews
- Formal proposals
- Industry best practices
- Strategic roadmaps
- Security and regulatory requirements (international, federal, local)

As the baseline set of requirements is being gathered from multiple sources, it is important to recognize that while they are all related, each requirement is separate and distinct. Generally, requirements can be grouped into one of the following categories:

- *Functional requirements* define features of the deliverable(s) that will specifically meet a business need or desire.
- *Operational requirements* describe the "behind the scene" functions needed to keep the deliverable(s) working over time.
- *Technical requirements* identify conditions under which the deliverable(s) must function.
- *Transitional requirements* outline aspects of the deliverable(s) that must be met to hand over support responsibilities.

As requirements are identified, each item should be documented in a centralized register that will be used throughout the analysis process, such as a database or spreadsheet.

A requirement analysis report template has been provided as a reference in the *Templates* section of this book which includes a matrix that can be used to capture requirements.

Phase #4: Interpret Requirements

Using the aggregated set of baseline requirements, stakeholders now need to review what was documented to ensure that proper business language used in the requirements was captured correctly. Depending on the availability and location of stakeholders, performing these reviews in person might not be possible and alternative methods of meeting can be used, such as conducting interviews, distributing surveys, or holding work-shops and focus groups.

Having stakeholders validate and verify the baseline set of requirements at this stage in the process is critical. Not only will stakeholder review ensure that requirements are as clear and concise as possible, but it also helps to eliminate any confusion related to having to translate business requirements into technical specifications by:

- Not combining separate requirements
- Removing subjective wording, ambiguities, or opinions
- Avoiding scope creep
- Preventing scheduling delays

Following the stakeholder review, it is important that the baseline set of requirements is signed off by all stakeholders as part of the requirements analysis report, which is discussed further in this appendix. Documenting stakeholder agreement is important because these individuals may not be present throughout the remaining phases of the analysis or afterward during the system design process.

Phase #5: Finalize Requirements

By now the baseline set of requirements has been agreed to by all stakehold-ers and can be finalized as the foundation for upcoming planning and archi-tectural design activities. For each requirement that has been accepted, the following additional contexts are needed to determine how it will be actioned and turned into a deliverable:

- *Aligning* the requirement to the scope of the project
- *Categorizing* the requirements based on how they relate to business needs and desires
- *Prioritizing* the requirements according to criticality to the business needs and desires by determining if they are:
  - Core requirements: those which the deliverable will not be able to function without
  - Essential requirements: those which a short-term work-around could be implemented; but in the long term must be addressed
  - Desirable requirements: those viewed as the "bells and whistles" that are not critical to deliverable(s) functionality

As part of the requirement analysis report template provided as a reference in the *Templates* section of this book, the requirements matrix can be used to further expand on the context of each requirement as discussed above.

Phase #6: Prepare Specification Documents

The specification document, also viewed as the final report, essentially outlines the organization's understanding of its business needs and desires as related to a specific business strategy. It provides a level of assurance that all stakeholders within the organization understand and agree to the requirements that were captured at that point in time.

This document is created in clear and concise business language that will be used as the basis for subsequent project activities such as design and architectural specifications, statements of work (SOW), and testing and validation plans. Because it will be used as a governing document, it is important that it remains objective by not providing suggestions, solutions, or information other than that related to the requirements analysis activities. When completed, the specification document will contain enough information that it:

- Provides assurance that all needs and desires have been well understood and translated into clear and concise requirements
- Structures the requirements in a way that helps organizations to maintain appropriate control over scope and schedule
- Contains sufficient details to serve as input into subsequent design specification activities
- Acts as a governing document for the testing and validation activities that will be used to verify the requirements

A requirement analysis report template has been provided as a reference in the *Templates* section of this book.

Summary

Requirements analysis is an essential part of the SDLC process to ensure that the needs and desires of an organization's business strategy are identified and documented as clearly and concisely as possible. Once completed, the specification document is used as a governing document to direct the subsequent activities of system design.

Appendixes

Introduction

As the digital forensic discipline was formalized as a scientific discipline, the principles, methodologies, and techniques have remained consistent despite the evolution of technology and can ultimately be applied to any form of digital data. Within a corporate environment, digital forensic practitioners are often relied upon to maintain the legal admissibility and forensic viability of digital evidence in support of a broad range of different business functions.

Digital Forensic Readiness requires organizations to strategically integrate its business functions and processes with its administrative, technical, and physical Information Security controls to maximize the use of digital evidence while minimizing investigative costs. By doing so, organizations are in a much better position to pro-actively detect and deter security events before they escalate into a more serious incident or reactive investigation.

While not directly related to how the digital forensic discipline is practiced, the supplemental business functions and processes discussed in this section of the book are essential to successfully implementing a Digital Forensic Readiness. Using these business functions and processes as part of a Digital Forensic Readiness program allows organizations to make much more appropriate and informed decisions about their business risks specific to the digital forensic investigations.

In this section, the business function and processes discussed throughout the book have been included as supplemental content to Digital Forensic Readiness. While these materials can be used as part of the Digital Forensic Readiness program, they have been included as standalone materials and can be referenced as independent functions and processes that can also be used in other contexts.

Appendix A: Investigative Process Models

Introduction

When technology was first involved with criminal activities, investigators did not follow any guiding principles, methodologies, or techniques when it came time to collect and process digital evidence. It was only in the 1980s that law enforcement agencies realized there was a need to have an established set of processes that could be consistently followed to support their forensic investigations and guarantee the legal admissibility of digital evidence.

Over the years, several authors have taken on the task of developing and proposing a process model to formalize the digital forensics discipline and transform "ad-hoc" tasks and activities into tested and proven methodologies. Displayed in Table AA.1 is a list of different process methodologies that have been developed and proposed for digital forensics investigations.

It is important to note that while this listing may not be complete, the inclusion of a process methodology does not suggest it is better or recommended over other methodologies that were not included in the table.

Table AA.1 Investigative Process Models

ID	Year	Author(s)	Model Name	Phases
P01	1995	M. Pollitt	Computer Forensic Investigative Process	4
P02	2001	U.S. Department of Justice	Computer Forensic Process Model	4
P03	2001	Palmer	Digital Forensic Research Workshop Investigative Model (Generic Investigation Process)	6
P04	2001	Lee et al.	Scientific Crime Scene Investigation Model	4
P05	2002	Reith et al.	Abstract Model of the Digital Forensic Procedures	9
P06	2003	Carrier and Spafford	Integrated Digital Investigation Process	5
P07	2003	Stephenson	End-to-End Digital Investigation	9
P08	2004	Baryamureeba and Tushabe	Enhanced Integrated Digital Investigation Process	5
P09	2004	Ciardhuain	Extended Model of Cyber Crime Investigation	13
P10	2004	Beebe and Clark	Hierarchical, Objective Based Framework for the Digital Investigations Process	6
P11	2004	Carrier and Spafford	Event-Based Digital Forensic Investigation Framework	5
P12	2006	Kent et al.	Four-Step Forensic Process	4
P13	2006	Kohn et al.	Framework for a Digital Forensic Investigation	3
P14	2006	Roger et al.	Computer Forensic Field Triage Process Model	12
P15	2006	Ieong	FORZA—Digital Forensics Investigation Framework	6
P16	2006	Venter	Process Flows for Cyber Forensics Training and Operations	3
P17	2007	Freiling and Schwittay	Common Process Model for Incident and Computer Forensics	3
P18	2007	Bem and Huebner	Dual Data Analysis Process	4
P19	2008	Selamat et al.	Mapping Process of Digital Forensic Investigations Framework	5
P20	2009	Perumal	Digital Forensic Model Based on Malaysian Investigation Process	7
P21	2010	Pilli et al.	Generic Framework for Network Forensics	9
P22	2011	Yusoff	Generic Computer Forensic Investigation Model	5
P23	2011	Agarwal et al.	Systematic Digital Forensic Investigation Model	11
P24	2012	Adams et al.	Advanced Data Acquisition Model (ADAM)	3

[P01] Computer Forensics Investigative Process (1995)

Consisting of four phases, this model was proposed as a means of ensuring appropriate evidence handling during a computer forensics investigation followed scientifically reliable and legally acceptable methodologies.

- *Acquisition*: Requires that digital evidence be collected using acceptable methodologies only after receiving proper approval from authorities
- *Identification*: Interprets digital evidence and converts it into a readable human format
- *Evaluation*: Determines the digital evidence's relevancy to the investigation
- *Admission*: Documents relevant digital evidence for legal proceedings (Figure AA.1)

[P02] Computer Forensic Process Model (2001)

Consisting of four phases, this model was proposed in the *Electronic Crime Scene Investigation: A guide to first responders* publication and focused on the basic components of a digital forensics investigation.

- *Collection* involves searching for digital evidence sources and ensuring their integrity is maintained while gathering.
- *Examination* evaluates digital evidence to reveal data and reduce volumes.
- *Analysis* examines the context and content of digital evidence to determine relevancy.
- *Reporting* includes presenting digital evidence through investigation documentation (Figure AA.2).

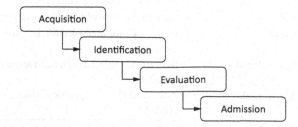

Figure AA.1 Computer forensic investigative process 1995.

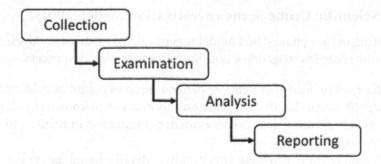

Figure AA.2 Computer forensic process model 2001.

[P03] Digital Forensic Research Workshop (DFRWS) Investigative Model (2001)

Consisting of six phases, this model was proposed as a general-purpose process for digital forensic investigations.

- *Identification* involves detection of an incident or event.
- *Preservation* establishes proper evidence gathering and chain of custody.
- *Collection* gathers relevant data using approved techniques.
- *Examination* evaluates digital evidence to reveal data and reduce volumes.
- *Analysis* examines the context and content of digital evidence to determine relevancy.
- *Presentation* includes preparing reporting documentation (Figure AA.3).

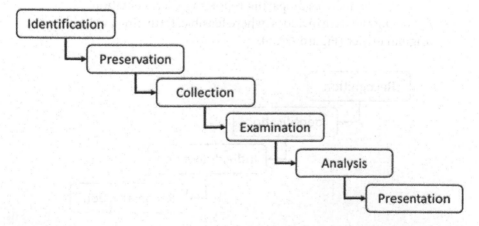

Figure AA.3 Digital forensic research workshop investigative model 2001.

[P04] Scientific Crime Scene Investigation Model (2001)

Consisting of four phases, this model was proposed to strictly address scientific crime scene investigations, not the entire investigative process.

- *Recognition* identifies items or patterns seen as potential evidence.
- *Identification* classifies evidence and compares it to known standards.
- *Individualization* determines evidence uniqueness in relation to the investigation.
- *Reconstruction* provides investigative details based on collective findings (Figure AA.4).

[P05] Abstract Model of the Digital Forensic Procedures (2002)

Consisting of nine phases, this model enhances the DFRWS model by including three additional phases; *preparation*, *approach strategy*, and *returning evidence*.

- *Identification* involves detection of an incident or event.
- *Preparation* includes activities to ensure equipment and personnel are prepared.
- *Approach strategy* focuses on maintaining evidence integrity during acquisition.
- *Preservation* establishes proper evidence gathering and chain of custody.
- *Collection* gathers relevant data using approved techniques.
- *Examination* evaluates digital evidence to reveal data and reduce volumes.
- *Analysis* examines the context and content of digital evidence to determine relevancy.
- *Presentation* includes preparing reporting documentation.
- *Returning evidence* includes, where feasible, returning evidence to its original owner (Figure AA.5).

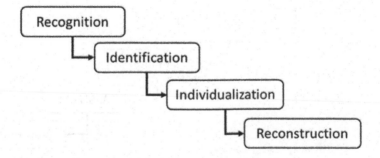

Figure AA.4 Scientific crime scene investigation model 2001.

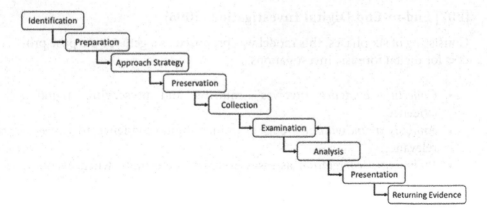

Figure AA.5 Abstract model of the digital forensic procedures 2002.

[P06] Integrated Digital Investigation Process (2003)

Consisting of five phases, this model was proposed with the intention of merging the various investigative processes into a single integrated model. This model introduced the idea of a digital crime scene created because of technology where digital evidence exists.

- *Readiness* includes activities to ensure equipment and personnel are prepared.
- *Deployment* enables the detection and validation of an event or incidents.
- *Physical crime scene* involves the collection and analysis of physical evidence.
- *Digital crime scene* involves the collection and analysis of digital evidence.
- *Review* assesses the entire investigative process to identify opportunities for improvement (Figure AA.6).

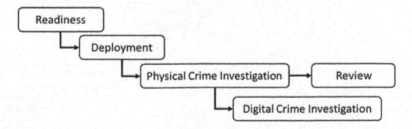

Figure AA.6 Integrated digital investigation process 2003.

[P07] End-to-End Digital Investigation (2003)

Consisting of six phases, this model was proposed as a general-purpose process for digital forensic investigations.

- *Collecting evidence* involves acquiring and preserving digital evidence.
- *Analysis of individual events* examines digital evidence to assess relevancy.
- *Preliminary correlation* assesses events to determine when events occurred and what technology is involved.
- *Event normalizing* de-duplicates and standardizes events into a unified structure.
- *Event deconfliction* consolidates multiple common events into a single event.
- *Second-level correlation* assesses the normalized events to further refine when events occurred and what technology is involved
- *Timeline analysis* builds the chronological sequence of events.
- *Chain of evidence construction* establishes the correlation based on sequential events.
- *Corroboration* validates evidence and events against other evidence and events (Figure AA.7).

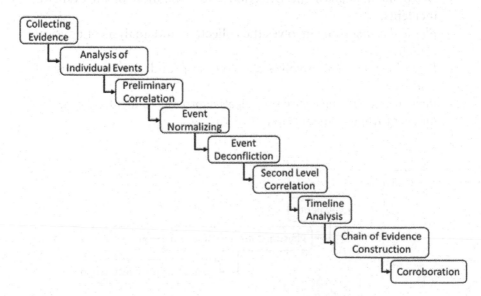

Figure AA.7 End-to-end digital investigation 2003.

[P08] Enhanced Integrated Digital Investigation Process (2004)

Consisting of five phases, this model is based on the integrated digital investigation process. This model introduces the *traceback* phase, which allows investigators to backtrack to the actual technology used in the crime.

- *Readiness* includes activities to ensure equipment and personnel are prepared.
- *Deployment* enables the detection and validation of an event or incidents.
- *Traceback* tracks back to the source crime scene including technology and location.
- *Dynamite* involves conducting investigations at the primary crime scene with intentions of identifying the potential offender(s).
- *Review* assesses the entire investigative process to identify opportunities for improvement (Figure AA.8).

[P09] Extended Model of Cyber Crime Investigation (2004)

Consisting of thirteen phases, this model was proposed as a generalized approach to the investigative process to assist the development of new tools and techniques.

- *Awareness* allows the relationship with investigation event to be identified.
- *Authorization* involves obtaining approval to proceed with the investigation.
- *Planning* scopes out how and where evidence will be collected.
- *Notification* informs stakeholders of the investigation.
- *Search for and identify evidence* locates and identifies evidence sources.

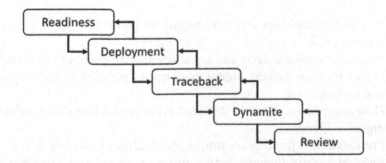

Figure AA.8 Enhanced integrated digital investigation process 2004.

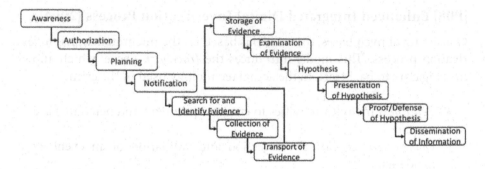

Figure AA.9 Extended model of cyber crime investigation 2004.

- *Collection of evidence* involves acquiring and preserving evidence.
- *Transport of evidence* includes moving evidence into a secure location.
- *Storage of evidence* includes placing evidence in protective custody.
- *Examination of evidence* evaluates evidence to reveal data and reduce volumes.
- *Hypothesis* constructs a theory based on the events that occurred.
- *Presentation of hypothesis* allows for a decision on the appropriate course of action.
- *Proof/defense of hypothesis* involves demonstrating the validity of the theory.
- *Dissemination of information* distributes information to stakeholders (Figure AA.9).

[P10] A Hierarchical, Objective-Based Framework for the Digital Investigations Process (2004)

Consisting of six phases, this model was proposed as a means of addressing all phases and activities described in preceding process models.

- *Preparation* includes activities to ensure equipment and personnel are prepared.
- *Incident response* detects and acknowledges an event or incident.
- *Data collection* gathers digital evidence in support of the response and investigation.
- *Data analysis* validates the detected event or incident using collected digital evidence..
- *Presentation of findings* communicates findings to stakeholders.
- *Incident closure* includes acting upon decisions and assessing the investigative process (Figure AA.10).

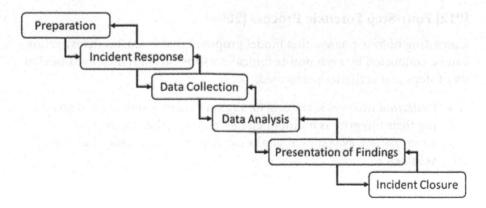

Figure AA.10 A hierarchical, objective based framework for the digital investigation process 2004.

[P11] Event-Based Digital Forensic Investigation Framework (2004)

Consisting of five phases, this model proposes following the processes for investigating physical crime scenes while considering the digital crime scene investigation as a subset.

- *Readiness* includes activities to ensure equipment and personnel are prepared.
- *Deployment* involves the detection of an incident and notification of investigators.
- *Physical crime scene investigation phases* is a series of steps and activities to search for, identify, and collect physical evidence to reconstruct physical events.
- *Digital crime scene investigation phases* is a subset of the physical crime scene investigation that involves a series of steps and activities to examine digital evidence.
- *Presentation* includes preparing reporting documentation (Figure AA.11).

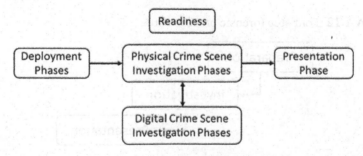

Figure AA.11 Event based digital forensic investigation framework 2004.

[P12] Four-Step Forensic Process (2006)

Consisting of four phases, this model proposes that forensics investigations can be conducted by even non-technical persons through increased flexibility of steps and activities performed.

- *Collection* involves searching for digital evidence sources and ensuring their integrity is maintained during the gathering process.
- *Examination* evaluates digital evidence to reveal data and reduce volumes.
- *Analysis* examines the context and content of digital evidence to determine relevancy.
- *Reporting* includes presenting digital evidence through investigation documentation (Figure AA.12).

[P13] Framework for a Digital Forensic Investigation (2006)

Consisting of three phases, this model proposes merging existing process models into a broader and more adaptable model.

- *Preparation* includes activities to ensure equipment and personnel are prepared.
- *Investigation* involves all steps and activities performed to preserve, analyze, and store evidence.
- Presentation includes preparing reporting documentation (Figure AA.13).

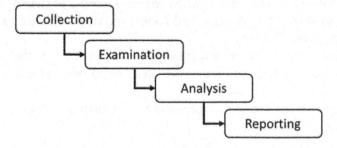

Figure AA.12 Four step forensic process 2006.

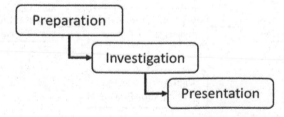

Figure AA.13 Framework for a digital forensic investigation 2006.

[P14] Computer Forensics Field Triage Process Model (2006)

Consisting of six primary phases and six sub-tasks, this model proposes performing investigative tasks onsite, in a short timeframe, without seizing technology or acquiring forensic images.

- *Planning* includes activities to ensure equipment and personnel are prepared.
- *Triage* identifies evidence and determines its relevance to the investigation.
- *User usage profile* focuses on analyzing user activity and behavior.
- *Chronology timeline* establishes a date/time sequence of digital evidence events.
- *Internet* examines artifacts from Internet-related service activities.
- *Case specific* places focus on digital evidence relating directly to the investigation (Figure AA.14).

[P15] FORZA—Digital Forensics Investigation Framework (2006)

Consisting of six layers, this model proposes linking the eight practitioner roles and their associated procedures throughout the investigative process.

- *Contextual investigation layer*: understands the background details of the event
- *Contextual layer*: recognizes the involvement of business elements with the event
- *Legal advisory layer*: determines the legal aspects of the event
- *Conceptual security layer*: explores the design of systems and relevant security controls
- *Technical presentation layer*: determines the strategies and steps required of the digital forensics investigation

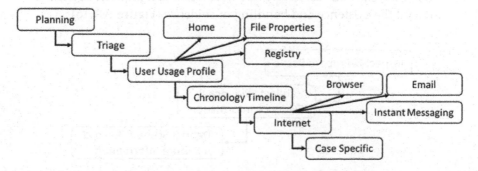

Figure AA.14 Computer forensic field triage process model 2006.

	Why (Motivation)	What (data)	How (Function)	Where (Network)	Who (People)	When (Time)
Case leader (contextual investigation layer)	Investigation Objective	Event Nature	Requested Initial Investigation	Investigation Geography	Initial Participants	Investigation Timeline
System owner (if any) (contextual layer)	Business Objective	Business and Event Nature	Business and System Process Model	Business Geography	Organization and Participants Relationship	Business and Incident Timeline
Legal advisor (legal advisory layer)	Legal Objective	Legal Background and Preliminary Issues	Legal Procedures for Further Investigation	Legal Geography	Legal Entities and Participants	Legal Timeframe
Security/system architect/ auditor (conceptual security layer)	System/Security Control Objective	System Information and Security Control Model	Security Mechanisms	Security Domain and Network Infrastructure	Users and Security Entity Model	Security Timing and Sequencing
Digital forensics specialists (technical preparation layer)	Forensic Investigation Strategy Objectives	Forensic Data Model	Forensic Strategy Design	Forensics Data Geography	Forensics Entity Model	Hypothetical Forensics Event Timeline
Forensics investigators/system administrator/operator (data acquisition layer)	Forensic Acquisition Objectives	On-site Forensics Data Observation	Forensics Acquisition / Seizure Procedures	Site Network Forensics Data Acquisition	Participants Interviewing and Hearing	Forensics Acquisition Timeline
Forensics investigators/ forensics analysts (data analysis layer)	Forensic Examination Objectives	Event Data Reconstruction	Forensics Analysis Procedures	Network Address Extraction and Analysis	Entity and Evidence Relationship Analysis	Event Timeline Reconstruction
Legal prosecutor (legal presentation layer)	Legal Presentation Objectives	Legal Presentation Attributes	Legal Presentation Procedures	Legal Jurisdiction Location	Entities in Litigation Procedures	Timeline of the Entire Event for Presentation

Figure AA.15 FORZA—digital forensic investigation framework 2006.

- *Data acquisition layer*: involves executing the identified digital forensics strategies and steps to collect evidence
- *Data analysis layer*: involves executing the identified digital forensics strategies and steps to examine evidence
- *Legal presentation layer*: involves discussing legal components as a result of the investigation (Figure AA.15)

[P16] Process Flows for Cyber Forensics Training and Operations (2006)

Consisting of three phases, this model proposes one workflow to govern general behavior related to an electronic crime scene.

- *Inspect and prepare scene* contains the preparation actions to survey the scene, equipment to be seized, and evidence to be collected.
- *Collect evidence and evidence information* contains the elements involved in the collection of information related to evidence.
- *Debrief scene and record seizure information* contains the actions to record the existence and handling of evidence (Figure AA.16).

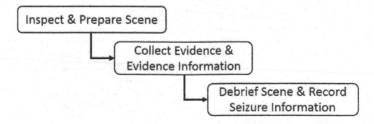

Figure AA.16 Process flows for cyber forensics training and operations 2006.

[P17] Common Process Model for Incident and Computer Forensics (2007)

Consisting of three phases, this model proposes combining incident response and computer forensics into an overall process for investigations.

- *Pre-analysis* contains all steps and activities that are initially completed.
- *Analysis* includes all steps and activities performed during evidence examination.
- *Post-analysis* documents all steps and activities completed throughout the investigation (Figure AA.17).

[P18] Dual Data Analysis Process (2007)

Consisting of four phases, this model proposes following parallel investigative streams. The first stream is with a less experienced "computer technician" and the second stream is with a "professional investigator."

- *Access* locates and identifies evidence sources.
- *Acquire* involves collecting evidence and ensuring its integrity is maintained.

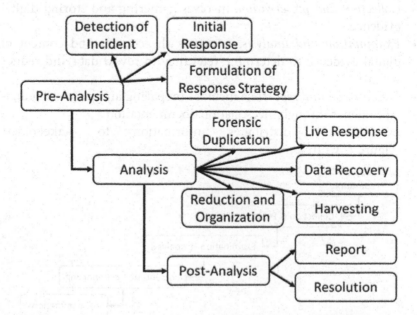

Figure AA.17 Common process model for incident and computer forensics 2007.

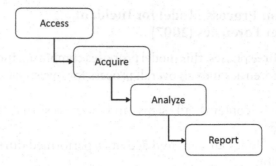

Figure AA.18 Dual data analysis process 2007.

- *Analysis* examines the context and content of digital evidence to determine relevancy.
- *Report* includes presenting digital evidence through investigation documentation (Figure AA.18).

[P19] Digital Forensic Investigations Framework (2008)

Consisting of five phases, this model proposes:

- *Preparation*: involves becoming familiar with the investigations and activities to ensure equipment and personnel are prepared
- *Collection and preservation*: involves gathering and storing digital evidence
- *Examination and analysis*: evaluates the context and content of digital evidence to determine relevancy to reveal data and reduce volumes
- *Presentation and reporting*: includes preparing and presenting digital evidence through investigation documentation
- *Dissemination*: distributes information to stakeholders (Figure AA.19)

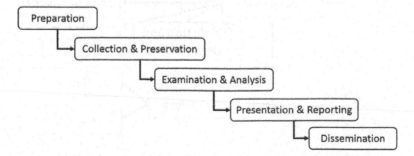

Figure AA.19 Digital forensic investigations framework 2008.

[P20] Digital Forensic Model Based on Malaysian Investigation Process (2009)

Consisting of seven phases, this model is based on the Malaysian investigation process focusing on data acquisition and fundamental phases in conducting analysis.

- *Planning* involves obtaining authorization and associated documentation to conduct an investigation.
- *Identification* identifies evidence to be seized while considering data volatility.
- *Reconnaissance* involves gathering and storing digital evidence.
- *Analysis* examines the context and content of digital evidence to determine relevancy.
- *Result* includes preparing reporting documentation.
- *Proof and defense* proves a hypothesis with supporting evidence.
- *Archive storage* maintains evidence for future reference (Figure AA.20).

[P21] Generic Framework for Network Forensics (2010)

Consisting of nine phases, this model was proposed to specifically formalize a methodology for network-based digital investigations.

- *Preparation and authorization* includes activities to ensure equipment and personnel are prepared.

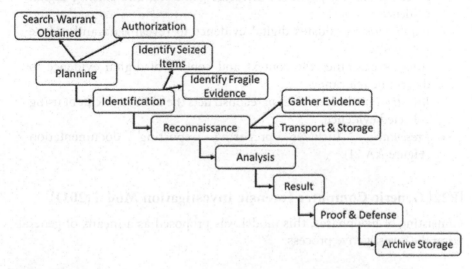

Figure AA.20 Digital forensic model based on malaysian investigation process 2009.

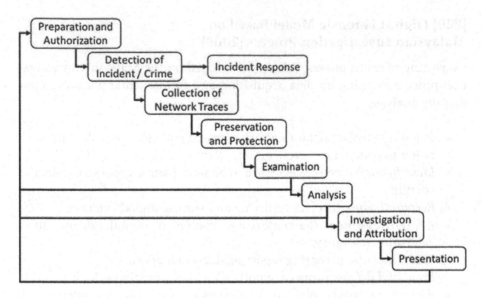

Figure AA.21 Generic framework for network forensics 2010.

- *Detection of incident/crime* indicates that an incident or event has occurred.
- *Incident response* consists of acknowledging and responding to an event or incident.
- *Collection of network traces* acquires data from sensors that collect network traffic data.
- *Preservation and protection* involves gathering and storing digital evidence.
- *Examination* evaluates digital evidence to reveal data and reduce volumes.
- *Analysis* examines the context and content of digital evidence to determine relevancy.
- *Investigation and attribution* reconstructs the event or incident using collected evidence.
- *Presentation* includes preparing reporting documentation (Figure AA.21).

[P22] Generic Computer Forensic Investigation Model (2011)

Consisting of five phases, this model was proposed as a means of generalizing the investigative process.

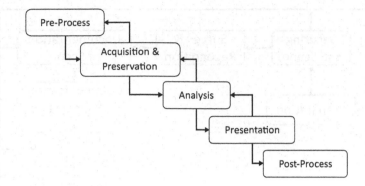

Figure AA.22 Generic computer forensic investigation model 2011.

- *Pre-process* includes obtaining approval to proceed and activities to ensure equipment and personnel are prepared.
- *Acquisition and preservation* involves gathering and storing digital evidence.
- *Analysis* examines the context and content of digital evidence to determine relevancy.
- *Presentation* includes preparing reporting documentation.
- *Post-process* includes returning evidence, where feasible, and identifying opportunities for improvement (Figure AA.22).

[P23] Systematic Digital Forensic Investigation Model (2011)

Consisting of eleven phases, this model was proposed with the goal of aiding in the establishment of appropriate policies and procedures in a systematic manner.

- *Preparation* involves becoming familiar with investigations and activities to ensure equipment and personnel are prepared.
- *Securing the scene* secures the crime scene from unauthorized access and mitigates evidence tampering.
- *Survey and recognition* involves assessing the crime scene for potential evidence sources and establishing an appropriate search plan.
- *Documenting the scene* ensures crime scene documentation is recorded, including photographs, sketches, etc.
- *Communication shielding* terminates all data exchange capabilities from technology.

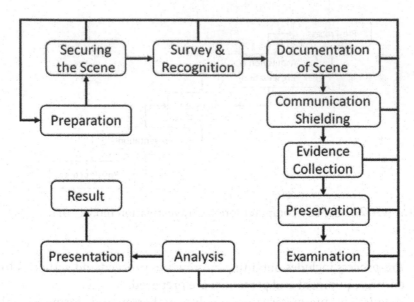

Figure AA.23 Systematic digital forensic investigation model 2011.

- *Evidence collection* focuses on gathering of relevant data using approved techniques.
- *Preservation* establishes proper evidence gathering and chain of custody.
- *Examination* evaluates evidence to reveal data and reduce volumes.
- *Analysis* examines the context and content of digital evidence to determine relevancy.
- *Presentation* includes preparing reporting documentation.
- *Result* identifies opportunities for improvement (Figure AA.23).

[P24] Advanced Data Acquisition Model (ADAM) (2011)

Consisting of three phases, this model was proposed to function as a generally accepted standard for the acquisition of digital evidence.

- *Initial planning* involves becoming familiar with the investigations and activities to ensure equipment and personnel are prepared.
- *Onsite planning* involves learning additional specific details about the investigations to facilitate the acquisition of evidence.
- *Acquisition* involves the gathering and storage of digital evidence (Figure AA.24).

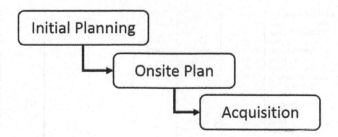

Figure AA.24 Advanced data acquisition model (ADAM) 2011.

Comparative Analysis

With an understanding of the phases and tasks within each process model, it is evident that each author has been variously influenced as they have developed their respective process models. Most notable is the use of non-parallel characteristics—such as the interchangeable use of procedures, processes, phases, functions, tasks, and steps—to describe their proposed investigative workflow.

Even though all identified process models have unique characteristics, each author developed theirs with the intention of upholding the application of forensic science to the investigative process. Having standardized the terminology being used to objectively compare these process models, we can easily recognize the phases of each model and extract them for further comparison.

NOTE: [M15] FORZA—Digital Forensics Investigation Framework 2006 was not included in the comparison below because of significant differences in the process model's characteristics; it uses layers and roles instead of phases for describing the investigative workflow (Figure AA.25).

As illustrated in Figure AA.25, we can easily see which phases are more often applied across multiple process models and how frequently they occur. Of special note, highlighted in the graphic below are seven phases that have the highest frequency of re-occurrence: *preparation, identification, collection, preservation, examination, analysis, and presentation*. Without getting caught up in the subtle differences in naming conventions, it is quite apparent that there is an opportunity to consolidate all phases identified throughout each process model into these common phases.

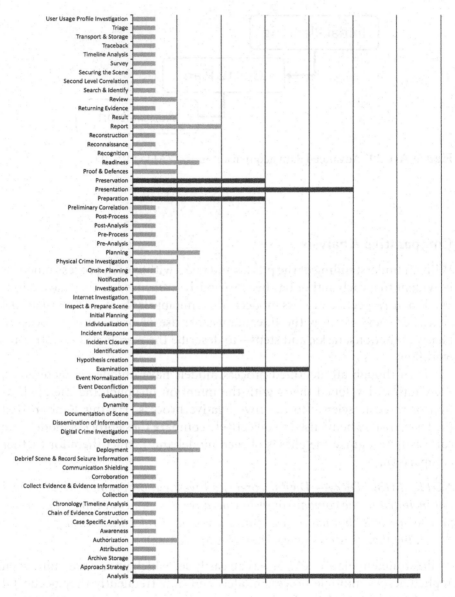

Figure AA.25 Process model phase frequencies.

Summary

Since the formalization of digital forensic science, several process models have been developed and proposed to meet specific investigative needs. Regardless of the difference in structure of each process model, the underlying fundamental workflow and concepts of mandatory investigative activities remains consistent as represented within the higher-level phases.

Appendix B: Education and Professional Certifications

Introduction

Digital forensics requires that individuals have strong information technology knowledge as well as formalized training of digital forensics principles, methodologies, techniques, and tools. These are essential and fundamental to maintaining the integrity, relevancy, and admissibility of digital evidence.

Professional Certifications

Internationally, there are several professional organizations that have established certifications and accreditations specific to the digital forensics profession. Predominantly, these certifications are provided by professional organizations with an industry-wide perspective on the digital forensics profession; however, there are a small number of certifications provided by merchants who sell digital forensics products and services.

It is important to keep in mind that while professional certifications provide assurance that an individual has met the required level of knowledge in digital forensics, these accreditations do not provide the in-depth level of education that formal academic program teach.

Although there may be some certifications missing in the list below, the following are examples of digital forensics accreditations grouped, and alphabetically ordered, by professional organization. It is also important to note that the inclusion of these certifying bodies does not suggest that they are better than or recommended over other professional organizations that are not included in the list below.

Industry-Neutral Certifications

- 7SAFE
  - Certified Corporate Digital Investigator
  - Certified Cyber Investigator
  - Certified Data Collection Technician
  - Certified Forensic Investigation Practitioner

- Certified Forensic Investigation Specialist
- Certified Linux Forensic Practitioner
- Certified MAC Forensics Specialist
- Certified Malware Investigator
- American Society for Industrial Security (ASIS) International
  - Professional Certified Investigator (PCI)
- Digital Forensics Certification Board (DFCB)
  - Digital Forensics Certified Practitioner
- International Council of Electronic Commerce Consultants (EC-Council)
  - Computer Hacking Forensic Investigator (CHFI)
- High Tech Crime Network (HTCN)
  - Certified Computer Crime Investigator (CCCI) Basic
  - Certified Computer Crime Investigator (CCCI) Advanced
  - Certified Computer Forensic Technician (CCFT) Basic
  - Certified Computer Forensic Technician (CCFT) Advanced
- Information Assurance Certification Review Board (IACRB)
  - Certified Computer Forensics Examiner (CCFE)
- International Association of Computer Investigative Specialists (IACIS)
  - Certified Forensic Computer Examiner (CFCE)
  - Certified Advanced Windows Forensic Examiner (CAWFE)
- International Information Systems Forensic Association (IISFA)
  - Certified Information Forensics Investigator (CIFI)
- International Society of Forensic Computer Examiners (ISFCE)
  - Certified Computer Examiner (CCE)
- SysAdmin, Audit, Networking, and Security (SANS)
  - Global Information Assurance Certification (GIAC)—Certified Forensic Analyst (GCFA)
  - Global Information Assurance Certification (GIAC)—Certified Forensic Examiner (GCFE)

Vendor-Specific Trainings and Certifications

- AccessData
  - AccessData Certified Examiner (ACE)
  - AccessData Mobile Phone Examiner (AME)
- BlackBag Technologies
  - Certified BlackLight Examiner (CBE)
  - Macintosh & iOS Certified Forensic Examiner (MiCFE)
- OpenText
  - Encase Certified Examiner (EnCE)
  - Certified Forensic Security Responder (CFSR)

Formal Education Programs

At the highest level of training, a working and practical knowledge of all areas of digital forensics must be gained. Individuals who must meet this level of knowledge are those who must have the skills and competencies necessary to ensure that all principles, methodologies, and techniques are upheld in support of their organization's digital forensics program.

Working directly in digital forensics requires individuals to have a significant amount of training and technical skills to comprehend and consistently apply the profession's well-established scientific fundamentals. The information provided at this level is extremely detailed and requires individuals to have strong working and practical knowledge.

The number of higher/post-secondary institutions offering education programs focusing specifically on digital forensics has grown extensively. While each education program is slightly different in the curriculum offered, they all cover the fundamental principles, methodologies, and techniques of digital forensics as required for individuals who are directly involved in the investigative workflow.

While there might be some higher/post-secondary institutions absent, the following is a list of digital forensics education programs grouped/ordered by geographical location and then ordered by the educational institution's name. It is important to note that inclusion of these digital forensics education programs does not suggest that these are better than or recommended over other digital forensics education programs that are not included.

Australia

- Charles Sturt University
  - Graduate Certificate in Information Systems Security (Digital Forensics)
  - Master of Information Systems Security (Digital Forensics)
  - Master of Cyber Security and Digital Forensics
- Edith Cowan University
  - Master of Digital Forensics
- Macquarie University
  - Postgraduate Diploma in Computer Forensics (PGDipCFR)
  - Postgraduate Certificate in Computer Forensics (PCertCFR)
- Melbourne University
  - Graduate Certificate in Digital Forensics
  - Master of e-Forensics and Enterprise Security
- University of New South Wales
  - Master of Cyber Security (Digital Forensics)

- University of South Australia (UniSA)
  - Graduate Certificate in Science (Forensic Computing)
  - Master of Science (Information Assurance)
- Swinburne University of Technology, Melbourne
  - Graduate Certificate in eForensics

Canada

- BCIT Centre for Forensics and Security Technology Studies
  - Bachelor of Technology (BTech) in Forensic Investigation—Digital Forensics and Cybersecurity Option
  - Advanced Certificate in Forensic Investigation—Digital Forensics and Cybersecurity Option
- Canadian Police College Technological Crime Learning Institute
  - Advanced Internet Child Exploitation (AICE)
  - Canadian Internet Child Exploitation (CICEC)
  - Cell Phone Seizure and Analysis (CSAC)
  - Computer Forensic Examiner (CMPFOR)
  - Digital Technologies for Investigators (DTIC)
  - Internet Evidence Analysis (IEAC)
  - Live Analysis Workshop (LAW)
  - Network Investigative Techniques (NITC)
  - Using the Internet as an Intelligence Tool (INTINT)
  - Advanced Computer Forensic Workshop (ACFW)
  - Registry Analysis Workshop (RAW)
  - Wireless Networks Workshop (WNETW)
- Ecole Polytechnique, University of Montreal's Engineering School
  - Certificat en cyberenquête
- Fleming College
  - Computer Security and Investigations program
- Ryerson University
  - Computer Security and Digital Forensics

England

- Canterbury Christ Church University
  - BSc (Hons) Forensic Computing
  - MSc by Research in Digital Forensics & Cybersecurity
- Coventry University
  - Forensic Computing MSc
- Cranfield University (based at the Defence Academy of the UK)
  - Forensic Computing MSc/PgDip/PgCert

- De Montfort University
  - Forensic Computing MSc/PG Dip/PG Cert
- University of Derby
  - BSc (Hons) Computer Forensic Investigation
  - MSc Computer Forensic Investigation
- University of Gloucestershire
  - Forensic Computing Honours degree (3 or 4 year sandwich)
  - Computer & Cyber Forensics BSc (Hons)
- University of Greenwich
  - BSc (Hons) Computer Security and Forensics
  - Computer Forensics and Systems Security, MSc
- Kingston University
  - Cyber Security and Computer Forensics BSc (Hons)
- Leeds Beckett University
  - BSc (Hons) Computer Forensics
  - BSc (Hons) Computer Forensics & Security
  - MSc Digital Forensics & Security
- University of East London
  - Information Security and Computer Forensics (ISCF) Block Mode MSc
- London Metropolitan University
  - Computer Forensics and IT Security (BSc Hons—Single)
  - Computer Networking and Computer Forensics (BSc Hons—single)
  - Computer Forensics and IT Security (MSc)
- Middlesex University
  - BSc Honours Forensic Computing
  - MSc E-security and Digital Forensics
- Northumbria University
  - Digital and Computer Forensics BSc (Hons)
  - Computer Networks and Cyber Security BSc (Hons)
- The Open University
  - Introduction to Computer Forensics and Investigations
  - Digital Forensics
- University of Portsmouth
  - BSc (Hons) Forensic Computing
  - MSc Forensic Information Technology
- Sheffield Hallam University
  - BSc (Honours) Computer Security with Forensics
- Staffordshire University
  - Forensic Computing BSc (Hons)
  - Cyber Security BSc (Hons)
  - Digital Forensics and Cybercrime Analysis MSc, Postgraduate Certificate (PgC), Postgraduate Diploma (PgD)

- University of Sunderland
  - BSc (Hons) Computer Forensics
- Teesside University
  - BSc (Hons) Computer and Digital Forensics
  - BSc (Hons) Computer and Digital Forensics (Extended)
  - BSc (Hons) Computer and Digital Forensics with Professional Experience
  - BSc (Hons) Computer and Digital Forensics with Professional Experience (Extended)
- University of the West of England
  - BSc (Hons) Forensic Computing

India

- Institute of Forensic Science, Mumbai
  - Post Graduate diploma in Digital and Cyber Forensic and related Law

Ireland

- Blanchardstown Institute of Technology
  - Bachelor of Science (Honours) in Computing in Digital Forensics and Cyber Security
- University College Dublin
  - Forensic Computing and Cybercrime Investigation (FCCI) Programme
  - MSc Digital Investigation and Forensic Computing
- Dublin City University
  - MSc in Security and Forensic Computing

Italy

- University of Bologna
  - Forensic Computer Science
- University of Piemonte Orientale
  - Corso di Informatica Forense

Netherlands

- Hogeschool Leiden
  - Forensisch ICT
  - Digital Forensics & E-Discovery

Scotland

- Edinburgh Napier University
  - Computer Security & Forensics BEng/BEng (Hons)
- Glasgow Caledonian University
  - Digital Security, Forensics and Ethical Hacking BEng/BEng (Hons)

South Africa

- University of Cape Town (UCT)
  - Postgraduate Diploma in Management in Information Systems (CG022)—INF4016W: Computer Forensics

Sweden

- Högskolan i Halmstad
  - IT-forensik och informationssäkerhet, 120/180 hp

United Kingdom

- Bournemouth University
  - Forensic Investigations BSc
  - Forensic Computing and Security BSc

United State of America

- American InterContinental University
  - Bachelor of Information Technology (BIT): Specialization in Digital Investigations
- Bloomsburg University of Pennsylvania
  - Digital Forensics (B.S.)
- Boston University
  - Digital Forensics Graduate Certificate
- Bristol Community College
  - Associate Degree in Science in Computer Information Systems (Computer Forensics)
- Bunker Hill Community College
  - Digital And Computer Forensics And Investigations Option—Computer Information Technology Program—(Associate in Science Degrees)

- Butler County Community College
  - Computer Information Systems—Computer Forensics and Security, A.A.S.
- California State University, Fullerton
  - Certificate In Computer Forensics I
- Carnegie Mellon University
  - Master of Science in Information Security Technology and Management (MSISTM)—Cyber Forensics and Incident Response
- Catawba Valley Community College
  - Cyber Crime Technology
- Central Piedmont Community College
  - Digital Evidence Training
- Century College
  - Computer Forensics—Associate in Applied Science Degree, Computer Forensics—Certificate
- Champlain College
  - Bachelor of Science, Computer & Digital Forensics
  - Bachelor of Science, Computer Forensics & Digital Investigations Degree (online)
  - Computer Forensics & Digital Investigations Certificate (online)
  - Master of Science in Digital Forensic Management
  - Master of Science in Digital Forensic Science
- Chestnut Hill College
  - Certificate in Computer Forensics and Electronic Discovery
- College of Western Idaho
  - Information Technology: Information Security and Forensics
- Colorado State University-Pueblo
  - Bachelor of Science (BS) degree in Computer Information Systems (CIS)—CIS 462/562, Computer Forensics and Investigations
- Community College of Philadelphia
  - Computer Forensics Courses
- Dakota State University
  - MSIS Information Assurance (Forensics Classes)
- Defiance College
  - Digital Forensic Science (Bachelor of Science degree)
- DeSales University
  - Master of Arts in Criminal Justice Online with a concentration in Computer Forensics
- DeVry University
  - Bachelor of Science, Computer Information Systems with a Specialized Track in Computer Forensics

- Dixie State University
  - BS in Criminal Justice—Digital Forensics Emphasis (PDF file)
- Drexel University
  - Minor in Computer Crime
  - B.S. in Computing and Security Technology—Concentration: Computing Security—CT 212 Computer Forensics (Elective)
- Florida State College
  - Computer Forensics Technician (6947)
- Fountainhead College of Technology
  - Network Security and Forensics
- George Mason University
  - MS in Computer Forensics
- Herkimer County Community College
  - Cybersecurity A.S.
- Highline Community College
  - Data Recovery / Forensic Specialist (Certificate & AAS options)
- Illinois Institute of Technology
  - Computer and Network Forensics, IT 538
- Iowa State University
  - CprE 536: Computer and Network Forensics
- James Madison University
  - Master's Degree in Computer Science concentration in Digital Forensics
- Johns Hopkins University
  - MSc Security Informatics (650.457 Computer Forensics, 650.657 Advanced Topics in Computer Forensics)
- John Jay College of Criminal Justice
  - Master of Science in Digital Forensics and Cybersecurity, Certificate in Applied Digital Forensic Science
- Kaplan University—Hagerstown Campus
  - Bachelor of Science in Criminal Justice
  - Master of Science in Criminal Justice
  - Associate of Applied Science in Criminal Justice
  - Computer Forensics Post Baccalaureate Certificate
- Kennesaw State University
  - ISA 4350. Computer Forensics. 3-0-3.
- Lamar Institute of Technology
  - ITDF 1300 Introduction to Digital Forensics 3:3:0
- Lawrence Technological University
  - Graduate Certificate in Information Assurance Management (MIS5213 High Tech Cyber Crime)

- Marshall University
  - Computer and Information Technology Major—Computer Forensics Area of Emphasis
  - Graduate Certificate in Digital Forensics
  - Master of Science Degree Program—Emphasis on Digital Forensics
- Middlesex Community College
  - Certificate and Associate Degree Programs in Computer Forensics
- Regis University
  - Information Assurance Certificate (options available in Computer Forensics and Network Forensics)
- Rochester Institute of Technology (RIT)
  - BS in Information Security and Forensics (ISF)
- St. Ambrose University
  - BA in Computer Investigations and Criminal Justice
- St. Petersburg College
  - Digital Forensics and Computer Investigations (A.S. Degree and Certificate)
- Solano Community College
  - Certificate and Associate Science Degree in Criminal Justice: Computer Forensics
- Stanly Community College
  - Cyber Crime Technology
- Stark State College
  - Cyber Security and Computer Forensics Technology
- The George Washington University
  - Master of Science in the field of High Technology Crime Investigation (HTCI)
- Tompkins Cortland Community College
  - Computer Forensics A.A.S. Degree
- University of Alabama at Birmingham (UAB)
  - Master of Science in Computer Forensics and Security Management (MSCFSM)
- University of Advancing Technology
  - BS in Technology Forensics
- University of Central Florida
  - Certificate Program
  - Master of Science in Digital Forensics (MSDF)
- University of Northwestern Ohio
  - Computer Forensics Associate Degree (pdf)
- University of Rhode Island (USA)
  - Digital Forensics Minor
  - Digital Forensics Professional Certificate (online)

- Digital Forensics Graduate Certificate (online)
- Computer Science Master's degree with a concentration in Digital Forensics
- PhD with a concentration in Digital Forensics
- University of Texas at Arlington
  - CRCJ 3320 Cybercrime (pdf)
- University of Texas at San Antonio
  - M.S. I.T. and Infrastructure Assurance—6363 Computer Forensics class
- University of Washington in Seattle
  - Certificate in Digital Forensics
- Utica College
  - Online Cybersecurity and Information Assurance Bachelor's program (Cybercrime Investigations and Forensics Concentration Courses)
- Walsh College
  - Digital Forensics Certificate
- Waynesburg University
  - Bachelor of Science in Computer Security (Computer Forensics)
- West Virginia University
  - Certificate in Computer Forensics
- Westchester Community College
  - Computer Security and Forensics Certificate
  - Computer Security and Forensics A.A.S.
- Westwood College
  - Major in Computer Forensics
  - Major in Computer Forensics Online
- Wilmington University
  - Computer and Network Security Bachelor of Science (credits in Electronic Discovery and Computer Forensics)

Wales

- Cardiff University
  - Computer Science with Security and Forensics (BSc)
  - Computer Science with Security and Forensics with a year in industry (BSc)

Appendix C: Investigative Workflow

Introduction

The logical flow from the time the initial event occurs requires organizations to follow a consistent and repeatable process that encompasses several stages of information (i.e., preserving digital evidence, conducting interviewing) gathering, communication (i.e., stakeholder reporting, escalations), and documentation (i.e., SOPs, incident/case management knowledge base).

The goal of following a logical investigative process is to reduce the possibility of quick and uninformed decisions being made at any time. However, with the understanding that the context of every investigation can be uniquely different, the logical workflow should still provide organizations with the ability to make the best and most educated decisions related to what actions are to be performed next.

The investigative workflow illustrated in Figures AC.1 through AC.4 encompasses each business risk scenario as discuss further in Chapter 7, "Defining Business Risk Scenarios." While the specific business risk–naming conventions have not been used in the workflow that follows, the methodology and approach take into consideration the workflow and activities required to address each risk scenario as it occurs.

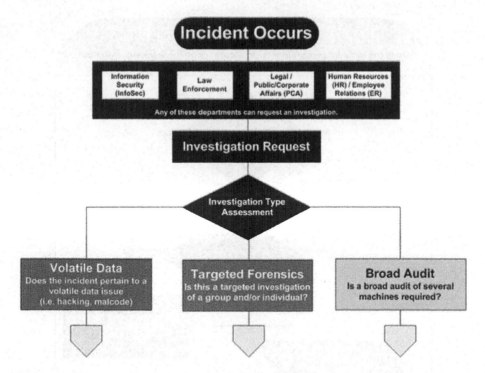

Figure AC.1 Investigative workflow—process initiation.

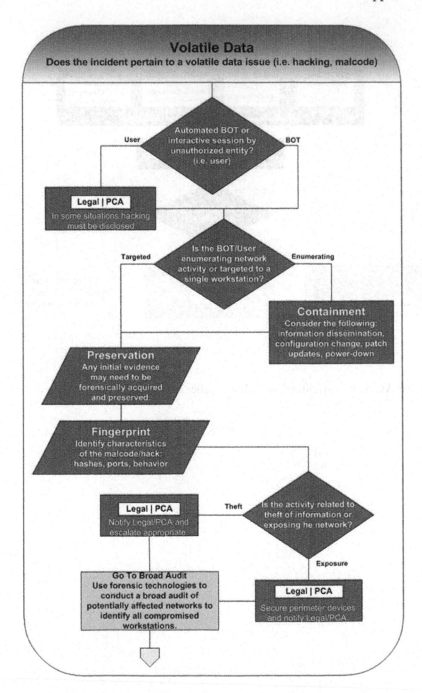

Figure AC.2 Investigative workflow—volatile data process.

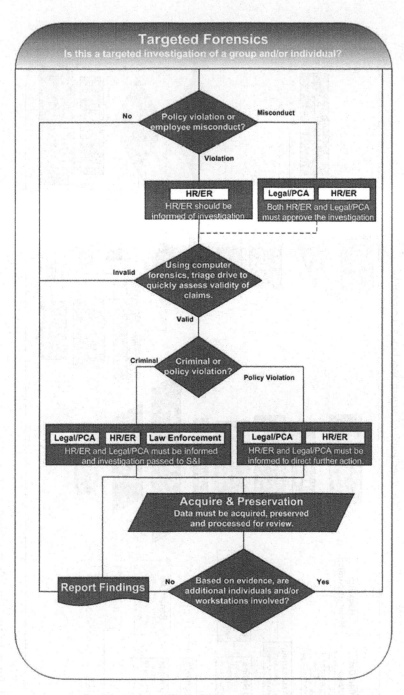

Figure AC.3 Investigative workflow—targeted forensics process.

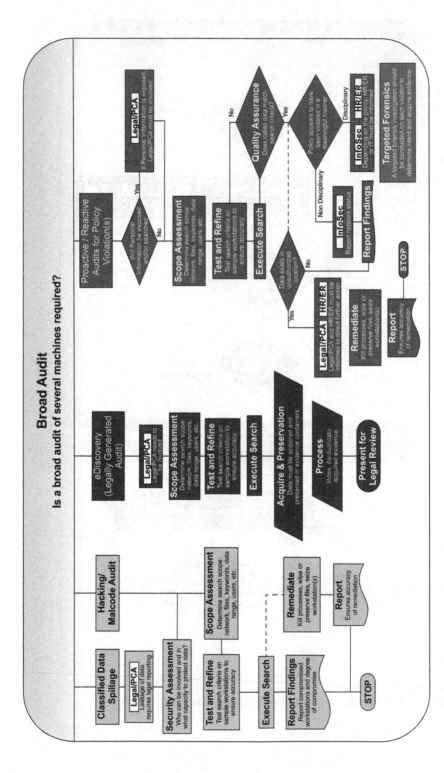

Figure AC.4 Investigative workflow—broad audit process.

Templates VI

Introduction

This section includes all template materials that are representative and supportive of both digital forensics readiness and business process documentation. The templates provided in this section contain instructions to the author, standardized text, and fields that should be modified and replaced with values specified at the time of writing, including:

- Italicized text enclosed in square brackets (*[text]*) provides instructions to the author or describes the intent, assumptions, and context for content included in the template document. These fields must be deleted prior to finalizing the template document.
- Italicized text enclosed in angle brackets (*<text>*) indicates a field that should be replaced with information specific to a particular section or text within the template document.
- Text and tables in *black* are provided as standardized examples of wording and formats that may be used or modified as needed. These are provided only as reference and/or suggestions to assist in developing the template document; they are not mandatory formats.

When using a template document, the following steps are recommended to perform modifications:

1. Replace all text enclosed in angle brackets (e.g., *<Project Name>*) with the correct field values. These angle brackets appear in the body of the template document as well as in headers and footers.
2. Modify standardized text as appropriate for the template document's specific topic.
3. To update the table of contents, right-click it, select "Update field", and choose "Update entire table".
4. Before submission of the first draft of this document, delete all instructions to the author throughout the entire template document.

Template 1: Test Case

<Test Case Name>
Test Case Document

<Date>

Presented by:
<team/department name>

Document History

Version	Date	Comments
0.1	<Date>	Initial Draft

Approvals

Item Name	Authorizer	Comments
Business Objectives	<Name & Title>	<approval terms or conditions, etc.>
Test Environment	<Name & Title>	<approval terms or conditions, etc.>
Test Cases	<Name & Title>	<approval terms or conditions, etc.>

Table of Contents

Introduction

Overview and Scope

[Provide a summary on the objective of the testing, the tool or equipment name/ version, and the business objectives for completing the testing]

This document outlines the results of assessing*<tool or equipment name/ version>* for use in the digital forensics investigative workflow, focusing specifically on:
  * *<high-level listing of focus areas for this testing>*

Summary of Findings

[Summarize the overall results from completing the test cases and note key observations and/or findings]

Conclusions/Recommendations

[Draw conclusions from the test results and provide recommendations, where/ if needed, with justifications]

Product Overview

<Vendor Name>

[A brief background of the company and the solutions they offer; including links to online resources]

<Product Name>
[Details about the tool or equipment being tested, including product name, current version, release date, key functionality]

Test Environment

Environment Baseline

[Administrative, physical, and technical specifications describing the applications, systems, processes, resources, etc. used as the controlled configurations for performing testing]

Flow of Events

[Describe the flow of events that would be expected in normal conditions as well as any potential alternate flow of events, and exceptions/errors that may occur]

Assumptions

The following circumstances and/or outcomes have been assumed for the duration of this testing:

- *<detailed listing of assumptions>*

Test Cases

<Phase Name>

Step	Date	Step Description	Test Data	Expected Results	Status	Comments
01.						
02.						
03.						
04.						
05.						
End						

<Phase Name>

Step	Date	Step Description	Test Data	Expected Results	Status	Comments
06.						
07.						
08.						
09.						
10.						
End						

Template 2: Logbook

Case/Incident	Date:	Description:	Investigator:

Time	Action(s) Taken		

Prepared By   Signature

Template 3: Chain of Custody

Case/Incident: _____   Exhibit/Property Number: _____

Date Acquired (mm/dd/yy): ____ /____ /____   Time Acquired (24 hr): ____ : ____

Location of Seized: _____   Seized By: _____

Description of Item (ex. Model, Quantity, Serial #, Condition, Markings, etc):

Notes / Additional Comments:

Chain of Custody			
Date / Time	Released By (Name & Signature)	Received By (Name & Signature)	Comments:

Authorization for Evidence Disposal

This item is no longer needed as evidence and is authorized for disposal through the following method:

☐ Return to Owner   ☐ Destruction   ☐ Donation   ☐ Other_____

Released by: _____ Signature: _____ Date: _____

Witness to Evidence Disposal

I, _____, witnessed on the _____ day of _____ 20__ the disposal of this item as performed by _____ in my presence.

Witness: _____ Signature: _____ Date: _____

Evidence Release to Lawful Owner

This item is no longer needed as evidence and has been released by me, _____
_____, to its lawful owner.

Owner _____

Address: _____

Telephone Number: (_____) _____

Signature: _____ Date: _____

Template 4: Investigative Final Report

<<*Case Number and Name*>>
Investigative Final Report

<<*Date*>>

Presented by:
<<*team/department name*>>

Document History

Version	Date	Comments
0.1	<Date>	Initial Draft

Table of Contents

Introduction

Background

[Description of the incident, including when it occurred, how it was detected, who identified it, where it took place, what happened, and who authorized the investigation]

Summary of Findings

[Summarize the significant findings of the investigation]

Conclusions

[Establish conclusions from the investigative findings and provide expert opinions where/when needed]

Investigative Details

Chain of Evidence

[Details describing where evidence was identified, techniques used to seize it, methods used to transport it to a secure location, and its continuous custody records]

Gathering of Evidence

[Methodologies, tools, and equipment used to collect and preserve digital evidence]

Processing of Evidence

[Methodologies, tools, and equipment used to perform examination of digital evidence]

Analysis of Evidence

[Details describing the meaningful, relevant, and factual findings from the analysis of digital evidence]

Addendums

References

[Details of professional references used during the investigation to validate and/or verify findings]

Glossary

[Definition of technical terms, phrases, or words used throughout the final report]

Template 5: Service Catalog

Service Catalog - ABC Company							
Service Name	Department	Service Owner	Service Manager	Description	Category	Group	Family
[Name of the service being offered]	[Name of department owning the service]	[Name of the Executive Management funding the service]	[Name of the individual functioning as the key contact for the service]	[Detailed description of the service]	[Illustrates the individual service function where the service aligns]	[Illustrates the individual business function where the service aligns]	[Illustrates the core business function where the service aligns]

Unit Cost / Driver / Year			Service Cost per Year	
Driver	Total Driver Units	Fixed Cost per Unit	Total Operational Costs	Total Service Cost
[Illustrated the Fixed/Variable units used to measure activity of the service]	[Number of Fixed/Variable units contained within the service]	[Calculated as: (Total fixed costs + Total variable costs)/Total units produced]	[Costs associated with fixed funding elements; including software licensing and capital expenditures]	[Calculated as: Total fixed costs + Total variable costs]

Business Line #1			Business Line #2			
Department #1	Department #2	Department #3	Department #1	Department #2	Department #3	Total %
[Percentage this department utilizes the service activities]	[Percentage this department utilizes the service activities]	[Percentage this department utilizes the service activities]	[Percentage this department utilizes the service activities]	[Percentage this department utilizes the service activities]	[Percentage this department utilizes the service activities]	[Total percentage the service is utilized by departments specified]

Template 6: Business Case

<Project Name>
Business Case

Recommendation

[Insert a new signature line for each additional stakeholder providing approval. The signature of each stakeholder confirms that all impacted business lines are informed and consulted. Approval of the business case provides agreement by stakeholders for shared responsibility of both one-time/ongoing cost and acceptance of project benefits. Delete this comment once completed.]

We recommend approval of this business case for *<Project Name>* initiative.

<Name – Technology Sponsor>
<Title/Department>

<Name – Business Sponsor>
<Title/Department>

I / We concur:

<Name – Executive Sponsor>
<Title/Department>

Date Prepared   *<Date>*

Presented By   *<team/department name>*

Document History

Version	Date	Comments
0.1	<date>	Initial Draft

Table of Contents

1. Executive Summary

[This section highlights the key points required to demonstrate the business rational for decision makers. It includes a summary of the current situation (i.e., risks/issues), identifies what needs to be done to remediate this situation, how the solution aligns to business strategies, and high-level illustration of costs and benefits. The executive summary should be no longer than one page in length. Delete this comment once completed.]

The costs and benefits illustrated below are in *<specify financial currency >*.

Cost/Benefit Analysis (in $000s)	V_0	V_1	V_2	V_3	Total
Capital Costs					
Expense Costs					
Resource Costs					
Total One-Time Costs					
Total Ongoing Costs					
Total Costs					
Benefit Total					
Net Benefit					
Net Present Value					

*For complete cost/benefit analysis details see NPV (section 10).

2. Business Analysis

2.1. Background/History

[Describe the risk/issues that need to be addressed, reasoning for why the recommended solution needs to be implemented, and implications of not approving the solution. Delete this comment once completed.]

2.2. Strategic Implications

Organizational Focus

☐ Revenue/Cost ☐ Risk Mgt. ☐ Regulatory
☐ Strategic ☐ Operational

[Select one or several of the strategic focus the recommended solution has on the organization. Delete this comment once completed.]

This initiative aligns with the business strategy by:

[Provide justifications, in bullet form, to illustrate the details of how the recommended solution aligns with the selected strategic focus. Specify details of how the solution will be implemented to support business functions throughout the entire organization and enhancements to operational efficiencies. Briefly highlight the impact on business plans, budgets, or forecasts. Delete this comment once completed.]

2.3. Purpose/Scope

[Document the objectives for evaluating alternatives specific to the details specified in Section 2.1. If this project is a subset of a larger project, ensure an overview of the larger project is provided. Delete this comment once completed.]

2.4. Business Need/Justification

[Elaborate on details related to the business justifications specified in Section 2.2, including any internal and external considerations that will influence the need for the recommended solution. Delete this comment once completed.]

3. Advantages/Disadvantages

[Briefly illustrate the advantages/disadvantages of the recommended solution. Delete this comment once completed.]

3.1. Advantages

[Provide advantages, in bullet form, to illustrate positive aspects of implementing the recommended solution. Delete this comment once completed.]

3.2. Disadvantages

[Provide disadvantages, in bullet form, to illustrate negative aspects of implementing the recommended solution. Delete this comment once completed.]

4. Risks & Assumptions

4.1. Risks

[Describe the significant events or conditions that, if they occur, will have either positive or negative effects on the objectives specified in Section 2.3. Delete this comment once completed.]

4.2. Assumptions

[Describe the circumstances and outcomes that if taken for granted in the absence of concrete information will have either positive or negative effects on the objectives specified in Section 2.3. Delete this comment once completed.]

5. Alternatives

[Document the recommended and alternative course of action for this project. The last alternative to be specified in this section is Do Nothing. Complete details about the recommended and alternative courses of action can be documented in Appendix A. Delete this comment once completed.]

- Alternative 1: *<Summarize the recommended course of action>*
- Alternative 2: *<Summarize the alternative course of action>*
- Alternative 3: Do Nothing

6. Timing/Schedules

[Include an implementation date for the project. Use multiple rows if the project is being implemented in several phases. Include a high-level schedule of the projected implementation plan as well as critical dates, including additional funding checkpoints and any interdependencies with other initiatives. Delete this comment once completed.]

Implementation/Phase/Major Milestone	Target Date (Month\Year)
<Specify the name of the phase>	*<Specify the delivery year/month>*
<Specify the name of the phase>	*<Specify the delivery year/month>*

7. Governance Structure

[Document the controls and mechanisms put in place to ensure compliance with rules and regulations for how the project functions. While the roles included in the governance structure may not initially have names allocated, at a minimum, representation from different levels throughout the organization should be specified: Executive Sponsor, Business Sponsor, Technology Sponsor, and where needed those located in other business areas of the organization such as project management, back offices, and operational support. Complete details about the governance structure can be documented in Appendix B. Delete this comment once completed.]

8. Key Success Metrics

[Baselines that will be used for measuring the success criteria against each test case, including the criteria for measuring success or failure, the scenario for how the test will be executed, tools or equipment subject to the test, and the business value for conducting the test case. Delete this comment once completed.]

#	Objective	Key Success Metric	Target	Baseline	Data Source
1					
2					
3					

[Details about the type of information to be provided in the above table is provided below:

Objective: description of benefit to be realized (e.g., improved operational efficiencies)

Key Success Metric: the item that will be measured (e.g., reduced work hours)

Target: the target of change, either percentage or actual value, which must be measureable

Baseline: the starting point, either percentage or actual value, used to measure against

Data Source: the origin from which metrics used to measure success will be provided (e.g., reporting system)

Delete this comment once completed.]

9. Funding

[Indicate the funding source(s) that have been allocated and are available within approved budgets. If necessary, provide alternative funding options where funding is not allocated or available. Delete this comment once completed.]

10. Financial Analysis

[Specify for each funding year: the year, total $$ amount to be funded, the business area providing funding, and the budget source from which funding is to be drawn. Delete this comment once completed.]

Details of cost/benefit analysis for the project are provided in the NPV schedule found in Appendix C.

[Complete details about the best and worst case scenarios identified through sensitivity analysis can be documented in Appendix C. Delete this comment once completed.]

10.1. Financial Assumptions

[Describe assumptions used during the financial analysis, including the drivers costs/benefits, business areas accepting ongoing costs or receiving benefits, justification for making the assumptions, and the effect on the project if the assumptions prove to be false. Complete details about assumptions made during sensitivity analysis can also be documented in Appendix C. Delete this comment once completed.]

10.2. Cost Allocation

[Using the service catalog as the authoritative source, indicate how ongoing funding of the implemented solution will be allocated across business areas sharing the costs. Delete this comment once completed.]

			1st Year Costs (V_0)		Ongoing Costs		
Business Line	% Total Allocation	$ Total Allocation	One-Time	Ongoing	V_1	V_2	V_3

Cost Driver Statement

[Describe the cost allocation driver, as documented in the service catalog, used to calculate the business line cost allocations. Delete this comment once completed.]

11. Contact Persons

[List the individuals who should be contacted for questions regarding the content of this document. Complete details about the roles and responsibilities for individuals involved with this project can be documented in Appendix B. Delete this comment once completed.]

In case of any questions, contact the following individuals:

Name	Title	Email	Phone Number

12. Appendix A: Alternative Analysis

[Describe the alternative recommendations that were considered and have been discarded as a final solution. Explain the justifications for why these alternative recommendations were not identified as the final solution. Delete this comment once completed.]

13. Appendix B: Roles & Responsibilities

[Provide detailed contact information for those individuals who are involved in this project as part of either the Governance Structure or a Contact Person. Specify the roles played by the individual, reporting hierarchy, and escalation process. Delete this comment once completed.]

14. Appendix C: Sensitivity Analysis

[Insert a print screen of the NPV. Provide details about the best and worst case scenarios identified during the sensitivity analysis. Delete this comment once completed.]

Template 7: Net Present Value (NPV)

Cost/Benefit Analysis *<insert project name>*		V_0	V_1	V_2	V_3	Total
One-Time Costs						
Capital Costs:						
<insert line for each capital cost>		$ -	$ -	$ -	$ -	$ -
<insert line for each capital cost>		$ -	$ -	$ -	$ -	$ -
Total Capital		$ -	$ -	$ -	$ -	$ -
Expense Costs:						
<insert line for each expense>		$ -	$ -	$ -	$ -	$ -
<insert line for each expense>		$ -	$ -	$ -	$ -	$ -
Total Expenses		$ -	$ -	$ -	$ -	$ -
Resource Workdays	V_0 wkd V_1 wkd V_2 wkd V_3 wkd					
<insert line for each business line>		$ -	$ -	$ -	$ -	$ -
<insert line for each business line>		$ -	$ -	$ -	$ -	$ -
Total Resource Workdays		$ -	$ -	$ -	$ -	$ -
Total One-Time Costs (Future Value)		$ -	$ -	$ -	$ -	$ -
Total One-Time Costs (Present Value)		$ -	$ -	$ -	$ -	$ -
Ongoing Costs						
<insert line for each ongoing cost>		$ -	$ -	$ -	$ -	$ -
<insert line for each ongoing cost>		$ -	$ -	$ -	$ -	$ -
Total Ongoing Costs (Future Value)		$ -	$ -	$ -	$ -	$ -
Total Ongoing Costs (Present Value)		$ -	$ -	$ -	$ -	$ -
Benefits						
<insert line for each benefit>		$ -	$ -	$ -	$ -	$ -
<insert line for each benefit>		$ -	$ -	$ -	$ -	$ -
Total Benefits (Future Value)		$ -	$ -	$ -	$ -	$ -
Total Benefits (Present Value)		$ -	$ -	$ -	$ -	$ -
Net Benefits / (Costs)		$ -	$ -	$ -	$ -	$ -
Cumulative Benefits / (Costs)		$ -	$ -	$ -	$ -	
Net Present Value		$0.00				
Benefit / Cost Ratio		0.00				

Template 8: Threat Risk Assessment

\<Initiative Name\>

Threat Risk Assessment Report

\<Date\>

Presented by:
\<team/department name\>

Document History

Version	Date	Comments
0.1	<Date>	Initial Draft

Table of Contents

Executive Summary

[Provides a high-level summary of the threat assessment, including why it was performed, key findings, and any conclusions or recommendations to be made. Delete this comment once completed.]

Assessment Details

Risk Statements

[Statements justifying the final and overall risk score of the threat modeling exercise. Delete this comment once completed.]

Confidentiality	Integrity	Availability	Authorization	Authentication	Non-Repudiation
<Score (i.e., Critical, High, Medium, Low>	<Score (i.e., Critical, High, Medium, Low>	<Score (i.e., Critical, High, Medium, Low>	<Score (i.e., Critical, High, Medium, Low>	<Score (i.e., Critical, High, Medium, Low>	<Score (i.e., Critical, High, Medium, Low>

Methodology

[Explanation of the stages, phases, steps, and processes used throughout the threat modeling exercise. Delete this comment once completed.]

Assumptions

[Identifies circumstances and/or outcomes that have been taken for granted. Delete this comment once completed.]

Threat Tree Workflows

Threat <#X: Threat Name>

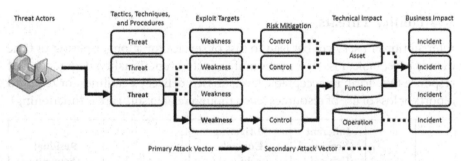

Figure T8.1 Threat tree workflow.

Threat Assessment Matrix

[Documents the details of each threat as they relate to the security principle it affects. Delete this comment once completed.]

Confidentiality Threats

Unauthorized viewing or disclosure of information that compromises privacy and/or secrecy.

UID	Threat	Inherent Scoring (Critical / High / Med / Low)	Mitigating Controls (technical / administrative / physical)	Residual Risk (description)	Residual Scoring (Critical / High / Med / Low)

Integrity Threats

Unauthorized additions, changes or deletions that affect the completeness, accuracy, authenticity, timeliness or currency of data or information.

UID	Threat	Inherent Scoring (Critical / High / Med / Low)	Mitigating Controls (technical / administrative / physical)	Residual Risk (description)	Residual Scoring (Critical / High / Med / Low)

Availability Threats

Interruptions in service that lead to loss of service for a longer period of time than is acceptable, loss of a portion of expected functionality, degradation of response time to an unacceptable level, missed delivery deadlines for required reports or loss of use of resources (even though related software is functioning).

UID	Threat	Inherent Scoring (Critical / High / Med / Low)	Mitigating Controls (technical / administrative / physical)	Residual Risk (description)	Residual Scoring (Critical / High / Med / Low)

Continuity Threats

Major interruption of facilities, such that a loss of processing capability is experienced that will last for an unacceptable period of time.

UID	Threat	Inherent Scoring (Critical / High / Med / Low)	Mitigating Controls (technical / administrative / physical)	Residual Risk (description)	Residual Scoring (Critical / High / Med / Low)

Authentication Threats

Proper identification of users and process requesting access into objects and assets.

UID	Threat	Inherent Scoring (Critical / High / Med / Low)	Mitigating Controls (technical / administrative / physical)	Residual Risk (description)	Residual Scoring (Critical / High / Med / Low)

Authorization Threats

Explicitly granting permissions to users or processes in order to read, write, or execute target information or processes.

UID	Threat	Inherent Scoring (Critical / High / Med / Low)	Mitigating Controls (technical / administrative / physical)	Residual Risk (description)	Residual Scoring (Critical / High / Med / Low)

Non-Repudiation Threats

Assurance that a user or process cannot deny the read, write, or execute access into target information or systems.

UID	Threat	Inherent Scoring (Critical / High / Med / Low)	Mitigating Controls (technical / administrative / physical)	Residual Risk (description)	Residual Scoring (Critical / High / Med / Low)

Template 9: Data Source Inventory Matrix

IMPLEMENTATION STATUS
Fully Implemented
Partially Implemented
In Progress
Plan in Place
Not Implemented

Overall Status	Business Scenario	Operational Service	Data Format	Data Origin	Data Category	Data Location	Data Owner
	Support litigation matters						
	Reduce impact of digital crime						
	Validate impact of digital crime						
	Demonstrate regulatory compliance						
	Support corporate policy violations						
	Aid contracual agreements						

Business Use Case	Technology Name	Technology Vendor	Technology Owner	Status	Status Details	Action Plan

Template 10: Project Charter

<Project/Initiative Name>

Project Charter

Recommendation

[Insert a new signature line for each additional stakeholders providing approval. The signature of each stakeholder confirms that all impacted business lines are informed and consulted. Approval of this project charter provides agreement by stakeholders for shared responsibility of deliverables scope, schedule, and cost of this project. Delete this comment once completed.]

We recommend approval of this business case for *<Project Name>* initiative.

<Name – Technology Sponsor>
<Title/Department>

<Name – Business Sponsor>
<Title/Department>

I / We concur:

<Name – Executive Sponsor>
<Title/Department>

Date Prepared   *<Date>*

Presented By   *<team/department name>*

Document History

Version	Date	Comments
0.1	<Date>	Initial Draft

Table of Contents

1. Executive Summary

[This section highlights the key points required to demonstrate the business rational for decision makers. It includes a summary of the current situation (i.e., risks/issues), identifies what needs to be done to remediate this situation, how the project aligns to business strategies, and a high-level illustration of costs and benefits. The executive summary should be no longer than one page in length. Delete this comment once completed.]

The costs and benefits illustrated below are in *<specify financial currency >*.

Cost/Benefit Analysis (in $000s)	V_0	V_1	V_2	V_3	Total
Capital Costs					
Expense Costs					
Resource Costs					
Total One-Time Costs					
Total Ongoing Costs					
Total Costs					
Benefit Total					
Net Benefit					
Net Present Value					

*For complete cost/benefit analysis details see NPV (section 10).

2. Introduction

[This section documents the high-level summary of the project. If this project is a subset of a larger project, ensure an overview of the larger project is provided. Delete this comment once completed.]

2.1. Background/History

[This section describes the details of the problem statement that will be addressed, the reasoning for why the project must be executed, and the implications of not completing this project. Delete this comment once completed.]

2.2. Purpose

This project charter documents and tracks the information required by stakeholders and decision maker(s) to approve project funding. This document also includes the needs, scope, justification, and resource commitments so project sponsors have necessary information to determine if the project will proceed or not.

The intended audience of this project charter is the project sponsor and senior leadership.

2.3. Project Scope

[This section explains what deliverables will be produced through this project. Delete this comment once completed.]

The following are considered in-scope deliverables as part of this project:

#	Business Functionality
1	*<detail the business functionality to be delivered>*
2	*<detail the business functionality to be delivered>*

#	Technical Functionality
1	*<detail the technical functionality to be delivered>*
2	*<detail the technical functionality to be delivered>*

2.3.1. Out-of-Scope

[This section explains what deliverables will not be produced through this project. Delete this comment once completed.]

The following are considered in-scope deliverables as part of this project:

#	Business Functionality
1	*<detail the business functionality to be delivered>*
2	*<detail the business functionality to be delivered>*

#	Technical Functionality
1	*<detail the technical functionality to be delivered>*
2	*<detail the technical functionality to be delivered>*

3. Business Justification

[Elaborate in detail the justifications, including any internal and external considerations that will influence the need for executing this project. Delete this comment once completed.]

3.1. Strategic Alignment

[For each goal this project will achieve, illustrate the details of its priority, how it aligns with the organization's strategic focus, and any additional comments decision makers need to know. Delete this comment once completed.]

Goal	Priority	Focus	Comments
<Goal description>	• High • Medium • Low • Not Applicable	• Revenue/Cost • Risk Mgt. • Regulatory • Strategic • Operational	*<Goal details>*
<Goal description>	• High • Medium • Low • Not Applicable	• Revenue/Cost • Risk Mgt. • Regulatory • Strategic • Operational	*<Goal details>*

4. Impact and Constraints

4.1. Risks

[Describe the significant events or conditions that, if they occur, will have an effect on the project. Delete this comment once completed.]

Risk	Severity	Mitigation
<Risk description>	• High • Medium • Low	*<Risk mitigating controls>*
<Risk description>	• High • Medium • Low	*<Risk mitigating controls>*

4.2. Assumptions

The following circumstances and outcomes, which if taken for granted in the absence of concrete information, will have an effect on this project:

- *<Assumption description>*
- *<Assumption description>*

4.3. Constraints

The following limitations and restrictions must be taken into consideration prior to the execution of this project:

- *<Constraint description>*
- *<Constraint description>*

4.4. Dependencies

The following preceding element must be in place prior to the execution of this project:

- *<Dependency description>*
- *<Dependency description>*

5. Timing/Schedules

[Include an implementation date for the project and use multiple rows if the project is being implemented in several phases. Include a high-level schedule of the projected implementation plan; critical dates, including additional funding checkpoints; and any interdependencies with other initiatives. Delete this comment once completed.]

Implementation Phase	Target Date (Month/Year)
<specify the name of the phase>	*<specify the delivery year/month>*
<specify the name of the phase>	*<specify the delivery year/month>*

5.1. Milestones

[Key deliverables that will be used for measuring the project's success or failure. Delete this comment once completed.]

Deliverable	Target Date (Month/Year)	Success Metric
<specify the deliverable>	*<specify the delivery year/month>*	*<specify how success is measured>*

6. Financial Statement

[Indicate the funding source(s) that have been allocated and are available within approved budgets. If necessary, provide alternative funding options where funding is not allocated or available. Delete this comment once completed.]

6.1. Funding Source

[Specify for each funding year: the year, total $$ amount to be funded, the business area providing funding, and the budget source from which funding is to be drawn. Delete this comment once completed.]

Details of cost/benefit analysis for the project are provided in the NPV schedule found in Appendix C.

[Complete details about the best and worst case scenarios identified through sensitivity analysis can be documented in Appendix C. Delete this comment once completed.]

6.2. Financial Assumptions

[Describe assumptions used during the financial analysis, including the drivers of costs/benefits, business areas accepting ongoing costs or receiving benefits, justification for making the assumptions, and the effect to the project if the assumptions prove to be false. Complete details about assumptions made during sensitivity analysis can also be documented in Appendix C. Delete this comment once completed.]

7. Project Structure

[Document the controls and mechanisms put in place to ensure compliance with rules and regulations for how the project functions. While the roles included in the governance structure may not initially have names allocated, at a minimum representation from different levels throughout the organizations should be specified: Executive Sponsor, Business Sponsor, Technology Sponsor, and where needed those located in other business areas of the organization such as project management, back offices, and operational support. Complete details about the governance structure can be documented in Appendix B. Delete this comment once completed.]

7.1. Contact Persons

[List the individuals who should be contacted for questions regarding the content of this document. Complete details about the roles and responsibilities for individuals involved with this project can be documented in Appendix B. Delete this comment once completed.]

In case of any questions, contact the following individuals:

Name	Title	Email	Phone Number
<full name>	*<job title>*	*<business email address>*	*<business phone number>*

8. Appendix A: Alternative Analysis

[Describe the alternative recommendations that were considered and have been discarded as the final solution. Explain the justifications for why these alternative recommendations were not identified as the final solution. Delete this comment once completed.]

9. Appendix B: Roles & Responsibilities

[The matrix below contains an example of common project roles and accompanying responsibilities. Depending on the organization, the roles outlined below may or may not be required or responsibilities may be distributed to other roles. Regardless, items within the matrix below must be assigned an individual who will function in each specific role. Delete this comment once completed.]

Project Role	Responsibilities	Assigned To
Project Sponsor	• Has ultimate authority over the project • Is responsible for the project's overall success • Approves changes to the scope and objectives • Provides all funding approvals • Approves budget-related deliverables • Controls business aspects • Assists in developing the charter and plans • Makes user resources available • Approves delivered products • Assists in tracking action items and budgets • Responsible for functional quality	*<specify the individual assigned to this role and related duties>*
Project Manager	• Controls the day-to-day aspects of the project • Develops and maintains the charter and plans • Executes formal reviews and management reviews • Tracks and closes issues, action items, and budgets • Helps resolve issues and change requests • Responsible for the quality of all deliverables	*<specify the individual assigned to this role and related duties>*
Team Leader	• Manages one or more functional aspects • Helps the project manager with formal reviews and • management reviews • Helps research issues and change requests • Helps the project manager create the work breakdown structure for his or her functional area • Helps the project manager develop the scope and estimates for his or her functional area • Maintains the scope, estimates, and work plans for his or her area	*<specify the individual assigned to this role and related duties>*

(Continued)

Project Role	Responsibilities	Assigned To
	• Tracks action items related to his or her functional area • Ensures the proper reporting of status by his or her team members	
Business Area Team Leader	• Responsible for the technical quality of deliverables assigned to his or her functional area	*<specify the individual assigned to this role and related duties>*
Procurement Officer	• Liaises and coordinates all procurement and contract management activities	*<specify the individual assigned to this role and related duties>*
Financial Officer	• Provides the financial information needed to manage the project • Helps the project manager to define the budget, estimates, and allocations • Helps the project manager with the tracking and reporting of costs and expenditures against budget	*<specify the individual assigned to this role and related duties>*
Business Analyst	• Documents and maintains models of business requirements • Documents and analyzes business processes using value-added or non-value-added, process modeling tools, cost-time charts, and root cause analysis	*<specify the individual assigned to this role and related duties>*
Project Management Officer	• Ensures effective communications about the project across the organization • Helps the project teams create a quality management approach and plan • Provides support to the project sponsor and project • manager • Assists in developing divisional implementation plans • Establishes standards (where necessary) for tool usage and project management • Reviews project performance	*<specify the individual assigned to this role and related duties>*
Subject Matter Expert (SME)	• Exhibits the highest level of expertise in performing a • specialized job, task, or skill within the organization • Understands a business process or area well enough to answer questions from people in other groups • Explains the current process to the project team and then answers their questions • Has in-depth knowledge of the subject • Represents the users' area in identifying current or future procedures	*<specify the individual assigned to this role and related duties>*

(Continued)

Project Role	Responsibilities	Assigned To
Senior Review Board	• Approves project investments • Reviews the business rationale, projects, and resources • Prioritizes projects based on specific criteria • Resolves all cross-project issues • Reviews all cross-divisional issues	*<specify the individual assigned to this role and related duties>*
Executive Steering Committee	• Discusses and resolves issues that cannot be resolved by the project team • Reviews all budget-related information regarding • deliverables for the project • Is responsible for organization-wide communications • Provides guidance and mentoring to the project sponsors, project manager, and teams • Ensures that requirements of the business are adequately represented to the individual projects • Represents all affected business areas as determined by the project sponsor and project manager (the executive sponsor extends invitations to members) • Reviews and makes recommendations on scope changes • Monitors project progress	*<specify the individual assigned to this role and related duties>*

10. Appendix C: Sensitivity Analysis

[Insert a print screen of the NPV. Provide details about the best and worst case scenarios identified during the sensitivity analysis. Delete this comment once completed.]

Template 11: Requirement Analysis Report

\<Project/Initiative Name\>

Requirements Specifications

Recommendation

[Insert a new signature line for each additional stakeholder providing approval. The signature of each stakeholder confirms that all impacted business lines are informed and consulted. Approval of this requirement's specification document provides agreement by stakeholders for shared responsibility of the business and technical requirements. Delete this comment once completed.]

We recommend approval of this business case for *\<Project Name\>* initiative.

_____   _____
\<Name – Technology Sponsor\>   *\<Name – Business Sponsor\>*
\<Title/Department\>   *\<Title/Department\>*

I / We concur:

_____
\<Name – Executive Sponsor\>
\<Title/Department\>

Date Prepared	*\<Date\>*
Presented By	*\<team/department name\>*

Document History

Version	Date	Comments
0.1	<Date>	Initial Draft

Table of Contents

1. Introduction

1.1. Purpose

This requirement specifications report documents and tracks the activities performed to determine the needs and/or desires for the architectural design of *<Specify the system name>*.

This document also includes an overview of the assessment methodology used and details the findings of the requirement analysis so stakeholders have necessary information to build system architectural designs.

1.2. Scope

[This section explains what business strategies will drive the results of this assessment. Delete this comment once completed.]

The following are considered in-scope deliverables as part of this project:

- *<Insert in-scope strategy>*
- *<Insert in-scope strategy>*

1.2.1. Out-of-Scope

[This section explains what business strategies will not drive the results of this assessment. Delete this comment once completed.]

The following are considered out-of-scope deliverables as part of this project:

- *<Insert out-of-scope strategy>*
- *<Insert out-of-scope strategy>*

2. Business Need

2.1. Benefits

[This section describes the benefit(s) to be achieved and the justification(s) for completing the assessment. Delete this comment once completed.]

2.2. Audience

[Modify the table in this section based on the individuals who have a vested interest in the outcome of this assessment, such as Executive Management, Subject Matter Experts, IT Support, or Sales. Delete this comment once completed.]

The intended audience of this requirements specification document includes the following:

- *<Insert the business lines or organizational role>*
- <Insert the business lines or organizational role>

2.3. Stakeholders

[This section lists the specific individuals and/or business lines who will participate either directly or indirectly in the completion of this assessment. The stakeholders listed in the table below are provided as examples and should be modified to match those individuals and/or groups specific to the organization. Delete this comment once completed.]

Stakeholder Group	Role
Chief Executive	• Functions as the overall champion for completing this assessment • Provides general sponsorship
Other executives	• Functions as an additional champion for completing this assessment • Provides mutual sponsorship
IT groups	• Concerned with data availability, definition, control and accessibility
Business Heads	• Governs consistency between their own reporting and any consolidated reporting
Head office departments	• Have interest in ensuring common data definitions, accounting methodologies and software choices

3. Impact and Constraints

3.1. Risks

[Describe the significant events or conditions that, if they occur, will affect this assessment. Delete this comment once completed.]

Risk	Severity	Mitigation
<Risk description>	☐ High ☐ Medium ☐ Low	*<Risk mitigating controls>*

3.2. Assumptions

The following circumstances and outcomes, taken for granted in the absence of concrete information, have affected this assessment:

- *<Assumption description>*
- *<Assumption description>*

3.3. Constraints

The following limitations and restrictions have been taken into consideration prior to the execution of this assessment:

- *<Constraint description>*
- *<Constraint description>*

3.4. Dependencies

The following preceding elements were performed prior to the execution of this assessment:

- *<Dependency description>*
- *<Dependency description>*

4. Timing/Schedules

[Include an implementation date for the project and use multiple rows if the project is being implemented in several phases. Include a high-level schedule of the projected implementation plan; critical dates, including additional funding checkpoints; and any interdependencies with other initiatives. Delete this comment once completed.]

Implementation Phase	Target Date (Month/Year)
<specify the name of the phase>	*<specify the delivery year/month>*

4.1. Milestones

[Describe the key deliverables that will be used for measuring the project's success or failure. Delete this comment once completed.]

Deliverable	Target Date (Month/Year)	Success Metric
<specify the deliverable>	*<specify the delivery month/ year>*	*<specify how success is measured>*

5. Assessment Methodology

The section outlines the methodology followed to gather and validate the requirements in support of the business strategies described in Section 1.2.

5.1. Reference Materials

In support of this assessment, the reference materials specified in the table below were used to gather the baseline set of requirements.

[In the table below, specify the documentation, roadmaps, best practices, etc. used to gather the baseline set of requirements. Delete this comment once completed.]

Reference Name	Author(s)	Publication Date	Location
<specify the reference name>	*<specify the reference author(s)>*	*<specify the date the reference was published >*	*<specify the location where the reference was retrieved>*

5.2. Assessment Techniques

In support of this assessment, the baseline set of requirements were validated with stakeholders identified in Section 2.3 using the approaches listed in the table below.

[In the table below, specify the interviews, surveys, workshops, etc. used to validate the baseline set of requirements with stakeholders. Delete this comment once completed.]

Validation Approach	Date Completed	Stakeholders
<specify the type of approach used>	*<specify the date performed>*	*<identify the stakeholders that participated in the validation>*

6. Requirements Analysis

The section outlines the finalized set of requirements in support of the business strategies described in Section 1.2.

6.1. Functional Requirements

This section describes the features of the deliverable(s) that will specifically meet a business need or desire.

ID	Requirement	Priority
<#>	*<input the requirement description>*	*<specify the priority>*

6.2. Operational Requirements

This section describes the "behind the scenes" functions needed to keep the deliverable(s) working overtime.

ID	Requirement	Priority
<#>	*<input the requirement description>*	*<specify the priority>*

6.3. Technical Requirements

This section describes the conditions under which the deliverable(s) must function.

ID	Requirement	Priority
<#>	*<input the requirement description>*	*<specify the priority>*

6.4. Transactional Requirements

This section describes the aspects of the deliverable(s) that must be met to hand over support responsibilities.

ID	Requirement	Priority
<#>	*<input the requirement description>*	*<specify the priority>*

6.5. Out-of-Scope Requirements

This section describes the requirements that have been identified as out of scope.

Requirement	Justification
<input the requirement description>	*<specify why this requirement is out of scope>*

Bibliography

Adams, Richard. The Advanced Data Acquisition Model (ADAM): A process model for digital forensic practice. 2013. https://www.researchgate.net/publication/258224615_The_Advanced_Data_Acquisition_Model_ADAM_A_process_model_for_digital_forensic_practice.

Agrawal, Ankit, Megha, Gupta, Saurabh Gupta, Subhash Chandra. Systematic digital forensic investigation model. *International Journal of Computer Science and Security (IJCSS)*, vol. 5, no. 1, 118–131, 2011.

Ahmad, Atif. The forensic chain-of-evidence model: Improving the process of evidence Collection in incident handling procedures. doi:10.1.1.87.8677. 2002.

Alabdulsalam, Saad, Schaefer, Kevin, Kechadi, Tahar, Le-Khac, Nhien-An. Internet of Things forensics: challenges and case study. 2018. https://arxiv.org/ftp/arxiv/papers/1801/1801.10391.pdf.

Alberts, Christopher, Dorofee, Audrey, Stevens, James, Woody, Carol. Introduction to the OCTAVE approach. Carnegie Mellon University, 2003. http://resources.sei.cmu.edu/asset_files/UsersGuide/2003_012_001_51556.pdf.

Alenezi, Ahmed, Hussein, Raid, Wills, Gary. A framework for cloud forensic readiness in organizations. *5th IEEE International Conference on Mobile Cloud Computing, Services, and Engineering*, 2017. https://ieeexplore.ieee.org/document/7944896.

American Bar Association. E-Discovery and electronic evidence in the courtroom. *Business Law Today*, vol. 17, no. 1, 2007. https://apps.americanbar.org/buslaw/blt/2007-09-10/chorvat.shtml.

Association of Chief Police Officers. Good practice guide for computer-based electronic evidence. 2007. http://www.7safe.com/electronic_evidence/ACPO_guidelines_computer_evidence.pdf.

Australian Government—Civil Aviation Safety Authority. Cost benefit analysis methodology procedures manual. 2007. http://www.casa.gov.au/scripts/257r005.pdf.

Australian Signal Directorate. Strategies to mitigate targeted cyber intrusions. Australian Government—Department of Defense, 2014. http://www.asd.gov.au/infosec/mitigationstrategies.htm.

Ayers, Rick, Brothers, Sam, Jansen, Wayne. *Special Publication 800–101 Revision 1: Guidelines on Mobile Device Forensics.* National Institute of Standards and Technology (NIST), Gaithersburg, MD, 2014. https://nvlpubs.nist.gov/nistpubs/specialpublications/nist.sp.800-101r1.pdf.

Bahadur, Parinita. Difference between guideline, procedure, standard and policy. 2014. http://www.hrsuccessguide.com/2014/01/Guideline-Procedure-Standard-Policy.html.

Baryamureeba, Venansius, Tushabe, Florence. *The Enhanced Digital Investigation Process Model.* Institute of Computer Science, Makerere University, Kampala Uganda, 2004. http://dfrws.org/2004/day1/Tushabe_EIDIP.pdf.

Beebe, Nicole Lang, Clark, Jan Guynes. A hierarchical, objectives-based framework for the digital investigations process. *Digital Forensics Research Workshop* (DFRWS), vol. 2, no. 2, 147–167, 2004. http://www.dfrws.org/2004/day1/Beebe_Obj_Framework_for_DI.pdf.

Bem, Derek, Huebner, Ewa. Computer forensic analysis in a virtual environment. *International Journal of Digital Evidence*, vol. 6, no. 2, 2007. https://www.utica.edu/academic/institutes/ecii/publications/articles/1C349F35-C73B-DB8A-926F9F46623A1842.pdf.

Bennett, Brian T. *Understanding, Assessing, and Responding to Terrorism: Protecting Critical Infrastructure and Personnel.* John Wiley & Sons, Hoboken, NJ, 2007.

Betts, Dominic, Shahan, Robin. Internet of Things security architecture. Microsoft, 2018. https://docs.microsoft.com/en-us/azure/iot-accelerators/iot-security-architecture.

Bragg, Roberta. *CISSP Training Guide.* Pearson IT Certification, 2002.

Bretherton, Francis P., Singley, Paul. T. *Metadata: A User's View.* IEEE, 1994. https://ieeexplore.ieee.org/document/336950.

Brunty, Josh. Validation of Forensic Tools and Software: A Quick Guide for the Digital Forensic Examiner. Forensic Magazine, 2011. http://www.forensicmag.com/articles/2011/03/validation-forensic-tools-and-software-quick-guide-digitalforensic-examiner.

Business Dictionary. *Jurisdiction.* WebFinance Inc, 2017. http://www.businessdictionary.com/definition/jurisdiction.html.

Campagna, Rich, Iyer, Subbu, Krishnan, Ashwin. *Mobile Device Security for Dummies.* John Wiley & Sons, 2011. https://www.amazon.ca/Mobile-Device-Security-Dummies-Campagna/dp/0470927534.

Canadian Government—Treasury Board of Canada Secretariat. Canadian cost-benefit analysis guide: Regulatory proposals. 2007. http://www.tbs-sct.gc.ca/rtrap-parfa/analys/analys-eng.pdf.

Carminati, F., Betev, L., Grigoras, A. *Grid and Cloud Computing: Concepts and Practical Applications.* IOS Press, 2016. https://www.iospress.nl/book/grid-and-cloud-computing-concepts-and-practical-applications/.

Carnegie, Mellon. CMMISM for Software Engineering (CMMI-SW, V1.1). 2002. http://resources.sei.cmu.edu/asset_files/TechnicalReport/2002_005_001_14069.pdf.

Carrier, Brian D., Spafford, Eugene H. An event-based digital forensic investigation framework. 2004. http://www.digital-evidence.org/papers/dfrws_event.pdf. Digital Forensics Research Workshop (DFRWS).

Casey, Eoghan. *Digital Evidence and Computer Crime: Forensic Science, Computers and the Internet.* Academic Press, San Diego, CA,2000.

Casey, Eoghan. *Digital Evidence and Computer Crime: Forensic Science, Computers and the Internet.* 3rd ed. Academic Press, 2011. https://www.elsevier.com/books/digital-evidence-and-computer-crime/casey/978-0-08-092148-8.

Ceresini, T. Maintaining the forensic viability of log files. System Administration, Networking, and Security Institute (SANS)—Global Information Assurance Certification (GIAC), 2001. http://www.giac.org/paper/gsec/801/maintaining-forensic-viability-log-files/101724.

Chike, Chike Patrick, D.Sc. The legal challenges of Internet of Things. 2018. https://www.researchgate.net/publication/322628457_The_Legal_Challenges_of_Internet_of_Things.

Choi, Seul-Ki, Yang, Chung-Huang, Kwak, Jim. Security hardening and security monitoring for IoT devices to mitigate IoT security vulnarabilities and threats. *Transactions on Internet and Information Systems*, vol. 12, no. 2, 2018. http://www.itiis.org/digital-library/manuscript/file/1937/TIIS+Vol+12,+No+2-22.pdf.

Choksy, Carol E.B. 8 Steps to develop a taxonomy. *The Information Management Journal*, 2006. http://www.arma.org/bookstore/files/Choksy.pdf.

Chow, Kam-Pui, Shenoi, Sujeet (Eds.). Advances in digital forensics VI. *Sixth IFIP WG 11.9 International Conference on Digital Forensics*, Hong Kong, China, 2010. http://www.springer.com/us/book/9783642155055.

Ciardhuáin, Séamus Ó. An extended model of cybercrime investigations. *International Journal of Digital Evidence*, vol. 3, no. 1, 2004. https://www.utica.edu/academic/institutes/ecii/publications/articles/A0B70121-FD6C-3DBA-0EA5C3E93CC575FA.pdf.

Cichonski, Paul, Millar, Tom, Grance, Tim, Scarfone, Karen. *Computer Security Incident Handling Guide*. National Institute of Standards and Technology (NIST), Gaithersburg, MD, 2012. http://nvlpubs.nist.gov/nistpubs/Special Publications/NIST.SP.800-61r2.pdf.

Cloud Security Alliance. Quick Guide to the Reference Architecture: Trusted Cloud Initiative. 2011. https://cloudsecurityalliance.org/wp-content/uploads/2011/10/TCI_Whitepaper.pdf.

Cloud Security Alliance. Security Guidance for Critical Areas of Focus in Cloud Computing V3.0. 2011. https://cloudsecurityalliance.org/guidance/csaguide.v3.0.pdf.

Communication safety establishment harmonized threat and risk assessment methodology. Royal Canadian Mounted Police, 2007. https://www.cse-cst.gc.ca/en/system/files/pdf_documents/tra-emr-1-e.pdf.

Computer Ethics Institute. The ten commandments of computer ethics. 1992.

Contesti,Diana-Lynnetal.*Official(ISC)2GuidetotheSSCPCBK*.AuerbachPublications, 2007. https://www.crcpress.com/Official-ISC2-Guide-to-the-SSCP-CBK/Contesti-Tipton/p/book/9780429195990.

Cornell University Law School. Admissible evidence. 2014. https://www.law.cornell.edu/wex/admissible_evidence.

Cornell University Law School. Brady rule. 2014. https://www.law.cornell.edu/wex/brady_rule.

Cornell University Law School. Daubert standard. 2015. https://www.law.cornell.edu/wex/daubert_standard.

Cornell University Law School. Federal rules of civil procedure. 2014. https://www.law.cornell.edu/rules/frcp/.

Cornell University Law School. Federal rules of evidence. https://www.law.cornell.edu/rules/fre. 2014.

de Rus, Gines. *Introduction to Cost-Benefit Analysis*. Edward Elgar Publishing Inc., Cheltenham, UK, 2010.

Digital Forensics Certification Board. *Code of Ethics and Standards of Professional Conduct*. 2016. https://dfcb.org/code-of-ethics-and-standards-of-professional-conduct/.

Dull, Tamara. Data lake versus data warehouse: Key differences. KDnuggets, 2015. https://www.kdnuggets.com/2015/09/data-lake-vs-data-warehouse-key-differences.html.

Dykstra, Josiah, Sherman, Alan. *Acquiring Forensic Evidence from Infrastructure-as-a-Service Cloud Computing*. Digital Forensics Research Workshop (DFRWS), 2012. https://www.dfrws.org/sites/default/files/session-files/pres-acquiring_forensic_evidence_from_infrastructure-as-a-service_cloud_computing.pdf.

Emmanuel, S. Pilli, Joshi, R.C., Niyogi, Rajdeep. A generic framework for network forensics. *International Journal of Computer Applications*, vol. 1, no. 11, 2010. http://www.ijcaonline.org/journal/number11/pxc387408.pdf.

Felix, C. Freiling, Schwittay, Bastian. A common process model for incident response and computer forensics. Laboratory for Dependable Distributed Systems, University of Mannheim, Germany, 2007. https://www1.informatik.uni-erlangen.de/filepool/publications/imf2007-common-model.pdf.

Fenu, Gianni, Solinas, Fabrizio. Computer forensics investigation an approach to evidence in cyberspace. http://sdiwc.net/digital-library/download.php?id=00000541.pdf.

Fernando, A.C. *Business Ethics and Corporate Governance*. Pearson Education India, Harlow, UK, 2010.

Finkle, Jim, Heavey, Susan. UPDATE 2-target says it declined to act on early alert of cyber breach. *Reuters*, 2014. http://www.reuters.com/article/2014/03/13/target-breach-idUSL2N0MA1MW20140313.

Foote, Keith D. A brief history of The Internet of Things. *Dataversity*, 2016. http://www.dataversity.net/brief-history-internet-things.

ForensicFocus. Computer forensics education. 2015. http://www.forensicfocus.com/education.

Forrester. Application control: An essential endpoint security component. 2012. http://www.forrester.com/Application+Control+An+Essential+Endpoint+Security+Component/fulltext/-/E-RES78502.

Forrester. Prepare for anywhere, anytime, any-device engagement with a stateless mobile architecture. 2012. http://www.forrester.com/Prepare+For+Anywhere+Anytime+AnyDevice+Engagement+With+A+Stateless+Mobile+Architecture/fulltext/-/E-RES61569.

Garrison. Clint P. *Digital Forensics for Network, Internet, and Cloud Computing: A Forensic Evidence Guide for Moving Targets and Data*. Syngress, Burlington, MA, 2010.

Gartner Research. Enterprise endpoint protection when the consumer is king. 2013. http://www.gartner.com/document/2402415.

Gerge, Mohay, Anderson, Alison, Collie, Byron, De Vel, Olivier, McKemmish, Rodnet. *Computer and Intrusion Forensics*. Artech House, Burlington, MA, 2003.

Ghorbani, A.A., Lu, W., Tavallaee, M. *Network Intrusion Detection and Prevention Concepts and Tecnniques*. Springer, Berlin, Germany, 2010.

Goodwin, Richard. The history of mobile phones from 1973 To 2008: The handsets that made it ALL Happen. *Know Your Mobile*, 2016.

Gregory, Peter. *CISSP Guide to Security Essentials*. Nelson Education, Toronto, Canada, 2014.

Grobler, C.P., Louwrens, C.P. Digital forensic readiness as a component of information security best practice. In Venter, H., Eloff, M., Labuschagne, L., Eloff, J., von Solms, R. (Eds.), *New Approaches for Security, Privacy and Trust in Complex Environments. SEC 2007*. IFIP International Federation for Information Processing, Vol. 232. Springer, Boston, MA, 2007.

Harrington, Sean. Professional ethics in the digital forensics discipline: Part 1. *Forensic Magazine*, 2014. https://www.forensicmag.com/article/2014/06/professional-ethics-digital-forensics-discipline-part-2.

Harrington, Sean. Professional ethics in the digital forensics discipline: Part 2. 2014.

Harris, Elizabeth A., Perlroth, Nicole. Target missed signs of a data breach. *New York Times*, 2014. http://www.nytimes.com/2014/03/14/business/target-missed-signs-of-a-data-breach.html?_r=0.

Hay, David C. *Requirements Analysis: From Business Views to Architecture*. Prentice Hall Professional, Upper Saddle River, NJ, 2003.

Hegarty, R.C. Lamb, D.J., Attwood, A. Digital evidence challenges in the internet of things. *Proceedings of the Ninth International Workshop on Digital Forensics and Incident Analysis*, 2016. https://www.cscan.org/openaccess/?id=231.

Hernan, Shawn, Lambert, Scott, Ostwald, Tomasz, Shostack, Adam. Uncover security design flaws using the STRIDE approach. *MSDN Magazine*, pp. 68–75, 2006. https://msdn.microsoft.com/en-us/magazine/cc163519.aspx.

Hernandez, Steven. *Official Guide to the CISSP CBK*, 3rd ed. CRC Press, Boca Raton, FL, 2012.

HG Legal Resources. Information technology law. HGEXPERTS, 2015. http://www.hg.org/information-technology-law.html.

Hoog, Andrew. *Android Forensics: Investigation, Analysis, and Mobile Security for Google Android*. Elsevier, New York, 2011.

Ieong, Ricci S.C. *FORZA: Digital Forensics Investigation Framework that Incorporate Legal Issues*. Elsevier, 2006. http://www.dfrws.org/2006/proceedings/4-Ieong.pdf.

InfoSec Reading Room. *An Overview of Threat and Risk Assessment*. SANS Institute, Redmond, WA, 2002. http://www.sans.org/reading-room/whitepapers/auditing/overview-threat-risk-assessment-76.

International Association of Computer Investigative Specialists (IACIS). Code of ethics. 2017.

International Organization for Standardization (ISO)/International Electrotechnical Commission (IEC). ISO/IEC 27005:2011 Information technology–Security techniques-Information security risk management. 2011.

International Society of Forensic Computer Examiners (ISFCE). Code of ethics and professional responsibility. 2017.

Investopedia. Market-orientation. 2015. http://www.investopedia.com/terms/m/market-orientation.asp.

Ionita, Dan, Hartel, Pieter. Current established risk assessment methodologies and tools. MS thesis. University of Twente, Enschede, the Netherlands, 2013. http://doc.utwente.nl/89558/1/%5Btech_report%5D_D_Ionita_-_Current_Established_Risk_Assessment_Methodologies_and_Tools.pdf.

ITIL v3 Study Guide. Taruu LLC, 2009. http://taruu.com/Documents/ITIL%20v3%20Foundation%20Study%20Guide%20v4.2.2.5.pdf.

Jarke, Matthias et al. *Fundamentals of Data Warehouse*. Springer Science & Business Media, Berlin, Germany, 2013.

Kabay, Michel E. A *Brief History of Computer Crime: An Introduction for Students*. 2008. http://www.mekabay.com/overviews/history.pdf.

Karake-Shalhoub, Zeinab, Al Qasimi, Lubna. *Cyber Law and Cyber Security in Developing and Emerging Economies*. Edward Elgar Publishing, Cheltenham, UK, 2010.

Kebande, Victor R., Karie, Nickson M., Venter, H.S. Adding digital forensic readiness as a security component to the IoT domain. *International Journal on Advanced Science, Engineering and Information Technology*, vol. 8, no. 1, 2018. https://www. researchgate.net/profile/Victor_Kebande/publication/323384894_Adding_ Digital_Forensic_Readiness_as_a_Security_Component_to_the_IoT_Domain/ links/5a9ea184aca2726eed57789e/Adding-Digital-Forensic-Readiness-as-a-Security-Component-to-the-IoT-Domain.pdf.

Kedar, Thakare J. *Advanced Database Management*. Technical Publications, Pune, India, 2008.

Kellermanns, Dave. Data lake vs data warehouse: What's the difference? *Automic*, 2016. https://automic.com/blog/what-difference-between-data-lake-and-data -warehouse.

Kemp, Richard. Legal aspects of the Internet of Things. Kemp IT Law, 2017. http:// www.kempitlaw.com/wp-content/uploads/2017/06/Legal-Aspects-of-the-Internet-of-Things-KITL-20170610.pdf.

Kent, Karen, Chevalier, Suzanne, Grance, Tim, Dang, Hung. Special publication 800-86: Guide to integrating forensic techniques into incident response. *NIST Special Publication*, vol. 10, no. 14, 800–886, 2006. http://csrc.nist.gov/publica-tions/nistpubs/800-86/SP800-86.pdf.

Kissel, Richard, Stine, Kevin, Scholl, Matthew, Rossman, Hart, Fahlsing, Jim, Gulick, Jessica. *Special Publication 800-64 R2: Security Considerations in the System Development Life Cycle*. National Institute of Standards and Technology (NIST), Gaithersburg, MD, 2008. http://csrc.nist.gov/publica-tions/nistpubs/800-64-Rev2/SP800-64-Revision2.pdf.

Ko, Ran, Choo, Raymond. *The Cloud Security Ecosystem: Technical, Legal, Business and Management Issues*. Syngress, Burlington, MA, 2015.

Kohn, Michael, Eloff, J.H.P., Olivier, M.S. *Framework for a Digital Forensic Investigation*. Information and Computer Security Architectures Research Group (ICSA), Department of Computer Science, University of Pretoria, Hatfield, Pretoria, 2006. http://icsa.cs.up.ac.za/issa/2006/Proceedings/ Full/101_Paper.pdf.

Krebs, Brian. The target breach, by the numbers. *Krebs on Security*, vol. 6, 2014. http://krebsonsecurity.com/2014/05/the-target-breach-by-the-numbers.

Kruse II, Warren G., Heiser, Jay G. *Computer Forensics: Incident Response Essentials*. Pearson, Indianapolis, IN, 2004.

Landoll, Douglas. *The Security Risk Assessment Handbook: A Complete Guide for Performing Security Risk Assessments*, 2nd ed. CRC Press, Boca Raton, FL, 2011.

Lang, Anthony, Bashir, Masooda, Campbell, Roy, Destefano, Lizanne. Developing a new digital forensics curriculum. *Digital Forensic Research Conference (DFRWS)*, vol. 11, S76–S84, 2014. https://www.dfrws.org/sites/default/files/ session-files/paper-developing_a_new_digital_forensics_curriculum.pdf.

Law Crossing. *Information Technology Attorney Job Description*. Employment Research Institute, Pasadena, CA, 2015. http://www.lawcrossing.com/ job-description/6048/information-technology-attorney-jobs.

Law Donut. Employment law – Discipline and grievance. 2015. http:// www.lawdonut.co.uk/law/employment-law/discipline-and-grievance/ disciplinary-issues-faqs#7.

Lee, H.C., Palmbach, T.M., Miller, M.T. *Henry Lee's Crime Scene Handbook*. Academic Press, San Diego, CA, 2001.

Legal Dictionary. Daubert test. 2008. http://legal-dictionary.thefreedictionary.com/Daubert+standard.

Linthicum, David. Three types of IoT data sources. *RTInsights*, 2016. https://www.rtinsights.com/three-types-of-iot-data-sources/.

Liu, Changwei, Singhal, Anoop, Wijesekera, Duminda. Identifying evidence for cloud forensic analysis. *Advances in Digital Forensics XIII*. Springer, Cham, Switzerland, 2017.

Lloyd, Ian. *Information Technology Law*. Oxford University Press, New York, 2014.

MacDonald, Neil. The future of information security is context aware and adaptive. *Gartner Research*, G00200385. 2010.

Malega, Peter. Escalation management as the necessary form of incident management process. *Journal of Emerging Trends in Computing and Information Sciences*, vol. 5, no. 6, 641–646, 2014. http://www.cisjournal.org/journalofcomputing/archive/vol5no8/vol5no8_8.pdf.

Mandia, Kevin, Prosise, Chris, Pepe, Matt. *Incident Response & Computer Forensics*, 2nd ed. McGraw-Hill, New York, 2003.

Marcella, Albert Jr., Menendez, Doug. *Cyber Forensics: A Field Manual for Collecting, Examining, and Preserving Evidence of Computer Crimes*, 2nd ed. CRC Press, Boca Raton, FL, 2007.

Marquis, Hank. *A Study Guide to Service Catalogue from the Principles of Itil V3, Volume 3*. The Stationery Office, 2010.

Mell, Peter, Grance, Timothy. *Special Publication 800-145: The NIST Definition of Cloud Computing*. National Institute of Standards and Technology (NIST), Gaithersburg, MD, 2011.

Microsoft. Secure boot overview. 2014. https://technet.microsoft.com/en-ca/library/hh824987.aspx.

Microsoft. The STRIDE threat model. 2005. https://msdn.microsoft.com/en-us/library/ee823878%28v=cs.20%29.aspx.

Microsoft. threat modelling. 2003. https://msdn.microsoft.com/en-us/library/ff648644.aspx.

The MITRE Corporation. About STIX. 2015. http://stixproject.github.io/about/.

The MITRE Corporation. STIX project. 2015. http://stixproject.github.io/about/.

Morgan, Brendan. Ensuring admissibility of mobile evidence in court. *The Federal Lawyer*, 2015. http://www.fedbar.org/Resources_1/Federal-Lawyer-Magazine/2015/March/Features/Ensuring-Admissibility-of-Mobile-Evidence-in-Court.aspx?FT=.pdf.

Morgan, Jacob. A simple explanation of "The Internet of Things". *Forbes*, 2014. https://www.forbes.com/sites/jacobmorgan/2014/05/13/simple-explanation-internet-things-that-anyone-can-understand/#6a853cf11d09.

Murphy, Cynthia A. *Developing Process for Mobile Device Forensics V3*. System Administration, Networking, and Security Institute (SANS), 2013. http://www.mobileforensicscentral.com/mfc/documents/Mobile%20Device%20Forensic%20Process%20v3.0.pdf.

National Institute of Standards and Technology (NIST). *Computer Forensic Tool Testing Project*. 2012. http://www.cftt.nist.gov/CFTT-Booklet-Revised-02012012.pdf.

Nelson, Bill, Phillips, Amelia, Enfinger, Frank, Steuart, Chris. *Computer Forensics and Investigations*. Thomson, Boston, MA, 2004.

Newsome, Bruce. *A Practical Introduction to Security and Risk Management*. SAGE Publications, Boston, MA, 2013.

NIST Cloud Computing Forensic Science Working Group Information Technology Laboratory. *NIST Cloud Computing Forensic Science Challenges*. National Institute of Standards and Technology (NIST), Gaithersburg, MD, 2014.

NIST Cloud Computing Security Working Group Information Technology Laboratory. *Special Publication 500-299: NIST Cloud Computing Security Reference Architecture*. National Institute of Standards and Technology (NIST), Gaithersburg, MD, 2013.

O'Loughlin, Mark. *The Service Catalog: Best Practices*. Van Haren, Norwich, UK, 2010.

Office of Legal Education Executive Office for United States Attorneys, Department of Justic. Searching and Seizing Computers and Obtaining Electronic Evidence in Criminal Investigations. 2009. http://www.justice.gov/criminal/cybercrime/docs/ssmanual2009.pdf.

OLAP.COM. OLAP definition. 2015. http://olap.com/olap-definition/.

Open Web Application Security Project (OWASP). 2010 T10 architecture diagram. 2010. https://owasp.org/index.php?title=File:2010-T10-ArchitectureDiagram.png.

Open Web Application Security Project (OWASP). Threat modeling. 2015. https://www.owasp.org/index.php/Threat_Modeling.

Open Web Application Security Project (OWASP). Threat risk modelling. 2015. https://www.owasp.org/index.php/Threat_Risk_Modeling.

Palmer, G. 2001. *A Road Map for Digital Forensic Research*. First Digital Forensic Research Workshop, Utica, NY, pp. 27–30.

Peltier, Thomas R. *Facilitated Risk Analysis Process (FRAP)*. CRC Press, 2000. http://www.ittoday.info/AIMS/DSM/85-01-21.pdf.

People's Law Dictionary. Bad faith. 2015. http://dictionary.law.com/Default.aspx?selected=21.

Perumal, S. Digital forensic model based on Malaysian investigation process. *International Journal of Computer Science and Network Security*, vol. 9, no. 8, 38–44, 2009.

Peterson, Gilbert, Shenoi, Sujeet. *Advances in Digital Forensics IX: 9th IFIP WG 11.9 International Conference on Digital Forensics*. Springer, Orlando, FL, 2013.

Pollitt, M.M. An ad hoc review of digital models. *Proceeding of the Second International Workshop on Systematic Approaches to Digital Forensic Engineering (SADFE'07)*, Washington, DC, 2007. https://www.researchgate.net/publication/221411294_An_Ad_Hoc_Review_of_Digital_Forensic_Models.

Ponniah, Paulraj. *Data Warehouse Fundamentals: A Comprehensive Guide for IT Professionals*. John Wiley & Sons, 2004. https://www.amazon.com/Data-Warehousing-Fundamentals-Comprehensive-Professionals/dp/0471412546.

Porterfield, Jason. *File Sharing: Rights and Risks*. The Rosen Publishing Group, 2014. https://www.amazon.ca/File-Sharing-Rights-Jason-Porterfield/dp/1477776397.

Press Release: Alexey Ivanov and Vasiliy Gorshkov: Russian Hacker Roulette. CSO, 2005. http://www.csoonline.com/article/2118241/malware-cybercrime/alexey-ivanov-and-vasiliy-gorshkov--russian-hacker-roulette.html.

Press Release: FBI "hack" raises global security concerns. CNET, 2002. http://www.cnet.com/news/fbi-hack-raises-global-security-concerns/.

Press Release: Pirate Bay file-sharing trial to start in Sweden. Telegraph Media Group Limited, 2009. http://www.telegraph.co.uk/technology/8580318/Top-five-internet-piracy-battles.html.

Press Release: Profile Gary McKinnon. *BBC News*, 2008. http://news.bbc.co.uk/2/hi/technology/4715612.stm.

Press Release: SEC Charges Company CEO and Former CFO with Hiding Internal Controls Deficiencies and Violating Sarbanes-Oxley Requirements. U.S. Securities and Exchange Commissions, 2014. http://www.sec.gov/News/PressRelease/Detail/PressRelease/1370542561150.

Queensland Government. Identifying business risk. 2014. https://www.business.qld.gov.au/business/running/risk-management/identifying-business-risk.

Ray, Daniel A., Bradford, Phillip G. Models of models: Digital forensics and domain specific languages. Department of Computer Science, University of Alabama, Tuscaloosa, AL. http://www.ioc.ornl.gov/csiirw/07/abstracts/Bradford-Abstract.pdf.

Ray, Indrajit, Shenoi, Sujeet. *Advances in Digital Forensics IV*. Springer, London, UK, 2008.

ReelLawyers. Lessons of AMD v. Intel. 2013. https://www.youtube.com/watch?v=jQ_9uLkw_Uo.

Reith, M., Carr, C., Gunsch, G. An examination of digital forensics models. *International Journal of Digital Evidence*, vol. 1, no. 3, 2002.

Rooney, Paul. Microsoft's CEO: 80-20 rule applies to bugs, not just features. *CRN*, 2002. http://www.crn.com/news/security/18821726/microsofts-ceo-80-20-rule-applies-to-bugs-not-just-features.htm.

Rowlingson, A. Ten step process for forensic readiness. *International Journal of Digital Evidence*, vol. 2, no. 3, 2004.

Royal Canadian Mounted Police. Crime prevention through environmental design. Government of Canada, 2011. http://www.rcmp-grc.gc.ca/pubs/ccaps-spcca/safecomm-seccollect-eng.htm.

Ruan, Keyun, Carthy, Joe, Kechadi, Tahar, Crosbie, Mark. *Cloud Forensics, Advances in Digital Forensics VII*. Springer, 2011. https://link.springer.com/chapter/10.1007/978-3-642-24212-0_3.

Saitta, Paul, Larcom, Brenda, Eddington, Michael. TRIKE V.1 methodology document. 2005. http://www.octotrike.org/papers/Trike_v1_Methodology_Document-draft.pdf.

Salama, Usama. Smart forensics for the Internet of Things (IoT). SecurityIntelligence, 2017. https://securityintelligence.com/smart-forensics-for-the-internet-of-things-iot/.

Sangaiah, Arun Kumar, Thangavelu, Arunkumar, Sundaram, Venkatesan Meenakshi. *Cognitive Computing for Big Data Systems Over IoT: Frameworks, Tools and Applications*. Springer, 2017. https://www.springer.com/gp/book/9783319706870.

SANS. Developing a computer forensics team. 2001. http://www.sans.org/reading-room/whitepapers/incident/developing-computer-forensics-team-628.

SANS. Information Security policy templates. 2015. https://www.sans.org/
    security-resources/policies/.
Schmitt, Veronia, Jordaan, Jason. Establishing the validity of MD5 and SHA-1 hashing
    in digital forensic practice in light of recent research demonstrating cryptographic
    weaknesses in these algorithms. *International Journal of Computer Applications*,
    2013. http://www.lex-informatica.org/2%20Ensuring%20the%20Legality%20
    of%20the%20Digital%20Forensics%20Process%20in%20South%20Africa.pdf.
Schniederjans, Marc J., Hamaker, Jamie L., Schniederjans, Ashlyn M. *Information
    Technology Investment: Decision-Making Methodology.* World Scientific Co.
    Pvt. Ltd., 2004. https://www.worldscientific.com/worldscibooks/10.1142/7433.
Scientific Working Group on Digital Evidence (SWGDE). Model standard opera-
    tion procedures version 3.0, 2012. https://www.swgde.org/documents/
    Current+Documents/SWGDE+QAM+and+SOP+Manuals/2012-09-13+SWG
    DE+Model+SOP+for+Computer+Forensics+v3.
Security Awareness Program Special Interest Group PCI Security Standards
    Council. Information supplement: Best practices for implementing a secu-
    rity awareness program. PCI Security Standards Council, 2014. https://www.
    pcisecuritystandards.org/documents/PCI_DSS_V1.0_Best_Practices_for_
    Implementing_Security_Awareness_Program.pdf.
Selamat, Siti Rahayu, Yusof, Robiah, Sahib, Shahrin. Mapping process of digital
    forensic investigation framework. *IJCSNS International Journal of Computer
    Science and Network Security*, vol. 8, no. 10, 163–169, 2008.
Smith, Ashley. *Mobile Device Management: What's Legal, What's Not?* Tom's IT Pro,
    2016.
State of North Dakota. Requirements analysis. New York State Office for Technology,
    2001. https://www.nd.gov/itd/files/services/pm/requirements-analysis-guide-
    book.pdf.
Stephenson, Peter. *A Comprehensive Approach to Digital Incident Investigation.*
    Elsevier, 2003. http://www.emich.edu/cerns/downloads/pstephen/Comprehen
    sive-Approach-to-Digital-Investigation.pdf.
Stephenson, Peter. *(ISC)2 Official Guide to the CCFP CBK.* CRC Press, 2014. https://
    www.amazon.ca/Official-ISC-Guide-CCFP-CBK/dp/1482262479.
Sule, Dauda. Importance of forensic readiness. *ISACA Journal*, vol. 1, 2014. http://
    www.isaca.org/Journal/archives/2014/Volume-1/Pages/JOnline-Importance-
    of-Forensic-Readiness.aspx#11.
Tan, John. Forensic readiness. 2001. http://home.eng.iastate.edu/~guan/course/
    backup/CprE-592-YG-Fall-2002/paper/forensic_readiness.pdf.
Tech Target. Cloud computing. 2015. http://searchcloudcomputing.techtarget.com/
    definition/cloud-computing.
Techtarget. Cloud provider. 2015. http://searchcloudprovider.techtarget.com/
    definition/cloud-provider.
TechTarget. IT asset. 2008. http://whatis.techtarget.com/definition/IT-asset.
TechTarget. Principle of Least Privilege (POLP). 2015. http://searchsecurity.techtar-
    get.com/definition/principle-of-least-privilege-POLP.
TechTarget. Total cost of ownership. 2015. http://searchdatacenter.techtarget.com/
    definition/TCO.

Thomson, Lucy L. Mobile devices: New challengers for admissibility of electronic devices. *American Bar*, 2013. https://www.americanbar.org/content/dam/aba/events/science_technology/mobiledevices_new_challenges_admissibility_of_electronic_device.authcheckdam.pdf.

Tipton, Harold F. *(ISC)2 Official Guide to the ISSAP CBK*. CRC Press, 2011a. https://www.crcpress.com/Official-ISC2-Guide-to-the-ISSAP-CBK/Corporate/p/book/9781466579002.

Tipton, Harold F. *(ISC)2 Official Guide to the ISSMP CBK*. CRC Press, 2011b. https://www.crcpress.com/Official-ISC2-Guide-to-the-CISSP-ISSMP-CBK/Steinberg/p/book/9781466578951.

Treasury Board of Canada. Guide to integrated risk management. Government of Canada, 2012. http://www.tbs-sct.gc.ca/tbs-sct/rm-gr/guides/girm-ggir02-eng.asp.

Treasury Board of Canada Secretariat. Guide to risk taxonomies. Government of Canada, 2011. http://www.tbs-sct.gc.ca/tbs-sct/rm-gr/guides/grt-gtr01-eng.asp.

Trenwith, Philip M., Venter, Hein S. *Digital Forensic Readiness in the Cloud*. Information Security for South Africa, 2013. https://www.researchgate.net/publication/261164697_Digital_forensic_readiness_in_the_cloud.

Tripathy, B.K., Anuradha, J. *Internet of Things (IoT): Technologies, Applications, Challenges, and Solutions*. CRC Press, 2017. https://www.crcpress.com/Internet-of-Things-IoT-Technologies-Applications-Challenges-and-Solutions/Tripathy-Anuradha/p/book/9781138035003.

U.S. Department of Justice. Electronic crime scene investigation: A guide to first responders. 2001. https://www.ncjrs.gov/pdffiles1/nij/187736.pdf.

United States District Court, Eastern District Court of Missouri, Eastern Division. United States of America v Joseph Schmidt, III. U.S. Government Publishing Office, 2009. http://www.gpo.gov/fdsys/pkg/USCOURTS-moed-4_09-cr-00265/pdf/USCOURTS-moed-4_09-cr-00265-0.pdf.

University of Cagliari, Department of Computer Science Cagliari, Italy, 2013.

University of Rochester. Mobile Device User Agreement. 2016.

U.S.-CERT. Computer Forensics. 2008. https://www.us-cert.gov/sites/default/files/publications/forensics.pdf.

van der Molen, Fred. *Get Ready for Cloud Computing*, 2nd ed. Van Haren, 2012. https://www.amazon.com/Ready-Cloud-Computing-Haren-Publishing/dp/9087536402.

Versprite. PASTA Abstract. 2013. http://versprite.com/docs/PASTA_Abstract.pdf.

Webopedia. Entity-relationship diagram. 2015. http://www.webopedia.com/TERM/E/entity_relationship_diagram.html.

Webopedia. Mandatory access control. 2015. http://www.webopedia.com/TERM/M/Mandatory_Access_Control.html.

Webopedia. Metadata. 2015. http://www.webopedia.com/TERM/M/metadata.html.

Webopedia. Role-Based Access Control (RBAC). 2015. http://www.webopedia.com/TERM/S/structured_data.html.

Webopedia. Structured data. 2015. http://www.webopedia.com/TERM/S/structured_data.html.

Webopedia. Unstructured data. 2015. http://www.webopedia.com/TERM/U/unstructured_data.html.

Wheeler. Evan. *Security Risk Management: Building an Information Security Risk Management Program from the Ground Up.* Elsevier, 2011. https://www.amazon.ca/Security-Risk-Management-Building-Information/dp/1597496154.

Wilson, Mark, Hash, Joan. Special Publication 800-50: Building an Information Technology Security Awareness and Training Program. National Institute of Standards and Technology (NIST), 2003. http://csrc.nist.gov/publications/nistpubs/800-50/NIST-SP800-50.pdf.

Yasinsac, A., Manzano, Y. Policies to Enhance Computer and Network Forensics. *IEEE Workshop on Information Assurance and Security,* 2001. https://www.researchgate.net/publication/255680113_Policies_to_Enhance_Computer_and_Network_Forensics.

Yusoff, Yunus, Ismail, Roslan, Hassan, Zainuddin. Common phases of computer forensics investigation models. *International Journal of Computer Science & Information Technology (IJCSIT),* vol. 3, no. 3, 2011. http://airccse.org/journal/jcsit/0611csit02.pdf.

Zeltser, Lenny. The many fields of digital forensics and incident response. SANS Digital Forensics and Incident Response. 2014. https://digital-forensics.sans.org/blog/2014/01/30/many-fields-of-dfir.

Zulkipli, Nurul Huda Nik, Alenezi, Ahmed, Wills, Gary B. IoT forensic: Bridging the challenges in digital forensic and the Internet of Things. *2nd International Conference on Internet of Things, Big Data and Security,* 2017. https://www.researchgate.net/publication/316867894_IoT_Forensic_Bridging_the_Challenges_in_Digital_Forensic_and_the_Internet_of_Things.

Resources

Digital Forensic Publications

There are countless resources available in today that are designed specifically to teach different the basics or specializations contained within the digital forensic discipline. While the volume of reference materials on digital forensics is beyond the intention to identify and include them all in the list below, the following are recent publications that can be used as a learning tool for digital forensics.

Digital Forensics with the AccessData Forensic Toolkit (FTK). McGraw-Hill Osborne Media, 05 Sep 2015. ISBN: 9780071845021

Handbook of Digital Forensics of Multimedia Data and Devices. Wiley-IEEE Press, 31 Aug 2015. ISBN: 9781118640500

Hacking Exposed Computer Forensics Third Edition: Secrets & Solutions. McGraw-Hill Osborne Media, 06 Jul 2015. ISBN: 978-0071817745

Operating System Forensics 1st Edition. Syngress, 01 Jul 2015. ISBN: 9780128019498.

Cybercrime and Digital Forensics: An Introduction. Routledge, 12 Feb 2015. ISBN: 978-1138021303

The Basics of Digital Forensics 2nd Edition. Syngress, 15 Dec 2014. ISBN: 9780128016350.

Computer Forensics and Digital Investigation with EnCase Forensic v7. McGraw-Hill Osborne Media, 28 May 2014. ISBN: 978-0071807913

Windows Forensic Analysis Toolkit 4th Edition: Advanced Analysis Techniques for Windows 8. Syngress, 10 Apr 2014. ISBN: 9780124171572.

Computer Incident Response and Forensics Team Management 1st Edition. Syngress, 22 Nov 2013. ISBN: 9781597499965.

Digital Forensics Processing and Procedures 1st Edition. Syngress, 17 Sep 2013. ISBN: 9781597497428.

Computer Forensics InfoSec Pro Guide. McGraw-Hill Osborne Media, 09 Apr 2013. ASIN: B00BPO7AP8

Malware Forensics Field Guide for Windows Systems 1st Edition. Syngress, 13 Jun 2012. ISBN: 9781597494724.

Digital Forensics with Open Source Tools. Syngress, 14 Apr 2011. ISBN: 9781597495868.

Handbook of Digital Forensics and Investigation. Academic Press, 26 Oct 2009. ISBN: 978-0123742674

Tools and Equipment

To identify and select the proper tools and equipment to perform their investigative activities and steps, the digital forensic team must have a good understanding of how different business environments functions respective to the hardware and operating system(s) they use. This assessment will determine what tools and equipment are required to gather and process evidence from the organizations data sources. While there might be some tools or equipment absent due to new ones being constantly developed, the websites below offer a listing of currently available digital forensic tools and equipment.

21 Popular Computer Forensics Tools, InfoSec Institute. http://resources.infosecin-stitute.com/computer-forensics-tools/. 2014.

Digital Forensic Tools and Equipment. ForensicsWiki. http://www.forensicswiki.org/wiki/Tools. 2015.

Forensic Hardware, Digital Intelligence. https://www.digitalintelligence.com/cart/ComputerForensicsProducts/Forensic-Workstations-p1.html.

Forensic Workstations, Forensic Computers. http://www.forensiccomputers.com/workstations/forensic-workstations.html.

Free Computer Forensic Tools, Forensic Control. https://forensiccontrol.com/resources/free-software/. 2015.

List of Digital Forensics Tools, Wikipedia. http://en.wikipedia.org/wiki/List_of_digital_forensics_tools. 2015.

OpenSource Tools, Digital Forensic Association. http://www.digitalforensicsasso-ciation.org/opensource-tools/.

Talino Forensic Workstation, InSig2. http://www.insig2.eu/talino-forensic-work station-31.

Tools, ForensicsWiki. http://www.forensicswiki.org/wiki/Tools. 2015.

Integrity Monitoring Compliance Objectives

Implementation of integrity monitoring is an essential security control to guarantee the authenticity and integrity of business records as digital evidence. In addition to the use of integrity monitoring as means of maintaining integrity and proving authenticity of data, these solutions have also been established as a requirement for several regulatory compliance objectives; including:

FISMA SP800-53 R4. Requirement SI-7. http://csrc.nist.gov/drivers/documents/FISMA-final.pdf. NIST, 2013.

HIPAA SP800-66. Section 4.16. http://csrc.nist.gov/publications/nistpubs/800-66-Rev1/SP-800-66-Revision1.pdf. NIST, 2008.

PCI DSS: Requirements and Security Assessment Procedures v3.1. Requirement
11.5.   https://www.pcisecuritystandards.org/documents/PCI_DSS_v3-1.pdf.
PCI Security Standards Council, 2015.

SOX Act of 2002. Section 404. https://www.sec.gov/about/laws/soa2002.pdf. U.S.
Securities and Exchange Commissions, 2002.

Risk Management Methodologies

Generally, all risk assessments follow a similar methodology consisting of
the same techniques to arriving at a final risk decision; including analyzing threats and vulnerabilities, asset valuation, and risk evaluation. However,
there is no single risk assessment methodology that meets the needs of every
organization because they were not designed to be "one-size-fits-all". Each
organization is unique in its own respect and has their own reasons for why
they would complete risk assessments. Therefore, a variety of industry recognized risk assessment methodologies have been developed to address the
varying needs and requirements of organizations. It is important to note that
inclusion of a methodology below does not suggest that these are better or
recommended over other models that were not included.

Alberts, Christopher; Dorofee, Audrey; Stevens, James; Woody, Carol; Introduction
to   the   OCTAVE   Approach.   http://resources.sei.cmu.edu/asset_files/
UsersGuide/2003_012_001_51556.pdf. Carnegie Mellon University, 2003.

Ionita, Dan; Hartel, Pieter; Current Established Risk Assessment Methodologies
and Tools. http://doc.utwente.nl/89558/1/%5Btech_report%5D_D_Ionita_-_
Current_Established_Risk_Assessment_Methodologies_and_Tools.pdf.
University of Twente, 2013.

Peltier, Thomas R; Facilitated Risk Analysis Process (FRAP). http://www.ittoday.
info/AIMS/DSM/85-01-21.pdf. CRC Press, 2000.

Laws and Regulations

In several geographic regions, there are laws and regulations that dictate how
technology can be used; such as information privacy, anti-spamming, and
data exporting. Designed to connect technology with risk, these laws and
regulations can be generally grouped into one of the following categories.

Computer Misuse Act of 1990. http://www.legislation.gov.uk/ukpga/1990/18/pdfs/
ukpga_19900018_en.pdf. Parliament of the United Kingdom.

Cybercrime   Act   of   2001.   https://www.comlaw.gov.au/Details/C2004A00937.
Australian Government.

Cybercrime Prevention Act of 2012 (Republic Act No. 10175). http://www.gov.
ph/2012/09/12/republic-act-no-10175. Congress of the Philipines.

Electronic Communications Privacy Act of 1986. http://www.loc.gov/law/opportunities/PDFs/ElectronicCommunicationsPrivacyAct-PL199-508.pdf. U.S. Congress.

ePrivacy Act of 2002. http://eur-lex.europa.eu/LexUriServ/LexUriServ.do?uri=OJ:L:2009:337:0011:0036:en:PDF. European Parliament.

FISMA SP800-53 R4. http://csrc.nist.gov/drivers/documents/FISMA-final.pdf. NIST, 2013.

HIPAA SP800-66. http://csrc.nist.gov/publications/nistpubs/800-66-Rev1/SP-800-66-Revision1.pdf. NIST, 2008.

Patriot Act of 2001. http://www.gpo.gov/fdsys/pkg/PLAW-107publ56/pdf/PLAW-107publ56.pdf. U.S. Congress.

PCI DSS: Requirements and Security Assessment Procedures v3.1. https://www.pcisecuritystandards.org/documents/PCI_DSS_v3-1.pdf. PCI Security Standards Council, 2015.

SOX Act of 2002. https://www.sec.gov/about/laws/soa2002.pdf. U.S. Securities and Exchange Commissions, 2002.

Cloud Computing Environments

Through the combination of several major technology concepts, cloud computing has evolved over several decades to become the next-generation of computing models. As cloud computing continues to mature, providing organizations with an inexpensive means of deploying computing resources, it is driving a fundamental change in the ways technology is becoming a common layer of service-oriented architectures. Cloud computing presents unique challenges to an organization's digital forensics capabilities because of the dynamic nature in which information exists and a shift where organizations have less control over physical infrastructure assets. This leads to the inherent challenge of maintaining best practices for cloud computing while continuing to enable digital forensic capabilities.

Cloud Security Alliance. Quick Guide to the Reference Architecture: Trusted Cloud Initiative. https://cloudsecurityalliance.org/wp-content/uploads/2011/10/TCI_Whitepaper.pdf.

Cloud Security Alliance. Security Guidance for Critical Areas of Focus in Cloud Computing V3.0. https://downloads.cloudsecurityalliance.org/assets/research/security-guidance/csaguide.v3.0.pdf.

NIST Cloud Computing Security Working Group – Information Technology Laboratory. NIST Cloud Computing Security Reference Architecture. http://collaborate.nist.gov/twiki-cloud-computing/pub/CloudComputing/CloudSecurity/NIST_Security_Reference_Architecture_2013.05.15_v1.0.pdf.

Mobile Devices

Since its inception, the world of mobile technologies has evolved quickly where new devices, operating systems, and threats are emerging every day. With mobile devices, achieving a state of digital forensic readiness is important because of the dynamic and portable nature by which these devices are used to interconnect and interface both business and personal information. Organizations need to optimize their investigative process by taking proactive steps to guarantee that evidence will be readily available when (and if) needed from mobile devices.

Choo, Kim-Kwang Raymond; Dehghantanha, Ali. Contemporary Digital Forensic Investigations of Cloud and Mobile Applications. Syngress Press, 2016. ISBN # 9780128054482.

Doherty, Eamon P. Digital Forensics for Handheld Devices. CRC Press, 2016. ISBN # 9781439898789.

Ho, Anthony T.S., Li, Shujun. Handbook of Digital Forensics of Multimedia Data and Devices. John Wiley & Sons, 2016. ISBN # 9781118757079.

Martin, Andrew. Mobile Device Forensics. https://www.sans.org/reading-room/ whitepapers/forensics/mobile-device-forensics-32888. SANS Institute, 2009.

National Institute of Standards and Technology (NIST) Special Publication 800-101 Revision 1. Guidelines on Mobile Device Forensics. http://nvlpubs.nist.gov/ nistpubs/SpecialPublications/NIST.SP.800-101r1.pdf.

NIST Special Publication 800-124 Revision 1. Guidelines for Managing the Security of Mobile Devices in the Enterprise. http://nvlpubs.nist.gov/nistpubs/ SpecialPublications/NIST.SP.800-124r1.pdf.

Glossary

airplane mode: a setting that prevents mobile devices from sending and receiving cellular and wireless communications.

application programming interface (API): a set of computer programming subroutines, definitions, protocols, and tools for building application software.

application-oriented: a methodology focused on interactions with complimentary modules that provide analytical or reporting capabilities.

assets: any resource of value such as people, information, or systems.

attack vectors: paths or means by which an attacker or intruder gains access in order to deliver an exploit.

backplane: a group of electrical connectors in parallel with each other, so that each pin of each connector is linked to the same relative pin of all the other connectors, forming a computer bus.

bad faith: the intentional dishonest act by not fulfilling legal or contractual obligations, misleading another, entering into an agreement without the intention or means to fulfill it, or violating basic standards of honesty in dealing with others.

base discount year: the time period used to first start measuring the effectiveness of cash flows.

best practice: a method or technique that has consistently shown results superior to those achieved with other means, and that is used as a benchmark.

best-of-breed: a term used to describe the solution that generates the most value by providing the greatest functionality for a specific niche or subject area.

black box: a methodology that examines the functionality of an application, system, or object without knowledge of internal structures or workings.

bring your own key: a security model that allows customers to use and manage their own encryption keys to protect data hosted in business applications

chain of command: the line of authority and responsibility along which orders and commands are passed between different units.

cleartext: a form of message or data which is in a form that can be immediately read, understood, and interpreted by humans without additional processing.

click-wrap agreement: a type of non-negotiable contractual agreement where consumers must agree to the terms and conditions set forth before using the product or service.

cloud service providers (CSP): companies that offer and manage components of distributed computing services over the Internet

cluster: a fixed number of contiguous and addressable units of storage space on electronic storage medium.

commercial-off-the-shelf (COTS): describes items that are available for purchase through the commercial marketplace; including, but not limited to, software or hardware products, installation services, training services.

common body of knowledge (CBK): encompasses the complete set of concepts, terms, and activities that make up a professional domain.

continuous improvement transformation: a condition by which any subject matter can achieve and sustain success.

cyclic redundancy check (CRC): an error-detecting calculation that is commonly used in digital networks and storage devices to identify accidental changes to raw data.

data in transit: the flow of information over any type of public or private network environment.

data-at-rest: refers to the protection of inactive data that is physically stored in any digital form (i.e., database, enterprise data warehouse, tapes, hard drives, etc.)

data-in-use: applies to data that is actively stored in a non-persistent state, such as memory, for consumption or presentation.

dimension tables: consist of descriptive attributes that are used in support of fact table measurements.

eggs-in-one-basket: a term used to describe the increased risk of losing an investment as a result of concentrating all resources into a single item

electronically stored information (ESI): for the purpose of the Federal Rules of Civil procedure (FRCP): is information created, manipulated, communicated, stored, and best utilized in digital form, requiring the use of computer hardware and software.

elevator speech: a short, clear, brief message used to quickly and simply share information.

enterprise data warehouse (EDW): a central repository used to store amalgamated data from one or more disparate sources to support analytics and reporting.

entity-relationship (ER) model: describes the connections between others objects typically used in regards to the organization of data or information aspects.

evaluation period: the time period in which effectiveness of cash flows is measured against subjective or objective standards.

exculpatory evidence: exonerates a subjects involvement in an event that establishes innocence.

fact tables: consist of measurements, metrics, or fact of a business process that are located at the center of a data warehouse schema.

false-negative: an error in which results improperly indicate no presence of a condition when it is present.

false-positive: an error in which results improperly indicate the presence of a condition when it is not present.

financial risk: associated with the financial structure, stability, and transactions of the organization.

forensically sound: qualifies and, in some cases, justifies the use of a specific technology or methodology in preserving the authenticity and integrity of electronically stored information.

form factor: a term commonly used to describe the specifications of a computing device, a computer case or chassis, or one of its internal components such as a motherboard.

fruit of crime: applies to material objects that are acquired during a crime

GREP: a utility for searching plain-text data sets for content that matches a specific pattern.

hard-delete: occurs when data is deleted and can no longer be accessed through the filesystem

hash value: a numerical value of fixed length used to uniquely identifies and/or represent large volumes of data.

hearsay evidence: second-hand or indirect evidence that is offered by a witness of which they do not have direct knowledge but, rather, their testimony is based on what another has said to them.

inculpatory evidence: demonstrates a subject's involvement in an event that establishes guilt.

intangible: costs are unquantifiable costs related to an identifiable source (e.g., employee productivity).

internal rate of return (IRR): the discount rate, commonly used in budgeting, that makes the net present value of all cash flows in a specific project equal to zero.

internet protocol security (IPsec): a protocol suite for securing network communications by establishing mutual authentication between nodes by encrypting each data packet of an entire communication session.

key performance indicators (KPI): a business metric used to evaluate factors that are crucial to the success of an organization.

least privilege access: the practice of limiting subjects' access to objects at the minimal level required to allow normal operations and functions.

legal risk: associated with the need to comply with the rules and regulations of the appropriate governing bodies.

level of inflation: the sustained increase in the level of costs measured as an annual percentage.

managed security service providers (MSSP): provide outsourced monitoring and managements of security systems and applications

mandatory access control (MAC): a type of access control mechanism where a subjects ability to access resource objects is controlled by the system or an administrator.

market-oriented: a methodology focused on discovering and meeting the needs and wishes of customers through products.

message digest algorithm family: a suite of one-way cryptographic hashing algorithms that are commonly used to verify data integrity through the creation of a unique digital fingerprint of differing length based on version used.

message digest version 5 (MD5): a one-way cryptographic algorithm used to verify data integrity through the creation of a unique 128-bit fingerprint.

metadata: data about data that is used to describe how and when and by whom a particular set of information was collected, and how the data is formatted.

net present value (NPV): the sum of the present values of incoming and outgoing cash flows, also described as costs and benefits, over a period of time.

objects are passive: elements that contain or receive information

online analytical processing (OLAP) system: a type of system that performs multidimensional analysis of data to provide complex modeling and trend reporting.

online transaction processing (OLTP): system is a type of system that manages and facilitates the operations of an application typically focused on data entry.

open systems interconnection (OSI) model: a conceptual model that characterizes and standardizes the communication function of a telecommunication or computer system.

operational risk: associated with the organization's business, operational, and administrative procedures.

other risks: associated with indirect, non-business factors such as natural disasters and others as identified based on the subjectivity of the organization.

passcode: a string of characters used to authenticate access to information technology resources, including lowercase and uppercase letters, numbers, and symbols.

payback period: the time required to regain costs of an investment or to reach the break-even point.

personally identifiable information (PII): is any data that can be used to identify and distinguish one person from another.

phreaking: a blend of the words *phone* and *freaking* and is used to describe activities performed to reverse engineer telecommunication systems to allow free calls to be made. Example: the plain old telephone system (POTS).

price year: any subsequent time period following the base year used to continue measuring the effectiveness of cash flows.

proof of concept (POC): a process by which the realization of a certain concept, theory, method, or idea demonstrates its feasibility or proves a principle.

recovery time objective (RTO): the targeted duration of time and service level within which a system, network, or application must be restored to avoid unacceptable consequences

repeatable: refers to obtaining the same results when using the same method on identical test items in the same laboratory by the same operator using the same equipment within short intervals of time.

reproducible: refers to obtaining the same results as those obtained when using the same method on identical test items in different laboratories with different operators utilizing different equipment.

return on investment (ROI): the benefit to the investor resulting from an investment of some resource.

role-based access control (RBAC): an approach where subjects have access to objects based on their associated roles.

runbooks: both electronic and physical, are a compilation of routine procedures and operations used as a reference.

secure boot: a security standard to ensure that a system only loads and uses know-good and trusted software.

secure hashing algorithm (SHA): a one-way suite of cryptographic algorithms used to verify data integrity through the creation of a unique fingerprint of differing length based on version used.

secure hashing algorithm family: a suite of one-way cryptographic hashing algorithms that are commonly used to verify data integrity through the creation of a unique digital fingerprint of differing length based on version used.

service level agreements (SLA): official commitments between parties that define the level of service expected by the customer from the provider.

service level objectives (SLO): specific quantitative characteristics used to measure service delivery in terms of availability, throughput, frequency, response time, or quality.

services: a means of delivering value outcomes to customers without requiring the customer to directly own the specific costs and risks.

shadow price: the gain from an increase, or loss from a decrease, of relaxing the constraint, or, equivocally, the change in the total cost of strengthening the constraint.

snowflake model: a database schema where a central table contains the bulk of data and the smaller sets of related tables containing both values for linked dimension tables as well as volumes of data volumes with further linked dimension tables.

soft-delete: occurs when data is marked for deletion and is only prevented from being accessed

someone with knowledge: describes any person who has awareness or familiarity gained through experience or learning.

star model: a database schema where a central table contains the bulk of data and smaller sets of related table contain values for each linked dimension tables.

strategic risk: associated with the organization's core business functions and commonly occurs because of business interactions (purchase/sale of goods and services), mergers and acquisitions, or investment relations management.

structured: data include information that resides in a fixed field within a record or file (i.e., databases, spreadsheets).

subject: an active element that operates on information or the system state.

subject-oriented: a methodology focused on building systems that can be used to analyze a particular focus area.

tactics, techniques, and procedures: describes the attack patterns, tools, exploits, infrastructure, victim targeting, and other methods used by the adversary or attacker.

tangible: costs are quantifiable costs related to an identifiable source or asset (e.g. software licensing).

technology-generated data: or background evidence, is any electronically stored information that has been created and is being maintained because of programmatic processes or algorithms.

technology-stored data: or foreground evidence, is any electronically stored information that has been created and is being maintained because of user input and interactions.

threat actors: describes the identification and/or characterization of the adversary or attacker.

threats: any intentional (e.g., cybercrime) or accidental (e.g., natural disaster) course of action with the potential to adversely impact people, processes, or technology.

time value of money (TVM): the principle that the value of money at the present time is worth more than the same amount in the future due to potential earning capacity.

tool of crime: applies to material objects used to perpetrate criminal activities.

total cost of ownership (TCO): a financial estimate to determine the direct and indirect expenses and benefits of an investment.

trier of fact: or finder of fact, is any person or group of persons in a legal proceeding who determines whether, from presented evidence, something existed or some event occurred.

true-positive: occurs when results properly indicate the presence of a condition.

unstructured: data include information that does not resides in a traditional row–column arrangement (e.g., email, productivity documents).

validation: the process of evaluating software to determine whether the products of a given development phase satisfy the condition imposed at the start of that phase.

verification: the process of evaluating software during or at the end of the development process to determine whether it satisfies specified requirements.

white box: a methodology that examines the non-functional, internal structures or workings of an application, system, or object.

Index

Note: Page numbers in italic and bold refer to figures and tables, respectively.